Free Time and Leisure Participation

International Perspectives

Free Time and Leisure Participation

International Perspectives

Edited by

Grant Cushman

Lincoln University
New Zealand

A.J. Veal

University of Technology, Sydney
Australia

and

Jiri Zuzanek

University of Waterloo
Ontario
Canada

CABI Publishing

CABI Publishing is a division of CAB International

CABI Publishing
CAB International
Wallingford
Oxfordshire OX10 8DE
UK

CABI Publishing
875 Massachusetts Avenue
7th Floor
Cambridge, MA 02139
USA

Tel: +44 (0)1491 832111
Fax: +44 (0)1491 833508
E-mail: cabi@cabi.org
Website: www.cabi-publishing.org

Tel: +1 617 395 4056
Fax: +1 617 354 6875
E-mail: cabi-nao@cabi.org

A catalogue record for this book is available from the British Library, London,
UK.

Library of Congress Cataloging-in-Publication Data
Free time and leisure participation : international perspectives / edited
    by Grant Cushman, A.J. Veal and Jiri Zuzanek
        p. cm.
    Updated and expanded ed. of: World leisure participation. 1966.
    Includes bibliographical references and index.
    ISBN 0-85199-620-5 (alk. paper)
    1. Leisure--Cross-cultural studies. 2. Recreation--Cross-cultural studies.
    3. Recreational surveys. I. Cushman, Grant. II. Veal, Anthony James.
    III. Zuzanek, Jiri. IV. World leisure participation. V. Title.

    GV181.3.F74   2004
    790.1--dc22   2004011056

ISBN 0 85199 620 5

Typeset in Optima by Servis Filmsetting Ltd, Manchester.
Printed and bound in the UK by Biddles Ltd, King's Lynn.

Contents

About the Contributors

C.J. Betz is Outdoor Recreation Planner, USDA Forest Service, Southern Research Station, Athens, Georgia, USA.

I.A. Butenko is Head of Research Methods Section, Russian Institute for Cultural Research, Ministry of Culture of the Russian Federation.

H. Ken Cordell is Research Scientist and Project Leader, USDA Forest Service, Southern Research Station, Athens, Georgia, USA.

Grant Cushman is Professor of Parks, Recreation and Tourism and Director of the Undergraduate School, Lincoln University, New Zealand.

Mary Donn is a policy adviser for the New Zealand Ministry for Culture and Heritage, and former researcher for Creative New Zealand.

Mark J. Fly is Associate Professor in Forestry in the University of Tennessee, Knoxville, Tennessee, USA.

Geoffrey C. Godbey is Professor in the Department of Hotel, Restaurant and Recreation Management, Pennsylvania State University, USA.

Chris Gratton is Professor and Director of the Sports Industries Research Centre, Sheffield Hallam University, UK.

Gary T. Green is Assistant Research Scientist, Warnell School of Forestry, University of Georgia, Athens, Georgia, USA.

Munehiko Harada is Professor of Sport and Recreation Management at the Osaka University of Health and Sport Sciences in Japan.

Bohdan Jung is Professor, Research Institute for Developing Economics, Warsaw School of Economics, Warsaw, Poland.

Wim Knulst is Professor in the Faculty of Social and Behavioural Sciences, Tilburg University, The Netherlands.

Allan Laidler recently retired from the Victoria University, Wellington, New Zealand.

V.R. Leeworthy is Chief Economist, National Oceanic and Atmospheric Administration, National Ocean Service, Silver Springs, Maryland, USA.

Mirja Liikkanen is Project Manager, Leisure Survey, Statistics Finland, Finland.

Concepción Maiztegui Oñate is in the Faculty of Philosophy and Educational Sciences, University of Deusto, Bilbao, Spain.

Harald Michels is a Sport Scientist and Lecturer in the Department of Leisure Science of the German Sport University in Cologne, Germany.

Hannu Pääkkönen is Project Manager, Time Use Survey, Statistics Finland, Finland.

Bob Robertson is Emeritus Professor in the School of Leisure, Sport and Tourism at the University of Technology, Sydney, Australia.

John P. Robinson is Professor of Sociology and past Director of the Americans' Use of Time Project at the University of Maryland, USA.

Hillel Ruskin was Professor of Physical Education and Chairman of the Cossel Center of Physical Education, Leisure and Health Promotion and Director of the Graduate Program of Physical Education in Public Health of the Faculty of Medicine, Hebrew University, Jerusalem, Israel. He died in 2003 while the book was in production.

Nicole Samuel recently retired from the position of Head of the CNRS research team: Temps Sociaux, Ages et Modeles Culturels, Paris, France.

Atara Sivan is Associate Professor in the Department of Education Studies at Hong Kong Baptist University.

R. Stephens is Senior Research Associate in Forestry in the University of Tennessee, Knoxville, Tennessee, USA.

Walter Tokarski is University Professor and President of the German Sport University, Cologne, Germany.

Hugo van der Poel is Senior Lecturer in the Faculty of Social and Behavioural Sciences, Tilburg University, The Netherlands.

A.J. (Tony) Veal is Adjunct Professor in the School of Leisure, Sport and Tourism, University of Technology, Sydney, Australia.

Sue Walker is Research Manager for the New Zealand Department of Internal Affairs; she was the Research and Information Manager for the Hillary Commission for Sport, Fitness and Leisure at the time of writing this contribution.

Jiri Zuzanek is Distinguished Emeritus Professor in the Department of Leisure Studies, University of Waterloo, Ontario, Canada.

List of Tables and Figures

_____

Tables

Figures

Preface

This book is an expanded and updated edition of *World Leisure Participation: Free Time in the Global Village*, published in 1996 (Cushman, Veal and Zuzanek, 1996). An updated version of the book is justified on a number of grounds.

First, since the mid-1990s, worldwide patterns of leisure participation have changed, as have the social, political, economic and cultural influences on leisure. In each of the chapters in the book, updated national survey data on leisure participation are included which, in some cases, provide a basis of comparison with earlier surveys to establish temporal trends.

Secondly, additional countries have been included, reflecting the increasing amount of survey activity taking place around the world.

Thirdly, more explicit reference has been given in this book to time-use, or time-budget, surveys. In the earlier book only a few chapters presented time-use data. An advantage of time-budget data is that cross-country comparisons are easier than for participation survey data. The methodological variation which bedevils participation surveys, is constrained, but not eliminated, in time-budget studies, due to the universal metric of 24 hours and 1440 minutes/day. This change is reflected in the changed title of the book, with its emphasis on *time*.

Fourthly, analysis of national patterns of leisure participation has been given a somewhat wider frame: in addition to addressing age, gender and socio-economic status, reference is also made in most chapters to the effects of globalization and new communication technologies, particularly the use of the Internet for leisure purposes.

The book concentrates on economically developed countries, with a particular focus on Europe. We have endeavoured to source contributions from other regions of the world, but have been only partially successful. There are various reasons for this. Some Third World, or developing, countries do not have the resources to devote to substantial research on leisure, including large-scale, national leisure participation surveys. In other cases, local or regional research on leisure does exist, but no national participation or time-budget surveys could be identified. Further, we have generally identified potential contributors through the various leisure studies conferences, cross-national research groups and discussion networks, and not all countries are represented in such networks.

The aim of the book is similar to that of the 1996 edition: to bring together, as a reference source, the results of survey research on patterns of national leisure participation from around the world. Our intention is to establish, as far as possible, the extent to which this research might provide insights into the general nature of, and levels of participation in, leisure activities and leisure involvement of populations within participating countries, and whether it is possible to make preliminary comparisons between countries.

As with the first edition, the book has an ambitious agenda and it contains a wealth of material that goes a long way to answering core questions about national and cross-national leisure participation. We trust that it will prove valuable to academic colleagues, students and policy-makers around the world.

Grant Cushman
A.J. Veal
Jiri Zuzanek
March, 2004

1 Leisure Participation and Time-use Surveys: an Overview

Grant Cushman, A.J. Veal and Jiri Zuzanek

Introduction: Why Leisure Participation Data?

What are the trends in the use of the Internet for leisure purposes around the world? Is leisure time increasing or decreasing? Is active participation in sport increasing or decreasing in developed, newly industrialized and developing countries? Which social groups patronize the arts, visit national parks or play sport, and which groups do not? Despite the increasing global significance of sport, entertainment, culture and the conservation and use of the environment, it is still not possible to provide definitive answers to simple questions like these on worldwide patterns of leisure participation. Data are collected on an internationally comparable basis on a wide range of phenomena, such as health, housing, education and economic activity,[1] but little if any comparable data exist for leisure activity. It might be thought that leisure is not sufficiently important to justify the cost of gathering such information, but at national level its importance is widely recognized, so that, over the years, governmental bodies, academics and commercial organizations in many countries have compiled national data on patterns of leisure participation and expenditure. In addition to its social and cultural significance, leisure, in its many forms, is a substantial sector of government and it is a growing market phenomenon, providing jobs, incomes and economic development. In aggregate, it could therefore be said to be an increasingly significant phenomenon internationally.

Further, leisure is one of the basic human rights safeguarded by the Universal Declaration of Human Rights, as the following articles indicate:

> Everyone has the right to rest and leisure, including reasonable limitation of working hours and periodic holidays with pay.
> (Article 24)

> Everyone has the right freely to participate in the cultural life of the community, to enjoy the arts and to share in scientific advancement and its benefits.
> (Article 27)[2]

In 1987, the then Secretary-General of the United Nations declared:

> One of the primary needs of the human person is leisure and such use of it as will provide psychological strength and refreshment.
> (Perez de Cuellar, 1987)

In Europe, the idea of leisure as a right has been embraced in relation to one aspect of leisure, namely sport, in the Council of Europe, in its 1978 *Sport for All Charter*, which stated:

> Every individual shall have the right to participate in sport.
> (Council of Europe, 1978)

Thus leisure has been recognized by national governments and international organizations as being of sufficient importance to be accorded the status of a human right and a human need. In the same way that other aspects of human rights and social and economic welfare are monitored internationally, there is therefore a case for leisure to be similarly monitored. Social and economic rights, however, generally attract less governmental attention than civil and political rights; indeed, referring to the Universal Declaration's articles on economic and social rights, David Harvey has said:

> What is striking about these articles . . . is the degree to which hardly any attention has been paid over the last fifty years to their implementation or application and how almost all countries that were signatories to the Universal Declaration are in gross violation of these articles. Strict enforcement of such rights would entail massive and in some senses revolutionary transformations in the political-economy of capitalism.
>
> (Harvey, 2000, pp. 89–90)

Whether or not the idea of rights is invoked, governments at national, regional and local levels, throughout the world, are heavily involved in supporting and promoting such sectors of leisure as: sport; physical recreation and education; outdoor recreation in urban and natural areas; children's play; the arts; natural and cultural heritage; and broadcasting. This involvement is justified on the grounds that such leisure activities make significant contributions to the quality of life of individuals and communities (Marans and Mohai, 1991) and overlap with other important governmental responsibilities, such as conservation, education, enhancement of national unity and identity and economic development. There are also aspects of leisure that can be harmful, such as abuse of legal and illegal drugs, problem gambling, sporting accidents and activities that cause environmental or cultural degradation. Here, governments become involved in regulation, education and sometimes prohibition. Whether promoting, providing for, regulating or combating forms of leisure activity, governments and the communities they serve need statistical data to indicate the scale of need and

demand, and to monitor the effects of government policy and activity.

But leisure is not only a public sector phenomenon: consumer expenditure on leisure in developed economies is estimated to be as high as 25% of all consumer expenditure (e.g. Martin and Mason, 1998; Veal and Lynch, 2001, pp. 136–139). Leisure industries are a significant aspect of the process of globalization, particularly in the area of international film, music, television, sport and tourism. It is also an intrinsic part of local economies, in the form of restaurants, bars, hotels and clubs, retail outlets and live arts, sport and entertainment venues. While most of the surveys reported on in this book are publicly available and government funded, used primarily by public bodies for policy and planning purposes, they are also of interest to the private sector. A number of surveys which collect data on consumer expenditure on leisure, as well as participation, are conducted in various countries around the world to serve the needs of the commercial sector, but are generally only available on a subscriber basis (e.g. Mintel in the UK (see Mintel, nd) and Simmons in the USA (see Kelly and Warnick, 1999)).

This book and its predecessor (Cushman et al., 1996) were designed to draw together existing information on patterns of leisure participation from a number of countries. The existence of these surveys, often conducted at considerable expense, is an indication of a growing worldwide recognition of the importance of leisure to communities, nations, economies and environments. The data from the various countries represented were collected at different times, using widely differing methodologies, so possibilities for comparison between countries are very limited. It is to be hoped that the act of publishing this book and demonstrating the problems of comparison, will stimulate consideration of ways in which future surveys might be designed with international comparison in mind.

In the remainder of this introductory chapter we consider first the role of national leisure participation surveys in leisure studies, and then review a number of predecessor publications which have sought to present international comparative research on leisure and aspects of leisure. This is followed by a discussion of the problems of conducting international, or cross-national, comparative research in general.

Leisure Surveys at National Level

Data are regularly collected by most governments for a limited number of aspects of leisure, as a by-product of taxation, licensing and other forms of regulation. Thus, for example, in countries where the activities are legal, data are generally available on expenditure on gambling, and on expenditure on and consumption of alcohol and tobacco. Data are also assembled by most countries on international travel, as a result of border controls. Data on working hours – in part the converse of leisure time – are gathered as a by-product of industrial and economic policy. Data on mass media use are generally gathered for commercial reasons and sometimes for licensing purposes. For more comprehensive, and in-depth, information on leisure participation, however, it is necessary to conduct special social surveys of the population. Such surveys can take two forms: *activity-based* or *time-based*.

Activity-based leisure participation surveys use questionnaires to gather information on people's recalled participation in leisure activities over a specified period of time (the 'reference period'), such as a month or a year.

Time-based surveys sometimes called 'time-budget' or 'diary' studies, these require respondents to keep diaries of all their activities over a specified period of time, usually 1 or 2 days. Start and finish times of activities are recorded in the diaries, including simultaneous activities (for example, listening to the radio while eating) and sometimes the location and company involved. In these surveys leisure time is just one element of the data collected.

Demographic and socio-economic characteristics of respondents, and sometimes other lifestyle or attitude data, are also gathered in both types of survey.

As far as its leisure content is concerned, the time-use survey can be seen as a participation survey with a short reference period. For studying leisure as a whole, broad categories of leisure, or a few individual activities which most people do on most days, such as watching television or listening to the radio, the short reference period of the time-use survey presents few difficulties. But if the researcher is interested in individual activities, a time-use survey will often include only a very small sample of participants, making detailed analysis difficult, if not impossible. For example, one time-use survey indicates that, on a typical day, an average of 5 minutes is spent visiting 'entertainment and cultural venues' (see Table 2.9). However, this involves only 4.3% of the population (ABS, 1998, p. 22). With a total sample of, say, 10,000 this means that 430 are cultural participants. This is a small sub-sample upon which to base the analysis of individual cultural activities, some of which might involve as few as perhaps 2% of all cultural participants – that is, a sub-sample of just eight or nine in the example. By contrast, a reference period of a month or a year produces much larger sub-samples of cultural participants – perhaps 50% or 60% of the sample – providing large enough sub-samples to facilitate detailed analysis, such as examination of the age, class or gender composition of participants in individual activities. Therefore, while time-use studies are invaluable for examination of broad patterns of leisure time availability and relationships between leisure and paid and unpaid work and other activities, leisure researchers and policy-makers also use participation surveys with longer reference periods for detailed analysis. Hence the chapters in this book generally present data from both types of survey.

While a few leisure participation and time-use surveys are known to have been carried out in the first half of the 20th century, the modern era of survey-based leisure research began in the 1960s, particularly with the work of the United States Outdoor Recreation Resources Review Commission (ORRRC, 1962), which utilized, among other techniques, large-scale national participation surveys to establish base data on levels of participation. Other Western countries rapidly followed suit with their own surveys. The impetus for conducting studies of leisure activity at this time was the challenge presented to planners in most Western countries by the combination of growing affluence, significant increases in car ownership and consequent growth in car-based recreation, and the rapid growth of the population, particularly of the then young 'baby boomer' population. At that time, large-scale, national or regional, time-use and questionnaire-based community leisure participation surveys vied with on-site surveys of users of individual recreation facilities or networks of facilities (usually outdoor recreation areas) as the main vehicle for empirical data collection on leisure.

Time-use surveys also have a history stretching back into the first half of the 20th century, but were recognized as an element of leisure studies with the advent, in the 1960s, of the Multinational Comparative Time-budget Research Project, which is described below (p. 6). Many individual countries have conducted time-budget surveys in the intervening 35 years, partly as a contribution to leisure policy, but also in regard to other policy concerns, such as gender equity in paid and unpaid work time.

The initiative and resources for the participation and time-use surveys have come largely from governments and government agencies, driven by policy concerns, while academics and consultants have been involved as advisers and as primary and secondary analysts. Early surveys were generally purely descriptive. Governments of the day, concerned about outdoor recreation, sport and physical recreation, or patronage of the arts, needed data in order to formulate, refine or monitor policies; the surveys provided an initial 'position statement' – for example, on the proportion of the population engaging in sporting or cultural activities and the variation in participation levels among various social groups. But in some cases, studies were also predictive. In situations of rapid economic and demographic growth, the data provided the basis for demand forecasting so that governments could be assisted in planning for the future.

The early surveys can therefore be seen as part of a general concern for social policy issues which was a feature of interventionist Western governments of the 1960s. In the former eastern European communist bloc they reflected government aims to establish 'socialist lifestyles' and to research ways and means of achieving this (Filipcova, 1972). While governments have generally become less interventionist over the intervening 30 years, many of the institutions established in the 1960s to administer government policies on various aspects of leisure, have continued to generate a demand for data on leisure participation and time-use.

In the area of social behaviour the 'facts' are continually changing, in contrast to the situation in most of the physical sciences where a discovery, once made, is forever true (even though its theoretical explanation may change). In the social sciences a discovery may be true only for the instant in which it is made; from that time on its value as a description of contemporary society begins to 'decay'. It therefore becomes necessary to update such data continually. This is certainly true of data on patterns of leisure behaviour and time-use. Indeed, it is the actual and potential *fluidity* of leisure behaviour that often gives rise to the need for data collection in the first place. Changes in patterns of leisure participation arise from cultural, social, economic and environmental influences, such as changes in social values, personal incomes or technology. Governments and other organizations seek to anticipate and monitor these changes, particularly when they seem to call for a policy response. For example, government agencies must cope with increased demand for recreation on remote and ecologically fragile public lands brought about by increased mobility, or pressure on water areas resulting from increased population. In other situations, governments and other organizations seek to stimulate change themselves – for example in promoting sports participation and exercise to counter increasing obesity arising from changed diet and lifestyles, or promoting participation in the arts to foster community spirit and urban regeneration. In these cases, data are required to monitor trends and to assess the 'before and after' effects of policy measures.

Thus, while surveys of leisure participation and time-use have had a chequered history, where governments have had an interest in leisure – or aspects of leisure, such as sport, outdoor recreation or tourism – and where the resources have been available, periodic surveys have become the norm. In many cases the surveys are conducted by the official national statistical agency, which is also responsible for the census of population and other official statistics. In other cases, the data collection is commissioned by government departments from commercial or academic survey organizations.

In addition to their policy roles, early leisure participation surveys, in particular, laid the groundwork for the development of a variety of research traditions in leisure studies. Researchers in the USA developed approaches based on quantitative modelling and demand prediction, and on quantitative behavioural models at the individual/psychological level (Cichetti, 1972). These models have tended to be prominent in leisure research in North America ever since. In the UK and Europe the quantitative/modelling approach was soon largely abandoned in favour of a more direct use of such data in policy formation and monitoring. Fred Coalter (1999) has referred to the contrasting traditions as the North American 'leisure science' tradition and the European 'leisure studies' tradition.

Academics in the social sciences – and in leisure studies in particular – do not themselves generally have access to resources to conduct large-scale empirical research, and so have been reliant on government-sponsored surveys when discussing general patterns of leisure behaviour. While theoretical and critical researchers in the leisure area have generally eschewed the survey method, they have nevertheless often drawn on the evidence of survey data as a starting point for their analyses, particularly in relation to social class and gender differences in participation levels, and in relation to publicly subsidized areas of leisure, such as elite sport, the arts and outdoor recreation. As the field of leisure studies has grown as an area of tertiary study, leisure participation survey data have found a role in textbooks and in the classroom, in providing students with an empirical picture of leisure participation patterns.

Large-scale national leisure participation surveys have become increasingly sophisticated over the years (Cushman and Veal, 1993) but they have often had a 'bad press' from academics, particularly those wedded to the increasingly popular – and indeed orthodox –

qualitative research methods in the field. In order to establish the case for undertaking, or placing more emphasis on, qualitative empirical research and non-empirical theoretical research, commentators often outline the limitations of quantitative methods, including surveys (e.g. Clarke and Critcher, 1985, pp. 26–27; Rojek, 1989, p. 70; Henderson, 1991, p. 26; Aitchison, 1993; Wearing, 1998, pp. 13–14). Critics often impute motives and attitudes to researchers who utilize survey methods, implying that they are somehow wedded to a somewhat outdated and extreme version of 'positivism', to the exclusion of other research approaches. The cumulative effect of repeated detailing of their failings and limitations has been to put surveys in a bad light with some of the leisure research community, and to create a 'phoney war' between alternative methodologies. The survey method has strengths and limitations, as do all research methods. For example, for the survey method, making definitive descriptive statements about the community as a whole is routine, but explanation of observed behaviour is often speculative at best. Conversely, qualitative methods are often strong on explanation but relatively weak with regard to reliable generalization to the wider community. Thus survey methods, other quantitative methods and qualitative research methods should, in our view, be seen as complementary (Kamphorst *et al.*, 1984).

Some of the implied criticism of surveys is that they consume substantial resources which are therefore denied to (and would go much further in) other forms of research. Roberts, for example, has stated: 'Sociologists are entitled to protest at this rampant and excessive fact-gathering' (Roberts, 1978, p. 28). But, as indicated above, large-scale surveys tend to be conducted for policy rather than theoretical purposes: they do not generally compete for the same resources as other forms of leisure research. The considerable resources devoted to the conduct of particular policy-orientated leisure participation surveys would probably not be available for purely academic research purposes. In fact, virtually all academic use of such survey data is secondary and is often undertaken with little or no specific funding. While non-survey methods also have a place in policy research, and this is being increasingly recognized by policy agencies, such research tends to be conducted in addition to, rather than instead of, survey work.

The need for governments to base policy development and evaluation on quantitative statements about the whole community is likely to remain; it would therefore appear that leisure participation and time-use surveys are 'here to stay' in many countries, and they are likely to be instituted in other countries which have not hitherto conducted them. It would seem wise, therefore, for the leisure research community to make use of this resource and, where possible, to seek to influence the design of official surveys to maximize their utility for wider research purposes. Surveys have a role to play in leisure studies alongside other research methods.

International Data on Leisure Participation and Time-use

As with national governments, some data are regularly collected by international organizations for a limited number of aspects of leisure. For example, the World Tourism Organization and the Organization for Economic Cooperation and Development both assemble data on international travel (WTO, Annual; OECD, Annual). Data on working hours, which can be seen as the obverse of leisure time, and paid holidays, which are specifically mentioned in the Universal Declaration of Human Rights, are collated by the UN's International Labour Office (ILO, Annual). International data are occasionally published on levels of ownership of some leisure goods, for example television sets and home computers.

In the field of leisure surveys, there have been few examples of truly multinational cooperation to produce data that could be compared between countries, but there have been a number of projects which have collated and compared data from a number of countries. Five relevant exercises can be identified:

- the Multinational Comparative Time-budget Research Project, 1967;
- the International Sociological Association series on sport and the arts, 1987/89;
- the *Leisure Policies in Europe* study, 1997;

- the European COMPASS study, 1999;
- the Eurostat compilation of European time-use studies, 2003.

These are reviewed briefly below. The pattern of country participation in these projects and in this book and its predecessor is shown in Table 1.1.

Multinational Comparative Time-budget Research Project

The Multinational Comparative Time-budget Research Project, conducted in 12 countries in the 1960s, was coordinated through the UNESCO-funded European Coordination Centre for Research and Documentation in Social Sciences, in Vienna, but was conducted by a variety of academic and governmental organizations in the participating countries (Szalai, 1972 (ed.); Feldheim and Javeau, 1977). Leisure is, of course, only one use of time, so this study was also concerned with such issues as paid and unpaid work and family life. The study established the considerable similarity in the daily patterns of life of the populations of the 12 countries studied, the major differences arising from variations in the economic status of women and the varying levels of television ownership that existed at the time (Feldheim and Javeau, 1977). Clearly, both of these factors will have changed substantially over the intervening 25 years, but no follow-up cross-national study has been attempted, although time-budget studies continue to be conducted in many countries and the Eurostat compilation, referred to below, has been conducted.

International Sociological Association series

Under the auspices of the International Sociological Association (Hantrais and Samuel, 1991), three volumes of collected papers on aspects of leisure in a number of countries were produced in the 1980s, covering the arts, sport and 'lifestyles'.

- *Trends in the Arts: a Multinational Perspective* (Hantrais and Kamphorst,

Table 1.1. Countries involved in cross-national leisure projects, 1967–2004.

	Time-budget study, 1967[a]	Trends in the arts, 1987[b]	Trends in sport, 1989[c]	Life-styles 1989[d]	Leisure Policies in Europe 1993[e]	COMPASS 1999[f]	Eurostat compilation[g]	First edn of this book, 1996	Current book, 2003
Albania									
Australia						•		•	
Austria									
Belarus						•			
Belgium	•			•		•	•		
Brazil	•			•		•			
Bulgaria			•			•			•
Canada		•	•			•		•	•
Cyprus		•	•			•			
Czechoslovakia/Czech Rep.	•	•	•			•			
Denmark						•	•		
Estonia							•		
Finland	•	•	•	•	•	•	•	•	•
France	•		•			•			•
Germany (GDR)	•						•	•	•
Germany (FDR)	•	•	•	•	•	•	•	•	•
Great Britain/UK		•	•	•	•	•	•	•	•
Greece					•				
Hong Kong	•	•						•	
Hungary	•		•	•			•		
India			•			•			
Ireland						•			
Israel									
Italy								•	•

Continued

Table 1.1. *Continued*

	Time-budget study, 1972[a]	Trends in the arts, 1987[b]	Trends in sport, 1989[c]	Life-styles 1989[d]	Leisure Policies in Europe 1993[e]	COMPASS 1999[f]	Eurostat compilation[g]	First edn of this book, 1996	Current book, 2003
Japan			•	•				•	•
Netherlands	•	•			•	•			•
New Zealand			•					•	•
Nigeria			•						
Norway			•			•	•		
Peru	•							•	•
Poland	•		•	•	•				
Portugal			•			•			
Puerto Rico		•		•					
Slovenia					•	•	•		
Spain						•		•	•
Sweden					•	•	•		
Switzerland	•	•	•	•		•			
USA	•	•	•		•			•	•
USSR/Russia	•								•
Yugoslavia	•								

Sources: [a]Szalai (1972), Feldheim and Javeau (1977); [b]Hantrais and Kamphorst (1987); [c]Kamphorst and Roberts (1989); [d]Olszewska and Roberts (1989); [e]Bramham *et al.* (1993); [f]Gratton (1999); [g]Aliaga and Winqvist (2003).

1987) included contributions from eight countries. Published in 1987, the book is based largely on data collected in the 1970s and early 1980s. The extent and quality of data available vary significantly from country to country. In addition to information on participation levels, data on attendances at arts venues and funding of arts organizations are also presented. One of the main conclusions drawn in the book is that participation in the arts is concentrated among the more highly educated, higher-income groups in society in most of the countries studied, and the editors call for more research, including qualitative research, to explore the processes that lead to this widespread situation.

- *Trends in Sports: a Multinational Perspective* (Kamphorst and Roberts, 1989) includes contributions from 15 countries. Despite the enormous variety of social, physical and economic environments represented by the 15 countries, the editors conclude that the universal nature of sporting participation is clear; that walking, running and swimming make up the bulk of sporting activity across the world; that there are widespread common perceptions of the importance of sport in modern social life; and that it is even possible to detect trends in participation, particularly the rapid growth of participation in the 1960s and 1970s and the slowing of growth in the 1980s.
- *Leisure and Lifestyle: a Comparative Analysis of Free Time* (Olszewska and Roberts, 1989) contains contributions on nine countries. While some of the contributions present survey data on leisure participation, overall they are less concerned with presentation of data than with painting a socio-political picture of the context of leisure in each country, particularly in the context of the economic recession of the late 1980s.

Leisure Policies in Europe

Leisure Policies in Europe (Bramham *et al.*, 1993), as the title implies, is concerned with policies rather than data on participation. The

contributions, from nine countries, are set against the background of the emerging 'new world order' of the early 1990s, involving the transformation of eastern Europe, including the collapse of the Soviet Union, the expansion of the European Community and the emergence of an international, post-industrial, post-Fordist, post-modern European society.

COMPASS study

The COMPASS (Coordinated Monitoring of Participation in Sports) programme involves 19 European countries and aims: 'to examine existing systems for the collection and analysis of sports participation data in European countries with a view to identifying ways in which harmonization may be achieved, so that greater comparability of data from different European countries will become possible' (COMPASS, 2002). In 1999 a review and secondary analysis of sport participation surveys from seven countries was published, but it was noted that comparison between countries was problematical since 'no two surveys are identical in survey methodology' (Gratton, 1999, p. 49). Problems encountered included variations in the definition of sport, the use or non-use of a 'prompt card' to indicate to survey respondents what was meant by 'sport', variation in the age range covered, differing interview methods (telephone, face-to-face, etc.) and differing sampling methods. The aim of the review was to provide a basis for future cooperation on standardizing sport participation data collection methods in Europe, including the possibility of conducting a common survey. At the time of writing, however, no joint surveys have been conducted.

Eurostat time-use compilation

In 2002–2003 Eurostat, the statistics arm of the European Communities, compiled time-use data from 13 European countries, drawing on time-use surveys conducted independently over the period 1999–2001. While the surveys varied in the time of year in which they were conducted and in the age range of their samples, a degree of comparability was achieved by most of the countries using the 'Harmonised European Time Use' activity coding list (Aliaga and Winqvist, 2003, p. 7). A number of tables relating to variables such as gender and age have been compiled and made available on the Eurostat website (Eurostat, 2003). Time-use studies are not, of course, concerned exclusively with leisure, so time-use studies have an independent existence and a body of specialist researchers (Pentland *et al.*, 1999). The Multinational Time Use Study (MTUS), based at the University of Essex, UK, compiles data on time-use studies on an ongoing basis (Gershuny *et al.*, 2000).

Participation by various countries in the above projects, and in this book and its predecessor, is partly fortuitous, reflecting networks between individual researchers, chance meetings at conferences, synchronization of projects and personal and organizational time and resources, and the availability of facilities to overcome language barriers (all the projects have used English as the common language). But it also reflects, to some extent, the degree to which the various participant countries are involved in leisure policy and research, particularly survey-based research. Altogether 40 countries have been involved in these projects, but it is notable that only one, France, has been involved in them all, although the USA took part in all except the European projects. Of the 40 countries, 16 have been involved in only one of the projects. It is notable that there has been little involvement from Africa, South America or South-east Asia.

Only the first of the studies reviewed above was designed from the beginning as a cross-national project: the rest have relied on the use of existing data sources. With the partial exception of the time-budget studies, these projects illustrate the lack of comparability between nation states in terms of data sources, definitions, research traditions and administrative arrangements. One of the long-term aims of this book is to stimulate discussion on how countries conducting leisure participation surveys might move towards more comparability in future surveys, so that comparisons and aggregation might be achieved. As the Eurostat exercise indicates, moves are already afoot to achieve this in the case of time-use studies.

Leisure and time-use surveys are, however, not alone in facing problems of comparability: cross-national comparative research generally is faced with a myriad of problems.

Cross-national Comparative Social Research: Studying Difference

Why conduct cross-national comparative research? One goal might be to produce 'league tables' – to show where different countries stand in relation to one another in addressing what Novak (1977) has termed 'nation-oriented problems'. This is done continually in relation to such phenomena as economic growth rates, per capita income levels, taxation levels and crime rates, and these league tables are often reported in the mass media. But implicit in even these comparisons, are quasi-scientific questions and answers – in Novak's terms, 'variable-orientated problems'. Media and political analysts rarely refer to comparative data without also providing some commentary; they usually seek 'explanations', often in order to pursue a particular political line of argument. For example, rates of economic growth are often causally linked to levels of taxation, or government expenditure, or levels of investment in education or research in different countries; and crime rates are linked to levels of gun ownership or inequalities in wealth distribution. Implicit in such statements are causal models, relating one variable to another. Warwick and Osherson (1973, p. 7) argue: 'Rather than being a second-order activity tacked onto more basic cognitive processes, comparison is central to the very acts of knowing and perceiving.' They explain how cross-national comparative research can contribute to theory building and theory testing in social research: it helps in developing 'clearly defined and culturally salient concepts and variables it enables theories to be tested against a wider range of conditions than single nation research, enabling a greater degree of generality to be achieved; and it is good for the researcher, developing a 'heightened sensitivity to the differential salience and researchability of concepts in varying cultural settings' (Warwick and Osherson, 1973, pp. 8–11).

This last point suggests a need for caution: reminding us that not all countries, even in the economically developed world, experience economic recession at the same time or in the same way. Some countries are still developing industrially, while others are experiencing de-industrialization or post-industrialism; some are grappling with the problem of a growing youth population, while others are experiencing an ageing of the population. There has been a tendency in leisure studies discourse to associate leisure with 'progress', to assume that more leisure time, more leisure activity and even more leisure expenditure is a 'good thing' and one of the dividends of social and economic progress. This raises the issue of the now questionable view that every society is seeking to achieve a 'one size fits all' form of Western modernity. The legacy of earlier modernist conceptualizations and constructions in the social sciences and in the related fields of leisure and tourism studies, in which it is assumed that the natural evolutionary development of societies is that of the modern, and post-modern, West, lives on. Elements of this teleological view of history are inevitably reflected in this book, including our own opening paragraphs above. Hall and Greben express this mind-set of Western modernity as follows:

> This belief that all societies could be laid out at different points along the same evolutionary scale (with, of course the West at the top!), was a very Enlightenment conception and one can see why many non-European societies now regard (this belief) as very Euro-centric.
> (Hall and Greben, 1992, p. 9)

In more recent times, it has been argued that we have moved beyond modernity to a new terrain, called post-modernity. Gradually, therefore, a more plural conception of the historical and contemporary process of development has emerged in the social sciences and in the related fields of leisure and tourism studies. It lays more stress on the validity of cultural specificity and on varied paths to developed, diverse outcomes, ideas of difference, unevenness, contradiction and contingency. Hall and Greben (1992, p. 9) explain how many social theorists now see unevenness and difference as a more powerful historical logic than evenness,

similarity and uniformity. These are contentious issues in social science, in leisure studies and, indeed, for world politics, and the questions they raise are far from settled.

The benefits of cross-national comparative research are easy to identify, but achieving the benefits in practice is more difficult. Numerous difficulties are presented to researchers attempting to overcome cultural and language barriers to conduct cross-national research. While researchers may struggle to overcome them, it is in the exploration of such differences that part of the value of cross-national comparison may lie. As Przeworski and Teune (1973, p. 123) put it: 'To say that a relationship does not hold because of systematic or cultural factors is tantamount to saying that a set of variables, not yet discovered, is related to the variables that have been examined.'

Nevertheless, common variables must be identified across countries for cross-national research to be of value. We have barely begun to address these issues in cross-national leisure research, even at the definitional level. For example, surveys may indicate certain levels of participation in 'football' in various countries, but 'football' includes a variety of different sports, including American grid-iron, soccer, rugby league, rugby union, Australian Rules and Gaelic football. Some of these codes are 'national' sports, some are regional and some are very much minority sports: thus the term 'football' implies a wide variety of phenomena, rather than a single one. Nominally identical activities may have totally different meanings and significances in different cultures. For example, in many countries much leisure activity revolves around the consumption of alcohol, while in others alcohol is forbidden. In some countries gambling is part of the culture, while in others it is frowned upon or banned. Such fundamental differences might eventually lead to the identification of a range of 'functional' activities for comparison in cross-national studies – for example the idea of a 'national sport' or 'focal cultural activity'. But this assumes that comparisons can be undertaken at all.

Much of the general social science literature on cross-national comparative research focuses on data collection projects designed from the outset to be conducted cross-nationally.

In the leisure area, apart from the Multinational Comparative Time-budget study, researchers have had to be content with making comparisons using data already collected in separate countries, at different times and for different purposes. Any level of comparison at all is therefore problematical. This is further confounded by the growing realization, resulting from experience with single-nation surveys, that leisure participation data are extremely sensitive to the methodology used in their collection. Responses are affected by the differing definitions of leisure itself, the age range of respondents included in surveys, the time of year when data are collected, the use or non-use of 'prompt lists' to indicate the range of leisure activity to be considered, and the participation 'reference period' used. These issues are considered in more detail in the concluding chapter of the book.

Global Trends

The data presented in this book have been collected in 15 individual countries, usually as a part of the public policy process of individual governments, as discussed above. They highlight the pattern of behaviour of the population of particular geographical areas at particular points in time. In bringing the data together, we seek to address not just the differences in patterns of leisure participation between countries, but also the similarities. It is widely posited that globalization is tending to produce a common culture across the developed world and, increasingly, among developing countries as well. In common with many aspects of modern life, leisure is affected by global forces, as can be seen in trends in activities as diverse as home-based leisure, sport, entertainment and tourism. The following broad global tendencies can be noted.

- Most leisure takes place in the home, particularly as standards of living increase and the size and range of equipment of homes increases. But increasingly the leisure 'products' which people consume in their homes are produced and distributed on a global scale, including film and television programmes, recorded music, books and magazines, computer games and the products of the Internet.
- Sport, which was once almost exclusively a neighbourhood leisure activity, is now also a global one. This is reflected not only in such overtly international phenomena as the Olympic Games and other international sporting championships, but in the internationalization of sporting culture via broadcasting and associated marketing of clothing and equipment.
- Modern entertainment industries, including film, popular recorded music and television, have been international in nature since they emerged in the early and middle 20th century, although the domination of Hollywood has resulted in Americanization as much as globalization.
- The ultimate international leisure activity, tourism, is now seen as one of the world's largest and fastest growing industries. Particularly affected by tourism are the natural environment and cultural heritage, which are the basis of much local and international tourism, giving rise to issues of 'ownership' and conservation.

Appadurai (1990) suggests that we can conceive of five dimensions of global cultural flows. First, there are *ethnoscapes* produced by flows of people: tourists, immigrants, refugees, exiles and guestworkers. Second, there are *technoscapes*, the machinery and plant flows produced by multinational and national corporations and government agencies. Third, there are *finanscapes*, produced by the rapid flows of money in the international currency markets and stock markets. Fourth, there are *mediascapes*, the repertoires of images and information, the flows which are produced and distributed by newspapers, magazines, television and film. Fifth, there are *ideoscapes*, linked to flows of images which are associated with state or counter-state movement ideologies which are comprised of elements of the Western Enlightenment world-view images of democracy, freedom, welfare, rights, etc. Clearly leisure, in its many forms, is affected by, and affects, every one of these dimensions.

Joffre Dumazedier (1982, p. 187) suggested that the 'comparative method' might be used to examine possible social futures – that is, one society can examine alternative futures for itself by studying the experiences of others, particularly those that are more economically developed. This can apply among economically advanced countries, since there is enormous variation in wealth and social practices even among members of the developed 'club', but it is particularly appropriate between developed and developing countries. The experiences of the handful of economically developed countries presented in this volume may provide the basis for such exercises. Further, the comparative method can be seen as relevant to the former communist countries of eastern Europe, facing the challenge of building mixed economies with new relationships between the state, the market and the individual, as indicated in the chapters on Poland and Russia in this volume. Such thinking emphasizes the point made above, that, even in the context of globalization, there is no longer, if there ever was, a 'one size fits all' pattern of economic and social development – there are alternative pathways. How a society develops its leisure institutions and practices is one component of the pattern of development.

Leisure phenomena are increasingly both local and international. The question of whether leisure participation patterns change simply because of variation in geographical and cultural focus is, at face value, straightforward. Of course, geography and culture heavily influence the leisure participation patterns of local populations. Surfing is a popular pastime where coastlines and waves make this sport possible. Indigenous forms of art and activity are significant features of most countries' culture. There are aspects of leisure, including alcohol, drugs, tobacco and gambling, as discussed above, which may be perceived as unhealthy, immoral or illegal in some cultures and places, but acceptable in others. Yet the question of the relative influence of local, in contrast to international, forces on leisure participation may be more problematic than first impressions might suggest.

Distinguishing the 'local' and the 'global' in leisure participation is not an easy task. At one level, the fundamental issue is the relationship of the universal (global) and the particular (local) in social science analyses, since there is a sense in which all social science is a search

for universals, and at the same time, there is the idea that all activity is particular. A fundamental issue which arises here is whether there is anything distinctive or particular about a local leisure experience. With regard to one of the contributions (New Zealand) in this book, Perkins argues that the local is distinctive:

> Even though it has become popular to think of ourselves as being part of a global economy, New Zealanders are still easily distinguishable from other peoples, and it is in the area of leisure that some of our differences are most obvious. This reflects a particular geographical location, history, landscape and economy and the mix of opportunities and constraints produced by them. Leisure and recreation studies has an important role to play in interpreting issues associated with New Zealand's regional and national cultural identity.
>
> (Perkins, 1997, p. 75)

Nevertheless, like so many aspects of modern life, leisure is undoubtedly being affected by global forces. As outlined in the earlier edition of this book, globalization processes, with their associated processes of exchange, circulation and commodification which characterize modern market societies (Jarvie and Maguire, 1994, p. 230; Rojek, 1995, p. 92) point to increasing international interrelatedness. This can be understood as leading to global *ecumene*, defined as a 'region of persistent culture interaction and exchange' (Kopytoff, 1987, p. 10; Featherstone, 1990) and is witnessed by a growing internationalization of ideas and consumer expectations in leisure and recreation (Mercer, 1994).

This Book

The book consists of individual chapters on leisure participation and time-use in 15 different countries. It has a particular focus on economically developed countries, but this does not mean that leisure is a concern only of nation states. Leisure is present in various guises in all cultures and forms of economic development. Most music and drama has deep cultural roots; modern sports were preceded by centuries-old local and regional sporting contests in non-industrial societies; and religious pilgrimages long pre-date modern mass tourism. Such issues as the need for open space for recreation in city environments, the role of sport in promoting health and national prestige, the status of indigenous culture in the face of mass media influences and the problems of conservation of natural and historic heritage in the face of growing population and tourist pressures are, if anything, more pressing in developing countries than in the developed world.

The contributors to this book were asked to provide information from their respective countries on: (i) national leisure participation and time-use surveys that have been conducted; (ii) overall patterns of leisure participation and time-use revealed by the surveys and, where possible, trends over time; (iii) inequalities in patterns of participation and time-use in relation to such factors as gender, age and socio-economic status; and (iv) the effects of globalization on leisure behaviour, including use of the Internet. Authors have broadly stuck to the brief, but nevertheless, the treatments vary considerably from country to country, depending on the social and economic context and availability of, and access to, data. Nevertheless some commonalities emerge: while leisure is nationally and culturally specific, it is also universal. These issues are addressed further in the final chapter of the book.

It is hoped that the experiences of the countries in this volume will be of interest to others as they consider the challenges of leisure participation, leisure policy and leisure development.

Notes

[1] See ILO (Annual), OECD (Annual, 1993), UN (Annual).
[2] Quotations from the Universal Declaration of Human Rights are from Brownlie (1992). See also Veal (2002, pp. 11–26) for further discussion of leisure and rights.

References

ABS (Australian Bureau of Statistics) (1998) *How Australians Use Their Time*. ABS, Canberra.

Aitchison, C. (1993) Comparing leisure in different worlds: uses and abuses of comparative analysis in leisure and tourism. In: Collins, M. (ed.) *Leisure in Industrial and Post-Industrial Societies*. Leisure Studies Association, Eastbourne, UK, pp. 385–400.

Aliaga, C. and Winqvist, K. (2003) *How Women and Men Spend their Time: Results from 13 European Countries*. Statistics in Focus: Population and Social Conditions, Theme 3 – 12/2003, Eurostat, European Communities, Brussels. Available at website: www.europa.eu.int/comm/eurostat (accessed July 2003).

Appadurai, A. (1990) Disjuncture and difference in the global cultural economy. In Featherstone, M. (ed.) *Global Culture, Nationalisation, Globalisation and Modernity*. Sage, London, pp. 295–310.

Bramham, P., Henry, L., Mommas, H. and Van der Poel, H. (eds) (1993) *Leisure Policies in Europe*. CAB International, Wallingford, UK.

Brownlie, I. (ed.) (1992) *Basic Documents on Human Rights*. Clarendon Press, Oxford, UK.

Cichetti, C. (1972) A review of the empirical analyses that have been based upon the National Recreation Survey. *Journal of Leisure Research* 4(1), 90–107.

Clarke, J. and Critcher, C. (1985) *The Devil Makes Work: Leisure in Capitalist Britain*. Macmillan, London.

Coalter, F. (1999) Leisure sciences and leisure studies: the challenge of meaning. In: Jackson, E.L. and Burton, T.L. (eds) *Leisure Studies: Prospects for the 21st Century*. Venture, State College, Pennsylvania, pp. 507–522.

COMPASS (2002) COMPASS website (based at University of Rome) at: http://w3.uniroma1.it/compass/index.htm (accessed April 2003).

Council of Europe (1978) *Sport for All Charter*. Council of Europe, Strasbourg.

Cushman, G. and Veal, A.J. (1993) The new generation of leisure surveys – implications for research on everyday life. *Leisure and Society* 16(1), 211–220.

Cushman, G., Veal, A.J. and Zuzanek, J. (eds) (1996) *World Leisure Participation: Free Time in the Global Village*. CAB International, Wallingford, UK.

Dumazedier, J. (1982) *The Sociology of Leisure*. Elsevier, The Hague.

Eurostat (2003) Available at website: www.europa.eu.int/comm/eurostat

Featherstone, M. (1990) Global culture: an introduction. In: Featherstone, M. (ed.) *Global Culture: Nationalism, Globalisation and Modernity*. Sage, London, pp. 1–14.

Feldheim, P. and Javeau, C. (1977) Time budgets and industrialization. In: Szalai, A. and Petrella, R. (eds) *Cross-National Comparative Survey*

Research: Theory and Practice. Pergamon, Oxford, UK, pp. 201–230.

Filipcova, B. (ed.) (1972) Special issue on socialist life style. *Society and Leisure* No. 3.

Gershuny, J., Fisher, K., Gauthier, A., Jones, S. and Baert, P. (2000) Appendix 2: a longitudinal multinational collection of time-use data – the MTUS. In: Gershuny, J. (ed.) *Changing Times: Work and Leisure in Postindustrial Society*. Oxford University Press, Oxford, UK, pp. 270–288 (see also: www.iser.essex.ac.uk/mtus/index.php).

Gratton, C. (1999) *COMPASS 1999: Sports Participation in Europe*. UK Sport, London.

Hall, S. and Greben, A. (eds) (1992) *Formations of Modernity*. Polity Press, Cambridge, UK.

Hantrais, L. and Kamphorst, T.J. (eds) (1987) *Trends in the Arts: a Multinational Perspective*. Giordano Bruno Amersfoot, Voorthuizen, The Netherlands.

Hantrais, L. and Samuel, N. (1991) The state of the art in comparative studies in leisure. *Loisir et Société/Society and Leisure* 14(2), 381–398.

Harvey, D. (2000) *Spaces of Hope*. Edinburgh University Press, Edinburgh.

Henderson, K. (1991) *Dimensions of Choice: a Qualitative Approach to Recreation, Parks, and Leisure Research*. Venture, State College, Pennsylvania.

ILO (International Labour Office) (Annual) *Year Book of Labour Statistics*. ILO, Paris.

Jarvie, G. and Maguire, J. (1994) *Sport and Leisure in Social Thought*. Routledge, London.

Kamphorst, T.J. and Roberts, K. (1989) *Trends in Sports: a Multinational Perspective*. Giordana Bruno Culemberg, Voorthuizen, The Netherlands.

Kamphorst, T.J., Tibori, T.T. and Giljam, M.J. (1984) Quantitative and qualitative research: shall the twain ever meet? *World Leisure and Recreation* 26(6), 25–27.

Kelly, J. and Warnick, R.B. (1999) *Recreation Trends and Markets: the 21st Century*. Sagamore, Champaign, Illinois.

Kopytoff, I. (1987) The international African frontier: the making of African political culture. In: Kopytoff, I. (ed.) *The African Frontier: the Reproduction of Typical African Societies*. Indiana University Press, Bloomington, Indiana, pp. 3–84.

Marans, R.W. and Mohai, P. (1991) Leisure resources, recreational activity, and quality of life. In: Driver, B.L., Brown, P.J. and Peterson, G.L. (eds) *Benefits of Leisure*. Venture, State College, Pennsylvania, pp. 351–364.

Martin, W.H. and Mason, S. (1998) *Transforming the Future: Rethinking Free Time and Work*. Leisure Consultants, Sudbury, UK.

Mercer, D. (1994) Monitoring the spectator society: an overview of research and policy issues. In: Mercer, D. (ed.) *New Viewpoints in Australian Outdoor Recreation Research and Planning*. Hepper/Marriott Publications, Melbourne, pp. 1–28.

Mintel International Group Ltd (nd) Available at website: http://reports.mintel.com (accessed June 2004).

Novak, S. (1977) The strategy of cross-national survey research for the development of social theory. In: Szalai, A. and Petrella, R. (eds) *Cross-national Comparative Survey Research: Theory and Practice*. Pergamon, Oxford, UK, pp. 3–48.

OECD (Organization for Economic Cooperation and Development) (Annual) *Tourism Policy and International Tourism in OECD Member Countries*. OECD, Paris.

OECD (Organization for Economic Cooperation and Development) (1993) *OECD Health Systems: Facts and Trends 1960–1991*. OECD, Paris.

Olszewska, A. and Roberts, K. (eds) (1989) *Leisure and Lifestyle: a Comparative Analysis of Free Time*. Sage, London.

ORRRC (Outdoor Recreation Resources Review Commission) (1962) *National Recreation Survey, Study Report No. 19*. Government Printing Office, Washington, DC.

Pentland, W.E., Harvey, A.S., Powell Lawton, M. and McColl, M.A. (eds) (1999) *Time Use Research in the Social Sciences*. Kluwer/Plenum, New York.

Perez de Cuellar, J. (1987) Statement. *World Leisure and Recreation* 29(1), 3.

Perkins, H. (1997) *Knowledge Base Profiles: Leisure and Recreation Studies*. Ministry of Research, Science and Technology, Wellington, New Zealand.

Przeworski, A. and Teune, H. (1973) Equivalence in cross-national research. In: Warwick, D.P. and Osherson, S. (eds) *Comparative Research Methods*. Prentice-Hall, Englewood Cliffs, New Jersey, pp. 119–137.

Roberts, K. (1978) *Contemporary Society and the Growth of Leisure*. Longman, London.

Rojek, C. (1989) Leisure and recreation theory. In: Jackson, E.L. and Burton, T.L. (eds) *Understanding Leisure and Recreation: Mapping the Past and Charting the Future*. Venture, State College, Pennsylvania, pp. 69–88.

Rojek, C. (1995) *Decentring Leisure: Rethinking Leisure Theory*. Sage, London.

Szalai, A. (ed.) (1972) *The Use of Time: Daily Activities of Urban and Suburban Populations in Twelve Countries*. Mouton, The Hague.

UN (United Nations) (Annual) *Statistical Yearbook*. UN, New York.

Veal, A.J. (2002) *Leisure and Tourism Policy and Planning*. CAB International, Wallingford, UK.

Veal, A.J. and Lynch, R. (2001) *Australian Leisure.* Longman, Sydney, Australia.

Warwick, D.P. and Osherson, S. (1973) Comparative analysis and the social sciences. In: Warwick, D.P. and Osherson, S. (eds) *Comparative Research Methods.* Prentice-Hall, Englewood Cliffs, New Jersey, pp. 3–41.

Wearing, B. (1998) *Leisure and Feminist Theory.* Sage, London.

WTO (World Tourism Organization) (Annual) *Yearbook of Tourism Statistics.* WTO, Madrid.

2 Australia

A.J. Veal

Introduction: Early Surveys

National leisure participation surveys in Australia were preceded by local, regional and state surveys (Veal, 1993a). One such local study, published under the simple title *Leisure*, was undertaken in 1958 for a religious charitable organization in an unidentified 'Australian housing estate', where 178 respondents were asked how they usually spent their weekday evenings and Saturdays and Sundays. Setting the tone for all future leisure participation surveys, the study report concluded:

> The most striking characteristic of the study was the concentration of leisure-time activities in and around the home. Home activities occupied most of the time of most people on Saturday mornings and afternoons, and Sunday mornings. It is difficult to know whether this preoccupation was by choice or necessity. However, most of the purely recreational and optional pursuits, such as reading and watching television, which absorbed a large amount of time, were also centred on the home.
> (Scott and U'Ren, 1962, p. 2)

The study noted that home-centred and privatized (as opposed to communal) leisure activities dominated people's leisure time, implying a limited role for communal leisure provision by 'churches, municipal councils and voluntary associations'.

The first supposedly 'national' survey was the federal government Cities Commission's 1974 study, *Australians' Use of Time*; however, this was not based on a national sample but was conducted in Melbourne, the capital of Victoria, and Aldbury-Wodonga, a developing twin city on the Victoria/New South Wales border. With a total sample size of some 1500 adults, it was primarily a 'time-budget' study rather than a 'participation' study and can be seen as the forerunner of later national time-budget studies, as discussed below.

National Surveys: 1975–2002

Survey activity in relation to leisure participation in Australia developed rapidly in the 1970s and 1980s. Table 2.1 lists the national surveys conducted between 1975 and 2002 in Australia, including information on the year conducted, sample size, activities covered, the age range of sample, survey type and participation reference period.

The surveys reviewed here fall into three groups:

1. Questionnaire-based leisure participation surveys covering a wide range of leisure activities;
2. Diary-based time-budget surveys in which leisure is just one of a number of time-uses; and

Table 2.1. National and regional leisure participation and time-budget surveys, Australia, 1975–2002.

Survey	Year	Organization	Survey type[a]	Activities covered	Reference period	Participation measure	Seasons covered[c]	Area covered	Sample size	Age range included	Report reference
GSS: Leisure Activities Away from Home	1975	ABS	QS	Leisure away from home	1 year	Acts in which you 'spend most time'	All	Urban areas	18,700	15+	ABS (1978)
National Recreation Participation Survey	1985	DSRT	QS	All leisure – list of 91 activities	1 week	At least once in last week	Winter	Nation-wide	2500	14+	DSRT (1986a)
	1985	DSRT	QS	All leisure – list of 91 activities	1 week	At least once in last week	Spring	Nation-wide	2500	14+	DSRT (1986b)
	1986	DSRT	QS	All leisure – list of 91 activities	1 week	At least once in last week	Summer	Nation-wide	2500	14+	DSRT (1986c)
	1986	DSRT	QS	All leisure – list of 91 activities	1 week	At least once in last week	Autumn	Nation-wide	2500	14+	DSRT (1986d)
	1987	DASETT	QS	All leisure – list of 91 activities	1 week	At least once in last week	Spring	Nation-wide	2068	14+	DASETT (1988a)
	1991	DASETT	QS	All leisure – list of 91 activities	1 week + 1 month	At least once in last week (+ monthy)	Summer	Nation-wide	2103	14+	DASETT (1991), Veal (1993b)
Physical Activity Levels of Australians	1984	DASETT	QS	'Physical activity' + participation in 17 listed activities	2 weeks	Frequency in 2 weeks	Winter	Nation-wide	3500	14+	DASETT (1988b)

1985	DASETT	QS	'Physical activity' + participation in 17 listed activities	2 weeks	Frequency in 2 weeks	Summer	Nation-wide	3480	14+	DASETT (1988b)
1985	DASETT	QS	'Physical activity' + participation in 17 listed activities	2 weeks	Frequency in 2 weeks	Winter	Nation-wide	3390	14+	DASETT (1988b)
1986	DASETT	QS	'Physical activity' + participation in 17 listed activities	2 weeks	Frequency in 2 weeks	Summer	Nation-wide	3360	14+	DASETT (1988b)
1986	DASETT	QS	'Physical activity' + participation in 17 listed activities	2 weeks	Frequency in 2 weeks	Winter	Nation-wide	3700	14+	DASETT (1988b)
1987	DASETT	QS	'Physical activity' + participation in 17 listed activities	2 weeks	Frequency in 2 weeks	Summer	Nation-wide	3590	14+	DASETT (1988b)
1997	Active Australia	QS	'Physical activity' + participation in 17 listed activities	2 weeks	Last week + weekly in last 6 months	Midwinter – early summer	Nation-wide	4800	18–75	Bauman et al. (2001)
1999	Active Australia	QS	'Physical activity' + participation in 17 listed activities	2 weeks	Last week + weekly in last 6 months	Midwinter – early summer	Nation-wide	4800	18–75	Bauman et al. (2001)
2000	Active Australia	QS	'Physical activity' + participation in 17 listed activities	2 weeks	Last week + weekly in last 6 months	Midwinter – early summer	Nation-wide	4800	18–75	Bauman et al. (2001)

Continued

Table 2.1. *Continued*

Survey	Year	Organization	Survey type[a]	Activities covered	Reference period	Participation measure	Seasons covered[c]	Area covered	Sample size	Age range included	Report reference
Participation in Sport and Physical Activities	1995/96	ABS (PSM)	QS	Sport and physical activities[b]	Year	Participation at least once in year	Year	Nation-wide	22,000	18+	ABS (1997)
	1996/97	ABS (PSM)	QS	Sport and physical activities[b]	Year	Participation at least once in year	Year	Nation-wide	26,000	18+	ABS (1998a)
	1997/98	ABS (PSM)	QS	Sport and physical activities[b]	Year	Participation at least once in year	Year	Nation-wide	12,500	18+	ABS (1998b)
	1998/99	ABS (PSM)	QS	Sport and physical activities[b]	Year	Participation at least once in year	Year	Nation-wide	13,000	18+	ABS (1999a)
	1999/2000	ABS (PSM)	QS	Sport and physical activities[b]	Year	Participation at least once in year	Year	Nation-wide	13,000	18+	ABS (2000)
	2001/02	ABS (GSS)	QS	Sport and physical activities[b]	Year	Participation at least once in year	Year	Nation-wide	15,500	18+	ABS (2003b)
Exercise, Recreation and Sport Survey (ERASS)	2001	ASC	QS	Sport and physical activities	Year	Participation at least once in year	Four quarterly surveys	Nation-wide	13,600	15+	Dale and Ford (2002)

Title	Year	Agency	Type	Activities	Reference period	Participation	Frequency	Coverage	Sample	Age	Source
	2002	SCORS	QS	Sport and physical activities	Year	Participation at least once in year	Four quarterly surveys	Nation-wide	13,600	15+	SCORS (2003)
How Australians Use their Time	1992	ABS	TB	All time	1 day	Time spent	Year	Nation-wide	9000	15+	ABS (1994)
	1997	ABS	TB	All time	1 day	Time spent	Year	Nation-wide	7000	15+	ABS (1999a)
Attendance at Selected Cultural Venues (and Events)	1991	ABS/MPS	QS	Selected venues/events	Year	At least once	Year	Nation-wide	16,000	18+	ABS (1992)
	1995	ABS/MPS	Qs	Selected venues/events	Year	At least once	Year	Nation-wide	26,000	15+	ABS (1995)
	1999	ABS/MPS	QS	Selected venues/events	Year	At least once	Year	Nation-wide	26,000	15+	ABS (1999a)
	2002	ABS/GSS	QS	Selected venues/events	Year	At least once	Year	Nation-wide	15,500	18+	ABS (2003a)
Australians and the Arts	1999	Australia Council	QS	Arts, entertainment, media			Not specified		1200	15+	Saatchi and Saatchi (1999)

ABS, Australian Bureau of Statistics; DSRT, Department of Sport, Recreation and Tourism; DASETT, Department of the Arts, Sport, the Environment, Tourism and Territories; MPS, Monthly Population Survey; PSM, Population Survey Monitor; GSS, General Social Survey; ASC, Australian Sports Commission; SCORS, Standing Committee on Recreation and Sport.

[a] QS, questionnaire survey; TB, time-budget survey.

[b] 'Physical activity' can include activities which are not always considered to be 'sport' – for example, non-competitive walking or cycling.

[c] Summer in Australia is the period November–February; winter is the period May–August.

3. Separate questionnaire-based surveys of participation in particular forms of leisure activity, notably: (i) sport and physical activities; (ii) the arts; and (iii) holiday-taking.

These groups of surveys are reviewed in turn below.

Leisure Participation Surveys

General Social Survey, 1975

The first national survey of leisure participation in Australia was the 1975 study, *Leisure Activities Away from Home*, which was part of the broader General Social Survey conducted by the Australian Bureau of Statistics (ABS, 1978). The survey involved a large sample of 18,700 persons from 8400 households. The main participation question asked was: 'In which activities do you spend most of your leisure time away from home?' A 'prompt' indicated that this was to include 'all activities for the last 12 months – that is for any season'. Space was provided for respondents to report up to seven activities. Extensive, expensive and competently conducted as this survey undoubtedly was, it did not provide a model for subsequent surveys, except in the list of individual activities which emerged. Asking people about the activities on which they 'spend most time' has not been widely accepted as the best approach to gathering participation data, since the term 'spend most time' lacks precision and, further, some activities which may be *significant* to the participant may not in fact take up very much of their time – for example playing squash. The 12-month reference period was also abandoned in some later surveys because of problems of accuracy.

National Recreation Participation Survey, 1985–1991

The most significant vehicle for collecting data on the broad range of leisure activities has been the series of six National Recreation Participation Surveys (NRPS), conducted by the market research company AGB:McNair on behalf of the federal Department of the Arts, Sport, the Environment, Tourism and Territories (DASETT) between 1985 and 1991. Each survey involved a nationwide sample of over 2000 individuals aged 14 years and over. The surveys were the fulfilment of a policy of the Commonwealth government, set out in a Ministerial statement in 1985:

> A first priority must be the creation of a comprehensive data base covering what Australians are doing in their leisure time . . . The Government will be working towards this end through the conduct of regular national recreation participation and attitudinal surveys which will take account of seasonal variations in recreation participation patterns and will provide a longitudinal perspective on recreation.
>
> (Brown, 1985, p. 26)

The NRPS used a precise methodology, asking respondents about participation in a specified list of 91 activities over the week prior to interview, with seasonality being addressed by conducting surveys at different times of the year. A report on historical comparisons and benefits of recreation activities was to be published but did not eventuate. Although the survey was conducted six times, its seasonal format precluded examination of trends in participation over time, since only two comparable pairs of seasonal surveys were conducted – spring 1985/1987 and summer 1986/1991.

Respondents were asked to indicate activities in which they had participated in their free time in the previous week. Showcards were utilized, providing lists of the selected activities in five groupings: (i) home-based activities; (ii) social/cultural activities; (iii) organized sports; (iv) informal sports (in the tables presented here, the latter two categories have been combined); and (v) recreational activities. In the final, 1991, survey information on participation in the previous month was also gathered. In addition to the basic participation questions, respondents were also asked about *frequency* of participation, leisure facilities visited, and activities and facilities which they had not participated in or visited but would like to have, and reasons for non-participation or non-visitation. Considerable socio-demographic detail was also collected on respondents, including: age, gender, marital status, education level, country of birth, employment status and occupation, personal and household income, and size and composition of household.

The results of all the surveys were published by DASETT and its predecessor department in brief, descriptive, individual reports (DSRT,1986a–e; DASETT, 1988a,b, 1991). There is no publicly available evidence of policy developments based on the survey findings, and only limited use was made of the data by state governments and local authorities in recreation planning and policy making. A collection of commentaries on the 1985/86 surveys, written by academics, was compiled and published in 1989 by DASETT (1989), and some use has been made of the data by independent academics for social analysis (McKay, 1990; Parker and Paddick, 1990; Darcy, 1993; Veal, 1993a,b; Veal and Cushman, 1993; Veal and Lynch, 2001) and forecasting (Veal, 1987, 1988; Veal and Darcy, 1993; Veal *et al.*, 1998; Lynch and Veal, 2001, pp. 418–419).

Although the NRPS is, at the time of writing, more than 10 years old, it still provides the most recently available, publicly accessible, national general leisure participation data in Australia. Following the summer (February) 1991 survey, government policy on data, including participation surveys, was reviewed by the Statistical Working Group of the Sport and Recreation Ministers Council (see Corporate Concern, 1994). The latter includes ministers for sport and recreation from the federal government, the six states and two territories. These ministers do not have responsibility for the arts, broadcasting or tourism or, in most cases, for national parks, or for local government, the level at which much of the planning and public provision for leisure takes place. Fortuitously, the federal department responsible for the NRPS during the 1980s did have responsibility for most of these areas, which may explain why the survey covered such a wide range of activities. It was therefore a small step to include activities outside of any direct ministerial responsibility, such as home-based leisure and social and entertainment activities. But ministers of sport and recreation have a narrower remit, so later surveys sponsored by the Sport and Recreation Ministers Council were confined to sport and physical recreation only, as discussed below.

Participation

The NRPS used a 1-week reference period, which is unusual, and has a number of advantages and disadvantages. Some of the disadvantages were partly overcome in the last, 1991, survey, which also included information on participation in the 4 weeks prior to interview. A feature of the NRPS data presented here is that it relates to summer, so for some activities, particularly winter sports, the data may be misleading. Other versions of the NRPS provide data for other seasons, but the latest winter season data relate to 1986, which is too out-of-date to be presented here. One of the major categories of activity affected by seasonality is sport, and more up-to-date data on this are presented later in the chapter.

Table 2.2 presents the basic participation data from the NRPS for summer 1991. The most popular activities, as in the 1950s study reported at the beginning of this chapter, were home-based. Even among the activities taking place outside the home, visiting other people's homes, was by far the most popular. While the physically undemanding activities of watching television/videos and 'relaxing, doing nothing' are the most popular home-based activities, the amount of physically active home-based activity is notable, with 37% reporting engagement in exercise and keep fit activities, 23% swimming in their own or friends' swimming pools; and 41% gardening. A unique feature of the 1991 NRPS was the inclusion of 'talking on the telephone' (for at least 15 min), which was engaged in by almost half the adult population.

Among the social/cultural activities, in addition to visiting friends and relatives, popular activities are dining out (32%) and shopping for pleasure (30%). The inclusion of the latter activity was an innovation of the 1991 NRPS and is rare in world terms (but see Chapter 12 for the use of shopping centres in New Zealand). Driving for pleasure (19%), church activities (14%), visiting pubs (14%) and going on picnics/barbecues (14%) are the other popular activities in this group.

Among the sporting activities, swimming is by far the most popular, with 15% participation, although it should be noted that this particular activity could include a significant amount of non-competitive, and even

Table 2.2. Leisure participation: Australia, summer 1991.

	% participating in last:			% participating in last:	
	Week	Month		Week	Month
Home-based leisure			Sport		
Watch TV	93.6	n/a	Athletics	0.5	0.9
Entertain at home	35.8	n/a	Gymnastics	0.4	0.6
Electronic and	11.2	n/a	Basketball	2.0	2.9
computer games			Netball –	0.6	0.8
Exercise, keep fit	35.7	n/a	indoors		
Swim in own/	23.3	n/a	Netball –	0.8	1.0
friends' pool			outdoors		
Play musical	8.8	n/a	Tennis	5.8	9.0
instrument			Squash	1.9	3.6
Arts, crafts	21.4	n/a	Badminton	0.2	0.4
Reading	70.4	n/a	Cricket –	1.5	2.0
Listen music	65.1	n/a	indoor		
Gardening for	41.3	n/a	Cricket –	3.9	7.2
pleasure			outdoor		
Indoor games	17.7	n/a	Baseball/softball	0.6	0.6
Outdoor play	28.9	n/a	Rugby League	0.2	0.6
with children			Rugby Union	0.1	0.1
Talk on telephone	48.8	n/a	Aust. Rules	0.3	1.0
(15 min +)			football		
Relax, do nothing	58.0	n/a	Soccer –	1.0	1.6
Social/cultural			outdoor		
Visit friends/relatives	62.8	80.2	Soccer – indoor	0.3	0.5
Dining, eating out	31.7	53.8	Touch football	0.9	1.4
Dancing, discotheque	5.9	12.7	Martial arts	0.9	1.3
Visit pub	13.8	22.8	Motor sport	0.4	1.0
Visit (licensed) club	9.7	18.2	Archery/shooting	0.5	0.9
Movies	8.0	25.3	Orienteering	.	0.2
Pop concerts	1.6	5.6	Hockey –	0.3	0.3
Theatre	1.1	4.4	indoor		
Music recital/opera	0.5	2.2	Hockey –	0.3	0.3
Other live	0.8	3.2	outdoor		
performances			Cycling	5.0	8.0
Special interest	1.6	3.4	Golf	4.1	7.9
courses			Swimming	15.5	22.9
Church activities	13.6	17.9	Surfing/lifesaving	2.5	4.2
Library activities	7.3	13.6	Horse riding	0.6	1.5
Museums, galleries	1.6	7.5	Rink sports	0.3	0.8
Exhibitions	0.9	3.9	Lawn bowls	1.5	2.0
Arts crafts	3.9	8.0	10-pin bowling	1.5	2.9
Hobbies	11.2	16.2	Recreation		
Picnic/barbecue	13.7	36.4	Walk dog	14.2	17.3
ex-home			Walk for	26.6	35.8
Visit parks	10.3	22.8	pleasure		
Horse races/trots/	1.7	5.0	Aerobics	5.4	7.2
dog races			Jogging/running	3.9	5.3
Sport spectator	6.6	13.4	Bushwalking/	2.3	5.6
Drive for pleasure	19.0	38.5	hiking		
Bird watching	2.6	4.3	Skateboarding	0.3	0.8
Play electronic	4.0	6.7	Shooting/	0.3	1.0
games			hunting		

Continued

Table 2.2. *Continued*

	% participating in last:			% participating in last:	
	Week	Month		Week	Month
Shopping for pleasure	29.6	48.1	Fishing	3.4	8.6
			Water activities – non-power	1.3	2.8
			Water activities – powered	0.9	3.1

n/a, Not available; ., less than 0.05%.
Source: National Recreation Participation Survey; sample size (persons aged 14+): 2103.

non-physical activity involved in being at the beach. Tennis comes a clear second, with only 6% participation, then cycling (5%) and golf (4%) are the only activities with 4% or more participants. Football is disadvantaged in this comparison, since it is a winter sport; however, the division of football into five codes in Australia, and the fact that it is overwhelmingly a male pastime, means that, even in winter, no one football code attracts more than 2 or 3% participation.

The 'recreation' category overlaps considerably with sport, but is intended to encompass the more informal physical recreation activities. The most popular of these is walking, with a dog (14%) or without (27%). The so-called boom activities of the 1980s, aerobics and jogging/running, attract only 5% and 4%, respectively.

The table also includes data on participation in the previous month. It illustrates very clearly that the length of the reference period affects different activities differently. Thus for activities such as visiting museums and art galleries, which are engaged in by most people comparatively rarely, the monthly participation rate is up to four times the weekly rate. For other activities, such as many of the team sports, where participation often involves some sort of regular commitment, such as once or twice a week, the monthly rate is not very different from the weekly rate.

Gender

Table 2.3 compares participation levels between men and women for those activities with at least a 5% participation level. Those activities where the levels of participation are significantly different between men and women are indicated with an asterisk. Exclusion of activities with less than 5% participation results in the exclusion of many sports, where men predominate. Of the 40 activities retained, for 11 there is no significant difference between the sexes; of the 30 remaining, 15 have higher participation rates among women and 14 among men. While this might suggest more equality between the sexes than anticipated, it does not, of course, indicate equality in any complete sense. In particular it is notable that, of the 15 activities where women's participation rates are higher, seven are home-based, illustrating the constraints on women in regarding access to activities outside the home environment.

Age

Table 2.4 presents participation levels by age group for the same 40 activities as included in Table 2.3. Two particular features should be noted: first, for 29 of the 40 listed activities, the lowest participation rate is among the 60-plus, age group. In surveys where the list of activities is dominated by sports and other physically demanding pastimes, this might be expected, but this is not the case here. Lower than average participation levels might be expected for the 60 and over age group, given that the group includes the 'old old'; and given that older age groups in Australia, as elsewhere, are, on average, economically disadvantaged compared with younger age groups. Nevertheless older people have large amounts of leisure time and it is generally believed that they are becoming more active, and many public programmes are directed at the elderly. These factors, however,

Table 2.3. Leisure participation by gender: Australia, summer 1991.

	% participating in week prior to survey		
	Male	Female	Total
Sample size (persons aged 14+)	1042	1059	2102
Home-based activities			
Watch TV/videos	93.5	93.7	93.6
Entertaining	32.6	38.9*	35.8
Electronic/computer games	13.7*	8.8	11.2
Exercising/keep fit	36.4	35.1	35.7
Swim in home pool	23.9	22.6	23.3
Play music instrument	9.8*	7.7	8.8
Art/craft/hobby	15.6	27.1*	21.4
Reading	64.5	76.2*	70.4
Listening to radio	77.1	75.5	76.3
Gardening	39.0	43.6*	41.3
Phone friends	36.3	61.1*	48.8
Listen to music	63.3	66.9*	65.1
Indoor games	17.4	18.0	17.7
Play outdoors with children	25.6	32.1*	28.9
Relax/do nothing	57.9	58.0	58.0
Out-of-home social activities			
Visit friends/relatives	59.5	66.0*	62.8
Dine/eat out	31.8	31.6	31.7
Dance/go to discotheque	7.5*	4.3	5.9
Visit pub	18.8*	8.9	13.8
Visit club	12.1*	7.5	9.7
Movies	8.3	7.6	8.0
Pleasure shopping	23.0	36.1*	29.6
Hobbies	11.4	11.1	11.2
Church activities	11.6	15.5*	13.6
Library activities	6.1	8.5*	7.3
Picnic/barbecue	13.8	13.6	13.7
Spectator at sport	7.6*	5.5	6.6
Drive for pleasure	20.3*	17.7	19.0
Visit parks	10.2	10.4	10.3
Electronic games	6.1*	1.9	4.0
Walking the dog	12.7	15.6*	14.2
Walk for pleasure	23.8	29.4*	26.6
Sport/physical recreation			
Aerobics	2.2	8.6*	5.4
Cricket/outdoor	6.4*	1.5	3.9
Cycling	6.0*	4.1	5.0
Fishing	5.2*	1.6	3.4
Golf	6.3*	2.0	4.1
Running/jogging	5.3*	2.5	3.9
Swimming	13.2	17.8*	15.5
Tennis	6.9*	4.7	5.8

* Statistically significant difference, at 5% level.
Source: National Recreation Participation Survey, 1991 (DASETT, 1991) – re-analysis of data
at University of Technology, Sydney.

Table 2.4. Leisure participation by age: Australia, summer 1991.

			% participating in week prior to interview				
Age:	14–19	20–24	25–29	30–49	50–59	60+	Total
Sample size	226	233	209	776	246	411	2102
Watch TV/videos	**98.5	94.0	93.9	92.9	92.6	92.5*	93.6
Entertaining	33.7	42.6	**44.9	38.5	34.6	24.1*	35.8
Electronic/computer games	**33.8	11.7	12.1	12.2	1.5	2.2*	11.2
Exercising/keep fit	**53.7	47.4	42.8	37.2	23.5	20.2*	35.7
Swim in home pool	**45.0	24.2	23.1	26.8	16.1	8.4*	23.3
Play music instrument	**17.7	11.3	8.5	9.0	4.6	4.5*	8.8
Art/craft/hobby	22.8	14.4	17.3	22.2	**32.2	18.5	21.4
Reading	67.7	69.5	66.5	**73.4	68.5	69.8	70.4
Listening to radio	80.5	**81.5	74.7	77.6	74.6	70.3*	76.3
Gardening	11.2	20.9	37.3	48.0	**54.3	51.2	41.3
Phone friends	**58.5	56.6	50.8	49.8	47.3	37.1*	48.8
Listen to music	**81.1	73.3	74.6	64.0	57.6	53.2*	65.1
Indoor games	**35.1	17.6	15.4	19.0	11.4	10.7*	17.7
Play outdoors	25.5	27.1	38.4	**39.4	19.8	12.5*	28.9
Relax/do nothing	66.9	**68.7	58.6	57.0	48.3	54.2	58.0
Visit friends/relatives	71.8	**75.5	73.3	60.2	69.3	46.4*	62.8
Dine/eat out	34.6	**38.2	36.2	32.9	30.1	22.5*	31.7
Dance/discotheque	**16.8	**16.2	10.0	2.4	1.6	1.1*	5.9
Visit pub	14.8	**31.0	23.6	13.8	6.2	3.3*	13.8
Visit club	6.8	10.1	9.5	8.6	**13.9	10.8	9.7
Movies	**22.6	11.5	10.1	6.5	3.7	2.1*	8.0
Pleasure shopping	**35.9	33.6	27.5	30.2	30.0	23.3*	29.6
Hobbies	**15.6	11.5	11.4	10.7	14.7	7.5*	11.2
Church activities	12.9	7.5	8.4	13.9	16.1	**17.8	13.6
Library activities	4.5	4.9	5.5	8.8	5.6	**9.3	7.3
Picnic/barbecue	9.8	15.6	**19.4	17.8	11.4	5.7*	13.7
Spectator at sport	**12.1	7.4	6.8	7.8	3.4	2.6*	6.6
Drive for pleasure	15.8	**24.2	19.6	21.4	18.6	13.2*	19.0
Visit parks	6.9	10.9	8.5	**15.4	6.7	5.4*	10.3
Electronic games	**12.9	4.3	3.8	4.4	0.5	0.2*	4.0
Walking the dog	**20.1	11.7	8.8	16.1	17.6	9.4	14.2
Walk for pleasure	19.2	24.5	26.2	**28.4	27.1	**28.5	26.6
Aerobics	9.5	**12.5	9.2	4.6	1.4	1.2*	5.4
Cricket/outdoor	**11.4	6.9	6.1	3.2	1.1	0.2*	3.9
Cycling	**8.6	**8.9	5.6	5.5	1.3	2.0	5.0
Fishing	**5.1	**4.6	2.8	3.8	2.1	2.0*	3.4
Golf	2.7	3.4	2.7	**5.4	**4.6	3.3	4.1
Running/jogging	5.9	**9.0	6.8	4.2	0.0	0.0*	3.9
Swim/dive/water polo	**24.0	19.9	19.0	18.6	8.0	5.4*	15.5
Tennis	**9.9	8.6	4.2	6.9	5.3	0.9*	5.8

*60+ age group lowest participation rate. ** Highest rate.
Source: Centre for Leisure and Tourism Studies, 1994.

do not appear to have overcome the traditional stereotype of an elderly population with a restricted range of leisure activity.

The second feature of the age-related data lies at the other end of the age range, namely the 14–19-year-old group. They are the most active group in 20 of the 40 listed activities. As a small age group (11% of the adult population), this does not mean that they dominate the activity in every case, but it does illustrate the 'life-cycle' thesis, that, as people age and family and work responsibilities accumulate, participation in many leisure activities declines. And the low participation rates for the elderly suggest that, once lost, leisure habits are not regained.

Economic status and occupation

Table 2.5 shows participation rates by economic status and occupation. The first four columns refer to people not in full-time paid employment. The 'retired' category overlaps with the elderly group already discussed and the 'student' group overlaps with the 14–19 year group. The 'home duties' category overlaps considerably with the discussion of gender, but separate data on women in all of the economic status categories would be needed to discuss this group fully.

The unemployed group are of special interest here, given that, at the time of the survey, the level of unemployment had reached 10% in Australia for the first time since the 1930s. Of the 40 activities, there are 19 where the participation rate for the unemployed was equal to or higher than the average (these are marked in the table). This suggests that the unemployed do use some of their largely unwelcome free time for leisure purposes. But in only one activity – fishing – are the unemployed the *most* active group. As with the elderly, this indicates that more than time is required for an active leisure life.

For those in full-time paid employment, social inequalities in leisure participation are starkly illustrated. In all cases except one (indoor games) the employed groups have higher participation rates than the average. For 23 out of the 40 activities the highest participation rate is among the managerial/professional group. The clerical/sales group is the second most active with 19 highs (eight being equal with the managerial/professional group). The 'supervisors' group has the highest participation rate in only one activity, tennis. The skilled manual workers have the highest rate in only four activities – dancing, pub-going, sport spectating and fishing – conforming very much to a working class stereotype. Unskilled manual workers have the highest rate only in playing indoor games and for most of the rest of the activities their participation rates are lower than the average.

Time-budget surveys

Although some limited time-budget surveys had been conducted in Australia in the 1970s and 1980s (Cities Commission, 1975; ABS, 1988; Bittman, 1991), the first nationwide time-budget study was conducted in 1992 by the Australian Bureau of Statistics (ABS), followed by a second in 1997. These surveys involved samples of 7000–9000 people in 3000 households, keeping diaries in February, May, September and November. The reports of these studies (ABS, 1994, 1998a) present an enormous amount of detailed information, in particular on the differences in time-use between men and women and between people in varying domestic situations (for example, with and without children, single-parent households, single-person households).

Table 2.6 shows the average daily time-budget for all respondents to the 1997 survey. The data are averaged over all individuals aged 15 and over and cover all types of day, including weekdays and weekends, which explains the low figures for those activities engaged in by only a proportion of respondents (e.g. education – 2% of time, or paid work – 14% of time). Nevertheless, the table gives a broad indication of the significance of leisure time in people's lives, since, on average, it takes up almost 22% of total time, compared with only 14% taken up by paid work. The table also indicates that men have more leisure time than women and engage in more paid work and less unpaid work.

The variation in leisure time availability among different age groups for men and women is shown in Table 2.7. These data show that, as might be expected, people have most leisure time at the beginning and end of their adult lives and that, in all age groups, women have less leisure time than men. Table 2.8 also shows a predictable pattern: that parents with children have less leisure time than those without children, although the differences are less than might have been expected.

Table 2.9 gives details of time spent on specific leisure activities; this contrasts with the measure from participation surveys, such as the NRPS, which is based on participation 'at least once' in the reference period, with no distinction being made between short and long periods of participation. The table reveals that the

Table 2.5. Leisure participation by occupation: Australia, summer 1991.

	Not in full-time paid employment				In full-time paid employment					Total
	Retired	Unemployed	F/T student (aged 14+)	Home duties	Manager/ professional	Supervisor	Clerical/ sales	Skilled manual	Unskilled manual	
Sample:	323	144	175	383	392	53	270	181	134	2055
					% Participating in week prior to interview					
Watch TV/videos	91.8	95.7!	99.6	94.7	93.7*	87.0	94.3*	90.0	91.5	93.7
Entertaining	22.9	33.9	31.2	37.6	45.0	33.3	46.6*	32.9	25.6	35.8
Electronic/computer games	2.2	13.1!	35.0	9.3	13.5*	5.4	10.5	5.1	9.3	11.1
Exercising/keep fit	21.5	36.0!	56.8	30.9	43.4*	30.4	40.3	32.4	29.6	35.6
Swim in home pool	7.0	22.0	48.5	18.1	28.6*	20.3	28.0	26.2	18.6	23.3
Play music instrument	4.1	7.7	22.5	6.8	12.0*	2.2	7.1	4.5	9.1	8.6
Art/craft/hobby	19.8	14.9	26.2	27.7	25.7*	17.6	23.0	11.2	10.7	21.6
Reading	66.8	64.1	77.6	72.2	79.3*	57.3	75.2	57.8	58.5	70.4
Listening to radio	72.0	79.5!	78.9	72.5	80.0	73.2	82.9*	72.4	72.6	76.3
Gardening	49.5	25.6	12.1	50.6	46.2*	44.9	41.8	35.8	41.0	41.4
Phone friends	32.3	45.6	63.0	61.6	54.1	36.1	55.5*	36.3	30.1	48.8
Listen to music	51.1	62.2	77.5	64.2	73.8*	57.3	73.8*	62.3	52.0	65.1
Indoor games	10.6	20.6!	36.7	20.0	16.4	10.0	17.1	11.1	17.5*	17.7
Play outdoors	12.5	18.8	29.7	41.6	31.1	25.2	33.3*	24.5	29.9	28.6
Relax/do nothing	56.0	60.6!	65.2	57.4	55.9	58.0	65.9*	48.3	54.5	57.9
Visit friends/rels	45.7	57.3	72.6	67.6	64.6	57.6	72.1*	61.0	62.5	62.7
Dine/eat out	22.8	27.4	36.2	21.7	45.5*	30.1	39.1	30.2	23.6	31.4
Dance/go to disco	1.2	8.8!	11.7	2.8	6.1	3.4	8.7*	8.9*	4.8	5.8
Visit pub	4.8	17.6!	12.7	4.7	19.6	16.2	18.4	24.5*	16.3	13.7
Visit club	14.0	10.9!	3.6	5.5	10.7	7.3	13.6*	10.7	8.3	9.8
Movies/drive-ins	2.7	5.6	25.6	3.2	10.3*	4.9	10.9*	6.6	2.4	7.9

Continued

Table 2.5. *Continued*

	Not in full-time paid employment				In full-time paid employment					Total
	Retired	Unemployed	F/T student (aged 14+)	Home duties	Manager/ professional	Supervisor	Clerical/ sales	Skilled manual	Unskilled manual	
Sample:	323	144	175	383	392	53	270	181	134	2055
	% Participating in week prior to interview									
Pleasure shopping	21.5	31.4!	34.0	35.1	33.4	33.9	36.7*	16.8	16.7	29.7
Hobbies	8.4	12.3!	14.1	10.5	14.2*	12.0	10.0	10.7	10.2	11.3
Church activities	14.2	9.4	14.9	16.1	16.3*	13.2	10.7	8.4	11.2	13.5
Library activities	9.9	7.9!	7.1	9.2	8.5*	2.6	6.5	2.4	3.3	7.4
Picnic/barbecue	6.2	10.8	11.1	11.7	22.6*	18.5	15.8	12.6	13.4	13.7
Spectator at sport	2.4	5.4	13.8	3.9	6.3	6.1	8.8	11.7*	5.1	6.5
Drive for pleasure	13.8	18.1	17.9	16.8	23.8*	16.7	24.7*	16.8	16.7	18.9
Visit parks	7.5	13.0!	8.7	10.3	15.3*	6.6	11.4	7.7	4.2	10.3
Electronic games	0.7	4.9!	13.8	2.1	4.6*	3.6	3.4	2.3	4.1	3.9
Walking the dog	9.9	14.6!	19.1	12.3	15.9	11.8	18.3*	10.1	14.8	14.1
Walk for pleasure	30.4	28.0!	17.3	30.8	29.2*	12.3	28.3*	16.2	22.3	26.4
Aerobics	0.8	2.8	12.3	6.1	5.1	2.4	9.5*	3.4	5.8	5.5
Cricket/outdoor	0.2	5.0!	11.2	0.9	5.6	1.9	5.7*	3.6	5.1	4.0
Cycling	2.2	7.0!	8.9	3.0	6.9*	4.3	6.9*	3.2	6.0	5.1
Fishing	1.7	9.2!	4.6	1.0	2.2	6.5	3.2	9.2*	2.2	3.4
Golf	3.6	0.9	2.0	2.1	8.1*	2.2	4.6	5.3	3.9	4.1
Running/jogging	0.0	3.1	9.1	0.4	9.0*	2.6	4.0	2.3	3.3	3.8
Swim/dive/water polo	4.6	12.6	30.8	14.0	21.9*	14.8	21.2*	9.3	9.0	15.6
Tennis	1.1	4.9	12.2	3.7	8.9	14.0*	6.9	4.2	2.5	5.7

! Unemployed equal to or higher than average. * Highest rates among those in full-time employment (1% differences or less ignored).
Source: Centre for Leisure and Tourism Studies.

Table 2.6. Average daily time spent on main activities, Australia, 1997.

	All persons aged 15 and over					
	Males		Females		Total	
Sample size:	3600 approx.		3600 approx.		7200	
Australian population aged 15+ ('000s):	6564		6690		13254	
	Time spent per day					
Activity groups	Minutes	%	Minutes	%	Minutes	%
Sleep	517	35.9	516	35.8	516	35.8
Personal care (personal hygiene, etc.)	141	9.8	155	10.8	149	10.3
Education	24	1.7	28	1.9	26	1.8
Domestic activities	167	11.6	303	21.0	237	16.4
Paid work	261	18.1	132	9.2	196	13.6
Leisure	325	22.6	301	20.9	313	21.7
Undescribed	5	0.3	5	0.3	5	0.3
Total (minutes in a day)	1440	100.0	1440	100.0	1440	100.0

Source: ABS (1998a, pp. 17–18).

Table 2.7. Daily leisure time by age and gender (min/day), Australia, 1997.

Age groups	Males	Females	Total
15–24	379	319	350
25–34	282	250	265
35–44	270	253	261
45–54	293	279	286
55–64	360	352	355
65 and over	441	420	429
Total	325	301	313

Source: ABS (1998a, p. 55).

Table 2.8. Leisure time by domestic situation and gender (min/day), Australia, 1997.

Domestic situation	Males	Females
Couples with dependent children	254	239
Couples with non-dependent children	323	306
Lone parents	353	288
Couples without children	356	282
Lone persons	373	338
Neither parent nor partner	384	273

Source: ABS (1998a, pp. 53–55).

leisure activity which takes up most time is watching television, and shows considerable differences between men and women, with men spending more time engaging in sport and watching television and women spending more time socializing, engaging in hobbies and crafts, relaxing and in talking. The gendered nature of leisure, as discussed elsewhere in the book, is therefore clearly illustrated in time-budget data.

Re-analysis by Bittman (1998) of earlier Australian time-budget data indicates that, between 1974 and 1992, free time for men in Australia increased only marginally (5 minutes a day), but increased by 40 minutes a day for women. Using the 1992 and 1997 ABS time-budget surveys to examine recent trends in leisure time as a whole is difficult, because of changes in coding of activities between leisure and personal care in the two surveys. In Table 2.10, leisure, sleep and personal care activities have been combined in order to overcome this problem. The data suggest that, overall, the pattern of time-use has been remarkably stable. There is a marginal tendency for women, on average, to increase the amount of time spent in paid work at the expense of domestic work and leisure/sleep/personal care, while the reverse is true for men. But the changes are of the order of less than 10 minutes a day. However, these averages no doubt hide considerable variation among different individuals and groups, which it is not possible to pursue here.

Table 2.9. Average daily time spent on leisure activities by gender, Australia, 1997.

| Activities | Min/day, main activity[a] | | |
	Males	Females	Total
Socializing (being visited, going to clubs, etc.)	11	11	11
Visiting entertainment and cultural venues	5	6	5
Attendance at sports event	2	1	2
Religious activities/ritual ceremonies	4	5	5
Community participation	7	9	8
Sport and outdoor activity	33	20	27
Games/hobbies/arts/crafts	18	15	17
Reading	24	26	25
Watching TV/video	131	108	119
Listening to radio, CDs	8	7	8
Accessing the Internet and other audio/visual	4	3	3
Resting/relaxing/doing nothing	12	14	13
Talking, including on the phone	27	44	35
Attendance at recreational course	1	1	1
Personal correspondence	1	2	1
Associated travel	23	20	22
Other	14	9	11
Total	325	301	313

[a] All data relate to 'main activity', i.e. when respondents are engaged in more than one activity, one is nominated as the 'main' activity. This particularly affects things such as listening to radio and watching television, which are often secondary activities. Data on 'all activities', including secondary, are available in the ABS report.
Source: ABS (1998a, pp. 17–18, 41).

Table 2.10. Changing time-use (min/day), Australia, 1992–1997.

| | 1992 | | | 1997 | | |
	Males	Females	Total	Males	Females	Total
Paid work	268	126	196	261	132	196
Education	32	28	30	24	28	26
Domestic work	165	306	237	167	303	237
Leisure/sleep/personal care	973	979	975	983	972	978
Undescribed	2	2	2	5	5	5

Source: ABS (1998a, pp. 17–18).

Sport, Physical Recreation and Exercise

Two main series of surveys have been conducted over the years on participation in sport and physical recreation rather than leisure as a whole. The first, the *Physical Activity Levels of Australians* surveys, were health-orientated surveys initiated by the federal Department of Sport, Recreation and Tourism[1] in 1984 and repeated five times in summer and winter between 1985 and 1987. Samples of some

3500 adults were asked whether they had participated in 'physical activity', 'physical exercise' or 'physical recreation' in the previous 2 weeks, and, if so, how often, together with questions about constraints on participation. The survey was taken up again in 1997–2000 by the 'Active Australia' campaign, part of the Australian Sports Commission, but the reference period was changed and other changes were made to the survey methodology, so that comparisons could not be made with the earlier survey results.

In 1993/94 the ABS, using its annual Population Survey Monitor omnibus survey, launched the *Participation in Sport and Physical Activities* series, but began publishing reports with the 1995/96 survey, continuing until 1999/2000. These surveys involved face-to-face interviews with a sample of some 13,000 residents aged 18 years and over, and collected information on participation in organized and informal sport and physical activities over a 1-year reference period. The results could not therefore be compared with those of the NRPS. Further, a number of changes were made to the survey design, particularly in the handling of 'organized' and 'non-organized' sport, so that no more than two consecutive surveys were comparable. Collection of this type of data then appeared to be taken over by a new survey, the 2001 Exercise, Recreation and Sport Survey (ERASS), conducted by ACNielssen (the successor company to AGB: McNair) on behalf of the Australian Sports Commission and the Standing Committee on Recreation and Sport (SCORS), representing the sport and recreation ministers of the federal, six state and two territory governments. There was a commitment to conduct the survey annually for at least 3 years. At the time of writing, the second, 2002, survey has been conducted. Changes in survey design involved reduction of the age range to 15 years and over, changes to the list of activities covered and conducting interviews by telephone rather than face-to-face. Curiously, the ABS conducted another survey in 2001/02, its General Social Survey omnibus, with other changes in survey design, which meant that the results were not comparable to ERASS or its own earlier surveys (for more detail see Veal, 2003).

The results for overall participation in sport, can be seen in Fig. 2.1. NRPS data on overall sport participation are included and, curiously, despite its use of a 1-week reference period, it shows a higher level of participation

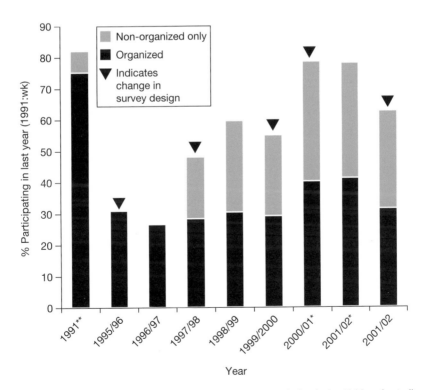

Fig. 2.1. Participation in organized and non-organized sport and physical activities, Australia, 1991–2002. Sources: NRPS (**), ABS/PSM, ABS/GSS, ERASS (*) (see Table 2.1), Veal (2003).

Table 2.11. Participation in any sport and physical activity by age and sex, Australia, 2000–2001.

	% participating in year prior to interview		
Age group	Males	Females	Total
15–24	90.7	86.8	88.8
25–34	88.3	82.2	85.3
35–44	82.3	78.9	80.6
45–54	78.3	72.5	75.4
55–64	69.8	70.5	70.2
65 and over	59.6	60.4	60.1
Total	79.8	75.9	77.8

Source: Dale and Ford (2002).

than subsequent surveys based on a 1-year reference period. Even ignoring the NRPS, there is little evidence of any increase in participation in organized sport over the period, despite the considerable public funds expended to promote such participation. However, because of the frequent changes in survey, after the conduct of eight surveys, involving an aggregate of 130,000 interviews, it is not possible to assess trends in participation reliably for more than 2 years at a time. Table 2.11 provides information on participation by age and sex for the 2001 ERASS, and Table 2.12 provides data on participation in 52 individual activities which make up 'sport and physical activities'. The full list of activities on which data were collected runs to 165, but activities with less than 0.2% participation are omitted. The 'top five' activities are: walking (29%), swimming (16%), aerobics and fitness (13%), cycling (10%) and tennis (9%).

noticeable decline in the museum attendance rate, which, however, 'bounced back' in 2002.

The main public arts organization, the Australia Council, commissioned a national survey of arts participation in 1999. The *Australians and the Arts* survey was based on a sample of only 1200 respondents aged 15 and over and referred to activities in the 2 weeks prior to interview; its design therefore precludes comparison with any other survey. As the summary of results in Table 2.14 indicates, the survey used a list of arts activities which was more detailed than any seen before in Australian surveys. For example, in the case of viewing and listening to the electronic media information is provided on whether drama, classical or popular music was involved, categories of reading material are explored and data are presented on direct involvement with the arts and whether or not this was for the enjoyment of the self or others.

The Arts and Entertainment

In the 1980s and up until 1991 the main source of data on participation in the arts and entertainment was the National Recreation Participation Survey, as discussed above. The ABS launched the *Attendance at Selected Cultural Venues* survey in 1991 and repeated it in 1995, 1999 and 2002. The results are summarized in Table 2.13 and show, over the 1990s, a static or declining level of attendance at a range of cultural venues, with a particularly

Use of the Internet

Australians have a reputation for rapid uptake of new consumer technology and use of the Internet is no exception. Table 2.15 shows that the proportion of households with home Internet access grew from 16% in 1998 to 46% in 2002, and was as high as 59% in households with children aged under 15. Further research by the Australian Bureau of Statistics indicates that more than 80% use home computers and the Internet for 'personal or private' purposes

Table 2.12. Participation in selected sports and physical activities, by sex, Australia, 2000–2001.

	Males %	Females %	Total %		Males %	Females %	Total %
Aerobics/fitness	9.0	16.9	13.0	Rock climbing	1.1	0.5	0.8
Aquarobics	**0.1	1.8	0.9	Roller sports	1.2	0.7	0.9
Athletics	0.7	0.7	0.7	Rowing	0.5	0.4	0.4
Aust. Rules football	4.5	*0.2	2.3	Rugby league	2.1	*0.1	1.1
Badminton	0.4	0.7	0.6	Rugby union	1.1	*0.1	0.6
Baseball	0.5	*0.2	0.3	Running	9.8	4.7	7.2
Basketball	4.4	2.7	3.5	Sailing	1.5	0.5	1.0
Boxing	0.5	*0.2	0.4	Scuba diving	0.8	*0.2	0.5
Canoeing/kayaking	0.9	0.5	0.7	Shooting sports	0.7	**0.1	0.4
Carpet bowls	*0.2	0.6	0.4	Soccer (indoor)	1.9	0.4	1.2
Cricket (indoor)	2.2	*0.3	1.3	Soccer (outdoor)	5.8	1.6	3.7
Cricket (outdoor)	4.7	0.8	2.7	Softball	*0.4	1.1	0.8
Cycling	13.0	6.1	9.5	Squash/racquetball	3.1	1.2	2.2
Dancing	0.7	3.2	2.0	Surf sports	4.5	0.4	2.4
Darts	*0.2	*0.2	0.2	Swimming	13.6	18.3	16.0
Fishing	4.1	0.7	2.4	Table tennis	0.7	0.4	0.5
Golf	13.4	3.2	8.2	Tennis	9.5	8.8	9.2
Gymnastics	*0.3	0.4	0.4	Tenpin bowling	0.9	1.1	1.0
Hockey (indoor)	*0.2	*0.2	0.2	Touch football	3.7	1.7	2.7
Hockey (outdoor)	1.0	1.1	1.0	Triathlons	0.4	**0.1	0.2
Horse riding/equestrian	0.9	2.0	1.5	Volleyball	1.9	1.5	1.7
Ice/snow sports	1.8	0.8	1.3	Walking (bush)	5.0	5.5	5.3
Lawn bowls	2.2	1.7	1.9	Walking (other)	19.5	38.0	28.8
Martial arts	2.0	2.2	2.1	Waterski/powerboating	1.7	0.7	1.2
Motor sports	1.8	*0.2	1.0	Weight-training	3.7	2.2	2.9
Netball	1.1	7.0	4.1	Yoga	0.4	2.5	1.5

% participating in year prior to interview, population aged 15 years and over.
* Estimate has a relative standard error of between 25% and 50% and should be used with caution.
** Estimate has a relative standard error greater than 50% and is considered too unreliable for general use.
Sources: ERASS (see Table 2.1), Dale and Ford (2002).

Table 2.13. Attendance at selected cultural venues and events, Australia, 1991–2002.

	% attending in last year			
	1991	1995	1999	2002
Age range:	18+	18+	15+	18+
Art gallery	23.9	22.3	21.2	24.9
Classical music concert	8.2	7.7	8.8	9.0
Dance performance	11.2	10.0	9.0	10.9
Museum	30.0	27.8	19.9	25.0
Opera/musical theatre	20.1	19.3	16.3	18.7
Pop music concert	28.6	26.9	25.4	26.4
Public library	36.7	38.4	38.1	42.1
Theatre	17.8	16.6	16.5	18.0
Cinema	na	60.4	65.6	69.9

Source: see Table 2.1.

Table 2.14. Arts and entertainment participation in Australia, 1999.

	% participating in last 2 weeks, persons aged 15 and over
Arts viewing/listening – electronic	
Watched a movie or TV drama	31
Listened to the radio (popular)	23
Listened to a CD (popular)	19
Watched a popular music concert (TV/video)	5
Listened to the radio (classical)	12
Listened to a CD (classical)	11
Watched a classical music concert (TV/video)	3
Watched an arts show on TV	17
Other electronic arts viewing/listening	2
Any arts viewing/listening – electronic	67
Reading books/stories	
Novels	39
Biographies/autobiographies	11
Short stories	8
Poetry	4
Plays	1
Any reading books/stories	58
Reading about the arts	
News about what's happening in the arts	17
News about who is who in the arts/the arts scene	9
Reviews/critiques on the arts	19
Book reviews	1
Movies/movie stars	13
Popular music/pop stars	5
Ballet and opera performance	2
Dance performance	2
Theatre/plays performance	1
Visual arts	2
Other	7
Any reading about the arts	54
Being part of audience	
Watch a show/band in a pub/club	7
See a popular music concert	5
See a classical music concert	3
School concerts	1
Opera	1
See a play/go to the theatre	6
Art gallery (local)	2
Art gallery (major)	1
Modern dance/ballet	2
Cinema/movie theatre	16
Sporting events	1
Other	6
Been part of any audience	44

Continued

Table 2.14. *Continued*

Direct participation	For own enjoyment	For others to enjoy
Creative writing (novels, stories, poetry)	18	9
Wrote letters	1	1
Theatre/drama/acting	1	2
Drawing	3	1
Painting	3	1
Design/graphic design	3	1
Photography	1	1
Sculpting	1	–
Playing a musical instrument	4	2
Composing music	3	2
Singing	1	1
Crafts (such as pottery, tapestry, etc.)	4	3
Gardening	1	–
Dancing	1	1
Other	4	4
Any direct participation	38	24

Source: Australia Council survey (Saatchi and Saatchi, 1999).

Table 2.15. Internet access, Australia, 1998–2002.

	% of households with home Internet access				
	1998	1999	2000	2001	2002
Households without children under 15 years	14	18	28	37	40
Households with children under 15 years	20	29	43	54	59
All households	16	22	32	42	46

Source: ABS (2003c, p. 8).

Table 2.16. Internet use by age and gender, Australia, 2001.

	% of persons aged 18+ using Internet at least once in the year
Gender	
Males	57
Females	51
Age (years)	
18–24	80
25–34	71
35–44	64
45–54	55
55–64	35

(purely 'leisure' purposes are not indicated); Table 2.16 indicates that the Internet is used more by males than females and that use is significantly age-related.

Tourism

Tourism is the best-served of the leisure sectors in Australia, partly because of the recognition of the tourism business, including planners, developers and marketers, of the need for data. A separate national government agency – the Bureau of Tourism Research – has been responsible for surveys of inbound tourists and domestic tourists since the 1980s; as of 2003 it will become part of the federal government department, 'Tourism Australia'. Domestic tourism patterns are monitored by the 'National Visitor Survey', which has been conducted annually, in various forms, for almost 20 years. Because of the requirement to track tourists' regional origins and destinations, and seasonal patterns, the sample is large – some 80,000 a year, spread over the whole year. For most other forms of leisure the commissioners of surveys are interested in rates of participation within a given community, but in the case of the tourism industry, both public and private sector interest is in the aggregate of visitors arriving in a destination from many communities – it is the volume of arrivals in destination areas that is of interest, rather than the rate of participation in origin communities. A further distinguishing feature of tourism is that it includes non-leisure trips – a tourist, for statistical purposes in Australia, is someone who spends at least one night away from home, at least 40 km from home. Using this definition, the 1999 survey estimated that Australians made 74.6 million domestic trips in the course of the year (almost five for each adult), involving 290 million nights away. Just 43% of trips were for holiday purposes, with 32% being to visit friends or relatives (some of which would be for leisure purposes), 20% were for business and 5% for 'other' purposes (e.g. education, health) (Bureau of Tourism Research, 2002).

Conclusions

The conclusion to the Australian chapter in the first edition of the book stated that the 'analysis indicates wide variations in patterns of leisure participation among social groups in Australia. Some of the differences may be due to taste differences, but it is also clear that social and economic constraints are also at work, presenting barriers to participation.' The conclusion to be drawn from the more recent data presented in this chapter remains substantially the same today. Unfortunately, due to changes in survey design, it has not been possible to monitor trends in participation over time. Further, the last publicly available survey which addressed leisure as a whole was undertaken in 1991 and is now very out of date. For the past 12 years, in order to obtain information on leisure participation, it has been necessary to piece

together data from a number of surveys, covering different aspects of leisure – but variations in survey design prevent compilation of these data into a coherent composite picture. The fragmentation has also left gaps in the picture, for example in visiting urban and national parks, social activities, such as visiting pubs, clubs and festivals, and home-based leisure. Fragmentation of government responsibility for different aspects of leisure in Australia suggests that this situation is unlikely to be remedied in the near future.

Notes

[1] The name of the federal government department responsible for leisure/recreation has been changed on numerous occasions over the past two decades. Beginning as the Department of Sport, Recreation and Tourism, it later became the Department of the Arts, Sport, the Environment, Tourism and Territories. First tourism and then the arts were removed, so that, at the time of writing, the department is the Department of the Environment, Sport and Territories.

[2] Data relate to formal and informal participation and are based on secondary analysis conducted at the University of Technology, Sydney.

References

ABS (Australian Bureau of Statistics) (1978) *General Social Survey: Leisure Activities Away from Home*, Cat. No. 4104.0. ABS, Canberra, Australia.

ABS (Australian Bureau of Statistics) (1988) *Information Paper: Time Use Pilot Survey – Sydney, May–June, 1987*, Cat. No. 4111.1. ABS, Sydney, Australia.

ABS (Australian Bureau of Statistics) (1992) *Attendance at Selected Cultural Venues, Australia, June 1991*, Cat. No. 4114.0. ABS, Canberra, Australia.

ABS (Australian Bureau of Statistics) (1994) *How Australians Use Their Time*, Cat. No. 4153.0. ABS, Canberra, Australia.

ABS (Australian Bureau of Statistics) (1995) *Attendance at Selected Cultural Venues, Australia, March 1995*, Cat. No. 4114.0. ABS, Canberra, Australia.

ABS (Australian Bureau of Statistics) (1997) *Participation in Sport and Physical Activities, Australia, 1996–97*, Cat. No. 4177.0. ABS, Canberra, Australia.

ABS (Australian Bureau of Statistics) (1998a) *How Australians Use Their Time*, Cat. No. 4153.0. ABS, Canberra, Australia.

ABS (Australian Bureau of Statistics) (1998b) *Participation in Sport and Physical Activities, Australia, 1997–98*, Cat. No. 4177.0. ABS, Canberra, Australia.

ABS (Australian Bureau of Statistics) (1999a) *Participation in Sport and Physical Activities, Australia, 1998–99*, Cat. No. 4177.0. ABS, Canberra, Australia.

ABS (Australian Bureau of Statistics) (1999b) *Attendance at Selected Cultural Venues, Australia, April 1999*, Cat. No. 4114.0. ABS, Canberra, Australia.

ABS (Australian Bureau of Statistics) (2000) *Participation in Sport and Physical Activities, Australia, 1999–2000*, Cat. No. 4177.0. ABS, Canberra, Australia.

ABS (Australian Bureau of Statistics) (2003a) *Attendance at Selected Cultural Venues, Australia, March 2002*, Cat. No. 4114.0. ABS, Canberra, Australia.

ABS (Australian Bureau of Statistics) (2003b) *Participation in Sport and Physical Activities, Australia, 2002*, Cat. No. 4177.0. ABS, Canberra, Australia.

ABS (Australian Bureau of Statistics) (2003c) *Household Use of Information Technology, 2001–02*, Cat. No. 8146.0. ABS, Canberra, Australia.

Bauman, A., Ford, I. and Armstrong, T. (2001) *Trends in Population Levels of Reported Physical Activity in Australia, 1997, 1999 and 2000*. Canberra, Australian Sports Commission/Active Australia. Available at: www.activeaustralia.org/facts/index.htm (accessed August 2003).

Bittman, M. (1988) The land of the lost weekend? Trends in free time among working age Australians, 1974–1992. *Society and Leisure* 21(2), 353–378.

Bittman, M. (1991) *Juggling Time: How Australian Families Use Time*. Office of the Status of Women, Canberra, Australia.

Brown, J. (Minister for Sport, Recreation and Tourism) (1985) *Towards the Development of a Commonwealth Policy on Recreation*. Department of Sport, Recreation and Tourism, Canberra, Australia.

Bureau of Tourism Research (2002) *Overnight Travel by Australians by Main Purpose of Journey, 2001*. BTR, Canberra, Australia. Available at: www.btr.gov.au/service/datacard/index.cfm (accessed December 2003).

Cities Commission (1975) *Australians' Use of Time*. Cities Commission, Melbourne, Australia.

Corporate Concern (1994) *Available Data and Sources for the Sport and Recreation Industry, Report to the Sport and Recreation Ministers Council Statistical Working Group*. Department of Environment, Sport and Territories, Canberra, Australia.

Dale, T. and Ford, I. (2002) *Participation in Exercise, Recreation and Sport, 2001*. Australian Sports Commission, Canberra, Australia.

Darcy, S. (1993) Leisure participation in Australia: the monthly data. *Australian Journal of Leisure and Recreation* 3(4), 26–32.

DASETT (Department of the Arts, Sport, the Environment, Tourism and Territories) (1988a) *Recreation Participation Survey: October/November 1987*. DASETT, Canberra, Australia.

DASETT (Department of the Arts, Sport, the Environment, Tourism and Territories) (1988b) *Physical Activity Levels of Australians*. AGPS, Canberra, Australia.

DASETT (Department of the Arts, Sport, the Environment, Tourism and Territories) (1989) *Ideas for Australian Recreation: Commentaries on the Recreation Participation Surveys*. AGPS, Canberra, Australia.

DASETT (Department of the Arts, Sport, the Environment, Tourism and Territories) (1991) *Recreation Participation Survey: February 1991*. DASETT, Canberra, Australia.

DSRT (Department of Sport, Recreation and Tourism) (1986a) *Recreation Participation Survey: April/May 1985*. DSRT, Canberra, Australia.

DSRT (Department of Sport, Recreation and Tourism) (1986b) *Recreation Participation Survey: Oct/Nov 1985*. DSRT, Canberra, Australia.

DSRT (Department of Sport, Recreation and Tourism) (1986c) *Recreation Participation Survey: February, 1986*. DSRT, Canberra, Australia.

DSRT (Department of Sport, Recreation and Tourism) (1986d) *Recreation Participation Survey: May, 1986*. DSRT, Canberra, Australia.

DSRT (Department of Sport, Recreation and Tourism) (1986e) *Recreation Participation Survey: July, 1986*. DSRT, Canberra, Australia.

Department of Tourism and Recreation (1975) *Leisure – a New Perspective: Papers presented at a National Seminar in Canberra, 22–24 April, 1974*. AGPS, Canberra, Australia.

McKay, J. (1990) Sport, leisure and social inequality in Australia. In: Rowe, D. and Lawrence, G. (eds) *Sport and Leisure: Trends in Contemporary Popular Culture*. Harcourt, Brace, Jovanovich, Sydney, pp. 125–160.

McKenry, K. (1975) *Recreation, Wilderness and the Public: a Survey Report for the Department of Youth, Sport and Recreation*. Department of

Youth, Sport and Recreation, Melbourne, Australia.

Mercer, D. (1985) Australians' time use in work, housework and leisure: changing profiles. *Australian and New Zealand Journal of Sociology* 21(3), 371–394.

Parker, S. and Paddick, R. (1990) *Leisure in Australia.* Longman Cheshire, Melbourne, Australia.

Saatchi and Saatchi (1999) *Australians and the Arts.* Australia Council, Sydney. Available at: www.ozco.gov.au (accessed June 2004).

SCORS (Standing Committee on Recreation and Sport) (2003) *Participation in Exercise, Recreation and Sport 2002.* Australian Sports Commission, Canberra. Available at: www.ausport,gov,au. info/statistics.htm (accessed January 2004).

Scott, D. and U'Ren, R. (1962) *Leisure: a Social Enquiry into Leisure Activities and Needs in an Australian Housing Estate.* F.W. Cheshire, Melbourne, Australia.

Veal, A.J. (1987) Leisure and the future. *Recreation Australia* 7(3), 1–3.

Veal, A.J. (1988) Future demand for outdoor recreation: planning implications. *Recreation Australia* 8(3), 12–17.

Veal, A.J. (1993a) Leisure participation surveys in Australia. *ANZALS Leisure Research Series* 1, 197–210.

Veal, A.J. (1993b) Leisure participation in Australia: 1985–91. A note on the data. *Australian Journal of Leisure and Recreation* 3(1), 37–46.

Veal, A.J. (2003) Tracking change: leisure participation and policy in Australia, 1985–2002. *Annals of Leisure Research* 6(2), 246–278.

Veal, A.J. and Cushman, G. (1993) The new generation of leisure surveys – implications for research on everyday life. *Leisure and Society* 16(1), 211–220.

Veal, A.J. and Darcy, S. (1993) Australian demographic change and leisure and tourism futures. In: Boag, A. *et al.,* (eds) *Proceedings of Australian and New Zealand Association for Leisure Studies Inaugural Conference.* ANZALS/Centre for Leisure Research, Griffith University, Brisbane, Australia, pp. 340–346.

Veal, A.J. and Lynch, R. (2001) *Australian Leisure.* Longman Australia, Sydney.

Veal, A.J., Gidlow, B. and Perkins, H.C. (1998) Interpreting leisure surveys in New Zealand and Australia. In: Cushman, G., Gidlow, R. and Perkins, H. (eds) *Time Off? Leisure and Recreation in New Zealand and Australia.* Longman, Auckland, New Zealand, pp. 64–85.

3   Canada

Jiri Zuzanek

Introduction

In 1978, I was asked to review Statistics Canada's programme of cultural and leisure statistics and comment on the state of Canada's leisure research in general. At that time, relatively few studies provided comprehensive information on Canada's leisure and cultural participation but by the turn of the millennium the situation had changed dramatically. Presently, we have at our disposal a series of national time-use and leisure participation surveys, which lend themselves to comparative as well as trend analyses. What do these surveys, past and present, tell us about everyday life and free time in Canada? How has the use of time and leisure participation changed over the past 20–25 years? How do time-use, leisure and cultural participation vary across different social groups? These are some of the questions addressed in this chapter.

The chapter is divided into four main sections. The first provides an overview of the history of leisure and time-use surveys in Canada; the second examines trends in time-use, feelings of time pressure and leisure participation; the third explores social differences; and the fourth presents observations on some conceptual, political and methodological issues of time-use and leisure research.

Canadian Studies of Leisure Participation and Time-use in Retrospective

This section provides a chronological account of leisure participation and time-use surveys conducted in Canada from 1967 to 2000. Technical information on the studies discussed is presented in Table 3.1.

First large-scale surveys of leisure participation and time-use: 1967–1978

In the 1960s, and particularly the 1970s, national statistical agencies in many countries began collecting systematic information about the involvement of their population in non-working time, leisure and cultural activities. Canada was no exception: in 1967–1972, Parks Canada conducted a series of Outdoor Recreation Demand surveys (CORDs) that focused on Canadians' participation in outdoor activities and park attendance. These surveys were designed to provide information about actual and potential demand for outdoor recreation in Canada.

In 1971/72, a team of researchers from Dalhousie University, under the direction of Andrew Harvey, conducted the *Halifax Time-budget Study*. This survey was designed along

Table 3.1. Canadian leisure participation and time-use surveys: 1967–2000.

Year of survey	Title of survey	Agency	Geographic area	Sample size	Sample age	Time referent	Measurement of participation
1967, 1968, 1969, 1972	Canadian Outdoor Recreation Demand (CORD) study	Parks Canada	Canada	3000–6000	10+; 18+	Per lifetime	% of participation
1971/72	Halifax Time-budget Study	Institute of Public Affairs Dalhousie University	Halifax–Dartmouth, N.S.	2141	18–64	Day/week	Minutes
1972	Leisure Study – Canada 1972	Statistics Canada	Canada	62,789	14+	Jan.–March	% of participation, frequency
1973/74	Tourism and Outdoor Recreation Planning Survey (TORPS)	TORP Commission of Ontario	Ontario	10,230	12+	12 months	% of participation, time estimates
1975	Leisure Study – Canada 1975	Statistics Canada	Canada	30,161	14+	12 months	% of participation, frequency
1976	Survey of Fitness, Physical Recreation and Sport	Statistics Canada	Canada	50,816	14+	12 months	% of participation, frequency
1978	Survey of Leisure Time Activities: Reading Habits	Statistics Canada	Canada	20,735	15+	12 months	% of participation, time estimates
1981	National Time-use Pilot Study	Statistics Canada	Canada: 14 metro areas	2686	18+	Day/week, autumn	Minutes
1981	Fitness and Lifestyle in Canada	Fitness Canada	Canada	23,400	12+	12 months	% of participation
1983/84	Leisure and Cultural Participation of Urban Canadians	Research Group on Leisure and Cultural Development, University of Waterloo	Kitchener–Waterloo–Brantford area of Ontario	418	18+	12 months	% of participation, frequency, time estimates
1986	General Social Survey: the Use of Time	Statistics Canada	Canada	9946	15+	Day/week, autumn	Minutes
1988	Well-being of Canadians	Canadian Fitness and Lifestyle Research Institute	Canada	2778	12+	12 months	% of participation, frequency

Year	Survey	Organization	Country	Sample	Age	Period	Measures
1990/91	Canadian Arts Consumer Profile Survey	Department of Communications Ottawa	Canada	11,106	16+	12 months	% of participation, frequency, time estimates
1992	General Social Survey: the Use of Time	Statistics Canada	Canada	8996	15+	Day/week year-round	Minutes, % of participation
1992	Survey of Consumer Product Preferences	Printing Measurement Bureau (PMB)	Canada	12,000	12+	12 months	% of participation
1998/99	General Social Survey: the Use of Time	Statistics Canada	Canada	10,749	15+	Day/week year-round	Minutes, % of participation
1994–2000	Longitudinal National Population Health Survey	Statistics Canada	Canada	1994: 17,276; 2000: 12,319	12+	3 months year-round	% of participation

the lines of the Multi-national Time Budget Survey, conducted in the mid-1960s under the auspices of UNESCO, and directed by Alexander Szalai (1972). The study provided one of the first glimpses into the use of time by urban Canadians.

National surveys of leisure and cultural participation in the 1970s were spearheaded by the Education, Science and Culture Division of Statistics Canada under the direction of Yvon Ferland. These surveys represented a conscious effort to collect data for the analyses of current and future trends in Canadians' leisure and cultural participation. In March 1972, Statistics Canada launched the survey *Leisure Study – Canada 1972*. Similar to a number of subsequent surveys, it was conducted as a supplement to the monthly Labour Force Survey. Respondents were asked to answer questions on how often they participated in selected leisure activities from the beginning of January 1972 to the day of the survey. Activities for which a response was sought included attending live theatre, opera, ballet, classical music, museums, art galleries, movies and sports events, watching television, reading, hobbies, participation in active sport and physical activities.

In October 1975, Statistics Canada administered a follow-up to the 1972 survey, *Leisure Study – Canada 1975*. Respondents aged 14 years and over were asked to report their participation in 45 selected leisure and cultural activities over a period of 12 months, as well as for the July–August and September–October periods. The 1976 *Survey of Fitness, Physical Recreation and Sport* focused on participation in a wide variety of physical activities. Similar to Statistics Canada's previous leisure studies, it was administered as a supplement to the annual Labour Force Survey, and monitored the frequency, intensity, location of, as well as motivations for and barriers to, participation in leisure activities. In February 1978, Statistics Canada conducted yet another leisure-related study, the *Survey of Leisure Time Activities: Reading Habits*, covering a broad spectrum of leisure and cultural activities, but paying particular attention to reading habits and preferences.

The national effort to collect data on Canadians' leisure participation was paralleled by surveys in several provinces. From May 1973 through April 1974, the Tourism and Outdoor Recreation Planning Commission of Ontario conducted an extensive survey of participation in leisure and recreational activities in Ontario (TORPS). Ontario residents aged 12 years and over were asked questions about their participation in outdoor recreation and tourism activities, as well as leisure preferences and constraints and barriers to leisure participation and travel. Some of the findings from these early studies were reported in the Canada chapter of the first edition of this publication (Zuzanek, 1996).

Studies of physically active leisure and time-use in the 1980s

The initial burst of leisure surveys subsided in the 1980s and interest shifted to the use of time and participation in physically active leisure, and moved institutionally from the Education, Science and Culture Division to the General Social Survey Division of Statistics Canada and Fitness and Amateur Sport Canada.

In 1981, Statistics Canada conducted its first *National Time-use Pilot Study*. Respondents in 14 urban centres across Canada were interviewed by telephone on their use of time. A number of traditional leisure and cultural participation questions were also included (Kinsley and Casserly, 1984). Also in 1981, Fitness and Amateur Sport (Canada) conducted the survey, *Fitness and Lifestyle in Canada*, which examined fitness behaviour extensively and included a battery of physical health and lifestyle measurements.

In 1983/84, the Research Group on Leisure and Cultural Development of the University of Waterloo was contracted by the federal Department of Communications to conduct the *Survey of Leisure and Cultural Participation of Urban Canadians*. An hour-long interview was administered to a random sample of household heads and their spouses from pre-selected urban census tracts representing lower-, middle- and upper-middle-class neighbourhoods in the Kitchener–Waterloo–Brantford area of south-western Ontario. The survey aimed at collecting information in six areas: (i) patterns of leisure and cultural participation; (ii) familiarity with the 'cultural code' – that is, levels of knowledge in the domain of arts and culture; (iii) value orientations and taste culture characteristics; (iv) mass media habits and preferences; (v) attitudes towards cultural policy issues; and (vi) 'mental' or 'semantic' images of culture and the arts (see Zuzanek, 1996).

In 1986, Statistics Canada administered, for the first time, a full-scale national time-use study as part of the *General Social Survey* (GSS). Telephone interviews were conducted with respondents 15 years and older from randomly selected households to gather information on time-use for 24 hours of the day preceding the interview. The interview gathered information on the primary activity in which the respondent was involved, the total duration of each activity involvement (reported in minutes), where the activity took place, and with whom the respondent was involved. Activities were classified into one of 99 specific categories, which were subsequently organized under general classes such as work for pay, domestic work, personal care, free time, etc. The survey also included a number of questions about respondents' satisfaction with various aspects of life, including the use of non-working time.

In 1988, the Canadian Fitness and Lifestyle Research Institute (Ottawa) conducted the survey, *Well-being of Canadians*. This survey involved a private sector sponsorship by the Campbell's Soup Company and examined participation in physically active leisure among Canadians aged 12 years and over. It was similar in design to the 1981 Canada Fitness Survey.

Surveys of leisure, cultural participation, population health and time-use in the 1990s

The 1990s were marked by a revival of interest in studies of cultural participation, an emerging interest in leisure and culture by commercial marketing agencies, a continuing interest in time-use studies, and the launching of national population health surveys that included relatively detailed questions on participation in physically active leisure and its health implications. Four surveys stand out in this period, as being of greatest interest for the study of trends in leisure participation and patterns of daily

life: the 1990–1991 Canadian Arts Consumer Profile Survey, the 1992 and 1998/99 time-use General Social Surveys, and the 1994–2000 longitudinal National Population Health Survey (NPHS).

In 1990/91, the federal Department of Communications conducted the largest ever study of arts participation in Canada, the *Canadian Arts Consumer Profile Survey*. It consisted of three components: the General Public Survey, the Performing Arts Survey and the Visual Arts Survey. Canadians 16 years of age and over were interviewed by telephone, with 5475 interviews completed in the first wave and 5631 in the second wave. The survey contained questions about Canadians' participation in a variety of leisure and cultural pursuits, and their attitudes towards leisure and cultural participation (see Zuzanek, 1996).

Statistics Canada's 1992 and 1998/99 *General Social Surveys* (GSS), similar to the GSS in 1986, collected detailed time-use information for the 24-hour period of the previous day. The 1992 survey was similar in design and sampling to that of 1986, but time-use data were collected over the entire year rather than a 2-month period. In addition to the duration of activities, respondents were asked questions on how subjectively rushed they felt and about their participation in selected leisure and cultural activities during the year preceding the survey. The 1998 GSS, in addition, contained questions about leisure preferences, feelings of psychological stress, life satisfaction and health.

In 1994, Statistics Canada launched a longitudinal National Population Health Survey (NPHS) with follow-up surveys conducted every 2 years. Respondents provided information on: physical, self-assessed and mental health; sense of being pressed for time; work-related and chronic stress; and participation in over 20 selected physically active leisure pursuits. From each sampled household, one person, aged 12 years and over, was randomly selected for an in-depth interview.

Trends in Time-use, Feelings of Time Pressure, and Leisure Participation

An important question, often asked by students of leisure, concerns long-term trends in the allocation of time to leisure, work for pay (contracted time), and domestic and family-related obligations (committed time). Dumazedier (1967), Linder (1970), Schor (1991), Gershuny (1991) and Robinson and Godbey (1997), among others, have provided different answers to the question of whether, in the past few decades, the lives of people in advanced industrial societies have become more 'leisurely' or more 'harried', that is more free or more constrained. It seems that the answer to these questions depends, to a certain extent, on the measurements of leisure used for the analysis of these trends.

Trends in the use of free, contracted and committed time

A comparison of the use of time in 1981 and 1986 suggests that the amount of free time available to Canada's employed population declined in that period, as indicated in Table 3.2. According to the authors of the 1986 GSS Report:

> Over the period from 1981 to 1986, free time appears to have decreased in Canada. Data directly comparable to the 1986 survey is not available for 1981. However, the 1981 sample can be matched by taking a subset of the sample. Such sample matching shows a decrease in free time over the five-year period from 1981 to 1986, of 0.6 hours per day or 4.2 hours per week. The decrease is virtually identical for women and men. This decline runs counter to the general trend in free time in recent decades.
>
> (Harvey *et al.* 1991)

Changes between 1986 and 1992 were relatively small and, likewise, do not substantiate the forecasts of an impending 'society of leisure'. Table 3.2 indicates that the amount of time spent by employed Canadians in paid jobs

Table 3.2. Time-use trends (based on time diaries) 1981–1998: employed population (hours:min/day), Canada.

Employed population: all days	1981[a]	1986	1992	1998
Workload	8:20	9:08	9:14	9:22
Paid work, including travel	5:38	6:36	6:29	6:22
Domestic work, family care, shopping, including travel	2:31	2:23	2:40	2:55
Housework	1:13	1:16	1:37	1:43
Child and family care	0:33	0:23	0:27	0:28
Shopping and errands	0:35	0:43	0:35	0:41
Study, continuing education	0:11	0:09	0:05	0:05
Personal needs (sleep, meals, personal care)	10:01	9:49	9:39	9:29
Night sleep	7:57	7:51	7:48	7:49
Naps	–	0:08	0:07	0:08
Meals at home	1:13	1:03	0:55	0:46
Personal care	0:52	0:47	0:48	0:46
Voluntary organizations	0:06	0:07	0:06	0:06
Religious activities	0:05	0:06	0:06	0:04
Free time	5:26	4:51	4:56	4:59
Watching TV	1:38	1:53	1:47	1:42
Social leisure	1:52	1:38	1:39	1:45
Reading	0:25	0:21	0:23	0:19
Physically active leisure (sports, outdoors)	0:19	0:21	0:31	0:34
Attending sporting events, movies, culture	0:09	0:09	0:08	0:10
Hobbies, crafts, games	0:11	0:07	0:07	0:06
Relaxing, resting	0:16	0:11	0:09	0:09

[a] Employment status in the 1981 survey was defined less 'tightly' than in subsequent surveys.
Source: 1981 National Time-use Pilot Study and GSS 1986, 1992, 1998 (see Table 3.1). All data reported in this table are weighted, save data for 1981.

declined over the 6-year period 1986–1992 by 7 min/day, but time spent in domestic work rose by 17 min. As a result, the combined load of employed Canadians' paid and unpaid work increased by 10 min/day, or approximately 1 h/week. Greater investment of time in domestic work was accomplished primarily at the expense of time spent in personal needs, in particular eating at home, rather than at the expense of free time. The amount of free time reported by employed Canadians in 1992 was 5 min higher than in 1986.

Trends between 1992 and 1998 resembled, by and large, those observed between 1986 and 1992. The amount of time spent in paid work declined by 7 min/day, while the amount of unpaid domestic work rose by 15 min, resulting in an increase of the combined weekly workload of paid and unpaid work by approximately 1 h. Similar to the 1986–1992 period, greater overall workloads of employed Canadians were accompanied by a reduction of time spent in personal needs and a marginal increase (by 3 min/day) in free time.

Apart from the changes in the allocation of time to paid and unpaid work, personal needs, and free time, time-use data collected since 1981, particularly after 1986, provide interest-ing information about the changing distribution of time to specific non-work activities. It is apparent that the amount of time spent eating at home has declined steadily since 1981, and was almost 40% shorter in 1998 than it was at the beginning of the 1980s. Another activity that shows a steady decline is study and adult education. The amount of time spent reading declined over the years and time spent watching television and videos increased between 1981 and 1986, but declined slightly thereafter. Some of the time freed from watching television was probably allocated to social leisure and computer use. The amount of time spent by employed Canadians in sporting and outdoor activities increased from around 20 min/day in the 1980s to 34 min by the end of the 1990s.

It is important to keep in mind that changes in time-use vary for different population groups. Table 3.3 indicates that the amount of free time available to *all* Canadians increased from 1986 to 1998 by 15 min/day or 1.5 h/week. But for the *employed population*, free time increased by only 8 min/day, and on workdays, total workloads increased by over 30 min, while free time declined by 14 min. These figures seem to tell us that: (i) compared to 1986, in 1998, proportionately fewer Canadians were in the

Table 3.3. Trends in time-use by different population and life-cycle groups: 1986–1998 (hours:min/day), Canada.

	Total workload	Personal needs	Night sleep	Free time
1986				
Entire population (weekdays and weekends)	7:30	10:25	8:14	5:47
Employed population (weekdays and weekends)	9:07	9:49	7:51	4:51
Employed population (workdays only)	11:02	9:13	7:23	3:38
Employed, single, 18–34	8:22	9:55	8:10	5:34
Employed, married, 25–44, no child	9:03	9:55	8:02	4:51
Employed, married, 25–44, child <12	9:57	9:42	7:41	4:32
Retired or housekeeping, 65+	3:39	11:44	8:49	8:15
1998				
Entire population (weekdays and weekends)	7:43	10:00	8:05	6:02
Employed population (weekdays and weekends)	9:22	9:29	7:49	4:59
Employed population (workdays only)	11:36	8:52	7:18	3:24
Employed, single, 18–34	8:23	9:28	8:04	6:01
Employed, married, 25–44, no child	9:22	9:32	7:54	4:58
Employed, married, 25–44, child <12	10:21	9:18	7:40	4:11
Retired or housekeeping, 65+	3:53	11:08	8:22	8:32

Source: GSS 1986 and 1998 (see Table 3.1). All data reported in this table are weighted.

labour force; (ii) those who were in the labour force were working fewer days per annum; and (iii) on those days when employed people were at work, they worked longer hours, and slept less than in 1986.

Further analysis of life cycle differences in time-use indicates that between 1986 and 1998 single employed respondents and employed childless couples managed to gain additional free time, while employed parents with children lost some. It would appear that both work and free time seemed to be more 'compressed' and 'segregated' between workdays and days off in 1998 than in 1986. This, in our opinion, may be at the root of changing subjective perceptions of time pressure that lately attracted considerable attention of researchers, policy-makers and mass media (Robinson and Godbey, 1997).

Table 3.4 shows that Canadians felt more pressed for time in 1998 than in 1992, the 2 years in which respondents were asked a number of identical questions on how 'rushed' or 'pressed for time' they felt. The comparison of the 1992 and 1998 responses shows that, in 1992, 35% of employed Canadians indicated feeling that they 'did not have time for fun any more'. In 1998, this figure rose to 46%. The number of respondents who felt that they 'did not have enough time for family and friends'

increased from 44% to 52%. In 1998, 80% of employed Canadians felt rushed daily or almost every day compared to 78% in 1992. The composite index of time pressure stood at 54 (out of 100) in 1998 compared to 50 in 1992.

Findings shown in Table 3.4 also suggest that employed Canadians were less satisfied with their lives in 1998 than they were in 1986. It may be indicative that levels of satisfaction with use of non-working or leisure time declined more steeply (by 9%) between 1986 and 1998 than the levels of satisfaction with job or life in general (which both fell by approximately 5%). It is tempting to speculate that part of the reason for the decline in life satisfaction is associated with an increasing sense of time pressure. This speculation is supported by the analysis of the relationship between feelings of time pressure and levels of life satisfaction in 1998, when data on both were collected as part of the GSS. The bi-variate correlations between the composite index of time pressure, satisfaction with use of non-working time, and general life satisfaction are negative and highly significant ($r = -0.37$ and $r = -0.29$; $P < 0.005$).

Time-use surveys provide vital information about changes in the distribution of common and frequently engaged in activities, but are not nearly as useful in monitoring changing levels

Table 3.4. Changing levels of perceived time pressure and life satisfaction, Canada 1986–1998.

	Per cent		
Employed population aged 20–64	1986	1992	1998
Feeling rushed daily or almost every day	n/a	77.7	80.3
Feeling more rushed than 5 years ago	n/a	56.6	59.8
Feeling not accomplished much at the end of the day	n/a	50.4	49.0
Worrying has no time for family and friends	n/a	43.6	51.9
Stressed trying to do more things than can handle	n/a	39.2	42.6
Feeling has no time for fun any more	n/a	35.0	45.9
	Mean scores		
Index of perceived time pressure		49.8	53.6
Satisfaction with life (1–4)	3.43	n/a	3.26
Satisfaction with job (1–4)	3.41	n/a	3.21
Satisfaction with health (1–4)	3.53	n/a	3.30
Satisfaction with self (1–4)	3.56	n/a	3.34
Satisfaction with non-work time-use (1–4)	3.38	n/a	3.03

Source: GSS 1986, 1992 and 1998 (see Table 3.1). All data reported in this table are weighted. n/a, Not applicable.

of participation in less-frequent activities. To fill this gap, statistical agencies administer special surveys of leisure participation, or incorporate questions about leisure participation into time-use and population health surveys. In such surveys conducted in Canada, respondents were asked to report whether, or how frequently, they participated in a set of selected leisure, cultural and sporting activities over a given period of time (e.g. past year, past month).

Unfortunately, unlike time-use studies, surveys of leisure participation are, generally, less standardized and more susceptible to methodological inconsistency. Slight changes in the wording or sequencing of questions, and discrepancies with regard to the period for which participation is reported result in dramatically different findings for the same activities. For example, a comparison of data from the Leisure Study – Canada 1972 and Leisure Study – Canada 1975 suggests that for most leisure activities participation rates in 1975 were considerably higher than in 1972. Yet this increase does not necessarily reflect lifestyle or social change, but rather is a product of a different 'time referent' used in the two surveys. In 1972, respondents were asked to report their participation in selected leisure activities for a period of approximately 2 months, from January to March 1972, while the 1975 survey recorded participation for a period

of 12 months preceding the survey. Clearly, the chances of participating for most activities are greater when recorded for a full year than for 2 winter months.

It is therefore necessary to be careful, when seeking to establish leisure trends on the basis of surveys that use recall activity questionnaires. These surveys provide useful information about the relative ranking of the popularity of leisure activities as well as social demographic differences in leisure participation, but may not be completely adequate for the analyses of historical trends. Table 3.5 presents a series of data on Canadians' cultural and recreational participation between 1981 and 1998. Judging by these data, participation in a number of 'high culture' activities, in particular going to opera, symphony, and possibly live theatre, declined over the period, while participation in other activities, such as attending ballet or visiting art galleries, parks, zoos and botanical gardens, underwent little change. Yet, even with the data collected as part of reasonably comparable GSS surveys caution must be exercised. The 1981 to 1992 decline of participation rates in activities such as attending live theatre or visiting history and science museums appears to be rather high and begs for further verification.

A similar comment should be made with regard to the participation trends in sporting

Table 3.5. Changing patterns of cultural and recreational participation: Canada 1981–1998.

	% of population aged 15+ participating at least once in past 12 months		
	1981	1992	1998
Attending movies	65.1	49.2	64.1
Attending live theatre	36.0	22.8	19.9
Attending opera	4.8	4.4	3.0
Attending ballet	6.6	4.9	6.8
Going to symphony/classical music performance	16.5	8.3	8.2
Going to jazz, popular music concert	39.9	23.6	19.6
Visited a history, community or science museum	40.6	21.8	18.3
Visited a public art gallery or art museum	24.8	19.3	22.1
Visited a historical or archaeological site	50.3	27.9	32.4
Visited park or conservation area		46.0	44.9
Visited zoo or botanical garden		35.2	32.2

Source: 1981 National Time-use Pilot Study and GSS 1992 and 1998 (see Table 3.1). All data reported in this table are weighted, save data for 1981.

Table 3.6. Participation in outdoor and sporting activities: Canada 1988–2000.

	1988		1994		2000	
	% of population aged 15 + participating in last:					
	12 months		3 months		3 months	
	%	Rank	%	Rank	%	Rank
Walking for exercise	67.9	1	61.9	1	67.6	1
Gardening	55.9	2	41.1	2	43.2	2
Home exercise	33.6	5	25.0	3	25.2	3
Bicycling	44.5	4	22.1	4	19.5	5
Swimming	46.1	3	20.6	5	19.9	4
Jogging and running	20.0	8	11.2	6	12.3	6
Weight training	13.3	14	10.1	7	11.2	7
Golfing	19.4	9	9.0	10	11.2	8
Bowling	18.8	10	9.7	9	9.1	9
Fishing	n/a	n/a	10.6	8	8.7	10
Aerobics	15.1	12	6.9	12	7.3	11
Ice skating	24.1	6	7.1	13	6.0	12
Volleyball	4.3	16	5.9	14	4.7	14
Tennis	13.5	13	4.3	15	2.9	17
Ice hockey	10.0	15	3.9	16	4.5	15
Downhill skiing	20.5	7	3.7	17	3.3	16

n/a = Not available.
Source: Data for 1988 are taken from the survey *Well-being of Canadians*; data for 1994 and 2000 from the longitudinal NPHS (see Table 3.1).

and outdoor activities. A comparison of data from the 1988 survey of Canadians' Well-being with the data from the 1994–2000 longitudinal National Population Health Survey (Table 3.6) suggests that reporting of sporting and outdoor activities is affected by the length of the referent period. Participation rates in 1988, reported for the entire year are, with very few exceptions, considerably higher than in 1994 and 2000, when participation was reported for the previous 3 months.

Thus, while the popularity ranking of outdoor and sporting activities remained quite stable over the years, with walking for exercise, gardening, home exercise, cycling and swimming topping the list, changes in annual participation rates do not seem to be clearly patterned. It is not clear, for example, why the 1996 NPHS rates of participation for many outdoor and sporting activities (not reported in tables) were higher than in both 1994 and 2000. In summary, leisure participation surveys, even when designed along similar lines, do not always provide reliable across-time information.

Social Differences in Time-use and Leisure Participation

Social differences in leisure behaviour have traditionally been studied from three different perspectives: (i) as differences in the amount and uses of free time; (ii) as differences in the diversity and frequency of leisure participation; and (iii) as differences in the amounts and composition of leisure spending. Authors using these measurements often arrived at seemingly contradictory conclusions with regard to the distribution of leisure resources between different social groups. The following analyses focus only on the first two of these measures, time and participation. In the discussion below, the effects of four social variables are considered: gender, ageing and life cycle, education and social–occupational status.

Effects of gender

Early time-use surveys showed that women in general, and particularly employed mothers with small children, were disadvantaged in terms of access to leisure time, when compared to men. Employed women interviewed in the 1971/72 time-use survey in Halifax, reported having an average of 4.0 hours of free time per day, compared to men's 4.9 h (Elliott *et al.*, 1973). According to the 1971 time-budget study in Greater Vancouver, employed married women with children had only 1.8 h of free time per day, compared to 3.4 h for the analogous category of men (Meissner *et al.*, 1975). These findings are corroborated by time-use data from the 1980s. The 1981 National Time-use Pilot Survey shows that employed married men aged 19–34 with children under the age of 5 had 4.5 h of free time per day, compared to only 3.3 h for women in the same employment and family status category.

The gender gap in access to free time began narrowing in the late 1980s and 1990s. According to the 1992 GSS time-use survey, the gap between the free time of employed men and women was 40 min on workdays and 66 min on weekends. In 1998, this gap narrowed to 29 min on workdays and 45 min on weekends (Table 3.7). Despite this narrowing of gender inequalities in time-use, psychologically the gap between men's and women's perceptions of how 'time free' or 'time pressed' they were remained wide. In 1998, 83% of employed women felt rushed daily or almost every day, 77% stated that weekdays were 'too short to do all the things one wants to do,' and 71% reported that they were stressed because of time shortage. For employed men, these figures were, respectively, 78%, 71% and 59%.

Table 3.7. Gender differences in time-use on workdays and weekends: employed population, Canada, 1998.

| | Time-use based on time diaries. Hours:min/day | | | |
| | Workdays | | Weekends | |
	Men	Women	Men	Women
Total workload	11:24	11:26	6:06	6:41
Paid work, including travel	9:49	8:45	2:35	2:01
Domestic work, family care, shopping, including travel	1:32	2:37	3:30	4:33
Housework	0:49	1:35	2:06	2:48
Child and family care	0:20	0:28	0:32	0:31
Shopping	0:21	0:31	0:49	1:10
Study, continuing education	0:03	0:05	0:02	0:07
Personal needs (sleep, meals, personal care)	8:43	9:09	10:11	10:19
Sleep	7:12	7:29	8:31	8:32
Meals	0:44	0:37	0:55	0:47
Personal care	0:40	0:57	0:36	0:51
Voluntary organizations	0:06	0:05	0:07	0:06
Religious activities	0:02	0:05	0:09	0:11
Free time	3:45	3:16	7:28	6:43
Watching TV	1:36	1:13	2:22	1:45
Social leisure	1:09	1:05	2:51	2:50
Reading	0:14	0:17	0:23	0:27
Physically active leisure (sports, outdoors)	0:20	0:16	0:57	0:50
Attending sporting events, movies, culture	0:04	0:06	0:16	0:19
Hobbies, crafts, games	0:04	0:06	0:09	0:09
Relaxing, resting	0:07	0:07	0:11	0:14

Source: GSS 1998 (see Table 3.1). All data reported in this table are weighted. Workday was defined as a week day if respondents reported 120 or more minutes of paid work, including travel to work.

Table 3.8. Feelings of time pressure, perceived stress and life satisfaction by gender: employed population, Canada, 1998.

	Men (%)	Women (%)
Feeling rushed daily or almost every day	77.7	82.9
Weekdays too short to do all the things one wants	71.3	76.9
Feeling stressed because of time shortage	59.3	70.7
Feeling more rushed than 5 years ago	57.3	62.4
Worry about not spending enough time with family and friends	51.3	51.2
Feeling that has not accomplished much at the end of the day	45.0	53.1
Feeling that has no time for fun any more	43.9	47.9
Feeling trapped in daily routine	41.9	48.0
Experienced a lot or moderate level of stress in past 2 weeks	57.1	70.0
Satisfied with life	93.3	91.4
Satisfied with job	88.1	85.1
Satisfied with use of non-work time	80.9	79.9
Satisfied with work–family balance	73.7	71.1

Source: GSS 1998 (see Table 3.1). All data reported in this table are weighted.

Among employed women 70% reported experiencing high or moderate levels of stress during the previous 2 weeks, compared to 57% of employed men. Perhaps not surprisingly, employed women reported lower levels of satisfaction with their life, job and work–family balance than men (Table 3.8).

Gender differences in participation in selected leisure activities do not reveal a clear or uniform pattern. Early Canadian studies, such as TORPS (1973), Leisure Study – Canada 1975 and the 1984 Kitchener–Waterloo–Brantford Survey (see Table 3.1) found that women engaged more actively than men in cultural activities but the reverse was true of sporting activities. There seemed, however, to be little difference in the number or diversity of leisure pursuits engaged in by men and women (see Zuzanek, 1996).

A similar pattern of gender differences in cultural and sporting participation emerges from the analyses of leisure surveys in the 1980s and 1990s. Activities such as attending opera, ballet, live theatre, going to the symphony, walking for exercise, aerobics and home exercise were somewhat more popular among women than among men. On the other hand, participation in golfing, fishing, bicycling, tennis and most sports attracted more men than women (Tables 3.10 and 3.11). In general, studies of leisure participation of the past 20 years show that gender differences in leisure participation are differences of preference rather than

of diversity or intensity of leisure participation. If anything, women appeared to be engaged in a more diverse spectrum of leisure pursuits than men.

Effects of ageing and life cycle

Early studies of time-use suggested that relationships between age and access to free time resembled a 'bipolar curve', with the largest amounts of free time reported by the youngest and the oldest respondents, and the lowest amounts by middle-aged groups. According to TORPS (1973), Ontario respondents in the 70+ age group reported having 6.3 hours of free time per day, compared to 4.3 hours among the 35–44-year-olds, and 5.3 hours in the 20–24 age group.

It has been said that age groupings often serve as substitutes for life-cycle transitions characterized by changing constellations of social roles (Zuzanek, 1979, 1988). The 'time crunch' in the middle of the life course results from a cumulative pressure of multiple career, employment, family and status roles rather than biological age *per se*. This multiple role strain is particularly obvious in the case of employed married women and men with small children at home.

According to the 1998 General Social Survey (Table 3.9), male students in the 18–24 age group reported having 6.4 hours of free

Table 3.9. Time-use and feeling of time pressure by gender and life-cycle group, Canada, 1998.

	Hours: min/day						Time crunch
	Total workload	Paid work	Study	Domestic work	Sleep hours	Free time	Mean score (1–100)
Men	7:47	4:42	0:33	2:32	5:58	6:14	43.5
Student, single, 18–24 years	7:43	1:29	4:58	1:16	8:31	6:23	47.2
Married, employed, 25–44, no children	9:27	7:20	0.00	2:04	7:42	5:07	55.3
Married, employed, 25–44, kid/s <11	10:24	7:15	0.00	3:06	7:32	4:18	57.3
Married, homemaker, 25–44, kid/s <11	8:50	2:31	0.00	6:19	8:05	5:33	48.0
Divorced, separated, 25–44, kid/s <11	8:46	4:25	0.00	4:22	7:34	6:09	55.1
Married, employed, 45–64, empty-nest	9:13	4:56	0.00	2:18	7:38	5:06	44.6
Retired or housekeeping, 65+	3:35	0:06	0.00	3:29	8:16	8:54	20.2
Women	7:20	2:54	0:36	4:10	6:11	5:50	46.1
Student, single, 18–24 years	8:55	1:09	6:22	1:24	7:58	5:19	56.2
Single, employed, 18–34 years	8:38	5:53	0:23	2:23	8:04	5:38	56.5
Married, employed, 25–44, no children	9:16	6:06	0:13	2:57	8:10	4:45	51.8
Married, employed, 25–44, kid/s <11	10:17	5:07	0:06	5:04	7:50	4:00	65.2
Married, homemaker, 25–44, kid/s <11	8:40	1:01	0:04	7:36	8:06	4:57	55.1
Divorced, separated, 25–44, kid/s <11	10:30	5:37	0:00	4:52	7:39	4:09	67.1
Married, employed, 45–64, empty-nest	8:40	5:12	0:01	3:27	7:48	4:58	49.8
Retired or housekeeping, 65+	4:05	0.04	0:00	4:01	8:26	8:17	23.9

Source: GSS 1998 (see Table 3.1).

time per day, compared to 4.3 hours by employed men who were fathers with children under the age of 11, and 8.9 hours by retired men. Likewise, female students under the age of 24 reported having 5.3 hours of free time per day, compared to only 4.0 hours by employed mothers with children under the age of 11, and 8.3 hours by women aged 65+ at home. Analyses of the subjective perceptions of time pressure among different age and life-cycle groups also indicate that middle-aged employed respondents with children at home experience greater time pressure than younger or retired respondents (Table 3.9).

Statistical evidence from leisure participation surveys of the 1970s suggests that, in spite of the growing amount of free time, the number of leisure activities engaged in by men and women declined with age. According to Leisure Study – Canada 1972, the highest rates of participation for all leisure activities, with the exception of opera attendance and reading, were reported by the 14–19 and 20–24 years age groups, and the lowest by the 65+ years age group. According to TORPS, the mean number of activities participated by those under 59 years of age was 13.8, compared to

only 5.3 for those aged 60+. The ageing pattern for leisure participation can be characterized, for the most part, as one of a gradual decline and is consistent with the 'disengagement' theory of activity decline among the elderly.

The surveys of the 1980s and 1990s lend further support to the above findings, yet suggest that the 'ageing slopes' for different leisure activities vary. According to Table 3.10, participation in most recreational and cultural activities declines with age, but participation in some 'high culture' activities, such as opera going and attending symphony concerts, increases with age, while reading books, attending live theatre, visiting historical and community museums, or doing crafts is affected little by age.

Participation in most sporting and outdoor activities also declines with age. In 1998, 58% of GSS respondents aged 15–19 reported participating regularly in sporting activities, compared to 20% among respondents aged 55 or older. There are, however, exceptions to this trend. Walking for exercise, gardening and golfing seem to resist the effects of ageing and attract sizeable proportions of older participants (Table 3.11).

Table 3.10. Cultural and recreational participation by gender, age, education, Canada, 1998.

	Men	Women	15–19 years	20–54 years	55+ years	Elementary school	High school	BA or more
	\multicolumn{8}{	% of population aged 15+ participating at least once in:}
				Last week				
Read magazine	40.0	41.2	41.7	40.3	40.8	24.6	31.8	56.5
Watched video	34.8	28.8	45.9	36.5	11.8	16.3	32.5	33.2
Listened to CD, tapes	69.4	68.3	90.7	72.1	47.3	43.8	72.3	82.3
				Last month				
Read a book	33.8	48.6	44.6	40.8	40.5	21.7	43.5	58.1
Went to a movie	17.7	13.1	38.8	13.2	4.8	3.2	13.9	20.5
				Last 12 months				
Practised								
Crafts	20.4	38.0	28.7	28.3	32.2	27.5	33.9	28.9
Musical instrument	18.4	15.9	28.7	16.2	11.8	7.3	14.2	25.2
Visited								
Park or conservation area	48.5	41.7	49.2	50.3	30.5	21.9	46.4	63.4
Historical or archaeological site	34.2	30.7	34.1	34.9	25.7	12.1	29.9	51.0
Zoo or botanical garden	30.8	33.7	33.4	36.6	21.8	16.1	32.7	48.2
Public art gallery/ museum	21.4	22.8	26.4	22.6	18.1	3.6	18.3	42.1
Jazz, popular music concert	20.8	18.4	33.5	20.5	8.6	5.9	17.1	31.8
Live theatre	18.0	21.8	21.3	20.0	18.9	9.1	19.0	36.5
Circus, ice show	15.1	16.1	18.4	17.8	8.8	6.8	15.9	19.3
Science centre or museum	13.2	12.6	16.1	14.0	8.4	3.5	9.6	23.5
Historical or community museum	10.9	10.9	11.5	11.1	9.9	5.0	7.2	19.1
Symphony/classical music	7.1	9.3	6.4	7.6	10.9	1.6	6.3	19.4
Ballet	5.7	7.9	8.3	7.4	4.5	2.4	6.7	14.4
Opera	2.5	3.4	2.9	2.9	3.1	0.1	2.2	7.4

Source: GSS 1998 (see Table 3.1). Data reported in this table are weighted.

Effects of education and social–occupational status

A number of authors (Wilensky, 1963; Ennis, 1968; Wippler, 1970; Cheek and Burch, 1976; Zuzanek, 1978) have argued that social–economic status (SES) represents an important determinant of time-use and leisure behaviour. According to the 1986 General Social Survey, respondents with the highest SES reported having less free time than respondents with lower economic status, measured on the Blishen's scale of occupational prestige (see Zuzanek, 1996). These trends are corroborated by the analyses of the 1998 GSS time-use data (Table 3.12). Managers interviewed in the 1998

GSS reported having 4.7 hours of free time per day, compared to 5.1 hours for clerical employees and 5.7 hours for blue-collar workers.

Higher education is not associated with lower amounts of free time, but rather with a different structure of its use. Higher status groups report spending a greater proportion of their free time than lower status groups in physically active leisure, reading and attending cultural events, and a lower proportion in watching television. Interestingly, higher occupational status is associated with higher levels of perceived time pressure and feelings of stress, while higher educational level carries higher level of perceived stress but not of time pressure (Table 3.12).

Table 3.11. Participation in sporting and outdoor activities by gender, age and education, 2000, Canada.

			% of population participating in the past 3 months					
	Men	Women	15–19 years	20–54 years	55+ years	Elementary school	High school	BA or more
Participated in sports regularly*	43.1	25.8	58.0	33.8	19.9	12.2	30.1	46.4
Walking for exercise	61.3	72.6	61.5	70.6	63.9	54.9	69.2	78.0
Gardening	46.2	40.8	31.0	47.3	38.9	31.3	46.0	50.1
Home exercise	21.9	27.8	36.0	26.3	19.9	17.0	24.1	31.4
Bicycling	23.5	16.2	32.3	23.4	8.3	13.4	18.8	25.8
Swimming	19.2	20.4	36.6	23.2	8.7	9.0	19.0	27.7
Jogging and running	15.3	9.9	40.4	13.6	1.7	9.3	8.9	19.0
Weight training	14.7	8.3	23.7	14.0	2.0	3.3	8.1	16.4
Golfing	17.1	6.5	8.5	13.3	8.1	3.3	11.3	17.1
Bowling	10.2	8.2	23.2	9.3	4.5	8.3	7.9	6.7
Fishing	13.7	4.7	9.1	10.6	5.0	5.5	10.7	6.3
Baseball, softball	7.6	3.2	10.6	6.8	0.5	3.1	6.5	4.3
Aerobics	3.6	10.3	11.8	8.7	3.3	2.8	6.2	11.9
Ice skating	7.2	5.1	22.0	6.4	0.8	5.9	4.5	6.7
Volleyball	5.2	4.3	28.7	3.5	0.2	8.6	3.2	4.3
Tennis	3.8	2.1	8.3	3.2	0.7	1.8	1.8	4.7
Ice hockey	9.1	0.8	18.8	4.7	0.1	5.5	3.4	4.1
Downhill skiing	4.2	2.6	13.1	3.2	0.7	3.9	2.0	5.3

Source: All data in this table are taken from the 2000 NPHS, except for the data on 'regular' participation (marked *), which are taken from the 1998 NPHS (see Table 3.1) .

Table 3.12. Time-use and feeling of time pressure by education: employed population aged 20–64 (hours:min/day), Canada, 1998.

	Elementary school	High school	BA or more	Blue collar	Clerical	Profes- sionals	Manage- ment
Total workload	10:24	9:30	9:35	8:12	8:56	9:04	9:59
Paid work	7:23	6:32	6:33	4:50	4:51	5:27	6:57
Domestic work	2:58	2:58	2:52	2:45	3:35	3:12	2:56
Study/education	0:03	0:00	0:10	0:37	0:30	0:25	0:05
Personal needs	9:34	9:31	9:19	9:56	9:50	9:33	9:08
Sleep	7:46	7:54	7:37	8:06	6:02	7:49	7:32
Voluntary organizations/religion	0:09	0:09	0:13	0:12	0:11	0:15	0:11
Free time	3:53	4:50	4:54	5:41	5:04	5:08	4:42
Watching TV and video	1:56	1:47	1:23	2:05	1:46	1:22	1:25
Social leisure	1:21	1:41	1:46	1:52	1:47	1:51	1:49
Physically active leisure	0:08	0:29	0:38	0:49	0:28	0:44	0:33
Reading	0:05	0:16	0:29	0:13	0:20	0:27	0:24
Attending cultural/sports events	0:02	0:09	0:13	0:12	0:09	0:16	0:07
	Mean scores						
Feeling of time pressure (1–100)	55.4	56.3	53.3	45.8	53.6	53.2	54.8
Perceived stress (1–5)	3.25	3.63	3.68	3.36	3.75	3.83	3.84
Life satisfaction (1–4)	3.14	3.25	3.27	3.35	3.24	3.32	3.30
Satisfaction with time-use (1–4)	2.94	3.05	3.00	3.16	3.05	3.00	2.96

Source: GSS 1998 (see Table 3.1).

The relationship between SES and leisure participation takes a different form than the relationship between SES and the use of free time. As in the case of gender and age, greater access to free time does not always go hand in hand with a greater interest in and diversity of leisure participation. The SES groups reporting highest levels of leisure and cultural participation are often also the most pressed for time and least 'leisurely'.

According to the 1984 survey in the Kitchener–Waterloo–Brantford area, higher educational and income status is associated with greater diversity and intensity of leisure participation. The few activities for which higher educational status does not signify increased participation include weaving, knitting, crocheting, playing bingo, attending auctions, playing ice hockey and, possibly, fishing and social dancing (see Zuzanek, 1996).

Most of the above findings were replicated in surveys of leisure and cultural participation in the 1990s. According to Tables 3.10 and 3.11, respondents with university education reported higher levels of participation in reading and 'high culture' activities such as attending theatre, opera, symphony and classical music concerts, visiting museums, art galleries, as well as most sporting and physically active pursuits. The few activities exempt from this trend were crafts, bowling, inline skating, ice hockey and, surprisingly, volleyball.

In general, the findings with regard to SES differences in the distribution of free time support Wilensky's (1963) observation that Veblen's notion of the 'leisure classes' did not apply to 1960s America. In modern societies, higher socio-economic status usually signifies greater access to financial and information resources, yet at the same time it is associated with functional responsibilities and career advancement expectations which predicate more intensive job involvement accompanied by greater time pressure. To paraphrase Wilensky, with economic growth, upper strata have probably lost rather than gained leisure. Yet these same high-status groups manage to compress more leisure and cultural activities into the limited amount of free time that they have available.

Conceptual, Political and Methodological Issues of Time-use and Leisure Research

Conceptually, one of the main issues facing both leisure participation and time-use surveys is how to define their respective survey universes as well as their units of analysis. More simply, the question is how to develop a functionally relevant classification of daily and leisure activities that will form a valid base for large-scale national leisure and time-use surveys. In discussing activity patterns of urban Americans, Chapin (1974) suggested that an 'activity class' might be, for example, simply *shopping*. But shopping can also be defined as driving from home to the shopping centre, buying groceries and driving back home. Further on, the same activity may be classified in even greater detail, as: (i) driving from one's home to the shopping centre; (ii) hunting for a parking space; (iii) picking up a cart, etc. The problem of leisure and time-use research is how to define an 'activity universe' that is both comprehensive and manageable. How many activities should be on our checklist? How detailed should the activity codes be? How much do we care about a difference between camping at 'developed' sites as opposed to the 'undeveloped' ones? Should we combine baseball and softball into one activity category or treat them separately? Should attendance at pop and rock concerts be one activity or two? How long can the list of recreational activities be, before it alienates the respondent? Without resolving some of these issues, practical relevancy and methodological consistency would be hard to achieve.

Practically, time-use surveys provide effective information about the distribution of time among most frequently engaged daily leisure activities, but are of more limited use for monitoring participation in specific leisure pursuits. Time-use surveys can be relied upon with regard to information on such activities as watching television, reading for pleasure, social leisure (visiting friends and entertaining at home), yet offer rather spotty information on arts attendance or sports participation. With the proliferation of telephone interviewing, the mean number of activities reported by respondents in time-use surveys has declined over the years. As a result, the emerging picture of daily time-use becomes increasingly 'broad stroked', occasionally blurring significant differences in human behaviour.

By contrast, leisure participation surveys are well-suited for the analysis of less frequent activities, such as active sports or culture. Yet they are almost entirely useless in examining participation in the more 'routine' leisure activities. For example, there is little to be gained from knowing that approximately 95% of all respondents in Canada and the USA, men and women, young and old, watched television at least once during the past 12 months.

Politically, leisure participation data are 'inflationary', while time-use findings provide us with more 'factual' or 'conservative' information. When filling out a checklist of leisure and cultural activities, respondents are often succumbing to the normative expectations of society and over-report participation in more desirable, socially approved or prestigious activities. 'Is it possible that I haven't been to the theatre this year? Surely, I must have been at least once, but have simply forgotten. Let's check it off. It will please the research team, anyhow, won't it?'

On the other hand, the very design of time-use diaries, with their focus on tedious reconstruction of the sequence of daily events, seems to take normative pressures off the respondent's shoulders. Not surprisingly, time-budget data show greater across-survey and across-time consistency. Yet, by 'pro-rating' time spent in worthy but infrequent cultural pursuits into minuscule daily averages they provide little political 'ammunition' for leisure and culture lobbyists. Compare, for instance, the political impact of the following two findings: (i) according to the 1984 Kitchener–Waterloo–Brantford survey, 46.4% of respondents attended at least one live theatre performance in the previous year; or (ii) analyses of GSS time-use data show that in 1998 Canadians spent, on average, *half a minute* per day for all 'high culture' activities, including attending theatre, concerts, opera, and visiting art galleries.

Methodologically, the most serious problem facing researchers engaged in cross-sectional and across-time comparisons of leisure participation and time-use is assuring across-survey consistency. Much confusion in

comparing leisure participation and time-use data from different surveys should be attributed to an inconsistent use of *age thresholds* in these surveys. Lowering the lower threshold from 18 to 15 years increases, as a rule, mean rates of physically active leisure participation and mean amounts of free time for the total sample.

Another problem, as indicated above, is the differences in time periods or '*time referents*' for which participation is reported. Participation rates reported for the entire year are higher than participation rates for the past 3 months or other shorter periods of time.

Yet another problem arises from the inconsistency in *defining surveyed activities*. Even surveys focusing upon specific areas of leisure involvement are rarely consistent in their choice and definition of surveyed activities. Of 35 cultural activities surveyed in 1972, 1975 and 1978, in Statistics Canada's surveys of leisure and cultural participation, only ten were defined identically. In Leisure Study – Canada 1972, respondents were asked about listening to records, tapes and cassettes 'as a conscious leisure activity', while the Leisure Study – Canada 1975 asked about participation in these same activities without any further qualification. Could this have contributed to a 14% increase in record listening in 1975? Is 'visiting an historic site (building, park, etc.)' from the 1972 survey, the same thing as 'visiting a historic site or restoration (pioneer homes and villages, architectural monuments, etc.)' in 1975? Could a seemingly innocuous difference in the wording of the question have caused the more than twofold increase in participation, from 10% to 24%, in a period of 3 years? According to Stynes *et al.* (1980, p. 226): 'When definitions or groupings of activities change even slightly from survey to survey or year to year, few clues about recreation trends for these activities can be discovered.'

A further concern involves differences in the *design and formatting* of questionnaires and the sequencing of the questions. A comparison of the findings from the 1976 Survey of Fitness, Physical Recreation and Sport and the 1981 Fitness Canada Survey suggests that participation in physically active leisure and sporting activities declined substantially during the 5-year period from 1976 to 1981. However, the lower rates of physically active and sporting participation in 1981 may have been caused by differences in the formatting of the survey questionnaires. In 1976, respondents were given a list of activities and asked to indicate whether they had participated in any of the listed activities during the past 12 months. In 1981, respondents had to name activities that they participated in without the help of an activity list. Recalling past participation without the assistance of a checklist is rather burdensome. Conceivably, the failure of an unprompted recall may have contributed to lower participation rates in 1981.

To provide reliable indicators of leisure participation, leisure researchers need to standardize their surveys to a considerably greater extent than has been the case in the past. Existing leisure participation surveys do not ensure the precision and consistency of data for effective across-time analyses. As of today, Canadian data on leisure participation are too 'soft' to allow credible trend analyses. Based on existing data, it is difficult to tell whether, in the past 20 years, Canadian society has become more passive or more active, more sedentary or more outgoing, more social or more 'cocooned'.

For time-budget surveys, one of the most important methodological problems is consistent *coding* and *grouping* of activities. Frequent changes in the definition, coding and grouping of activities are among the most common reasons for discrepancies in survey findings. While changes in grouping of activities can be rectified by recodes, different coding instructions may irreparably reduce across-survey comparability.

Conclusion

Methodologically, time-use surveys provide information about the distribution of free time as a leisure resource and opportunity, but they do not offer sufficient detail on how this opportunity is used. Such information is provided, at least in part, by leisure participation surveys. The data on leisure and recreation participation serve as an indication of a respondent's or a group's interest in, and competence to live up to the challenge of free time. In short, time-use and leisure participation surveys provide complementary rather than competing strategies for studying leisure behaviour.

Substantively, analyses reported in this chapter suggest that access to free time and its uses evolved along different, and at times divergent, lines among different population groups. Under these circumstances, the statistics of central tendency, which average time-use for the total population, may be inappropriate for the study of time-use trends. Tremblay and Villeneuve (1997), using official Canadian labour statistics, showed that while the average length of the working week in Canada did not change much from 1976 to 1995, the proportion of long-hour workers in the labour force (41 hours per week or more) and the proportion of those working short hours (35 hours per week or less), increased. In other words, the two ends of the workload spectrum have risen at the expense of the middle. A similar tendency towards polarization of the labour force along workload lines was observed by Zuzanek and Smale (1997) in their analyses of Canadian time-use data from the 1980s and 1990s. Some population groups work longer hours, lost free time, and experience greater time pressure and stress. Others have more relaxed schedules and gained greater access to free time. The gender gap in time-use and access to free time has probably narrowed during the past 20 years, while the time-use cleavage between the young and the older age groups has, on the contrary, widened.

The observation about potential polarization of time-use, if correct and broadly applicable, has serious policy implications. The process of polarization implies that there is not a single reality, but rather several divergent realities. Consequently, the question of whether people in modern societies have gained or lost free time may be the wrong question to ask, and we should be asking *who* in modern societies is gaining and *who* is losing the strife for time.

Bibliography

Blishen, B.R., Carroll, W.K. and Moore, C. (1987) The 1981 Socioeconomic Index for Occupations in Canada. *Canadian Review of Sociology and Anthropology* 24, 465–487.
Canadian Fitness and Lifestyle Research Institute (1991) *The Well-being of Canadians. Highlights of the 1988 Campbell's Survey.* Canadian Fitness and Lifestyle Research Institute, Ottawa.

Chapin, F.S., Jr (1974) *Human Activity Patterns in the City*. John Wiley & Sons, New York.

Cheek, N.H., Jr and Burch, W.R., Jr (1976) *The Social Organization of Leisure in Human Society*. Harper & Row, New York.

Cushman, G., Veal, A.J. and Zuzanek, J. (eds) (1996) *World Leisure Participation: Free Time in the Global Village*. CAB International, Wallingford, UK.

Decima Research and Les Consultants Cultur'inc Inc. (1992) *Canadian Arts Consumer Profile: 1990–1991. Findings*. Decima Research and Les Consultants Cultur'inc Inc., Ottawa.

Dumazedier, J. (1967) *Toward a Society of Leisure*. The Free Press, New York.

Elliott, D.H., Harvey, A.S. and Prokos, D. (1973) *An Overview of the Halifax Time-budget Study*. Dalhousie University, Institute of Public Affairs, Halifax, Nova Scotia, Canada.

Ennis, P.H. (1968) The definition and measurement of leisure. In: Sheldon, E.B. and Moore, W.E. (eds) *Indicators of Social Change: Concepts and Measurement*. Russell Sage, New York.

Fitness Canada (1983) *Fitness and Lifestyle in Canada*. Fitness and Amateur Sport, Ottawa.

Gershuny, J. (1991) Allons-nous manquer de temps? *Futuribles*, July–August, 3–18.

Harvey, A.S., Marshall, K. and Frederick, J.A. (1991) *Where Does Time Go?* Statistics Canada, Ottawa.

Kinsley, B.L. and Casserly, C.M. (eds) (1984) *Explorations in Time-use*. Employment and Immigration Canada, Ottawa.

Kirsh, C., Dixon, B. and Bond, M. (1973) *A Leisure Study – Canada 1972*. Culturcan Publications for the Arts and Culture Branch, Department of the Secretary of State, Ottawa.

Linder, S.B. (1970) *The Harried Leisure Class*. Columbia University Press, New York.

Meissner, M., Humphreys, E.W., Meiss, S.M. and Scheu, W.J. (1975) No exit for wives: sexual division of labour and the cumulation of household demands. *Canadian Review of Sociology and Anthropology* 12, 424–439.

Parks Canada (1976) *Canadian Outdoor Recreation Demand Study. An Overview and Assessment*. Ontario Research Council on Leisure, Toronto, Canada.

Robinson, J. and Godbey, G. (1997) *Time for Life: the Surprising Ways Americans Use Their Time*. Pennsylvania University Press, University Park, Pennsylvania.

Schliewen, R.E. (1977) *A Leisure Study – Canada 1975*. Comstat Services, Ottawa.

Schor, J. (1991) *The Overworked American*. Basic Books, New York.

Stynes, D.J., Bevins, M.T. and Brown, T.L. (1980) Trends or methodological differences? Paper presented to the *National Outdoor Recreation Trends Symposium, Durham, New Hampshire*.

Szalai, A. *et al.* (1972) *The Use of Time*. Mouton, The Hague.

TORPS Committee (1978) Tourism and recreation behaviour of Ontario residents: free time. In: *Tourism and Outdoor Recreation Planning Study*, Vol. 4. TORPS Committee, Toronto.

Tremblay, D.G. and Villeneuve, D. (1997) Aménagement et réduction du temps de travail: réconcilier emploi, famille et vie personnelle. *Loisir et Societe/Society and Leisure* 20(1), 107–157.

Veblen, T. (1953) *The Theory of the Leisure Class*. A Mentor Book, New York.

Wilensky, H. (1963) The uneven distribution of leisure: the impact of economic growth on free time. In: Smigel R.C. (ed.) *Work and Leisure*. College and University Press, New Haven, Connecticut, pp. 107–145.

Wippler, R. (1970) Leisure behaviour: a multivariate approach. *Sociologia Neerlandica* 6(1), 51–65.

Zuzanek, J. (1978) Social differences in leisure behaviour: measurement and interpretation. *Leisure Sciences* 1(3), 271–293.

Zuzanek, J. (1979) Leisure and cultural participation as a function of life-cycle. Paper presented to the *Annual Meeting of the Canadian Sociology and Anthropology Association, Saskatoon*.

Zuzanek, J. (1988) The fads and foibles of cultural statistics. *Journal of Cultural Economics* 14(1), 2–4.

Zuzanek, J. (1996) Canada. In: Cushman, G., Veal, A.J., and Zuzanek, J. (eds) *World Leisure Participation: Free Time in the Global Village*. CAB International, Wallingford, UK, pp. 35–76.

Zuzanek, J. and Smale, B. (1997) More work – less leisure? Changing allocation of time in Canada. *Loisir et Societe/Society and Leisure* 20(1), 73–106.

4 Finland

Mirja Liikkanen and Hannu Pääkkönen

History of Leisure and Time-use Surveys in Finland

Studying leisure in the past: leisure as part of consumption

Although the first national leisure survey in Finland was not conducted until the 1970s, the roots of studying leisure go back to social research on workers' living conditions in the 19th century (Liikkanen, 2000). For example, Vera Hjelt's study on the subsistence conditions of skilled workers in 1908–1909 included questions about cultural and educational expenditure (literature, magazines, children's schooling), association membership fees and entertainment (theatre, concerts, dances, etc.) (Ahlqvist, 2000).

Since the 1960s data about leisure expenditure have been collected regularly as part of Finnish consumption expenditure surveys. The 1971 Household Budget Survey was the first extensive study on leisure expenditure and use of leisure services. The object of the survey was to gain 'a comprehensive view of living conditions' and examine the use of all 'free services', including cultural services (Linnaila, 1972).

Leisure surveys and the social indicators movement

The study of leisure and cultural participation is closely associated with the concept of the Nordic welfare state and, in a broader international setting, with the so-called 'social indicators movement'. This movement proposed the development of a social statistical system comparable to the system of national accounts, that could compensate for the shortcomings of macro-economic statistics and be used for comprehensive social reporting (see Lehto, 1996, pp. 13–19). International organizations, such as the United Nations, the Organization for Economic Cooperation and Development and especially the European Union, have actively advocated this approach.

Concerns with the growth of free time and its effects on society were at the centre of the 1972 Report of the Finnish government's Economic Council (Yhteiskuntapolitiikan Tavoitteita Ja Niiden Mittaamista Tutkiva Jaosto, 1972a,b), which discussed, among other things, problems associated with the construction of social indicators that could serve social policy goals and objectives. According to the report:

Ways of thinking apparently need to be changed in a situation where leisure time clearly begins to dominate time use in society . . . To look for the socially optimal way of increasing leisure time we should, on the one hand, be aware of the *valuations* or preferences related to different possibilities and, on the other hand, try to establish the costs of different alternatives to society, that is the social *expenses* of alternative ways of increasing leisure time. A prerequisite of this is to identify social factors that control leisure time-use.

Yhteiskuntapolitiikan Tavoitteita Ja Niiden Mittaamista Tutkiva Jaosto (1972b, pp. 251–252)

Leisure surveys and cultural politics

The first extensive study on cultural participation in Finland was conducted in 1970 by Katarina Eskola for the National Council for Literature (Eskola, 1976b). The launching of this survey was closely associated with changes in Finland's cultural policies. The age of the 'pure art' policy was over: culture was now seen as a part of welfare policy and the objective was to examine the use, availability and distribution of cultural services to the entire population. Equal rights to cultural services had become the objective of the policy (see Kulttuuritoimintakomitean mietintö, 1974; Eskola, 1976a; Heiskanen, 1994).

Statistics Finland began developing a comprehensive system of cultural statistics in 1972. The results of these efforts were presented in a draft report entitled: *A General Outline for a System of Cultural Statistics* (Tapio Kanninen, 1973 Statistics Finland, Helsinki, unpublished). This draft suggested that the collection of leisure and cultural participation data be linked

with the broader system of social statistics, such as the national accounts and the Consumption Expenditure Surveys. The compilation of leisure and cultural statistics in Finland was also affected by UNESCO's efforts, during the 1970s, to build a system of comprehensive international cultural statistics. Leisure statistics were expected to include data on participation in institutional, organized, self-directed, active and passive leisure activities, as well as participation in organizations, associations and youth activities, and expenditure on leisure services and equipment, cultural commodities, leisure facilities and equipment, and recreation and entertainment services. Art and media statistics were to include data on music, theatre, physical art, visual art, festivals, exhibitions and other cultural events (including non-artistic), fiction and non-fiction reading, libraries, cinema and photography, radio, TV, cultural heritage and information services.

1977, 1981 and 1991 Studies of leisure and cultural participation

The first major Finnish compendium of leisure and cultural statistics was published in 1977. It contained data from a sample of 1300 persons collected as part of Statistics Finland's Leisure Survey, structured along lines suggested in Tapio Kanninen's draft on cultural statistics. An effort was made to make the contents of the 1977 survey as comparable as possible with Katarina Eskola's 1970 study. The close connection between the study of leisure and culture was reflected in the name of the survey, which referred to both cultural and leisure participation. Details of sample sizes and other technical information on this and other surveys discussed in this chapter are presented in Table 4.1.

Table 4.1. National leisure participation and time-use surveys conducted by Statistics Finland.

No.	Year of survey	Title of survey	Sample size	Sample age	Time referent	Measurement of participation
1	1977	Leisure Survey	1300	15 +	12 months	% participating
2	1979	Time-use Survey	6057	10–64	Day	Minutes
3	1981	Leisure Survey	2910	10 +	12 months	% participating
4	1987/88	Time-use Survey	7800	10 +	Day	Minutes
5	1991	Leisure Survey	5600	10 +	12 months	% participating
6	1999/2000	Time-use Survey	5300 (2600)	10 +	Day	Minutes

The 1981 survey of leisure and cultural participation was conducted along similar lines to the 1977 survey. The sample was slightly larger, at 2910 persons, and the data were collected by personal interviews from persons aged 10 years and older.

The 1991 Leisure Survey, for the first time, separated the collection of cultural and leisure statistics, and since then the Leisure Survey has been seen as an independent study. New kinds of approaches were introduced which challenged the assumption of 'universal leisure values' and turned attention towards everyday life and the meanings associated with it by various population groups. The survey questioned the active/passive dichotomy imposed on people 'from above', as reflected in the long tradition of popular education and welfare state 'leisure policies'. The 1991 Leisure Survey may also have been the first Statistics Finland study to combine, in the same research process, both traditional quantitative data collection methods and qualitative methods, thematic and semi-structured interviews and qualitative coding of open questions. The sample for the survey was larger than in the two previous studies, at 5600 persons. At the time of writing, the next Leisure Survey was to be carried out in 2002.

Time-use surveys in Finland

The first time-use surveys in Finland were conducted in the 1930s and 1940s (Niemi *et al.*, 1981, pp. 7–8; Niemi, 2000). They concerned time-use of schoolchildren and farmers' wives. Later on, surveys were conducted of time-use by other population groups. The Finnish Broadcasting Company carried out time-use surveys of the whole population by a mail enquiry for the purposes of programme planning in 1967, 1969, 1971 and 1975, but ceased when the non-response rate rose to unacceptable levels. Similarly to leisure surveys, Statistics Finland's Time-use Surveys were spurred by the recommendations of the 1972 *Report of the Economic Council*, which observed that: 'so far no exhaustive studies are available in Finland on the structure of real time-use in different population groups' (1972b, p. 251).

Statistics Finland's first Time-use Survey was administered in the autumn of 1979 in connection with the Labour Force Survey. The target population was the population aged 10 to 64, with the exception of permanent or temporary residents of institutions. The Ministry of Education funded the data collection for 10–14-year-old children. Diaries were kept on 2 consecutive days, the first of which was drawn by lot. The total number of survey days was 12,057.

The next Time-use Survey was conducted after 8 years in 1987/88. The data were collected over the entire year and the target population was again the resident population aged 10 years and older, living in a household, but there was no upper age limit. The Ministry of Education again covered the costs of the sample of the 10–14-year-olds. The additional sample of the pension-age population was financed by the Ministry of Social Affairs and Health. As in the previous survey, the respondents kept a diary on 2 successive days. Total survey days numbered 15,350.

Statistics Finland's third Time-use Survey was conducted in 1999/2000 and was part of the European Time-use Survey harmonized by Eurostat, the Statistical Office of the European Union. Data collection was financed by the Ministries of Education, Labour, Agriculture and Forestry, and Transport and Communications, as well as the Finnish Broadcasting Company, the Social Insurance Institution, the National Consumer Research Centre, the Research Institute of the Finnish Economy (ETLA), and the National Research and Development Centre for Welfare and Health (STAKES).

Data collection procedures changed somewhat compared to the earlier surveys. The survey now sampled households, so that all household members aged 10 and older kept a diary. The diaries were completed for 1 weekday and 1 weekend day. Household members kept the diary on the same days. The number of survey days was around 10,500.

Leisure as Time, Activity and Experience: Analysis of Trends

Changes in daily time-use patterns

The term 'free time', as used in the Time-use Surveys, means time remaining from the

24 hours, after the time devoted to sleep, meals, gainful employment, domestic work and full-time studies has been subtracted. Free time is thus 'residual' time, free from these activities.

As can be seen from Table 4.2, the allocation of time to major groups of daily activities remained almost unchanged during the 1980s. Personal needs took up more than 40% of daily time (of this sleeping took more than one-third, and meals and personal hygiene almost one-tenth). On average, a fifth of daily time was used for gainful employment and education, and domestic work took, on average, more than one-tenth. The remaining one-quarter was free time.

The amount of free time increased, on average, by 1 hour per week in the 1980s, from 40 hours in 1979 to 41 hours in 1987. Men's free time remained unchanged, whereas women's increased by nearly 2 hours/week. Men still had more free time than women, but the difference diminished from 5 hours to 3 hours/week.

The youngest and the oldest age groups had the greatest amounts of free time and showed its largest increase among the oldest age groups in the 1980s. People in the 45–64-year age group had two more hours of free time per week in the late 1980s than at the end of the 1970s.

The greatest change in the structure of time-use was an increase in the amount of television-watching. In 1987, some 29% of free time was spent in front of the television set. In 1979 the proportion of television-watching was 23%. Resting has decreased to the same degree as television-watching has increased. It seems as if resting moved in front of the television screen.

The second largest portion of free time, after television-watching, is used for socializing with family members and friends. A quarter of free time is spent socializing and, contrary to expectations, this did not decrease during the 1980s. Free time did not become more home-centred either: in 1979 63% of all free time was spent at home and in 1987 the percentage was 62. Women spend a greater part of their free time (64%) at home than men (60%).

There was no discernible reduction in reading over the period, accounting for the same portion in 1987/88 (14%) as in 1979. Sports and outdoor recreation also retained their 10% proportion of free time.

Table 4.2. Use of time by gender, Finland (hours.min/day), 1979 and 1987.

	Total		Men		Women	
	1979	1987	1979	1987	1979	1987
Gainful employment, total	3.41	3.53	4.18	4.29	3.07	3.17
Domestic work, total	2.47	2.47	1.50	2.01	3.39	3.35
Physical needs, total	10.34	10.23	10.35	10.25	10.33	10.21
Education, total	1.12	1.00	1.10	0.97	1.14	1.05
Free time, total	5.44	5.53	6.05	6.06	5.25	5.40
Leisure-time studies	0.05	0.05	0.04	0.04	0.06	0.05
Voluntary activities	0.08	0.07	0.10	0.07	0.07	0.07
Sports and outdoor recreation	0.32	0.32	0.42	0.39	0.23	0.24
Entertainment and culture	0.06	0.05	0.07	0.06	0.05	0.05
Reading	0.48	0.49	0.52	0.50	0.45	0.48
Watching TV	1.18	1.41	1.27	1.51	1.10	1.31
Listening to radio (primary activity)	0.08	0.10	0.10	0.12	0.06	0.08
Socializing with family	0.12	0.12	0.12	0.11	0.13	0.13
Socializing with friends	1.00	0.58	0.59	0.53	1.01	1.04
Hobbies	0.27	0.25	0.18	0.20	0.36	0.30
Resting	0.27	0.12	0.30	0.14	0.25	0.10
Other free-time activity	0.05	0.05	0.05	0.06	0.04	0.04
Travel related to free time	0.27	0.32	0.31	0.34	0.25	0.30
Unspecified time-use	0.02	0.03	0.03	0.03	0.02	0.03
Total	24.00	24.00	24.00	24.00	24.00	24.00
Diary days	12,057	4764	5807	2395	6250	2369

Source: Niemi et al. (1981) and Niemi and Pääkkönen (1990).

Changes in the structure of men's and women's free time were similar, with few exceptions. The proportion of socializing diminished for men but increased for women. Another difference between men and women was in the amount of time spent on hobbies, with involvement declining for women but increasing slightly for men. This may have resulted from the decrease in women's involvement with handicrafts and an increase in men's technical hobbies (see Niemi and Pääkkönen, 1990).

Old and new communication technologies at home

The mass media and electronic means of communication occupy an increasingly prominent role in modern life at home. Watching television forms a permanent part of everyday life. As Table 4.3 indicates, in 1991 more than 70% of the respondents reported that they watched television every day. Today in Finland about 40% of families have more than one television set, and television-watching is becoming more individualized (Finnish Mass Media 2000, p. 79).

There was an increase in the frequency of television-watching through the 1980s and the 1990s. In 1981, less than 60% of respondents reported watching television every day. In 1991, this figure was over 70%. In 1987/88, television viewing as a primary activity accounted for 1 h 41 min/day. If television-watching as a secondary activity is added, it amounts to 1 h 50 min, compared to 1 h 29 min in 1979 (Niemi and Pääkkönen, 1990, p. 47). Women in Finland watch television slightly less frequently than men. Elderly and unemployed people are the most keen television viewers, and young adults the least frequent (see Table 4.4). The so-called television meter studies carried out continuously by Finnish television companies show that the increase in daily television viewing time continued throughout the 1990s. According to these studies, television and video viewing amounted to, on average, 2 h and 47 min in 1999 (Finnish Mass Media, 2000, p. 72).

According to the data collected by Finnish Mass Media, about two-thirds of Finnish households have a VCR (Finnish Mass Media, 2000, p. 72). Video watching is most popular among

young respondents and students, and men watch videos more often than women. The most common use of the VCR in Finland is watching recorded television programmes (the so-called 'time-shift' use) (Liikkanen, 1995a).

The importance of radio listening declined somewhat in the 1980s and 1990s, although radio remains, like television, a part of everyday life (Liikkanen, 1994a). Some 70% of respondents aged 10 or over reported that they listened to the radio daily in 1991, while only 2% of the population never listened to it. The number of daily listeners declined over the 1980s. The habit of radio listening is slightly more common among men, but women in almost all age groups considered the radio more important than men. The radio is mostly used for listening to music, although four out of five respondents of both sexes also used record and cassette players for listening to music (Liikkanen, 1994b).

A relatively new element in electronic household technology is the computer, which has spread rapidly in Finnish homes. In 1991, a quarter of the Leisure Survey respondents reported that they had a computer at home. According to the *Finns and the Future Information Society* study, carried out by Statistics Finland in 1999, as many as a half of the population aged 10–74 had access to a computer at home. In 1991 and in 1999 boys and men used home computers more often than girls and women, but this difference diminished in the course of the 1990s (see Nurmela *et al.*, 2000). Young people in general, and especially young boys, are the most eager home computer users, reporting the greatest variety of computer use and frequent regular playing of computer games. Men play computer games and use CD-ROMs more frequently than women, but the differences in other uses of the computer are relatively small. For instance, women and men seem to use e-mail and word processing equally. Only in the older age groups do men report considerably more e-mail and word processing than women. 'Chatting' over the Internet is common among both boys and girls under the age of 20, with about one-seventh reporting chatting often in their leisure time. Among older age groups Internet chatting is a very rare activity (see also Nurmela *et al.*, 2000).

Table 4.3. Leisure participation (%), Finland, 1981 and 1991.

	Total		Males	Females
	1981	1991	1991	1991
Use of media and reading				
Watches television every day	59	72	75	69
Listens to the radio every day	79	71	73	69
Listens to recorded music	87	82	83	80
Reads at least one newspaper regularly	97	96	96	95
Reads some magazine at least once a week	79	69	67	70
Has read books during the past 6 months	76	75	70	80
Creative hobbies				
Plays an instrument	20	15	15	15
Takes an interest in visual arts	13	13	11	15
Takes an interest in handiwork	65	63	52	74
Cultural attendance (during past 12 months)				
Concert	35	34	27	39
Theatre	45	37	28	46
Dance performance	25	18	14	22
Art exhibition	37	44	38	50
Museum	43	43	42	44
Cinema (during past 6 months)	41	35	35	35
Library (during past 6 months)	53	59	55	62
Social participation (during past 12 months)				
Attended a religious meeting	63	53	44	62
Participated in an association or club	57	52	52	52
Sports and outdoors (at least once a week for 2 months)				
Does sport in the summer	85	82	80	84
Does sport in the winter	81	81	79	84
Jogging, running	–	22	25	19
Walking	–	59	51	68
Swimming	–	28	25	31
Cycling	–	44	38	50
Keep-fit gymnastics at home	–	22	15	29
Soccer	–	6	11	2
Cross-country skiing (incl. biathlon)	–	20	21	19
Downhill skiing	–	11	13	9
Ice hockey (including ringette)	–	5	9	1
Hunting (at least once in the past 12 months)	10	9	17	1
Other fishing (at least once in the past 12 months)	–	45	62	30
Berry picking (at least once in the past 12 months)	–	65	58	71
Mushroom picking (at least once in the past 12 months)	–	41	37	44
Other pastimes (at least once in the past 12 months)				
Goes out dancing or to a restaurant	63	70	75	65
Video or TV games	–	31	39	24
Slot machines	54	43	58	30
One-arm bandit, solid state pinball or similar	30	46	59	35
Roulette or pool	21	25	37	14
Bingo	8	7	7	6
Chess	17	13	20	7
Card games	59	57	62	52
Crossword puzzles	53	49	39	57
Sample size	2506	4378	2108	2270

Source: Liikkanen and Pääkkönen (1994).

Table 4.4. Leisure participation by age (%), Finland, 1991.

	Age (years)				
	10–14	15–24	25–44	45–64	65+
Use of media and reading					
Watches television every day	72	64	67	75	84
Listens to the radio every day	28	55	74	82	83
Listens to recorded music	96	99	90	76	47
Reads at least one newspaper regularly	76	97	98	98	98
Reads some magazine at least once a week	57	73	69	71	65
Has read books during the past 6 months	90	86	80	66	61
Creative hobbies					
Plays an instrument	43	24	13	10	5
Takes an interest in visual arts	36	22	11	8	5
Takes an interest in handiwork	56	62	66	67	56
Cultural attendance (during past 12 months)					
Concert	31	48	34	32	22
Theatre	35	36	36	43	31
Dance performance	17	21	18	22	11
Art exhibition	49	53	44	45	30
Museum	60	49	45	41	25
Cinema (during past 6 months)	62	81	40	14	4
Library (during past 6 months)	94	82	65	45	28
Social participation (during past 12 months)					
Attended a religious meeting	65	48	44	59	65
Participated in an association, club	67	48	53	52	45
Sports and outdoors (at least once a week for 2 months)					
Does sport in the summer	93	87	82	83	77
Does sport in the winter	92	86	80	83	74
Jogging, running	32	41	28	12	2
Walking	19	46	61	71	69
Swimming	53	32	25	30	16
Cycling	70	42	43	48	32
Keep-fit gymnastics at home	16	19	21	24	26
Soccer	36	11	6	0	–
Cross-country skiing (incl. biathlon)	24	8	19	31	12
Downhill skiing	34	20	12	6	0
Hunting (at least once in the past 12 months)	–	8	12	9	4
Fishing (at least once in the past 12 months)	–	49	51	48	23
Berry picking (at least once in the past 12 months)	–	45	69	78	51
Mushroom picking (at least once in the past 12 months)	–	20	41	56	33
Other pastimes (at least once in the past 12 months)					
Goes out dancing or to a restaurant	–	82	86	65	24
Video or TV games	69	58	37	14	2
Slot machines	43	65	50	35	18
One-arm bandit, solid state pinball or similar	66	78	55	32	11
Roulette or pool	37	54	30	12	3
Chess	31	24	13	8	3
Card games	76	82	65	44	26
Crossword puzzles	49	56	54	47	29
Sample size	324	646	1603	1144	661

Source: Liikkanen and Pääkkönen (1994).

In the course of the 1990s, another product of new technology – the mobile phone – spread rapidly in Finland. There are now more mobile phones in Finland than fixed phones. This has had many effects on how people handle their social networks, as well as how they arrange and plan their time-use. According to the above-mentioned *Information Society* study, more than 70% of men and 60% of women aged 15–74 have a mobile phone for their private use. Mobile phones are most common in the 15–30 years age group, with four out of five of both sexes reporting having one. Using mobiles for sending text messages is also most common among younger age groups. In the 10–14-year age group, 25% of boys and 30% of girls had a mobile phone of their own and about half of the boys and 60% of the girls used a mobile phone at least sometimes. The availability of mobile phones has changed sociability patterns in Finland, especially among young respondents and families. The use of mobile phones decreases in older age groups, and gender differences are greater in these age groups. Among 60–74-year-old respondents, two in five men but only one in five women use mobile phones (see also Nurmela *et al.*, 2000).

Reading

Reading occupies a prominent position in Finland's life, for historical reasons. In the 1991 Leisure Survey this was reflected not only in the popularity of reading reported by respondents but also in the significance attached to it.

Reading of newspapers is very common in Finland among people of all kinds, irrespective of age, sex, education or social status. In 1991, about 90% of the adult population were daily newspaper readers. Three out of four respondents aged 15–24 reported reading newspapers, and even among those aged 10–14, the proportion was 40%. It seems that some changes have occurred since then, although data on the present situation are scarce. The reading habits of older age groups may not have changed, but there is some evidence that the frequency of newspaper reading has diminished among young people.

In contrast, reading magazines and comic books declined in the course of the 1980s. In 1991, 70% of the population aged 10 or over reported reading magazines and 30% reported reading comic books at least once a week. Comic-book reading is especially popular among young age groups. Higher-income employees read magazines more frequently than other social groups.

Reading of books is also common in Finland, with three out of four persons aged 10 or over reported having read at least one book during the past 6 months in 1991. The habit of reading is more common among women than men, with 80% of the former and 70% of the latter reporting reading at least one book during the past 6 months. Between 1981 and 1991 the reading of books declined slightly among men, but increased among women. Although young age groups continue to be the most eager readers, the biggest decline in the frequency of book reading during the 1980s occurred among young boys, with a smaller decline among young girls. This development among younger age groups seems to have continued during the 1990s (see also Eskola, 1994; Liikkanen, 1995a).

Cultural and other social attendances

Attending cultural and artistic events, similar to reading and participation in social organizations, has traditionally been considered an active and significant form of leisure in Finland. Finns have always been keen visitors to cultural events. In 1991, almost 80% of people aged 10 or over reported attending at least one cultural event or visiting a museum during the year of the survey. The figure for females was higher than that for men (see also Pääkkönen, 1994; Liikkanen, 1995a). Women valued artistic events more than men and were, in general, more active visitors to cultural functions. Approximately 60% of persons who had attended a cultural event (other than cinema or museums) during the year preceding the survey were women, and women accounted for some 70% of opera visitors, and slightly more than a half of cinema-goers and museum visitors.

In general, cultural attendance declined during the 1980s, only art exhibitions attracting an increasing number of visitors, in particular men. The most noticeable decline in the 1980s was in visits to theatre and dance performances. The number of tickets sold in the course of the 1990s would indicate, however, that this trend may have changed again (Cultural Statistics, 1999, p. 212). Visits to the cinema declined more among men than among women, while the proportion of people going to concerts and museums remained almost unchanged for both sexes during the 1980s.

The proportion of women among frequent visitors to cultural events is clearly greater than that of men. Cultural attendance is one of the most socially exclusive of all groups of leisure activities. Salaried employees and students are the most active visitors, although people from a wide range of social groups can be found among audiences (Liikkanen, 1995b).

A wide range of types of event are included under the heading 'cultural'. For instance, in 1991: more than half of the population attended religious meetings; almost half attended sports events; about a third visited an agricultural or sales show; a third reported visiting an amusement park and a quarter reported visiting a zoo or an animal park. Sports events, motor racing sports, trotting races and agricultural shows are far more popular among men than women. Women, on the other hand, are more active in attending religious meetings.

Sports and outdoor recreation

By international comparison, Finns report a high level of sports and outdoor recreational participation. In 1991, the proportion of the population aged 10 or over participating in physical activities at least once a week was over 80%, in both summer and winter. According to the time-use and leisure surveys, participation in physically active leisure changed little in the 1980s. The proportion of free time devoted to sports and outdoor recreation was 10% in 1987, the same as in 1979 (Niemi and Pääkkönen, 1990, p. 52). The number of active participants in sports and outdoor recreation has declined slightly in the summer, but has remained unchanged in the winter. Children and young people are the most active participants and were also the group most involved in sports associations and clubs (see Aaltonen, 1994).

In 1991, the most favoured types of physical activities for Finns were walking, cycling, swimming, keep-fit gymnastics at home, jogging and cross-country skiing. These activities were practised by over one-fifth of respondents aged 10 years or over. Walking, cycling and skiing continued to be the most popular activities for adults at the end of the 1990s (Finnish Sports Federation, 1999). Reflecting the Finnish environment and traditions, fishing and berry and mushroom picking are also common leisure interests, with as many as two-thirds of those aged 15 or over having picked berries during 1991 and almost a half of the population having fished or picked mushrooms.

Time-use surveys and leisure participation surveys produce varying impressions with regard to gender differences in physically active leisure participation. According to the 1987 Time-use Survey, men spent an average of 44 min/day on physical activities, but for women the figure was just 27 min/day (Niemi and Pääkkönen, 1990, p. 52). However, according to the 1991 Leisure Survey, women practise more sports than men both in the summer and winter (Aaltonen, 1994, p. 115). This difference may be explained by the research methods used, in that men's definition of physical activities appears to correspond closely to that used in the Time-use Survey classification and analysis, while women may have included walking or cycling to work or shops as physical activities (cf. Niemi, 1985), activities which, in time-use surveys, were classified as a part of gainful employment or domestic work.

Dancing and eating out

There was no major change in the course of the 1980s in the frequency of going out dancing. In 1991, 34% of the population aged 15 or over had been out dancing at least once during the past 6 months, compared with 31% in 1981. The distinctively Finnish culture of dancing in open-air pavilions in the summer was also still alive in 1991. One in four respondents had been to open-air dances. However, restaurants had clearly taken over from dance pavilions as the chief place of dancing, with almost half of the population aged 15 or over having been to a restaurant for dancing during the past 6 months, and one in ten having been to 'ladies' choice' dances. The number of those going to afternoon dances remained very low.

Going to discos has also become increasingly common, with one in four respondents aged 15 years and over having been during the past 6 months. Virtually all visitors to discos were in the age group under 45. Among those aged 15–24, as many as four-fifths had frequented discos.

Men tend to go dancing and to restaurants more than women. Young people went to dances less than before, whereas in other age groups the frequency increased. More young people, however, went to discos than 10 years previously (see Pääkkönen, 1994).

Games

Cards and other parlour games are the most popular types of games played in Finland. In 1991, 57% of respondents reported playing such games. About a half of respondents said that they did crosswords, and pinball and other slot machines were almost equally popular. One-quarter of respondents reported playing roulette or snooker. Chess and bingo are less common, with 13% of respondents reporting playing chess, and 7% playing bingo. The popularity of parlour games and slot machines increased considerably in the 1980s. There was also some increase in playing roulette and snooker. On the other hand, the traditional *Pajatso* slot machine lost players. Some decline was also reported for crosswords and chess playing. Men are more active in playing such games than women. The only category where women are more active than men is doing crosswords. Playing bingo has now become equally popular among men and women.

It is a popular theory in Finland that pensioners spend a lot of time playing slot machines. Indeed, the findings of the Leisure Survey indicated that, in 1991, some 17% of Finnish pensioners played on slot machines during the past 12 months while, in the groups aged over 65, only one in ten respondents reported playing slot machines (see also Pääkkönen, 1994).

Leisure as a subjective phenomenon

Time-use surveys define leisure time as a residual concept. Defined in this manner, leisure time does not include eating, lovemaking, childcare, tending of house or garden plants, sleeping or preparing festive meals or eating with friends. As a consequence, in many instances this definition does not correspond with respondents' subjective experiences of leisure in their everyday lives. Furthermore, in cultural terms, leisure does not represent merely time spent, but is rather a qualitative concept laden with a number of different meanings. If leisure is defined 'residually', numerous activities regarded by individuals as part of their leisure time can be excluded. Leisure in a subjective sense is determined to a great extent by individual situations. It means different things to different groups in society, and involves different types of activities depending on one's stage in life, although there are, of course, certain common and compelling forms of thinking about leisure in Western culture.

If leisure is perceived as a qualitative concept, and elements of enjoyment and fun are attached to it, even work can, at times, be regarded as leisure. In some situations in life, when the children are young, for example, many people regard work as the sphere in which they can enjoy their own life and spend time in their own way, particularly if the content of their work is interesting. Mixing work and leisure nowadays seems to be a trend, especially in the new technologies and media industries.

According to the 1991 Leisure Survey, neither men or women regard domestic work as always merely routine or a duty. These attitudes may apply to washing, ironing and cleaning, but many men, and even women, attach elements of pleasure and interest to cooking and shopping. As Table 4.5 indicates, almost 70% of all respondents surveyed in 1991 considered cooking and shopping to be fun at least occasionally, although only one-tenth regarded them as being fun at all times (Liikkanen, 1995a). The most enjoyment from household maintenance activities is derived from gardening, with 36% of women and 30% of the men in households where gardening was practised

Table 4.5. Attitudes towards domestic work by gender (%), Finland, 1991.

	Always a routine and duty	Sometimes a pleasure	Always a pleasure	Never takes part
Cooking				
Males	20	37	17	25
Females	28	57	12	2
Cleaning				
Males	54	19	5	20
Females	59	33	4	4
Laundry, care of clothing				
Males	35	10	2	51
Females	62	28	4	5
Gardening				
Males	16	33	30	19
Females	10	39	36	13
Shopping				
Males	42	39	8	10
Females	28	55	11	4
House repairs				
Males	41	40	9	8
Females	17	18	5	58

Source: Leisure Survey, 1991 (see Table 4.1) and Liikkanen and Pääkkönen (1994).

regarding it as being always fun and looking on it as a hobby. Three-quarters of women and three-fifths of men approached gardening in this way at least occasionally.

Conclusion

Many changes in Finnish use of leisure time parallel international trends. For example, in the past, time spent by Finns watching television was low by international standards, but use of electronic media, especially television viewing, is on the increase and is now close to the international average, but still far below the corresponding figures for some countries, such as the USA.

Changes in cultural life that began in the 1980s, appeared to have deepened in the 1990s. The most evident change is probably the transition from involvement with national and literary culture towards international and audio-visual and electronic media and, most recently, the Internet. Moreover, mobile phones are so popular in Finland that the country has been called 'a mobile information society' (Kopomaa, 2000).

It has long been predicted that the significance of national cultures will be eroded as a result of 'globalizing' international trends. This was clearly reflected in the results of the 1991 Leisure Survey, which showed that many nationally important institutions were losing ground. The first signs of the fall in newspaper and book reading were visible. The same applies to the popularity of folk music and religious practices. The decline of interest in national culture was particularly evident among younger age groups who, unlike older age groups, often preferred international to national media content.

Similar changes have affected all Western cultures, but have probably been experienced particularly dramatically in Finland. Finland became independent from Russia over 80 years ago. Before that the country was, for a long period, under Swedish rule, and the re-establishment of the Finnish language as a national and official main language in the place of Swedish was not fully achieved until the 1930s. In these circumstances Finland was consciously built as an ethnically mono-cultural country of one language and one people, despite the position of Swedish as the official minority language. Literary production was constructed as the foundation of national culture. In the 1990s, new communication technologies took the country, particularly young people, by storm. Computers, the Internet and mobile phones became part of everyday life, and became widely used, even when travelling abroad. However, national feelings have not disappeared in the globalized world, but are interestingly intertwined with the new phenomena. For example, Nokia is strongly felt to be a Finnish enterprise, of which Finns are particularly proud.

A surprising boom in the 1990s took place in the Finnish film industry, when all of a sudden a number of films were produced, drawing from the history of Finnish wars and popular culture, and achieving enormous popularity among all age groups. An interesting development took place in the recording industry as well. The sales of Finnish recordings clearly fell in the course of the late 1980s, but this trend has turned around in the 1990s (Finnish Mass Media, 2000). There may be several reasons for this. In part, Finnish production has become more international in style and performance, while at the same time, a comparable rise has occurred in the popularity of more traditional national musical forms. Of course, as with the film industries, this may be temporary and even slightly nostalgic.

Participation in sports and outdoor recreation has also followed international trends, since many conventional types of sports, such as athletics and cross-country skiing, have lost in popularity, while the diversity of sports participation has increased. Business-like approaches have penetrated sports in Finland, as in many other countries, but these developments have also been coupled with a strong national feeling and great pride in the success of Finns in the globalized world of sports. This pride naturally extends to those successful in cultural businesses as well, such as conductors, opera singers and pop stars. Cultural icons, such as Darude, Bomfunk MC's and HIM, may, like Nokia, be recognized as Finnish only by Finns, yet these success stories are meaningful from the perspective of the citizens of a small country.

Bibliography

Aaltonen, K. (1994) Sports and physical culture in Finland. In: Liikkanen, M. and Pääkkönen, H. (eds) *Culture of the Everyday: Leisure and Cultural Participation in 1981 and 1991.* Statistics Finland, Helsinki.

Ahlqvist, K. (2000) Kulutustutkimuksen historia ja yhteiskunnan muutos [*History of the consumption expenditure survey and social change* (in Finnish only)]. In: *Hyvää Elämää. 90 Vuotta Suomalaista Kuluttajatutkimusta* [*Good Life. 90 Years of Finnish Consumer Research* (in Finnish only)]. National Consumer Research Centre and Statistics Finland, Helsinki.

Central Statistical Office of Finland (1976) *Finnish Survey on Relative Income Differences.* Study No. 35, Central Statistical Office of Finland, Helsinki.

Eskola, K. (1976a) Taidehalli ja Taiteen Yleisö [*Kunsthalle Helsinki and the arts audience* (in Finnish only)]. In: *Taidehalli 76 (Kunsthalle 76).* Kunsthalle, Helsinki.

Eskola, K. (1976b) *Suomalaisten Kulttuuriharrastukset. [Finns' Cultural Participation* (in Finnish only)]. Publication No. 7, Finnish Arts Administration, Helsinki.

Eskola, K. (1994) Reading books. In: Liikkanen, M. and Pääkkönen, H. (eds) *Culture of the Everyday. Leisure and Cultural Participation in 1981 and 1991.* Statistics Finland, Helsinki.

Finnish Mass Media (2000). *Culture and the Media 2000,* vol. 1. Statistics Finland, Helsinki.

Finnish Sports Federation (1999) Available at website: www.slu.fi (accessed 22 June 1999).

Heiskanen, I. (1994) Kulttuuripolitiikan pitkät linjat. Kansallisen kulttuurin prototyypistä hyvinvointivaltiollisen kulttuuripolitiikan kautta kohti uutta kenties monikansallista kulttuuria. [Long lines of cultural policy. From the prototype of national culture via the welfare state's cultural policy towards new possibly multinational culture (in Finnish only)]. *Hyvinvointikatsaus* [*Welfare Review*] 2, 6–9.

Kopomaa, T. (2000) *The City in Your Pocket. Birth of the Mobile Information Society.* Gaudeamus, Helsinki.

Kulttuuritoimintakomitean mietintö [Report of Committee for Cultural Activities] (1974) *Committee report 1974,* vol. 2 [in Finnish only]. Kulttuuritoimintakomitea, Helsinki.

Lehto, A.-M. (1996) *Työolot tutkimuskohteena* [*Working Conditions as a Subject of Investigation*]. Research Reports 222, Statistics Finland, Helsinki.

Liikkanen, M. (1994a) Television, video, radio and home computers: recent trends and breakthroughs. In: Liikkanen, M. and Pääkkönen, H. (eds) *Culture of the Everyday. Leisure and Cultural Participation in 1981 and 1991.* Statistics Finland, Helsinki.

Liikkanen, M. (1994b) Television and radio programmes: the choices of viewers and listeners. In: Liikkanen, M. and Pääkkönen, H. (eds) *Culture of the Everyday. Leisure and Cultural Participation in 1981 and 1991.* Statistics Finland, Helsinki.

Liikkanen, M. (1995a) Leisure time. In: Veikkola, E.-S. and Palmu, T. (eds) W*omen and Men in Finland: Living Conditions 1995.* Statistics Finland, Helsinki.

Liikkanen, M. (1995b) Participation in cultural life. In: *Cultural Policy in Finland. National Report. European Programme of National Cultural Policy Reviews.* Council of Europe, Arts Council of Finland, Helsinki.

Liikkanen, M. (2000) Kulttuuritilastoja ja vapaa-aikatutkimuksia vuodesta 1977 [in Finnish only]. In: Marjoma, P. (ed.) *Tilastokeskus 1971–2000 [Statistics Finland 1971–2000].* Statistics Finland, Vantaa.

Liikkanen, M. and Pääkkönen, H. (eds) (1994) *Culture of the Everyday. Leisure and Cultural Participation in 1981 and 1991.* Statistics Finland, Helsinki.

Linnaila, J. (1972) *Kotitaloustiedustelun Vuosihaastattelu [Annual Interview of the Household Budget Survey* (in Finnish only)]. Central Statistical Office of Finland, Helsinki.

Niemi, I. (1985) *Harrastusmittareiden Luotettavuus [The Validity of Measuring Leisure Activities* (in Finnish only)]. Tilastokeskus, Tutkimuksia 117, Helsinki.

Niemi, I. (2000) Ajankäyttötutkimukset 1979, 1987–88 ja 1999–2000 [Time-use Surveys in 1979, 1987–1988 and 1999–2000 (in Finnish only)]. In: Pertti, M. (ed.) *Tilastokeskus 1971–2000.* Statistics Finland, Vantaa.

Niemi, I. and Pääkkönen, H. (1990) *Time-use Changes in Finland in the 1980s.* Study No. 174. Statistics Finland, Helsinki.

Niemi, I., Liikkanen, M. and Kiiski, S. (1981) *Use of Time in Finland 1979.* Study No. 65. Statistics Finland, Helsinki.

Nurmela, J., Heinonen, R., Ollila, P. and Virtanen, V. (2000) *Mobile Phones and Computers as part of Everyday Life in Finland. Phase II of the project 'The Finns and the Future Information Society',* Report 1. Reviews 2000/5, Statistics Finland, Helsinki.

Pääkkönen, H. (1994) Cultural participation. In: Liikkanen, M. and Pääkkönen, H. (eds) *Culture of the Everyday. Leisure and Cultural Participation in 1981 and 1991.* Statistics Finland, Helsinki.

Yhteiskuntapolitiikan Tavoitteita Ja Niiden Mittaamista Tutkiva Jaosto (Division Examining the Objectives of Social Policy and Their Measurement) (1972a) *Elämisen Laatu, Tavoitteet ja Mittaaminen [Quality of Life, Objectives and Measurement* (in Finnish only)]. Economic Council, Helsinki.

Yhteiskuntapolitiikan Tavoitteita Ja Niiden Mittaamista Tutkiva Jaosto (Division Examining the Objectives of Social Policy and Their Measurement) (1972b) *Liite 6 Erillisselvityksiä [Appendix 6 Special Surveys* (in Finnish only)]. Economic Council, Helsinki.

5 France

Nicole Samuel

Introduction

It was not until after the Second World War that leisure research – including national leisure participation surveys – emerged in France. This became possible for at least two reasons. First, the social sciences, having gained increased recognition and official support, became attractive to a wider number of researchers, whose interests spread from the traditional fields of investigation, such as work, law, religion, the family and education, to new areas of study. Secondly, leisure had slowly but surely become a social right and a significant social phenomenon in French society (Samuel and Romer, 1984). As a result, knowing about leisure as a social phenomenon *per se* and about leisure participation as a feature of contemporary society became an important matter, not only for social scientists, but also for planners and politicians, and for business people interested in the leisure market. The convergence of these two factors explains why leisure studies came into existence and gathered momentum in the late 1940s, both theoretically and empirically. This take-off was stimulated by the fact that it became possible to obtain statistical information about leisure from research conducted by several institutions, most of which were established during the post-war period.

This chapter presents the contribution of such surveys to the knowledge of leisure participation in France. It includes three sections: first, a brief history and description of French leisure participation surveys; second, a summary of results from a diachronic perspective; and third, some comments about leisure participation today as related to gender, age, size of community, occupation and educational level. Concluding remarks discuss theoretical and methodological problems concerning the conduct of national surveys and their use.

Brief History and Description of French National Surveys on Leisure Participation

In this section an overview is presented of the surveys conducted by five different organizations. Basic data on the surveys are summarized in Table 5.1.

The IFOP surveys

The Institut Français d'Opinion Publique (IFOP) was a commercial enterprise established to conduct opinion surveys in 1938. Its first leisure survey was conducted in 1947. A journal entitled *Sondages* (surveys), published by the Institute, first appeared in June 1939; and two issues of the journal focused on leisure, in 1947 and 1949 (*Sondages*, 1947, 1949). IFOP

Table 5.1. Time-budget studies and leisure participation surveys in France.

Survey/organization	Year	Type	Sample size	Area	Age range	Reports
IFOP – vacation surveys	1961–1963	Quest.	700/500	Paris	18+	Sondages (1962)
		Quest.	2800	France, urban	18+	–
		Quest.	3500	France, 280 sites	18+	Sondages (1964)
INSEE – international time-budget	1965/66	Time-budget	2800	6 towns	18–65	Goguel (1966); Szalai et al. (1972)
INSEE – time-budget	1967	Time-budget	1800/1000	Paris/Nimes	18–65	Lemel (1972)
INSEE – time-budget	1974/75	Time-budget	6600	France, urban	15+	Documentation Française (1988)
INSEE – time-budget	1985/86	Time-budget	24,400		15+	
INSEE – time-budget	1998/99	Time-budget	16,000	France	15+	Dumontier and Pan Ké Shon (1999, 2000)
INSEE – leisure behaviour of the French	1967	Quest.	6637	France	14+	Leroux (1970a,b); Debreu (1973)
INSEE – leisure behaviour of the French	1987/88	Quest.	10,872	France	14+	Dumontier et al. (1987–88)
INSEE – Conditions de Vie des Ménages	1993/94	Quest.	8000 hholds	France	0–70	Manon (1996)
INSEE – vacation surveys	1949	Quest.	6500 hholds	18 large cities	18+	
	1950	Quest.	13,200 resp.	18 large cities	18+	
	1951	Quest.		18 large cities	18+	
	1957	Quest.	5275	Cities 50k+	14+	Gounot (1958)
	1961	Quest.	13,300	France	14+	Gounot (1961)
	1964	Quest.	17,300	France	14+	Goguel (1965)
	1965–1993 (annual)	Quest.	8000 hholds	France	Adults and children	Mémento du Tourisme (1993)
SOFRES – trips by French tourists	Annual, 1990–	Quest.	10,000	France	15+	SOFRES (annual since 1990)
Ministry of Culture: *Cultural Activities of the French People*	1973	Quest.	2000	France	15+	Ministère de la Culture (1974)
	1981/82	Quest.	4000	France	15+	Ministère de la Culture (1982)
	1988/89	Quest.	5000	France	15+	Ministère de la Culture (1990); Donnat and Cogneau (1990)
	1997	Quest.	3000	France	15+	Donnat (1998); Ministère de la Culture (1998)
Ministry of Culture: leisure activities of young people	1996/97	Quest.	4900	France	8–19	Ministère de la Culture (1999b)

Ministry of Culture: participation in multimedia	1999	Quest.	450 hholds	France	10+	Ministère de la Culture (1999a)
CREDOC – living conditions of the French	1978–1981	Quest.	2000	France	18+	CREDOC (1983)
CREDOC – participation in informal sport	1994	Quest	1000	France	14–65	Pouquet (1995)
Ministry of Youth and Sports – sports participation survey	1985	Quest.	3000	France	12–74	Erlinger *et al.* (1985)
Ministry of Youth and Sports – sports participation survey	2000	Quest.	6500	France	15–75	Mignon (2001)

CREDOC, Centre de Recherche et de Documentation sur la Consommation; hhold, household; IFOP, Institut Français d'Opinion Publique; INSEE, Institut National de Statistique et d'Études Economiques; Quest., questionnaire; Resp., respondents; SOFRES, Société Française d'Études et de Sondages.

also carried out vacation surveys in 1961, 1962 and 1963. The first was concerned with workers around Paris and in the north of France (*Sondages*, 1962). The second, which remained unpublished, dealt with a representative sample of the population in communities of at least 5000 inhabitants and studied their vacations in 1962. The third took place in 1963 and covered preferences for various types of holidays in the event of a reduction of working time, and ownership of second homes (*Sondages*, 1964). An effort was made to design the questionnaire so that the answers were comparable with those of the 1962 IFOP study and with the 1961 INSEE study, described below.

The INSEE surveys

The Institut National de Statistique et d'Études Economiques (INSEE) was founded in 1946 to analyse statistics concerning many topics, on a national scale. Two types of data gathered through national representative surveys provide information about leisure participation, namely time-budget studies and leisure participation surveys, which include surveys dealing with leisure activities in general and specifically with vacations.

In France, the preoccupation with time-budgets can be traced back to Le Play's research in the 19th century (Le Play, 1877). Later this type of study developed in the USSR and in the USA. In France, time-budget studies were conducted in the 1940s and the 1950s (Stoetzel, 1948; Fourastie, 1951; Girard, 1958; Girard and Bastide, 1959; Dumazedier, 1962a,b). But the first such study carried out on a national scale involved participation in the extensive UNESCO funded 'International Time-budget Study of Human Behaviour' conducted in 12 countries, as discussed in Chapter 1 (Szalai, 1972). In this study, the concept of free time was preferred to the concept of leisure. It was defined as the daily 24 hour time-budget minus work time – professional and domestic – and physiological time (sleep, meals, washing, etc.). This definition, which was adhered to in later French studies, includes within free time, time spent on political and religious activities, as well as time spent on leisure activities.

The French part of this international study was first carried out in six towns, with a total sample of 2800 persons (Goguel, 1966). In 1967, the study was replicated in two urban areas, Paris and Nimes (Lemel, 1972, 1974). In 1974/75 INSEE carried out a new time-budget study in urban areas only, and in 1985/86 it conducted a large-scale time-budget study covering the entire country, including the rural areas, and involving a sample of 16,000 households and 24,400 respondents (Documentation Française, 1988). Data were collected in two ways. For frequent activities, one or two persons in each household kept a detailed diary of the use of their time during a given day. For irregular or rather infrequent activities, average frequency of participation over a long period was determined by interview (Grimler and Roy, 1987). Where two or more activities took place simultaneously, results quoted later refer only to what were recorded as 'main' activities. In 1998–1999 a third time-budget survey was conducted by INSEE using a national sample of 16,000 people aged 15 and over, who were interviewed and also kept a diary of time-use for a day (Dumontier and Pan Ké Shon, 2000).

INSEE carried out leisure participation surveys in 1967, 1987/88 and 1993/94. It has also conducted specific surveys about vacations in 1949, 1950, 1951, 1957, 1961 and every year since 1964. The 1967 survey on the *Leisure Behaviour of the French People* took place during the last three months of the year, with a random sample of 6637 persons. In addition to results about the whole sample, the report presented a breakdown of leisure behaviour according to socio-cultural variables such as age, sex, occupation, income, level of education and size of the town of residence. A pre-established list of leisure activities was presented to the respondents, who were requested to indicate whether they were, or have been, practising each activity, and how often, during the preceding year (Leroux, 1970a,b; Debreu, 1973).

The second INSEE study (1987/88) took place during a whole year, which made it possible to study the impact of seasons upon leisure activities. It was held on a random sample drawn from 15,000 households (10,872 respondents). The questionnaire was more detailed than the one devised in 1967[1] and included new leisure activities which had appeared in the meantime. Some of the questions were designed to obtain information about the leisure lifestyles of some specific categories of the population (the young; elderly people). One of the aims of the second study was to attempt a measure of the evolution of leisure behaviour since the first study, 20 years before (Dumontier and Valdelievre, 1989). The third INSEE study was conducted with a random sample from 17,500 households. In all three cases, results were tabulated according to socio-cultural variables such as gender, age, educational level, occupation and size of the place of residence.

In 1996/97 INSEE, together with an organization called 'Media-metre', conducted a survey of the leisure activities of a nationally representative sample of 4900 young people aged between 8 and 19 years (Ministère de la Culture, 1999b).

Combining information from three of its own surveys, in 1988 INSEE published a report on the evolution of sporting activities from 1967 to 1984 (Garrigues, 1988).

The INSEE surveys on *vacations* are based on the following definition of vacation: 'any trip away from home for at least 4 consecutive days is said to be a 'vacation' if it is not taken for reasons of work, study, health care in specialised places, illness or death in the family' (Goguel, 1965). INSEE conducted vacation surveys in 1949, 1950 and 1951 in 18 large cities. In 1957, the field of investigation was widened to all cities of more than 50,000 inhabitants – about one-third of the French population at the time (Gounot, 1958). Finally, in October 1961, the INSEE vacation survey included the whole of metropolitan France (rural as well as urban areas), and a sample of 13,300 persons (Gounot, 1961). A similar survey followed in 1964, with a random sample of over 17,000 persons (Goguel, 1965). In addition, some questions are asked every 5 years on holiday-taking and leisure participation within an INSEE general survey on the economic situation, using a sample of 8000 households. The latest available results relate to 1998/99 (Manon, 1996; Rouquett, 2000).

Ministry of Tourism/SOFRES

Since April 1990, the Ministry of Tourism has conducted vacation surveys in collaboration with an organization called the Société Française d'Études et de Sondages (SOFRES). It involves a sample of 10,000 persons aged 15 and over, and is conducted on a monthly basis throughout the year, asking respondents about trips made within France and abroad during the previous month, for whatever reason. Results are published in the *Memento du Tourisme*.

The Ministry of Culture surveys

The Ministry of Culture was founded in 1959. Until 1969, it was headed by André Malraux (1901–1976), a famous writer who later became a minister in de Gaulle's governments. The Department of Studies and Prospective, set up by Malraux, carried out four studies, entitled *Cultural Activities of the French People*, in 1973, 1981, 1989 and 1997. Each survey was conducted in an identical way using a representative sample of 2000 (rising to 5000) people aged 15 and over, stratified by region and size of community. Details are given in Table 5.1.

The surveys were conducted on the basis of questionnaires administered through interviews at the homes of the respondents. They were based on a wide definition of culture, including participation in sporting activities, do-it-yourself activities, and social leisure activities such as going to the café or belonging to voluntary associations. This was clearly meant to go beyond the traditional French identification of culture with the arts.

The results of these four studies can be compared since the same basic questions were asked to comparable representative samples of persons aged 15 and over. In each case, the results are tabulated, for the whole sample, according to gender, age, occupation, educational level, marital status and size of the place of residence.

The CREDOC surveys

The *Centre de Recherche et de Documentation sur la Consommation* (CREDOC) is a public agency, established in 1953. It has a wide field of investigation – the general living conditions of the French population – but its surveys include information on leisure behaviour, including sporting activities and holiday-taking. It publishes a journal called *Consommation*. Upon the request of several bodies (Caisse Nationale des Allocations Familiales, Commissariat Général au Plan, Ministère de l'Environnement, Centre d'Étude des Revenus et des Coûts), in 1978 it started its series of surveys on the living conditions of the French population. In 1981/82 new participants joined the project – among them the recently created Ministry of Free Time, the Directorate of Tourism and the Service for the Study and Planning of Mountain Tourism (SEATM). This explains why more interest in leisure activities and in holiday going appeared in the CREDOC surveys from this date. The CREDOC sample of 2000 people, drawn using the quota method, is deemed representative of the French population aged 18 and over.

In October 1994, CREDOC conducted a survey on sporting activities and sport equipment, using a representative sample of 1000 people aged 14–65 (Pouquet, 1995).

The Ministry of Youth and Sports surveys

The Ministry of Youth and Sports carried out a survey of participation in sporting activities in 1985. The investigation was conducted by members of the Research Department of the National Institute for Sport and Physical Education (INSEP), an institute that is part of the Ministry of Youth and Sports network. The sample included 3000 persons aged 12–74, and a wide definition of sport was adopted, including walking, relaxation exercises, aerobics, gym at home and bathing without necessarily swimming (Erlinger *et al.*, 1985).

INSEP carried out a new survey of participation in sporting activities in May–June 2000, using a sample of 6500 persons aged 15–75.

Some Results of Time-budget and Leisure Participation Surveys

Some of the results of the above surveys are presented below, in two sections, relating to time-budget surveys and leisure participation surveys, respectively.

Time-budget studies

As mentioned above, some time-budgets were established in France during the 1940s and the 1950s. According to IFOP, leisure time amounted to an average of 2 hours per evening between 1945 and 1948 (Raymond, 1968). From the second IFOP survey we know what were the most frequent occupations during an evening of January 1948. To the question 'What did you do last night?', the answers were as shown in Table 5.2.

In 1951, Jean Fourastié gave an estimate of an average of 3 hours of leisure per day for the French adult worker (Fourastié, 1951). On the basis of a non-random sample (120 working families in the Paris area), Chombart de Lauwe's estimation (1958) for the 1950s was from 1.5 to 2 hours of daily leisure time for the Paris area; his computation excluded do-it-yourself activities, which he evaluated at an additional average daily 1.5–2 hours, but he admitted that only part of these activities was perhaps felt to be true leisure. In contrast, Dumazedier (1962a,b) included do-it-yourself activities in leisure time, for which he gave an estimate between 2 and 3 h/day in the 1950s, insisting

Table 5.2. Evening leisure activities, France, January, 1948.

Activity	% participating (multiple answers possible)
Leisure	
Reading	24
Radio listening	20
Resting	12
Inviting/visiting friends	7
Go to a show	6
Playing card games	5
Go to dance hall	1
Other leisure	5
Work	
Professional work	7
Domestic work	23

Source: Raymond (1968).

that the leisure time experienced after the midday meal as well as before the evening meal should be added to the evening computation of leisure time suggested by Stoetzel (1948). With regard to free time, the more systematic INSEE 1966 time-budget study indicated that the average daily free time for the whole adult population, including adult education, political and religious activities, was 3.9 hours. The results for subsequent surveys, for employed men and women, are as shown in Table 5.3. In each case, the time spent on adult education and participation in political and religious activities was practically non-existent, so that the figures quoted may, roughly speaking, be considered as a fair estimate of the time spent on leisure and rest.

Considerable differences concerning the definitions, the sample and the wording of questions make it impossible to compare the 1966 data with the 1974/75, 1985/86 and 1999 sets of figures, even in terms of general trends. But they were adjusted by statisticians to ensure their comparability with each other. The two later sets of data, which involved the whole population, urban and rural, are comparable with only a few adjustments. Table 5.4 shows that, in the 13 years between 1986 and 1999, French adults (employed and not employed) acquired, on average, 26 minutes more leisure time per day. The change was obviously due to the fact that, over the same period of time, the length of non-discretionary time decreased by a corresponding amount, on average: professional working time by 16 minutes, domestic work time by 4 minutes, physiological time by 2 minutes and non-work related travel by 4 minutes

(this small change hidden by rounding of figures in Table 5.4). Working time in France was reduced to 35 hours a week for wage-earners by laws enacted in June 1998 and January 2000.

The main leisure activities which benefited from the change were television-watching (+21 minutes) and, to a much lesser degree: games (+6 minutes), walking (+5 minutes) and sports (+1 minute). In 1985/86, the average leisure time for the whole population amounted to 4 h/day. More than 40% of this time was used for television-watching. On average, going out for shows and social life took up more than 1 h/day. Time devoted to walking and sport totalled 30 min, the same as was spent on reading (Grimler and Roy, 1987). In 1999 the average leisure time for the whole population amounted to 4.5 h/day; 47% of this was used for television-watching. On average, time for going out for shows and social life had decreased by 2 min but still amounted to about an hour, the same trend being observed for reading (down from 27 to 25 min). Time devoted to sport and walking increased slightly, from 23 to 29 min (Dumontier and Pan Ké Shon, 1999).

The results of the 1999 time-budget survey show that, between 1986 and 1999, the proportion of working time in a typical day diminished by an average of 16 min/day over the total adult population. During the same period, free time increased by an average of 26 min/day, reaching a daily average of 4.4 h. It is notable that this free time is more than ever taken up by television-viewing, taking 2.1 h/day in 1999, compared with 1.8 h in 1986 (Dumontier and Pan Ké Shon, 1999) (see Table 5.4).

Table 5.3. Daily free time, France, 1966–1999.

| | Hours of free time per day, including adult education and participation in political and religious activities | |
	Employed men	Employed women
1966	4.1	3.7
1974/75	3.2	2.4
1985/86	3.6	2.8
1999	3.7	3.0

Sources: Goguel (1966, p. 179); Grimler and Roy (1987); Dumontier and Pan Ké Shon (1999).

Table 5.4. Changes in time-use by adults, France, 1985/86, 1998/99.

Activities	Hours/day	
	1985/86	1998/99
Physiological time	12.1	12.0
Sleep	9.2	9.0
Personal care	0.9	0.8
Meals	2.0	2.2
Professional and training time	3.7	3.4
Professional work	2.8	2.5
Travel related to work	0.4	0.4
Study	3.5	3.4
Domestic time	3.5	3.4
Housework (cooking, dishwashing, laundry)	2.6	2.5
Caring for people	0.3	0.3
Do-it-yourself	0.2	0.3
Gardening, caring for animals	0.3	0.3
Other travel	0.6	0.6
Leisure time	4.0	4.6
Television	1.8	2.1
Reading	0.5	0.4
Walking	0.2	0.3
Games	0.1	0.3
Sport	0.1	0.1
Conversation, telephone, mail	0.5	0.3
Visits, going out	0.3	0.4

For each main activity category, only activities showing major change have been selected. Figures are averaged over the whole week, including Saturday and Sunday; multiply by 7 to obtain estimate of weekly time. Source: Dumontier and Pan Ké Shon (1999).

Leisure participation surveys

Since systematic comparative analysis of the data in the INSEE and Ministry of Culture surveys is impossible for methodological reasons, it seems appropriate to concentrate on the results of the latter, which allow a comparison of trends over time, once certain statistical adjustments have been made to the data. However, results from other sources are referred to when deemed useful, as, for example, in the case of sports participation or holiday-taking. The results may be classified under six headings: (i) leisure activities involving the media; (ii) artistic leisure activities; (iii) social leisure activities; (iv) physical leisure activities; (v) do-it-yourself leisure activities; and (vi) holiday-taking. This classification is an update of the one suggested by Dumazedier and Ripert (1966). Each of these groups of activities is discussed in turn below.

Activities involving the media

The trends indicated by the results of the 1997 Ministry of Culture survey, as shown in Table 5.5, indicate a continued increase in daily television-watching, as already discussed. But the striking increase in listening to records and cassettes, which took place between 1973 and 1988, had levelled off by 1997, as had reading of books and attendance at movies. Radio listening, which had been in decline up to 1988, experienced an increase in the 1990s. There was a decrease in newspaper reading while the reading of magazines fell, following the dramatic increase in 1973–1988. Being registered with, and visiting, a library experienced a small increase.

Table 5.5. Participation in leisure activities involving the media, France, 1973–1997.

| | | Ministry of Culture Surveys | | | |
| | | % participating, aged 15+ | | | |
	Frequency	1973	1981	1988	1997
Television-viewing	Every day or almost every day	65	69	73	77
Radio listening	Every day or almost every day	72	72	66	69
Listening to cassettes or records	Every day or almost every day	9	19	21	21
Reading a newspaper	Every day	55	46	43	36
Reading a magazine	Regularly	29	–	84	80
Reading books	At least once in past 12 months	70	74	74	73
Being registered in a library	–	13	14	17	21
Going to a library	At least once in past 12 months	–	–	23	31
Going to the movies	At least once in past 12 months	52	50	49	49

Source: Donnat (1998).

Artistic leisure activities

Looking for trends in arts-based activities, we observe an overall stability, as shown in Table 5.6. There is, however, growing interest in theatre attendance and visits to museums (probably including science and technology museums, which are becoming increasingly popular, but can not strictly be termed 'artistic'). Playing music seems to have lost some of its popularity, while, in contrast, there was an increase in non-musical amateur activities (writing, drawing, painting, dance, etc.).

Social leisure activities

There is no dramatic change in trends related to social leisure activities, as shown in Table 5.7. There is some increase in membership of associations, going out in the evening, inviting relatives home for a meal and in playing music or singing with a group. Other social activities are static and none shows a decrease in participation.

Physical leisure activities

Among physical leisure activities, the surveys paid particular attention to formal sport until the CREDOC survey of 1994 provided information on more informal physical activities (Pouquet, 1995). The main results from leisure participation surveys concerning sports are shown in Table 5.8. As was the case for other activities, method-

ological obstacles make an accurate diachronic comparison impossible, but trends can again be observed. In the period between 1967 and 1988, there was an overall increase in participation in sports, particularly: cycling, skiing and gymnastics. Participation in windsurfing and table tennis also increased, while team sports, except football, became less popular. It should be noted that the definition of gymnastics used in the 'Clothing survey' in Table 5.8 was much wider than that used in the other surveys, so the figures are not comparable. The overall participation for the 1993/94 INSEE survey is much lower than that for the other surveys, probably due to the wider age range used. Early results from the 2000 INSEP study confirm the pattern of the 1985 survey, although the survey was based on a sample with a narrower age range.

A new and most welcome type of information was provided by the 1994 CREDOC survey of informal sport participation, as shown in Table 5.9. This indicated that, while 68% of respondents participated in at least one sport, only half belonged to a formal club or federation. Indeed, the main trend of the 1990s appears to have been the development of informal, non-competitive physical activities, as opposed to formal, competitive sport.

Often combined with this trend, and visible from informal observation but not yet supported by available statistics, is the development of many new leisure activities, mostly centred on nature. About 40 sporting and physical activities have become popular in France since the 1970s,

Table 5.6. Participation in artistic leisure activities, France, 1973–1997.

	Ministry of Culture Surveys			
	% participating at least once a year, aged 15+			
Going to:	1973	1981	1988	1997
Museums	27	30	30	33
Theatre	12	10	14	16
Historic monuments	32	32	28	30
Concerts				
Classical	7	7	9	9
Jazz/pop/rock	6	10	13	13
Opera	3	2	3	3
Lyric theatre	4	2	3	2
Music hall	11	10	10	10
Playing music	–	–	18	13
Non-musical, amateur activity	–	–	27	32
Artistic exhibitions	19	21	23	25

Source: Donnat and Cogneau (1990); Donnat (1998).

Table 5.7. Participation in social leisure activities, France, 1973–1997.

		Ministry of Culture Surveys			
		% participating, aged 15+			
Activity	Frequency	1973	1981	1988	1997
Going out in the evening	At least once in a while	63.0	–	–	80
	At least once a month	15.9	25.8	48	–
Inviting friends home for a meal	Once in a while/often	–	–	73	75
Inviting relatives home for a meal	Once in a while/often	–	–	66	74
Belonging to at least one association	–	19.5	23.4	27	37
Playing cards or other games	In past year	Chess 7.9 Other 41.9	Chess 8.4 Other 45.5 Chance 55.1 Electronic 14.9	–	53
Playing music/singing with a group	In past year	5.1	5.1	–	10
Going to a fair	In past year	47	43	45	48
Dancing	At public dancing hall in past year	25.4	28	28	30

Source: see Table 5.1.

mostly mountain- and water-based. Especially popular are 'soft adventure' activities – a collection of outdoor activities which are not too difficult to master but provide fulfilment to outdoor nature enthusiasts (e.g. hiking, mountain climbing, cycling, canoeing). Water sports are in great demand, not only canoeing, but also rafting, hydro-speeding (swimming in water torrents with neoprene exposure suit, helmet, plastic floating shield and flippers), 'tubing', 'hot dogging' and body-board surfing.

'Practical' leisure activities

The leisure participation surveys give limited information on 'practical' leisure activities,

Table 5.8. Participation in sports, France, 1967–1997.

Activity:	INSEE					INSEP	Ministry of Culture
Survey:	1967 Time-budget	1974/75 Time-budget	1983/84 Clothing	1988	1993/94	1985	1997
Age range:	14+	18+	14+	14+	0–70	12–74	15+
	%	%	%	%	%	%	%
At least one sport	39.0	48.8	43.2	47.7	27.9	about 75	20
Swimming	25.0	29.8	18.1	13.0	–	22.5	19
Gymnastics	11.1	12.9	36.0*	15.1	–	26.3	3
Bowling	13.1	24.9	0.9	–	–	3.3	–
Football	5.1	5.5	4.2	3.7	–	6.8	–
Basketball	2.7	2.3	1.2	–	–	1.4	
Volleyball	–	–	1.1	–	–	2.3	
Rugby	1.0	1.1	1.1	–	–	0.6	
Skiing	4.9	9.7	5.8	16.5	–	10.0	
Athletics	3.5	3.7	–	–	–	–	
Sailing	3.4	5.1	2.5	–	–	2.3	
Tennis	3.0	5.9	8.6	8.3	–	12.8	
Mountain climbing	1.5	–	–	–	–	1.0	
Horse riding	1.4	2.8	1.0	–	–	2.8	
Martial arts	0.8	1.2	–	1.3	–	0.7	
Cycling	–	–	9.2	13.8	–	15.4	34 (inc. hiking)
Running	–	–	3.6	4.8	–	12.7	18 (inc. jogging)
Windsurfing	–	–	1.1	1.8	–	4.0	
Table tennis	–	–	1.0	3.1	–	3.9	
Body building/ weight lifting	–	–	–	2.6	–	0.8	

Source: see Table 5.1. *Different definition of gymnastics used, so not comparable with figures from other surveys.

Table 5.9. Participation in informal sport, France, 1994.

Activity	% informal among those engaged in sport
Roller/ice skating	97
Skiing/winter sports	92
Walking/hiking	92
Swimming/aqua-gym	88
Sailing/windsurfing	87
Jogging/running	85
Diving	72
Mountain climbing	64
Tennis	63
Horse riding	55
Golf	54
Dancing	49
Body building/fitness	35
Gym/aerobics	26
Team sports	20
Athletics	15
Martial arts	4

Source: Pouquet (1995).

such as do-it-yourself, gardening, hunting and fishing, probably because of the reluctance of many researchers to include them within their definition of leisure. We know, however, from INSEE that in 1987/88, 23.5% of male respondents stated that they repaired their car with pleasure once in a while, while 67.2% of female respondents said that they enjoyed sewing once in a while. From the trends shown in Table 5.10, it can be seen that participation in do-it-yourself activities increased from the late 1960s until the 1980s, with a decrease in the 1990s, possibly from an improvement in economic conditions which make do-it-yourself less necessary and less a priority for many people. No statistical conclusions can be drawn about gardening. Hunting and fishing are both reported as decreasing but it must be noted that the INSEE figures for hunting and fishing given for 1967 and 1987/88 are not comparable because the seasons of reference are not the same.

Holiday-taking

Since 1965, as mentioned before, yearly data concerning holiday-taking have been collected on a strictly comparable basis. Also, data from earlier INSEE surveys have been adjusted by statisticians, so that they could be compared to the series starting in 1965. The surveys therefore provide a continuous record of the proportion of the population taking a summer holiday away from home, for a least four consecutive days, and, as Table 5.11 shows, there has been a dramatic increase, from 30% in 1951 to 57% in 1999. Other sources provide similar results: according to INSEE, a higher figure of 69% is given for 1994, while the Ministry of Culture

Table 5.10. Participation in 'practical' leisure activities, France, 1967–1997.

		INSEE			INSEP	Ministry of Culture		
		1967	1987/88	1993/94	1985	1973	1981	1988	1997
	Age range:	14+	14+	14+	12–74	15+	15+	15+	15+
					At least once in		In last year		
	Frequency				a while				
Activity		%	%	%	%	%	%	%	%
Do-it-yourself	Once or twice a week	16	20.5	36.5	–	37.5	58.5	–	50
Gardening	Every day/almost every day in 'good' season	20.2	18.2		–	54.1	–	38	40
Hunting	Regularly during the hunting season	6.9	4.5		2.2	9.2	6.5	5	4
Fishing	Regularly during the fishing season	17.8	11.1	–	2.2	20	17	16	14

Source: see Table 5.1.

Table 5.11. Holiday-taking*, France, 1951–1999.

	Holidays over the whole year (%)	Summer holidays (%)	Winter holidays (%)	Winter sports (%)
1951	–	30.0†	–	–
1957	–	39.0†	–	–
1961	–	39.0†	–	–
1964	43.6	41.7†	–	–
1970	56.0	44.6	–	–
1975	57.5	50.2	17.1	–
1980	56.2	53.3	22.7	–
1985	57.5	53.8	24.9	8.8
1990	59.1	55.1	26.7	7.1
1992	60.0	55.3	28.9	8.8
1994	62.0	58.0	30.0	10.0
1999	62.0	57.0	28.0	–

– Not available; * For at least 4 consecutive days; † Estimates to ensure data comparability.
Sources: INSEE, *Données Sociales* (1973, 1987); Bertrand (1984); Christine (1987); Manon (1996); Monteiro (1996); *Mémento du Tourisme* (1993, 2000).

reports a figure of 61% for long holidays and 46% for weekends away (Donnat, 1998).

Trends in leisure participation: conclusions

In summary, important leisure trends in the period 1967–1987 are the growth of activities involving the media (especially television) and the popularity of music in a way that can be described as an individualization of the relationship between people and culture, or 'individuation' as Rojek (1985, p. 19) terms it. Television competes with other leisure activities, such as movies or reading newspapers and books, with a decline in reading in the population except for the highly educated. More than half of the population ignores leisure activities which are often seen as characteristic of the French 'traditional culture', such as going to the theatre, to a concert of classical music, to a dance performance, to an art exhibition or to museums and historic monuments – in 1990 more French people visited an industrial site or a technological museum (67%) than art museums (57%) (Ficquelmont, 1991; Samuel, 1993).

The overall increase in social leisure activities is confirmed by other studies, which link this intensification to a need for 'belonging' in a society which is often felt as alienating, and to a preference for achieving this aim through activities oriented toward self-realization (leisure) rather than through political or religious participation,

which is another option for the use of free time (Hatchuel and Valadier, 1992).

Concerning 'practical' leisure activities, the increase observed in the 1960s and 1970s, which was probably a response to the growing cost of repair and construction work done by professionals, was followed by a decrease, almost certainly as a result of the improved economic situation of French households. While no statistical trend can be identified in participation in gardening for methodological reasons, informal observation suggests a growing interest in gardening, perhaps linked to the enthusiasm for nature, and is confirmed by the development of 'garden centres' and the popularity of books, magazines, radio and television programmes dealing with the subject. The decrease in hunting and fishing may be a consequence of the action of environmentalists and the subsequent strengthening of hunting and fishing regulations; the growing pollution of the waters and the disappearance of many valuable species may also play a part in the case of fishing.

There has been an increase in participation in sport in France, and the range of sporting activities has widened. Favourite sports are those that can be performed all year round, at any age, either alone or with the family (Garrigues, 1989). It may be said that the 1980s were characterized by a rediscovery of the body and by a growing awareness of its importance as a health and happiness factor. The development of informal and non-competitive sport, preferably in a natural environment, was a development of the 1990s.

Finally, holiday-taking has been a growing phenomenon since the 1950s (with the increase in paid vacation time), but has remained static since the end of the 1980s, probably as a result of economic crises and high levels of unemployment. Perhaps also, a reflection of increasing prosperity is that some people are less willing to leave their homes to travel by means of congested transportation for a holiday in an increasingly crowded environment!

Leisure Participation and Socio-economic Variables

As mentioned above, the results of both the INSEE and the Ministry of Culture surveys are tabulated relating participation in 30 activities according to a number of socio-cultural variables. The percentage participation rates for different activities are not all comparable because of differences in the choice of categories for the analysis of responses. But, as in overall participation rates, trends may be observed. In the tables, for each activity, the highest participation rate is indicated in bold and the lowest rate is underlined. For the sake of brevity and clarity, comments will only be made about the leisure activities showing significant differences in participation between the categories of population under observation. The relationships between leisure and gender, age, occupation, size of community and level of education are discussed in turn.

Gender

As indicated in the discussion of time-budget studies above, working women have less leisure than working men, respectively 3.0 h and 3.7 h/day in 1998/99 (Dumontier and Pan Ké Shon, 1999). Indeed, the unfair division of domestic labour between men and women persists: working women spend an average of 3 h/day on domestic labour while working men spend an average of just 1 h/day. Men not in paid employment (whether they wish it or not)

have the highest amount of daily free time: 6.3 h, compared with 5.0 h for women not in paid employment. Men spend more time than women watching television; reading is the only activity to which men and women devote an equal amount of time. Working men spend twice as much time as working women on sport and games, the gap being even wider among those not in paid employment.

As shown in Table 5.12, the membership of women in associations is lower than that of men, but they are more inclined to visit libraries. While women's participation in do-it-yourself is lower than men's, participation in gymnastics and physical education is higher. On the whole, it appears that the gap between leisure participation levels of men and women has diminished somewhat during the 1990s.

Age

The 1999 time-budget study information on daily average free time according to age, as presented in Table 5.13, shows that the groups at either end of the age spectrum enjoy the largest amount of free time and those aged 25–54 the lowest (Dumontier and Pan Ké Shon, 1999).

It is not surprising to observe, in Table 5.14, that young people aged 15–19 have the highest rate of participation in almost half the 30 leisure activities listed, and the lowest rate in only four. They also have the highest rate of participation in sport overall (Manon, 1996). By contrast, the oldest age groups, aged 55–64 and 65 and over, have the highest participation rate in only four activities and the lowest participation rate in 22.

Former leisure participation surveys did not include young people aged 14 and under, but a recent survey conducted by the Ministry of Culture in 1996/97 focused on young people aged 8–19. Table 5.15 presents results from this survey for four sub-groups. The children in the youngest group (8–10) engage in a wider range of activities, principally sport, cycling, outdoor activities, card etc. games and computer games. Many of these activities take place in the family circle, even though they express a desire for more freedom for their outings.

At about age 11 there is a desire for more autonomy: members of the 11–13 age group choose and buy their own records, and

Table 5.12. Leisure participation by gender, France, 1997.

	Males (%)	Females (%)	Total (%)
TV every day	76	**78**	77
Radio listening every day	**71**	68	69
Listening to records/cassettes every day	**28**	26	27
Newspaper reading every day or almost every day	**40**	33	36
Reading books (1–50) in past year	70	**76**	73
Using computer for games/entertainment (% of persons using computer)	**49**	40	45
Going to the movies in past year	**51**	48	49
Going to the theatre in past year	16	**16**	16
Going to classical music concert in past year	9	**10**	9
Going to opera in past year	3	**4**	3
Going to an art exhibition in past year	**16**	14	15
Going to a museum in the past year	**34**	32	33
Inviting friends home for a meal (often or once in a while)	**75**	72	74
Inviting relatives home for a meal (often or once in a while)	72	**77**	75
Playing cards/other games in past year	51	**54**	53
Being a member of at least one association	**42**	32	36
Being registered in a library	17	**24**	21
Going to a library in past year	27	**34**	31
Do-it-yourself activities in past year	**66**	35	50
Repairing a car or motorcycle in past year	**55**	24	39
Gardening for pleasure in past year	38	**42**	40
Playing music in past year	**15**	11	13
Painting, sculpture, engraving in past year	9	**11**	10
Collecting	28	**29**	29
Yoga/relaxation in past year	4	**5**	4
Gymnastics or physical education in past year	16	**21**	19
Bowling in past year	**27**	14	20
Walking/cycling in past year	**37**	32	34
Fishing in past year	**20**	8	14
Hunting in past year	**6**	1	4

Highest percentage in bold.
Source: Donnat (1998).

Table 5.13. Daily free time by age, gender and employment status, France, 1999.

	Free time (hours/day)			
	Males		Females	
Age	Employed	Non-employed	Employed	Non-employed
15–17 years	–	4.95	–	4.38
18–24 years	4.03	5.10	3.35	4.18
25–54 years	3.50	5.62	2.65	3.70
55–64 years	3.48	5.73	2.72	4.32
65–74 years	–	5.98	–	4.88
75 years and over	–	5.88	–	4.73
Overall average		4.00		

Source: INSEE (1999), see Table 5.1.

Table 5.14. Leisure participation by age, France, 1997.

	15–19 (%)	20–24 (%)	25–34 (%)	35–44 (%)	45–54 (%)	55–64 (%)	65+ (%)	All (%)
TV every day	74	69	74	74	73	86	88	77
Radio listening every day	70	72	72	73	74	69	58	69
Listening to records/cassettes every day	56	62	42	28	15	8	4	27
Newspaper reading every day or almost every day	16	26	23	30	46	51	53	36
Reading books (1–50) in past year	84	87	75	76	72	67	62	73
Using computer for games/entertainment (% of persons using computer)	73	39	43	40	36	30	31	45
Going to the movies in past year	87	79	59	53	46	34	18	49
Going to the theatre in past year	27	21	14	15	18	15	9	16
Going to classical music concert in past year	5	7	9	10	14	10	9	9
Going to opera in past year	3	4	4	3	5	3	2	3
Going to an art exhibition in past year	14	15	17	15	19	15	9	15
Going to a museum in the past year	44	35	37	34	33	32	22	33
Inviting friends home for meal (often/once in a while)	70	74	87	81	77	73	53	74
Inviting relatives home for meal (often/once in a while)	44	49	79	78	84	88	77	75
Playing cards/other games in past year	72	68	62	52	43	45	41	53
Being a member of at least one association	45	34	34	35	37	37	39	36
Being registered in a library	40	31	21	23	21	11	10	21
Going to a library in past year	63	48	33	32	27	19	15	31
Do-it-yourself activities in past year	32	42	56	59	54	59	38	50
Repairing a car or motorcycle in past year	27	47	47	46	38	42	24	39
Gardening for pleasure in past year	19	17	30	46	51	53	49	40
Playing music in past year	40	27	16	9	11	4	3	13
Painting, sculpture, engraving in past year	20	12	13	12	10	6	5	10
Collecting	50	42	31	27	26	27	15	29
Yoga/relaxation in past year	6	3	6	4	6	4	2	4
Gymnastics or physical education in past year	53	33	21	17	14	11	7	19
Bowling in past year	21	20	22	27	19	19	12	20
Walking/cycling in past year	43	41	39	41	38	30	14	34
Fishing in past year	15	15	17	17	13	12	8	14
Hunting in past year	2	2	3	3	7	4	3	4

Highest percentage in bold, lowest underlined.
Source: Donnat (1998).

Table 5.15. Leisure participation, young people, France, 1996/97.

Participation rate	Age groups			
	8–10 years	11–13 years	14–16 years	17–19 years
Over 70%	Sport, movies, watch TV, cycling, computer games	Sport, records, movies	Records, talk with friends, movies, radio	Records, talk with friends
50–70%	Walking, records, talk to friends, study on computer, video games, outdoor games, play cards, etc., read comic books	Talk with friends, watch TV, cycling, study on computer, video games, outdoor games, walking, pop concerts, listen to radio, read comic books	Watch TV, sport, pop concerts	Go to movies, watch TV, listen to radio, sport, walking, pop concerts
40–49%	Drawing, pottery, sculpture, do-it-yourself, model-making, pop concerts	Play cards, etc., reading: books, newspapers, magazines	Walking, reading: newspapers, magazines, study on computer	Computer games, cycling
Under 40%	Reading: newspapers, magazines, listen to radio	Drawing, pottery, sculpture, do-it-yourself, model-making	Video games, read comic books, outdoor games, play cards, etc., drawing, pottery, sculpture, do-it-yourself, model-making	Read books, study on computer, cycling, video games, read comic books, play cards, etc., drawing, pottery, sculpture, do-it-yourself, model-making

In households equipped with a computer, the latter is used by: 5% of children aged 0–4, 21% of children aged 5–10.
Source: Ministère de la Culture (1999b).

listening to them becomes their primary leisure activity. Reading newspapers and magazines replaces the reading of books, and a new type of sociability appears, orientated to their own friends, independent of their parents.

Around age 14, about half of respondents made their own decisions about choosing friends, types of sport, books, records, newspapers and games. All this leads to a re-organization of patterns of leisure activity in which meeting friends becomes their highest priority. Traditional leisure activities, such as reading, are neglected in favour of audio-visual activities.

In the 17–19 age group audio-visual activities increase, with radio satisfying their interest in music and an increasing curiosity about the wider world. There is also an increase in interest in reading magazines. A growing importance is given to friends, while parental influence is on the decline: at this age only 17% are accompanied by parents when they go out (Ministère de la Culture, 1999b).

Occupation

From the 1999 time-budget survey, we know that students, and retired men and women have the highest daily average leisure time, while farmers and independent workers have the lowest (Dumontier and Pan Ké Shon, 1999).

Leisure participation related to occupation is shown in Table 5.16. As may be expected, managers and professionals have the highest rate of participation in more than half of the activities listed. By contrast, unskilled manual workers do not have the highest participation rate in any of the activities. Farmers have the lowest participation rates in 11 activities. Of particular interest is the skilled non-manual group, the growing 'new middle class', which includes secretaries, financial workers, nurses, social workers and IT workers, all working in the tertiary economic sector. They have the highest participation rate in five activities and are second to managers/professionals in 13 activities.

Size of community

The 1999 time-budget study indicates that inhabitants of medium-sized towns (20,000–100,000) have the highest daily average of leisure time, followed by those living in larger cities (>100,000), while rural areas and the Paris region have the lowest daily average leisure time (Dumontier and Pan Ké Shon, 1999).

The notable feature of the pattern of participation portrayed in Table 5.17 is the polarization between rural areas and the most urban part of the country: Paris. Residents of Paris have the highest participation rate in half of the activities listed, particularly in arts and culture-related activities which depend on the infrastructure of a large city. In nine other activities, rural residents have the highest participation rates, particularly home-based activities, 'practical' leisure and the rural pursuits of fishing and hunting. The extreme difference between these groups is indicated by the fact that in 21 cases, where one has the highest participation rate the other has the lowest. While this pattern is to be expected, the clearcut nature of the disparity is perhaps surprising.

Level of education

According to the 1998/99 time-budget survey, level of education and amount of leisure time are inversely related, with people with no educational qualifications having the largest amount of leisure time and people with univer-

sity degrees having the least (Dumontier and Pan Ké Shon, 1999).

Table 5.18 clearly shows that university education is associated with high levels of participation in a wide range of activities, with the highest rate shown in 19 of the 30 activities listed. In particular these high levels are recorded in arts and culture-related activities. Correspondingly, those with primary education only show the lowest participation rate in two-thirds of the activities – it should be noted, however, that this is a relatively small group who are old enough to have left school before the introduction of universal secondary education.

Holiday-taking and socio-economic variables

Table 5.19 provides a summary of the 1997 data on holiday-taking and its relationship with socio-economic characteristics. The patterns are as might be expected, with younger, higher-status and more highly educated people having the highest rate of holiday-taking.

Socio-economic variables: summary

In brief, leisure participation surveys show that, on the whole, being young, male, living in Paris, being a university graduate and having a managerial or professional occupation are associated with high levels of participation in most leisure activities.

New technology

New audio-visual technology has been important in orientating choices of leisure activity of the French people in recent years. While the country was well-equipped with television sets by the 1980s, that decade also saw an increase in other audio-visual equipment (hi-fi systems; VCRs; individual stereo; CD players), followed in the 1990s by the spread of home computers. All this ushered in a new audio-visual age and associated home-based audio-visual leisure activity, the latter taking up a large proportion of free time (Donnat, 1999). In 1977 22% of the French population had access to a home computer, of which 6% were connected to the

Table 5.16. Leisure participation by occupation, France, 1997.

	Farmers (%)	Independent workers (%)	Managers/ professionals (%)	Skilled non-manual (%)	Other non-manual (%)	Skilled manual (%)	Unskilled manual (%)	Retired (%)	Other not employed (%)	All (%)
TV every day	70	75	61	70	73	82	81	**87**	70	77
Radio listening every day	64	**80**	74	**80**	72	70	65	64	51	69
Listening to records/cassettes every day	8	27	**43**	33	37	31	33	7	33	27
Newspaper reading every day or almost every day	50	35	31	30	28	29	29	**54**	29	36
Reading books (1–50) in last year	53	76	**93**	87	81	64	70	73	67	73
Use computer for games etc. (% of those using computer)	43	59	66	62	50	48	48	70	**82**	45
Going to the movies in past year	32	59	**82**	72	61	48	38	24	40	49
Going to the theatre in past year	5	11	**44**	21	16	7	5	10	18	16
Going to classical music concert in past year	3	7	**27**	11	6	4	1	10	8	9
Going to opera in past year	0	2	**13**	3	2	1	1	3	3	3
Going to an art exhibition in past year	2	18	**39**	21	13	6	7	11	14	15
Going to a museum in the past year	20	33	**65**	43	34	23	22	25	30	33
Inviting friends home for meal (often/once in a while)	82	83	**86**	**86**	76	79	66	60	53	74
Inviting relatives home for meal (often/once in a while)	**96**	80	77	76	67	75	68	79	57	75
Playing cards/other games in past year	43	50	59	**63**	52	55	59	43	50	53
Being a member of at least one association	49	35	**49**	45	27	30	19	40	37	36
Being registered in a library	14	19	**42**	32	23	15	9	12	21	21
Going to a library in past year	21	28	55	**56**	37	25	16	17	36	31
Do-it-yourself activities in past year	59	49	51	**60**	50	52	54	44	39	50
Repairing a car or motorcycle in past year	48	48	37	44	38	**49**	44	29	26	39
Gardening for pleasure in past year	46	46	45	44	28	35	27	**50**	23	40

Continued

Table 5.16. Continued

	Farmers (%)	Independent workers (%)	Managers/ professionals (%)	Skilled non-manual (%)	Other non-manual (%)	Skilled manual (%)	Unskilled manual (%)	Retired (%)	Other not employed (%)	All (%)
Playing music in past year	7	13	**27**	17	16	12	12	4	17	13
Painting, sculpture, engraving in past year	2	16	**20**	16	9	9	7	4	12	10
Collecting	17	31	32	36	**35**	30	31	20	26	29
Yoga/relaxation in past year	2	7	**10**	6	5	2	1	3	3	4
Gymnastics or physical education in past year	6	15	**34**	27	24	19	15	10	17	19
Bowling in past year	14	17	12	24	17	**31**	27	15	14	20
Walking/cycling in past year	17	30	**56**	47	37	36	26	20	27	34
Fishing in past year	20	11	6	17	11	**23**	21	9	1	14
Hunting in past year	**20**	7	0	3	1	6	1	3	4	4

Figures in bold are highest; underlined are lowest.
Source: Donnat (1998).

Table 5.17. Leisure participation by size of community, France, 1997.

Population, '000s:	Rural (%)	<20 (%)	20–100 (%)	100+ (%)	Paris (%)	Paris region (%)	All (%)
TV every day	80	**81**	74	78	<u>67</u>	67	77
Radio listening every day	67	70	70	70	<u>63</u>	**73**	69
Listening to records/cassettes every day	<u>21</u>	27	32	28	**40**	29	27
Newspaper reading every day or almost every day	39	**41**	32	37	<u>27</u>	29	36
Reading books (1–50) in past year	72	<u>68</u>	70	73	**91**	78	73
Use computer for games, etc. (% of those using computer)	48	47	**49**	43	<u>33</u>	47	45
Going to the movies in past year	<u>38</u>	43	52	54	**69**	63	49
Going to the theatre in past year	<u>9</u>	<u>9</u>	17	16	**48**	25	16
Going to classical music concert in past year	<u>7</u>	8	8	10	**27**	10	9
Going to opera in past year	<u>1</u>	2	2	4	**13**	5	3
Going to an art exhibition in past year	<u>9</u>	12	14	17	**44**	17	15
Going to a museum in the past year	<u>26</u>	27	31	36	**57**	42	33
Inviting friends home for meal (often/once in a while)	**78**	72	<u>70</u>	71	76	74	74
Inviting relatives home for meal (often/once in a while)	**85**	77	70	70	<u>59</u>	72	75
Playing cards/other games in past year	53	**54**	52	52	<u>51</u>	52	53
Being a member of at least one association	**38**	<u>35</u>	36	37	<u>35</u>	37	36
Being registered in a library	<u>14</u>	18	16	24	**33**	30	21
Going to a library in past year	<u>24</u>	30	26	34	**49**	36	31
Do-it-yourself activities in past year	**55**	53	48	46	<u>38</u>	47	50
Repairing a car or motorcycle in past year	**47**	44	38	33	<u>14</u>	34	39
Gardening for pleasure in past year	**59**	41	35	28	<u>16</u>	39	40
Playing music in past year	11	<u>10</u>	<u>10</u>	15	**30**	15	13
Painting, sculpture, engraving in past year	<u>8</u>	11	10	11	**17**	13	10
Collecting	<u>24</u>	29	29	31	**33**	30	29
Yoga/relaxation in past year	<u>3</u>	4	6	4	**11**	5	4
Gymnastics or physical education in past year	<u>14</u>	20	19	23	**26**	18	19
Bowling in past year	**25**	22	20	19	<u>6</u>	14	20
Walking/cycling in past year	<u>31</u>	35	32	35	35	**38**	34
Fishing in past year	**18**	16	11	12	<u>4</u>	11	14
Hunting in past year	7	3	3	2	<u>1</u>	2	4

Highest percentage in bold, lowest underlined.
Source: Donnat (1998).

Internet; 14% had used a computer in the past year and 4% did so daily. Perhaps not surprisingly, the highest rate of access was found among male executives aged under 55, with a university degree and living in Paris. In 1997, among the 22% who had a home computer, 20% used it for leisure purposes only (56% of executives, 25% of men, 20% of women) (Donnat, 1998). The importance of the use of computers for leisure was confirmed in a study carried out in January–March,

1999 on people aged 10 and over in a sample of 450 households equipped with at least one computer: almost half (46%) said they used the computer only, or mostly, for leisure purposes (Ministère de la Culture, 1999a).

But new technologies are also being introduced in other fields of leisure, including libraries, museums, do-it-yourself activities, sport (including clothing and equipment) and even fishing, with resultant changes in leisure behaviour. In this way it may be said that technology is continually invading leisure (Samuel, 1996).

Table 5.18. Leisure participation by level of education, France, 1997.

	Primary school only (%)	4 years high school (%)	Tech. cert. (%)	Full high school (%)	University (%)	All (%)
TV every day	**84**	76	77	67	<u>59</u>	77
Radio listening every day	<u>63</u>	75	71	76	**80**	69
Listening to records/cassettes every day	<u>19</u>	37	29	35	**38**	27
Newspaper reading every day or almost every day	**41**	<u>28</u>	35	33	31	36
Reading books (1–50) in last year	<u>59</u>	87	75	90	**94**	73
Use computer for games, etc. (% of those using computer)	<u>43</u>	44	59	70	**72**	45
Going to the movies in past year	<u>29</u>	69	51	76	**82**	49
Going to the theatre in past year	<u>8</u>	22	10	29	**38**	16
Going to classical music concert in past year	<u>5</u>	10	<u>5</u>	13	**29**	9
Going to opera in past year	<u>1</u>	3	<u>1</u>	6	**12**	3
Going to an art exhibition in past year	<u>8</u>	13	11	24	**39**	15
Going to a museum in the past year	<u>21</u>	40	27	48	**67**	33
Inviting friends home for meal (often/once in a while)	<u>61</u>	79	85	83	**88**	74
Inviting relatives home for meal (often/once in a while)	74	<u>68</u>	**80**	70	77	75
Playing cards/other games in past year	<u>45</u>	**66**	55	62	60	53
Being a member of at least one association	<u>31</u>	42	35	47	**50**	36
Being registered in a library	<u>10</u>	34	14	37	**47**	21
Going to a library in past year	<u>17</u>	49	24	49	**62**	31
Do-it-yourself activities in past year	44	<u>41</u>	**61**	53	58	50
Repairing a car or motorcycle in past year	<u>33</u>	34	**51**	41	40	39
Gardening for pleasure in past year	39	<u>33</u>	44	37	**45**	40
Playing music in past year	<u>8</u>	20	12	21	**23**	13
Painting, sculpture, engraving in past year	<u>7</u>	14	10	14	**18**	10
Collecting	<u>22</u>	**40**	31	37	32	29
Yoga/relaxation in past year	<u>2</u>	4	4	7	**9**	4
Gymnastics or physical education in past year	<u>11</u>	**37**	17	27	30	19
Bowling in past year	20	22	**26**	15	<u>13</u>	20
Walking/cycling in past year	<u>23</u>	41	39	42	**54**	34
Fishing in past year	13	14	**22**	10	<u>8</u>	14
Hunting in past year	3	3	**6**	3	<u>2</u>	4

Highest percentage in bold, lowest underlined.
Source: Donnat (1998).

Table 5.19. Holiday-taking, France, 1997.

		% taking trips away from home in last year	
		Holiday	Weekend
Gender	All	61	46
	Male	61	47
	Female	60	45
Age	15–19	**76**	**61**
	20–24	61	63
	25–34	64	55
	35–44	61	47
	45–54	64	47
	55–64	60	42
	65+	<u>47</u>	<u>26</u>
Occupation	Farmers	<u>45</u>	45
	Independent workers	65	44
	Managers/professionals	**85**	**68**
	Skilled non-manual	75	60
	Other non-manual	59	49
	Skilled manual	57	46
	Unskilled manual	51	42
	Retired	52	<u>31</u>
	Other non-employed	49	43
Size of community '000s	Rural	56	44
	<20	42	<u>42</u>
	20–100	<u>31</u>	45
	>100	61	52
	Paris	**83**	**57**
	Paris region	71	52
Level of education	Primary school	<u>47</u>	<u>33</u>
	4 yrs high school	76	59
	Tech. cert.	63	49
	Full high school	72	60
	University	**84**	**68**

For each category highest percentage in bold, lowest underlined.
Source: Department of Studies and Prospective, Ministry of Culture and Communications.

Conclusion

As may be gathered from the preceding sections, the problems usually listed as plaguing survey methodology in general (Cushman and Veal, 1993, p. 212) are indeed present in the French leisure participation surveys. The most important among these problems relate to the scope of leisure, to sampling, to the choice of the period of reference and to the choice of categories for the analysis of responses.

As to the scope of leisure, this problem goes back to the old quarrel about the definition

of leisure, which has been going on for decades (Dumazedier, 1974, pp. 88–134) and which, of course, is strongly associated with the listing of leisure activities. The French surveys tend to define leisure in a broad sense, including a wide range of home-based, social and entertainment activities as well as outdoor activities. But each survey is focused according to the central interests of its sponsoring institution (for example, the Ministry of Culture surveys emphasize artistic leisure activities). Some leisure activities are, however, in practice excluded from French surveys: for example cigarette or pipe smoking was only investigated in the first INSEE (1967) study (Debreu, 1973, p. 6); going to cafés is included; but no mention of drinking is to be found; there is no reference whatsoever to sexual activity, which obviously plays a role in leisure activities, *a fortiori* for drugs.

Sampling, a matter of importance, is done in different ways in practically each survey, with a particularly striking lack of uniformity about the age ranges of the respondents.

The choice of the period of reference varies from one survey to another and even, sometimes, within the same survey for different questions. The most usual procedure is to ask the respondents to indicate their participation over the course of the previous year. But, in some cases, a shorter reference period, namely the month prior to the interview, has been used, which makes it difficult to construct the leisure behaviour of the respondents, and which may introduce a bias in the case of seasonal leisure activities.

Finally, there is a lack of uniformity in the choice of the socio-cultural categories used in the analysis of responses: age groups vary from one survey to another; the same goes for occupational groups and educational groups. The only socio-cultural variable which is treated uniformly is gender!

It may be hoped that these shortcomings will be remedied in the future,[2] so that leisure participation surveys will increase their potential as a resource for leisure research. Of course, it may be argued that we do not need large participation surveys to know that leisure participation changes over time and varies according to gender, age, occupation, level of education and place of residence, but the basic principle of the scientific method reminds us that any statement has to be tested against the evidence before we can be sure of its validity, and surveys are one means of providing such evidence.

Notes

[1] Making the diachronic comparison difficult, if not impossible. But this is called progress!

[2] But the comparison with previous surveys might then become even more difficult than it is today.

References

Bertrand, M. (1984) Les vacances. *Données Sociales*, 253–257.

Chombart De Lauwe, P.H. (1958) *La Vie Quotidienne Des Familles Ouvrieres. Recherches sur les Comportements Sociaux de Consommation*. CNRS, Paris.

Christine, M. (1987) Les vacances. *Données Sociales*, 382.

CREDOC (Centre de Recherche et de Documentation sur la Consommation) (1983) *Le Système d'Enquêtes sur les Conditions du Vie et Aspirations des Français: 1978–1981*, Phase 4, Vol. 7: *Le temps Libre, les Vacances*. CREDOC, Paris.

Cushman, G. and Veal, A.J. (1993) The new generation of leisure surveys: implications for research on everyday life. *Loisir et Société* 16(1), 211–220.

Debreu, P. (1973) *Les Comportements de Loisir des Francais*, Coll. INSEE, No.102, Serie M, 25, August (also *Economie et Statistique*, No. 51, December).

Documentation Française (1988) *L'enquête Emploi du Temps*. Documentation Française, Paris.

Donnat, O. (1998) *Les Pratiques Culturelles des Français: Enquête 1977*. Documentation Française, Paris.

Donnat, O. (1999) *Changes in the Cultural Activities of the French People, 1973–1997*. Ministère de la Culture, Circular 11, New Series, Paris.

Donnat, O. and Cogneau, D. (1990) *Les Pratiques Culturelles des Français*. Documentation Français, Paris.

Dumazedier, J. (1962a) Contenu culturel du loisir ouvrier dans 6 villes Européennes. *Revue Français de Sociologie* 4(1), 12–21.

Dumazedier, J. (1962b) *Vers une Civilisation du Loisir?* Le Seuil, Paris.

Dumazedier, J. (1974) *Sociologie Empirique du Loisir*. Le Seuil, Paris.

Dumazedier, J. and Ripert, A. (1966) *Loisir et Culture*. Le Seuil, Paris.

Dumontier, F. and Pan Ké Shon, J.L. (1999) En 13 ans, moins de temps contraint et plus de loisirs. *INSEE Première*, No. 675, Oct. Institut National de Statistique et d'Études Economiques, Paris.

Dumontier, F. and Pan Ké Shon, J.L. (2000) Enquête emploi du temps 1997–1998: description des activitiés quotidiennes. *INSEE Résultats*, No. 693–694/Consommation Modes de Vie, No. 101–102, Jan. Institut National de Statistique et d'Études Economiques, Paris.

Dumontier, F. and Valdelievre, H. (1989) *Les Pratiques de Loisir: Vingt Ans Aprés: 1967/1987–88*. INSEE

Resultats No. 13. Institut National de Statistique et d'Études Economiques, Paris.

Erlinger, P., la Louveau, C. and Metoudi, M. (1985) *Pratiques Sportives des Français*. Mininstère de Jeunesse et Sports, Paris.

Ficquelmont, G.M. de (1991) La visite d'entreprise, un loisir culturel. *Espaces* 107, 31–34.

Fourastié, J. (1951) *Machinisme et Bien-être*. Editions de Minuit, Paris.

Garrigues, P. (1988) *Evolution de la Pratique Sportive des Français de 1957 à 1984*. Coll. de l'INSEE, 134 M., October. Institut National de Statistique et d'Études Economiques, Paris.

Garrigues, P. (1989) Une France un peu plus sportive qu'il y a 20 ans . . . grace aux femmes. *Economie et Statistique*, No. 224, September.

Girard, A. (1958) Le budget-temps de la femme mariée dans les agglomerations urbaines. *Populations*, No. 4, October–December.

Girard, A. and Bastide, H. (1959) Le budget-temps de la femme mariée a la campagne. *Populations*, April–June.

Goguel, C. (1965) Les vacances de Français en 1964. *Economie et Statistiques*, No. 6, June.

Goguel, C. (1966) Recherche comparative internationale sur les budgets-temps. *Études et Conjoncture*, No. 9, September.

Gounot, Ph. (1958) Les vacances des Français en 1957. *Études et Conjoncture*, No. 7, July.

Gounot, Ph. (1961) Les vacances des Français en 1961. *Études et Conjoncture*, 17th year, May, 413–434.

Grimler, G. and Roy, C. (1987) *Time Use in 1986–87, Paris, First Results*. INSEE Results, No. 100, October. Institut National de Statistique et d'Études Economiques, Paris.

Hatchuel, G. and Valadier, J.L. (1992) *Les Grands Courants d'Opinion et de Perception en France de la Fin des Années 70 au Début des Années 90*, Coll. des Rapports, No. 116, March. CREDOC, Paris.

Huet, M.T., Lemel, Y. and Roy, C. (1978) *Les Emplois du Temps des Citadins*. Resultats Provisoires de l'Enquête Emploie du Temps 1974–1975. Institut National de Statistique et d'Études Economiques, Paris.

INSEE (Institut National de Statistique et d'Études Economiques) (1973) Les vacances 1951–1970, *Données Sociales*, INSEE, Paris, pp. 87–89.

INSEE (Institut National de Statistique et d'Études Economiques) (1987) *Données Sociales*. INSEE, Paris.

Lemel, Y. (1972) Elements sur les budgets-temps des citadins. *Economie et Statistiques*, 33, April.

Lemel, Y. (1974) Les budget-temps des citadins. *Coll. de l'INSEE*, M. 33, October. INSEE, Paris.

Le Play, F. (1877) Les ouvriers Européens. *Mame* 6 (2).

Leroux, P. (1970a) Le comportement de loisirs des Français. Paris, *Coll. INSEE*, 24, M, 2, July. INSEE, Paris.

Leroux, P. (1970b) Les loisirs des Français. *Economie et Statistiques*, May.

Manon, N. (1996) *Condition de vie des Ménages: Enquêtes 1986–87 et 1993–94*. INSEE Results, No. 450/Consommation Modes de Vie, No. 79, Feb. Institut National de Statistique et d'Études Economiques, Paris.

Mémento du Tourisme (1993) *Transports et Tourisme*. Direction du Tourisme, September. Min. Equipment, Paris.

Mémento du Tourisme (2000) *Transports et Tourisme*. Direction du Tourisme, September. Min. Equipment, Paris.

Ministère de la Culture (1974) *Pratiques culturelles des Français. Service des Études et Recherches*, vol. 2. La Documentation Française, December.

Ministère de la Culture (1982) *Pratiques Culturelles des Français, Description Socio-démographique: Evolution 1973–1981*. Dallox, Paris.

Ministère de la Culture (1990) *Nouvelle Enquête sur les Pratiques Culturelles des Francais en 1989*. La Documentation Française, Paris.

Ministère de la Culture (1998) *Les Pratiques Culturelles des Français. Evolution 1989–1997*, No. 124, June. Ministère de la Culture, Paris.

Ministère de la Culture (1999a) Les usages de loisir de l'informatique domestique. *Développement Culturel*, No. 130, Oct.

Ministère de la Culture (1999b) Les loisirs de 8–19 ans, *Développement Culturel*, No. 131, Dec.

Monteiro, S. (1996) *Les Vacances des Français*. INSEE Results, No. 451–452/ Consommation Modes de Vie, No. 80–81, March. INSEE, Paris.

Pouquet, L. (1995) *Le Sport en Liberté*. CREDOC: Consommation et Modes de Vie, No. 94, Jan.

Raymond, H. (1968) Loisir, travail, culture 1955–1968. *Current Sociology* 16(1), 5.

Rojek, C. (1985) *Capitalism and Leisure Theory*. Tavistock, London.

Rouquette, C. (2000) Chaque année, 4 Français sur 10 ne partent pas en vacances. *INSEE Première*, No. 734, August.

Samuel, N. (1993) Leisure research for a world in turmoil. Paper to the World Leisure and Recreation Association Congress, Leisure, Tourism and Environment, University of Rajahstan, Jaipur, India, December 5–10.

Samuel, N. (1996) Technology invades leisure. *World Leisure and Recreation* 38(3), 12–18.

Samuel, N. and Romer, M. (1984) *Le Temps Libre: Un Temps Social*. Klincksieck – Les Meridiens, Paris.

Société Française d'Études et de Sondages (SOFRES) (Annual since 1990) *Le Suivi de la Demande Touristique des Français.* SOFRES, Paris.

Sondages (1947) *Distraction et Culture en France,* November. IFOP, Paris.

Sondages (1949) *Les Loisirs,* January. IFOP, Paris.

Sondages (1962) *L'étalement des Congés.* IFOP, Paris.

Sondages (1964) *Les Vacances en 1963,* No. 2. IFOP, Paris.

Stoetzel, J. (1948) Une étude du budget-temps de la jeunesse dans les agglomerations urbaines. *Populations* 1, Jan.–Mar.

Szalai, A. *et al.* (eds) (1972) *The Use of Time: Daily Activities of Urban and Suburban Populations in Twelve Countries.* Mouton, The Hague.

6 Germany

Walter Tokarski and Harald Michels

Introduction

Leisure includes a multitude of activities and associated organizational structures and services. The extensive field of leisure embraces sport, culture, tourism, use of the media, entertainment and social activity (Tokarski, 1999). Leisure plays an increasingly significant role in the time-budgets of German citizens, both qualitatively and quantitatively. Two-thirds of the population, and four-fifths of 14–29-year-olds, consider leisure to be an important part of their life (Tokarski, 1999). Today increased leisure indicates a high standard of social welfare which represents an important aspect of the quality of life for the individual. Ownership of expensive leisure equipment involves prestige, and leisure-wear is predominant in urban areas.

Leisure is a characteristic indicator of the quality of life of highly developed societies and it is a benchmark of freedom, participation in social life and well-being of the citizenry. While leisure encompasses fun, entertainment and relaxation from work, it also means education and political and social involvement, as well as health-oriented behaviour. However, the term leisure is far from being accurately defined in contemporary society: it means whatever the individual wishes it to mean.

Furthermore, work and leisure are no longer entirely distinct spheres for many: work can become leisure and leisure can become work.

Both the subjective appreciation of leisure and the investment of individuals in leisure have seen a considerable growth over recent years, based primarily on the fact that, in spite of economic crises, non-work time has increased considerably and work time has been reduced. In Germany in 1993, women in the paid workforce had about 4.8 hours and men in the paid workforce had about 5.4 hours of leisure at their disposal on weekdays, while on weekends they had almost twice as many hours available for leisure.

Moreover, leisure itself has changed considerably: the view of leisure as being predominantly recreation time and consumer-oriented time, which was characteristic of the period from the 1950s to the 1970s, has been replaced by a perspective which sees it as a time of excitement and consumption, involving increasing expenditure on leisure activities and goods, and the search for exceptional attractions and new challenges and demands. Today, leisure is seen as a sphere in which individuals can develop new lifestyles and new dimensions for everyday life routines, and where they search for self-fulfilment (Tokarski, 1996).

Studies of Leisure Behaviour in Germany

There are no regularly implemented compre-hensive, representative, empirical, national studies of the leisure behaviour of individuals in Germany. Data on the role of leisure in German public life are derived from a variety of topical surveys of consumer behaviour of readers of magazines, or they result from surveys of market research institutes, statistical data from organ-izations such as sports federations, and case-studies regarding single aspects of leisure behaviour. The data are compiled into leisure reports published yearly by the Deutsche Gesellschaft für Freizeit (German Leisure Association; DGF). The chapter on Germany in the first edition of this book included a brief summary of results of a leisure survey conducted by a commercial organization in 1991 (Tokarski and Michels, 1996), but given the social change that has taken place in Germany since that time, it would not be appropriate to use those data to describe leisure in Germany now.

Leisure Policy

Government responsibility for leisure in Germany rests with state and local govern-ments. The Federal Government influences leisure issues only indirectly by setting the legal and administrative framework enabling indi-viduals and communities to make their own leisure choices and to establish leisure facil-ities. Such initiatives are implemented by state and local community governments, which take responsibility for programmes for specific groups of the community and provide public parks, sport and cultural facilities and leisure centres, and they make public land available for commercial leisure facilities.

In Germany, leisure policy is not an inde-pendent function of government: being a 'cross-sectional' issue, it is dealt with in many policy areas, such as housing and urban devel-opment, agriculture, social policy and family affairs, labour, health and transport, as well as in economic policy. Over the past 50 years, it was specifically *labour* policy, focusing on reduction of working hours towards 35 hours a week, increased holiday entitlements, flexible

transition into retirement and creation of part-time positions, which has contributed to the considerable increase in the significance of leisure in German society (Tokarski, 1999).

Leisure Behaviour

The aspect of leisure which is most frequently studied is leisure behaviour or participation. The analysis of leisure behaviour is, however, often confined to quantitative aspects, thus ignoring qualitative aspects, such as leisure motivation, leisure attitudes and leisure experi-ence. Leisure *behaviour* is the generic term for partial aspects of leisure, such as leisure *activ-ities*, leisure *routines* and leisure *patterns*. The totality of all individual activities participated in, together with frequency of participation, reflects the range of possibilities open to members of a society, a class or a group and their relative significance. Thus, data on leisure activities are the indices for the socially accepted behaviour repertoire for a society, class or group.

Comparing the results of more than 40 years of compiled statistical data on participa-tion in leisure activities in Germany, the fol-lowing broad leisure patterns can be outlined.

Beginning in the early 1950s, watching television became a leisure activity and, over the years, it has become the most popular of all leisure activities, leaving behind use of more traditional media such as newspapers, maga-zines and radio. Over recent years, new media have become more important, but they still involve only around 15% of the population. Travelling and excursion activities increased substantially during the 1950s and 1960s, subsequently levelling out. Participation in sport/fitness/health-related activities also increased, but has reached a plateau of around 35% of the population. Since the beginning of leisure research in Germany, cultural activities have ranked last in popularity.

Differentiating these results according to social groups, it can be observed that sport, games, media and events are more popular with children and youth than with the adult population. For adults, the popular activities are health-related activities, home-based pastimes, gardening, reading, and caring for children and grandchildren (DGF, 1998). Among the favourite leisure activities of adult Germans are: listening to music (90%), watching television (86%), reading newspapers (79%), dining out (78%) and partying/being with friends (72%) (DGF, 1999). There has been a slight increase in exercise activities, such as cycling and jogging, inline-skating, water sports and skiing (DGF, 1999). The use of the media as a resource of relaxation and entertainment plays a central role and frequently forms the background for other activities – for example, listening to music on the radio while engaged in other activities, such as reading newspapers or eating.

Due to new information and communication technologies, such as computers, the Internet and mobile phones, future leisure habits may be expected to change considerably. Already 40% of German households own a computer. During recent years the number of private computer owners and users has risen continuously (DGF, 1999). Young Germans, in particular, use their computers as 'intelligent toys' to experiment with hardware and software, as a tool for communicating with friends and the Internet, as well as for playing games. Through the Internet, the possible range of domestic leisure activities has significantly increased – for example, as a result of e-commerce, virtual shopping and window-shopping can take place in front of the computer. Time will show whether and to what extent these technologies will gain acceptance in future everyday life (DGF, 1999).

Over recent years, sport and physical exercise have gained increasing importance. Besides the traditional forms of physical activities, new forms of non-competitive physical exercise have been created, aimed at playful physical activity in order to enhance health and well-being. The traditional competitive sports are attractive to children and young adults and have a formative influence in their lives, but are less relevant to the majority of adult Germans, who see fun, health and fitness as their main reason for engaging in physical exercise.

As the traditional sport associations have continuously adapted to the changed motivations of the exercising group, there has been a steady increase in membership figures. Today there are almost 90,000 sport clubs in Germany, with some 27 million members. In addition, a flourishing fitness market has been developed, with about 5000 fitness centres serving up to 5 million customers. During the past 10 years, sport development in Germany has been successful in integrating a number of social groups, such as adults generally, senior citizens, families, and women, which were not formerly involved in sporting activity. Consequently, today, it is now possible to speak of Germany as a 'sport-oriented society'.

Tourism

During the 1990s, German tourism showed a tendency towards increasing numbers of short trips with the length of the average holiday becoming shorter. Following a period of decline, the end of the 1990s saw an increase in domestic tourism. In all, the Germans spend about 92 billion Marks per year on extended vacation trips (5 days or longer). Germany is the main destination, with a 20% share of trips. In 1998 65% of German tourists travelled abroad, Majorca being the most popular destination (DGF, 1999). Depending on how precisely tourism is defined, the industry employs up to 2.5 million people nationwide. The share of tourism in the gross national product amounts to 8%.

The Leisure Budget: Financial

During the German 'leisure boom' of the late 1990s, expenditure on leisure also increased, economic crises notwithstanding. About 15% of the disposable income of German families of two adults and two children with average income is spent on leisure goods and services (DGF, 1999). Households with lower incomes still spend about 11% on leisure. The leisure industry accounts for approximately 12% of the gross domestic product and, along with the waste disposal sector, is the only branch of industry that has continued to grow significantly during times of recession (Horch and Tokarski, 2000). As Table 6.1 indicates, three items in leisure expenditure account for 60% of the total, namely: holidays, other trips for leisure purposes and radio/television/video (DGF, 1998).

Table 6.1. The household leisure budget in Germany (West), 1994–1998.

| | Annual expenditure, employee household, four persons, average income | | | | | |
| | 1994 | | 1996 | | 1998 | |
	Marks	%	Marks	%	Marks	%
Vacation	2271	24.9	2406	25.0	2544	25.2
Car (leisure purposes)	1251	13.7	1382	14.3	1392	13.7
Sport, camping	1344	14.7	1380	14.3	1332	13.2
Radio, TV, video	1026	11.2	946	9.8	1044	10.4
Books, newspapers	725	7.9	787	8.2	804	8.0
Gardening, pets	607	6.6	603	6.3	612	6.1
Games	438	4.8	479	5.0	482	4.4
Photography	213	2.3	219	2.3	231	2.9
Movies, theatre	218	2.4	258	2.7	292	2.3
Do-it-yourself	80	1.0	74	0.8	96	0.9
Other	962	10.5	1105	11.5	1272	12.6
Total	9135	100.0	9639	100.0	1008	100.0

Source: Deutsche Gesellschaft für Freizeit (1998).

In the 30-year period from 1965 to 1995, the leisure budget of private households increased by 650% (DGF, 1999), although families in the new federal states in East Germany, with lower levels of income, spend less on leisure than their West German counterparts, as discussed below.

The Leisure Budget: Time

On an average day, Germans aged 12 years and over spend about 4 hours in education, training and/or paid work. Some 20% of time is spent on housekeeping and family care; a third is used for sleeping and 8% for personal care, dressing and eating. The rest of available time, about 20%, or 5 hours, is leisure. However, there are considerable differences in time-budgets of different social groups, such as employees, retirees or young persons. Thus the full-time employed person spends twice as much time on work and homemaking as on leisure, while those who are not in full-time employment have a higher leisure/work time ratio (Tokarski, 1999).

On average, adult Germans have about 2500 hours of leisure per year at their disposal, including holidays and vacation time, compared with about 1600 hours spent in paid work (DGF, 1999).

Leisure Time in West and East Germany

Since the reunification of East and West Germany in 1990, questions of the relationships between living conditions and lifestyles, including leisure, in East and West have been of ongoing interest. In the Eastern part of the country, due to the relative economic backwardness of the former German Democratic Republic, there is an immense, unsatisfied demand for living conditions and lifestyles to match those in the West.

In 1998, nearly 10 years after reunification, there was still a considerable difference in the average working hours of the employed population in East and West Germany. Nearly half of East German employees worked 40 hours or more per week, while in West Germany, this applied to only a small minority of about 3% (DGF, 1999). Average weekly working hours were 39 in the East but only 36 in the West. At the same time, the proportion of employees working part-time (less than 21 hours per week) was higher in the East (15%) than in the West (5%).

In 1998, in the East, 45% of adults reported a feeling that they had little or very little time available for leisure purposes, compared with just 38% in the West (Statistisches Bundesamt, 2000). Closely connected herewith is the fact that West Germans are satisfied with their leisure to a higher degree, which especially applies for persons older than 55 years.

Economic Dimensions of the Leisure Sector

The leisure industry turnover amounts to about 440 billion Marks per year, which is about twice as much as in the chemical or construction industry. Table 6.2 provides details of sales in selected leisure markets.

Table 6.3 provides estimates of the level of employment in the leisure industries, resulting from an overview of different economic sectors of the leisure industries, based on an extensive statistical survey carried out in 1994 by DGF (Horch and Tokarski, 2000). According to the DGF (1998), the number of full-time and

Table 6.2. The German leisure industry, sales, 1997.

Sales by sector	Marks, billion
Tourism	183.0
Excursions	35.0
Sport (total sales)	64.2
Entertainment and communication electronics	28.5
Culture (total sales)	45.0
Tourism	
Accommodation and catering trade (leisure sales)	61.0
Camping equipment	0.9
Travel agencies*	55.0
Leisure and theme parks	0.7
Camping sites	6.5
Leisure mobility	
Car sales (leisure share 50%)	186.9
Motorbikes (manufacturers, trade)	12.5
Vacation trips	88.6
Bikes (manufacturers, trade)	4.8
Vacation trips abroad	77.0
Caravans, mobile homes (manufacturers)	2.3
Sport	
Sports articles (trade)	14.0
Sports events	1.9
Sports articles (manufacturing)	5.4
Aquatic parks (pools)	0.9
Fitness facilities	3.6
Sport schools	0.6
Water sports	3.0
Saunas	0.3
Print media	
Book sales*	17.4
Culture	
Community expenditure	8.3
Movies	1.5
Theatres	4.8
Cultural scene, musicals	0.5
Electronic media	
Radio, TV (fees. commercials – revenues)	25.6
Phonographic market	4.9
Entertainment electronics	16.8
Video shops (sales/rentals)	1.9
Personal computers	7.3
Video games	1.4

Continued

Table 6.2. Continued

Sales by sector	Marks, billion
Gardening and pets	
Horticultural centres	19.6
Pet shops	4.5
Horticulture	8.4
Do-it-yourself/hobbies	
Do-it-yourself	30.2
Needlework	1.6
Crafts and hobbies	2.5
Music instruments (trade)	1.4
Stamps, philately	2.0
Dance schools	0.3
Play, games and gambling	
Gambling (betting, lotteries and casinos)	31.2
Toys and games (trade)	5.8
Gambling (slot machines)	10.5
Slot machines (manufacturing, import, trade)	1.8
Gambling halls	6.0
Fairgrounds	1.6
Photography	
Photo market (hobby)	6.1
Light and sound events (technology)	0.8

* Non-leisure sales included.
Due to the frequent overlap of sectors and the fact that some categories also include non-leisure sales, the leisure total sales volume cannot be obtained by adding the figures stated above. The DGF conservative estimate also includes public sector expenditure and joint expenditures of clubs, societies and associations.
Source: Based on DGF (1998).

part-time jobs in the leisure sector was about 5 million in 1997. Sport, culture and do-it-yourself created more jobs than any other service sector in the 1990s.

Leisure Trends in Germany

In the past two decades, the leisure system, with its various elements, has become a more diversified phenomenon. Leisure is regarded as a component of citizens' rights and it represents an important part of contemporary life. Not only is the demand for leisure growing in Germany, there is also an increasing number of potential suppliers in the leisure market, which has experienced a dynamic pace of development over recent years. New trends follow one another increasingly rapidly, new groups become the focus of attention of the leisure

market (as for example the 50+, 'baby boomer' generation) and ever-new demands are expressed to suppliers of leisure opportunities (e.g. excitement, thrills, staging of the extraordinary). Table 6.4 summarizes some of these trends as seen by German commentators Wenzel and Franck (1998) and Steinecke (1997). Furthermore, most individuals seem to have accepted as natural that they should pay the full cost of attractive leisure products.

In Germany, leisure is increasingly being viewed as 'mega-leisure', which is characterized by the bringing together of leisure activities, interests, desires and excitement qualities into 'leisure styles' and 'leisure packages' in multi-dimensional and multi-complex developments. Multi-functional sport and leisure facilities are increasingly dominating the leisure sector and may therefore offer a pattern for the future forms of leisure and sport.

Table 6.3. The German leisure industry as employer, 1993.

Sector	No. of employees
Tourism: tourism industry, travel organization and selling (travel agencies), tourism, catering, accommodation, cures and spas	1,300,000
Leisure mobility: manufacturing and trade of cars, motorbikes and bikes, including traffic and service trade (about 30% of current expenditure for leisure purposes)	1,250,000
Sport: sports articles industry, camping, caravanning, boating and yachting, sports organizations, spas, sport and fitness facilities	604,000
Print media: manufacturing and trade of books and magazines, newspapers; libraries, reading circles	475,000
Culture: movies, theatres, orchestras, stage productions, fairground companies, cultural institutions	380,000
Electronic media: manufacturing and trade of radios, TVs and video, public broadcasting and TV companies	323,000
Gardening and pets: public parks and gardens, gardening, horticulture, pets, forestry and hunting, pets, plants and flower supplies	234,000
Do-it-yourself: crafts, hobbies, do-it-yourself, needleworking (trade)	170,000
Playing, games and gambling: toy industry, slot machine industry, casinos, clubs, bets and lotteries	105,000
Photography: manufacturing and trade of photo and film appliances	60,000
Total	4,901,000

Source: DGF (1998) and Statistisches Bundesamt/Wiesbaden (Federal Statistical Office), BBE-Unternehmensberatung (management consultancy), Bundesanstalt für Arbeit, (Federal Office for Employment), Bundesinstitut für Sportwirtschaft (Federal Institute for Sport Science), Deutsches Fremdenverkehrspräsidium (German Tourist Office Chairmanship), GHS Paderborn (Comprehensive University), Künstlersozialkasse (Artists' Social Fund).

Table 6.4. Trends in leisure and sport, Germany.

I. Flexibility and differentiation
  – increasing need for socializing and communication
  – maximizing freedom of action and selection
  – increase of unorganized leisure behaviour
  – increasing desire for individuality, flexibility and short-term actions
  – increasing differentiation of leisure behaviour and leisure styles
  – short life cycles in leisure sports sector
  – trend towards short trips, two and three times per year
  – trend towards topic-focused events in the convention, seminar and congress market
  – complex motive and activity packages
  – diversification of target groups
II. Commercialization/professionalization
  – increasing overall quality standards for leisure and tourist services
  – commercialization and professionalization
  – tendency towards passive and consumption-oriented leisure behaviour
  – high standards for variety and complexity of leisure facilities
  – competitive pressure and specialization of accommodation companies
  – increasing significance of cooperation in smaller accommodation companies
  – change of prestige sports to commercially attractive mass sports

Continued

Table 6.4. *Continued*

III. Excitement-orientation
 – growing need for excitement
 – increasing significance of multi-sensual excitement transfer
 – increasing expectance for innovation and change
 – growing demand for cultural events
 – trend towards theme-oriented offers and facilities
 – high acceptancy of weather-independent leisure offers
 – increasing standards (e.g. additional services with high emotional excitement values are
   expected)
 – growing importance of cross-over-offers
IV. Health/wellness
 – increasing demand for sport and health-oriented leisure activities and offers
 – growing significance of beauty and slimming awareness
 – trend towards holistic offers: beauty + health + fitness = wellness
 – development of activity-supporting tourism (e.g. biking, biking without luggage)
 – high awareness of nature and ecology

Source: Steinecke (1997); Wenzel and Franck (1998).

References

DGF (Deutsche Gesellschaft für Freizeit) (1998) *Freizeit in Deutschland '98.* DGF, Erkrath.

DGF (Deutsche Gesellschaft für Freizeit) (1999) *Freizeit in Deutschland B Freizeittrends 2000plus.* DGF, Erkrath.

Horch, H.-D. and Tokarski, W. (2000) *Qualifizierungsfelder in der Sport- und Freizeitwirtschaft im Hochsauerlandkreis.* Gesellschaft für Innovative Beschäftigungsförderung, Bottrop.

Statistisches Bundesamt (1994) *Wo bleibt die Zeit?* Statistisches Bundesamt, Bonn.

Statistisches Bundesamt (2000) *Wiesbaden/WZB Berlin/ZUMA Mannheim: Datenreport 1999.* CD-ROM-Ausgabe, Statistisches Bundesamt, Wiesbaden/Berlin/Mannheim.

Steinecke, A. (1997) Inszenierung im Tourismus: Motor der künftigen touristischen Entwicklung. In: Steinecke, A. and Treinen, M. (eds) *Inszenierung im Tourismus. Trends – Modelle – Prognosen.* Trier.

Tokarski, W. (1996) Stichwort 'Freizeit'. In: Landeszentrale für Politische Bildung (eds) *NRW Lexikon.* Verlag Leske Budrich, Opladen.

Tokarski, W. (1999) *Stichworte der Freizeitwissenschaft.* Materialien Band 4, Institut für Freizeitwissenschaft, Deutsche Sporthochschule, Köln.

Tokarski, W. and Michels, H. (1996) Germany. In: Cushman, G., Veal, A.J. and Zuzanek, J. (eds) *World Leisure Participation: Free Time in the Global Village.* CAB International, Wallingford, UK, pp. 107–112.

Weber, W., Schnieder, C., Kortlüke, N. and Horak, B. (1995) *Die wirtschaftliche Bedeutung des Sports.* Hofmann Verlag, Schorndorf.

Wenzel, C.-O. and Franck, J. (1998) Trends: Die Ferienwelt von morgen. In: Isenberg, W. (Hrsg.) *Kathedralen der Freizeitgesellschaft.* Bergisch Gladbach.

7 Great Britain

Chris Gratton and A.J. Veal

Introduction

This chapter reviews statistics on British time-use and leisure participation as revealed in government and other time-use surveys conducted since the 1960s, and official leisure participation surveys conducted since the 1970s. Details of the surveys discussed are presented in Table 7.1. Because of the constant changes to methodology and lack of coordination between data collection in different sectors of the field, it is not possible to present data on all aspects of the field, such as time-use, participation, sport or the arts, in a common format. Time-use research is therefore discussed separately from participation research. Different surveys have been conducted for different parts of the UK and this is indicated in Table 7.1.[1]

Time-use

Time-use has been studied in Britain since the 1930s, when the BBC commissioned the first of a series of time-budget studies to provide data on the behaviour of radio, and later television, audiences (Gershuny, 1983). In the post-Second World War era, findings from five time-use surveys conducted by the BBC and other agencies between 1961 and 1995 (Gershuny, 2000, p. 273) have been subject to secondary analysis by Gershuny and Fisher (1999) and a

summary is shown in Table 7.2. Overall, it shows leisure time increasing up until 1975, but then becoming static or declining up to 1995. It is particularly notable that, despite 30 years of public promotion, the amount of time spent participating in sporting and physical recreation did not increase during this period. Averages can, however, hide shifts taking place within the population – average leisure time can be increasing overall but falling for some groups, or it may be increasing on average because those groups with more leisure time (for example retired people) are increasing as a proportion of the total population. Some of these more detailed aspects of time-use trends have been analysed by Gershuny (2000).

More recent time-use data, from the UK time-use survey conducted by the Office for National Statistics (ONS) in 2000/01, are presented in Table 7.3. The data relate to the UK, rather than just Great Britain (that is, Northern Ireland is included) and indicate that average leisure time was 313 min/day. It should be borne in mind that the averages presented here cover both weekdays and weekends and all age groups. The overall figure is a little higher than that for 1995 shown in Table 7.2, providing no evidence for a significant 'time crunch' as referred to in some of the literature and discussed in Chapter 1, but again the detail is hidden by the averages. Women's leisure time is, on average, 28 min/day less than men's,

Table 7.1. Surveys of time-use and leisure participation, Britain, 1961–2000.

Survey	Organization	Year	Area	Type	Sample	Refs
The People's Activities	BBC	1961	GB	TBS	2400	BBC (1965)
People's Activities and Use of Time	BBC	1975	GB	TBS	3500	BBC (1978)
Social Change and Economic Life	ESRC	1985	GB	TBS	2000	Gershuny and Fisher (1999)
Social Change and Economic Life	ESRC	1995	GB	TBS	1900	ESRC (1995)
UK Time-use Survey	ONS	2000/01	UK	TBS	10,300	ONS (2001); Aliaga and Winqvist (2003)
General Household Survey	OPCS	1973	GB	QS	20,000	OPCS (1974)
General Household Survey	OPCS	1977	GB	QS	23,000	OPCS (1978), Veal (1979)
General Household Survey	OPCS	1980	GB	QS	22,600	OPCS (1981)
General Household Survey	OPCS	1983	GB	QS	19,000	OPCS (1984)
General Household Survey	OPCS	1986	GB	QS	19,200	OPCS (1987)
General Household Survey	OPCS	1987	GB	QS	19,500	OPCS (1988) ONS (1991)
General Household Survey	ONS	1990	GB	QS	17,600	Matheson (1990)
General Household Survey	ONS	1993	GB	QS	17,550	ONS (1994)
General Household Survey	ONS	1996	GB	QS	15,700	ONS (1997)
Arts in England (via ONS Omnibus)	ONS	2001	England	QS	6042	Skelton et al. (2002)

ONS, Office for National Statistics; OPCS, Office of Population Censuses and Surveys; ESRC, Economic and Social Research Council; QS, questionnaire survey; TBS, time-budget survey.

Table 7.2. Trends in leisure time, UK, 1961–1995.

	Min/day, persons aged 16+			
	1961	1975	1985	1995
TV and radio	139	128	135	129
Other leisure at home	74	79	84	65
Eating out, visiting pubs, cinema, theatre, etc.	28	47	42	61
Socializing	35	42	35	40
Sports and walking	9	10	14	10
Total leisure	285	306	310	305

Source: Gershuny and Fisher (1999), based on surveys listed in Table 7.1.

reflecting the tendency for women to shoulder the greater burden of housework and childcare while, at the same time, increasing their involvement in the paid workforce.

Table 7.4 provides a snap-shot picture of variation in leisure time by life-cycle groups in 2000. As might be expected, those at each end of the age spectrum have the greatest amount of leisure time, and those with young dependent children have the least. Women have less leisure time than men in all categories, but the difference between men's and women's leisure time varies considerably, from just 8 min/day for young single adults to 44 min/day for older couples.

Leisure Participation Surveys

The main source of information on leisure participation in Britain is the General Household Survey (GHS), an annual 'omnibus' survey with

Table 7.3. Time-use by gender, UK, 2000/01.

	Min/day, persons aged 16 and over		
	Males	Females	Total
Sleep	517	523	520
Personal care	124	136	130
Employment	205	117	161
Household/family care	131	232	181
Study	40	40	40
Volunteer work	9	12	10.5
Travel	87	81	84
Total leisure	327	299	313
Social life, entertaining, culture	62	73	67
Sport, hobbies, resting	75	57	66
TV/video	157	136	147
Other mass media	33	33	33
Total	1440	1440	1440

Source: UK 2000 Time-use Survey – Office for National Statistics (2001).

a sample of around 20,000 adults (aged 16 and over) which has been carried out in Great Britain by the Office for National Statistics (formerly the Office of Population Censuses and Surveys; OPCS) annually since 1972. It is a wide-ranging survey covering a number of topics of interest to government, such as housing, education and health. Questions on leisure activities have not been included every year, but were included on a regular basis up until 1996 and then again in 2001, but the results of the 2001 survey were not available in time to be included in this chapter.

The first time leisure questions were included in the GHS was 1973. Questions were asked on sports participation, watching sport, informal recreation trips, arts activities, entertainment, home-based leisure activities and various social activities. Leisure questions were asked again in 1977, but changes in the prompt card given to respondents resulted in substantial changes to recorded participation rates in some activities between 1973 and 1977 and, as a result, 1977 became the 'base year' for comparative purposes. The methodology used in

Table 7.4. Leisure time by age/life-cycle stage, UK, 2000.

		Males	Females	Difference
Age (years)	Domestic/life-cycle situation		Min/day	
8–24	Single, no children, living with parents	356	319	+37
25–44	Single, no children, living with parents	326	318	+ 8
Under 45	Couple, no children	321	296	+25
Under 45	Single, no children	265	253	+12
All ages	Single parent, youngest child < 18	301	264	+37
All ages	Parent, couple, youngest child 0–6	233	217	+16
All ages	Parent, couple, youngest child 7–17	269	236	+33
45–64	Mid-age couple, no children at home	319	291	+28
45–64	Mid-age single, no children at home	372	331	+41
65+	Older couple	427	383	+44
65+	Older single	445	416	+29
Average		327	299	+28

Source: see Table 7.3.

1977 was repeated in 1980, 1983 and 1986, giving a consistent series of participation data over this period. By 1986, the list of leisure activities other than sports participation had, however, become more restricted, mainly by limiting the range of social activities and hobbies included.

Questions on sports participation were again included in 1987, but several significant changes were made to the way participation data were collected. In particular, instead of the conventional 'open-ended' leisure question used in the 1977–1986 surveys, a pre-coded sports and physical exercise section was introduced, with 32 categories of sport being prompted. The consequence of this change was that reported participation rates for some sports increased dramatically. As a result, for sporting activities, 1987 became the new 'base year'. The new methodology was followed again in 1990, 1993 and 1996, with some minor modifications (most importantly an additional distinction was made between activities done mainly indoors and those done mainly outdoors). After 1996 the gap between inclusions of leisure questions in the GHS increased to 5 years.

In view of the fact that arts participation questions had been dropped from the GHS survey in the 1990s, the Arts Council of England eventually commissioned a survey on arts participation from the Office for National Statistics 2001, and data from this survey are presented below.

Trends in Leisure Participation Over Time

Because of changes in leisure categories included in various rounds of the GHS, and differing treatments of these categories, as discussed above, trend data are available for different time-periods for different groups of activities, namely: home-based leisure; the arts, entertainment and cultural visits; and sport and physical activities. These activity groups are discussed in turn.

Home-based leisure

Table 7.5 gives the participation rates in home-based leisure activities included in the GHS on a consistent basis since 1977. As indicated in the time-use data, there was virtually no change in participation levels in television-watching or radio listening over the 20-year period, but for the other activities there appears to be a difference between the 1980s and the 1990s, with participation levels in everything except dressmaking/needlework/knitting increasing.

Arts, entertainment and cultural visits

Trend data on arts participation are available only for the period when questions on arts, entertainment and cultural activities were included in the GHS, from 1977 to 1987.

Table 7.5. Trends in participation in selected home-based leisure activities, Great Britain, 1977–1996.

Activity	% participating in 4 weeks before interview, persons aged 16+							
	1977	1980	1983	1986	1987	1990	1993	1996
Watching television	97	98	98	98	99	99	99	99
Visiting/entertaining friends/relations	91	91	91	94	95	96	96	96
Listening to radio	87	88	87	86	88	89	89	88
Listening to records/tapes	62	64	63	67	73	76	77	78
Reading books	54	57	56	59	60	62	65	65
Gardening	42	43	44	43	46	48	48	48
Do-it-yourself	35	37	36	39	43	43	42	42
Dressmaking/needlework/knitting	29	28	27	27	27	23	22	22
Sample	23,000	22,600	19,000	19,200	19,500	17,600	17,550	15,700

Source: General Household Survey, ONS (1997).

Table 7.6. Trends in participation in selected arts/entertainment/cultural visits, Great Britain, 1977–1987.

Activity	% participating in 4 weeks before interview, persons aged 16+				
	1977	1980	1983	1986	1987
Films	10	10	7	8	11
Plays, pantomime, musicals					7
Ballet, modern dance					1
Opera or operetta					1
Classical music	5	5	4	5	2
Jazz, blues, soul, reggae					2
Other musical shows					7
Art galleries or museums	4	3	3	4	8
Visit historic buildings, sites, towns	8	9	8	9	8
Sample					19,500

Source: General Household Survey, ONS (1997).

Table 7.6 shows that there was little change in participation rates in these activities over the period, although the more detailed categorization of musical events in the 1987 survey produced higher overall rates, suggesting that earlier surveys may have been under-counting in this area.

Sport and physical activities

Table 7.7 indicates trends over the period 1987 to 1996 in participation in those sport and physical activities which have a participation level of at least 1% in a 4-week period. Despite a decade of public sector activity in promoting sport participation, overall participation (in at least one activity) was quite static, at 64%, if walking is included, but showed a small decline if walking is excluded. Two activities, snooker and squash, experienced a decline, while two, walking and cycling, experienced an increase. The Great Britain chapter in the first edition of this book (Gratton, 1996) examined the effect of including within the definition of 'sport and physical activity' such activities as snooker/billiards and darts, which are largely pub-based and lacking in any significant form of physical exercise. The chapter also considered the effect of the inclusion of walking, an activity which is largely self-defined by the survey respondent and may also include lim-

ited activity which is not physically demanding. This analysis is not repeated here, but Table 7.7 does present overall participation figures including and excluding walking. This is significant for public policy purposes, since the bulk of public funding is directed towards the more physically demanding sporting activities.

Current Participation Patterns

Again, because of changes in survey design, it is not possible to provide current participation data for a common date for all activities. For the arts there are data from a 2001 survey, but for other activities, the most recent data relate to 1997.

Home-based leisure

The most recent information on home-based leisure participation relates to 1996, as shown in Table 7.5 and discussed above.

Arts, entertainment, culture

Table 7.8 provides information on attendance at arts events for England for 2001. A wide range of cultural activities is included, although it is notable that sport spectating is not included. Two measures of participation are presented, in the

Table 7.7. Trends in participation in sports and physical activities, Great Britain, 1987–1996.

	% participating at least once in 4 weeks, persons aged 16+			
	1987	1990	1993	1996
Walking	38	41	41	45
Any swimming**	13	15	15	15
Keep fit/yoga	9	12	12	12
Snooker/pool/billiards	15	14	12	11
Cycling	8	9	10	11
Weight training	5	5	5	6
Weight lifting †	1	1	1	1
Soccer	5	5	4	5
Golf	4	5	5	5
Running/jogging	5	5	5	5
Ten-pin bowls/skittles	2	4	4	3
Badminton	3	3	3	2
Tennis	2	2	2	2
Bowls	1	2	2	2
Fishing	2	2	2	2
Table tennis	2	2	2	2
Squash	3	3	2	1
Horse riding	1	1	1	1
At least one activity (excluding walking)*	45	48	47	45
At least one activity*	60	64	64	64
Sample	19,500	17,600	17,550	15,700

* Includes activities not separately listed; ** 1987 figure estimated; † 1990, 1993, 1996 figures estimated.
Source: General Household Survey, ONS (1997) – see Table 7.1.

last year and the last month, and frequency of participation, indicating that, even for the most popular activities, the average frequency of participation is quite low. Attendance at events as audience is the traditional way in which 'participation in the arts' has been measured; Table 7.9 presents information on active engagement with the arts, such as reading, involvement with amateur drama and music, and crafts. It is notable that reading is far and away the most popular of the activities recorded.

Sport and physical activities

Table 7.10 provides information on 1996 participation levels for a wider range of activities than covered in Table 7.7 and also provides 4-week and 1-year participation rates and frequency. It indicates how the 12-month reference period, which is widely used in participation surveys, inflates participation rates, compared with the 4-week period, the basic measure used in the GHS, which is half the rate for many activities. The information on frequency of participation is particularly important for sport and physical activities, since frequent and regular participation gives the maximum benefits for health. For most activities the participation frequency is at least four times a month, or once a week, for participants.

Socio-economic Variation

Gender

In Tables 7.11–7.13, which present information on gender differences in participation, the higher participation rate for each activity is indicated in bold format.

Table 7.8. Attendance at arts events, England, 2001.

	% of persons aged 16+ attending in last:		Average frequency, times pa (participants)
	12 months	4 weeks	
Film at a cinema or other venue	55	19	5.3
Play or drama	27	5	2.7
Carnival, street arts or circus	23	4	1.5
Art, photography or sculpture exhibition	19	6	3.2
Craft exhibition	17	4	2.7
Pantomime	13	–	–
Cultural festival	10	2	1.8
Event connected with books or writing	8	2	2.7
Event including video or electronic art	7	2	2.2
A musical	24	4	2.3
Pop or rock concert	18	4	2.3
Classical music concert	10	3	2.7
Opera or operetta	6	1	2.0
Jazz concert	5	2	2.8
Folk or country and western concert	3	–	2.8
Other music	9	–	3.0
All types of live dance performance	12	–	2.8
Contemporary dance	3	–	2.1
Ballet	2	–	1.8
Other dance	7	–	3.4
Sample	6042	6042	

– zero/not asked; pa, per annum.

Time

It has already been noted above that women have less leisure time than men.

Home-based leisure

Table 7.11 indicates a very 'traditional' pattern of participation in home-based activities on the part of men and women.

Arts, entertainment and culture

Table 7.12 presents information on gender differences in arts event attendance and participation. With regard to attendance at events, the *Arts in England* report does not provide information on every activity, but states:

Similar proportions of men and women attended most of the events covered by the survey, with just a few exceptions. Women, for example, were more likely than men to have attended pantomimes (16% had done so, compared with 9% of men) or plays (mentioned by 30% of women, but only 24% of men). A higher proportion of men, on the other hand, said they had been to a live music event; 30% had, compared with 27% of women.

(Skelton *et al.*, 2002, p. 23)

The data relating to event attendance therefore reflects this statement. In relation to arts participation, the report is more detailed, but still not fully detailed. The picture presented is therefore incomplete and mixed – there is no very clear pattern of difference in the involvement of men and women in the arts.

Table 7.9. Participation in arts activities, England, 2001.

Type	Activity	% of persons aged 16+ participating in past 12 months
Literature	Read for pleasure	73
	Buy a novel, fiction, play or poetry for yourself	49
	Write any stories or plays	3
	Write any poetry	3
Dance	Clubbing	25
	Other dance (but not fitness class)	8
	Ballet	1
Music	Play a musical instrument for own pleasure	9
	Sing to an audience (or rehearse)	4
	Play a musical instrument to an audience (or rehearse)	3
	Write or compose a piece of music	2
	Perform in opera or operetta	*
Drama	Perform or rehearse in a play or drama	2
Visual arts	Painting, drawing, print making or sculpture	14
	Photography as an artistic activity	6
	Buy any original works of art	6
	Make any films or videos as an artistic activity	2
Crafts	Textile crafts such as embroidery, sewing, etc.	14
	Buy any original handmade crafts	12
	Wood crafts	6
	Other crafts (e.g. calligraphy, pottery, jewellery making)	4
Other	Create original artworks or animation using computer	4
	Help run an arts/cultural event or arts organization	4
Sample		6042

* less than 0.5%.
Source: Arts in England – see Table 7.1.

Sport and physical activities

The dominance of men in sport is well-known and is confirmed by Table 7.13. Women's participation rate is higher than men's in only three activities and equal in two.

Age

Table 7.4, discussed above, provides some indication of age-related leisure time availability. As indicated above, leisure time is most plentiful at the two ends of the age spectrum – the young and the old.

Home-based leisure

Although it might be expected that the elderly would give emphasis to home-based leisure activities, and that they would devote their relatively abundant leisure time to such activities, they are the least active in all except two of the home-based leisure activities (Table 7.14). The exceptions are gardening and dressmaking/needlework/knitting, where the youngest age group are least active.

Arts, entertainment and culture

As with gender, the data on the relationship between age and participation in arts activities

Table 7.10. Participation in sports and physical activities, Great Britain, 1996.

	% of persons aged 16+ participating in:		
	4 weeks before interview	Year before interview	Frequency of participation per participant in 4 weeks
Walking (at least 2 miles)	44.5	68.2	n/a
Any swimming	14.8	39.6	4
Swimming: indoor	12.8	35.1	4
Swimming: outdoor	2.9	14.9	6
Keep fit/yoga	12.3	20.7	7
Snooker/pool/billiards	11.3	19.2	4
Cycling	11.0	21.4	8
Weight training	5.6	9.8	7
Any soccer	4.8	8.5	5
Soccer: outdoor	3.8	6.9	5
Soccer: indoor	2.1	4.8	4
Golf	4.7	11.0	4
Running/jogging	4.5	8.0	6
Darts	–	8.6	–
Tenpin bowling/skittles	3.4	15.5	2
Badminton	2.4	7.0	3
Tennis	2.0	7.1	4
Any bowls	1.9	4.6	6
Carpet bowls	1.1	3.0	5
Lawn bowls	0.9	2.8	6
Fishing	1.7	5.3	3
Table tennis	1.5	5.3	3
Squash	1.3	4.1	4
Weight lifting	1.3	2.6	8
Horse riding	1.0	3.0	8
Cricket	0.9	3.3	3
Shooting	0.8	2.8	4
Self-defence	0.7	1.7	6
Climbing	0.7	2.5	2
Basketball	0.7	2.0	3
Rugby	0.6	1.3	4
Ice skating	0.6	3.2	1
Netball	0.5	1.4	3
Sailing	0.4	2.3	4
Motor sports	0.4	1.6	3
Canoeing	0.4	1.6	2
Hockey	0.3	1.1	4
Skiing	0.3	2.6	4
Athletics – track and field	0.2	1.2	5
Gymnastics	0.2	0.7	6
Windsurfing/boardsailing	0.2	1.1	2
At least one activity (excluding walking)	45.6	65.9	–
At least one activity	63.6	81.4	–
Sample	15,700	15,700	15,700

n/a, not available.
Source: General Household Survey, ONS (1997) – see Table 7.1.

Table 7.11. Participation in home-based leisure activities by gender, Great Britain, 1996.

	% of 16+ population participating in 4 weeks prior to interview		
	Males	Females	Total
Watching television	98	**99**	99
Visiting/entertaining friends or relations	91	**94**	96
Listening to radio	**78**	75	88
Listening to records/tapes	**51**	42	78
Reading books	57	**66**	65
Gardening	**59**	40	48
Do-it-yourself	**42**	11	42
Dressmaking/needlework/knitting	3	**36**	22

Higher numbers in bold.
Source: General Household Survey, ONS (1997) – see Table 7.1.

present a mixed picture (Table 7.15). The young are most active, particularly in participant activities and in movie attendance, as might be expected. But in event attendance generally, the 55–64 age group is the most active.

Sport and physical activities

As might be expected, the age-related participation pattern in sporting activities is bi-polar, with the young by far the most active and the elderly by far the least active (Table 7.16). In many cases the participation rate for the youngest, 16–19, age group is more than double the average – five times the average in the case of soccer.

Socio-economic Group

Time

No information is available on the relationship between time-use and socio-economic group.

Home-based leisure

Television-watching and visiting friends and relatives are virtually universal (Table 7.17). Apart from these two pastimes, the broadly bi-polar pattern in home-based leisure patterns reflects to some extent the cultural divide in out-of-home activity – that is, the professional

group have high levels of participation in the more cultural activities, while unskilled manual workers and their household members have the highest participation rate only in dressmaking/needlework/knitting.

Arts, entertainment and culture

Information is not available on the participant arts activities, but event attendance shows a clear bi-polar pattern, with the managerial/professional group being the most active and those in 'routine' (mostly manual) occupations being generally the least active (Table 7.18). The jibe that publicly subsidized arts are 'middle class welfare' held true in Britain in 2001.

Sport and physical activities

The bi-polar pattern is repeated in relation to sport and physical activities (Table 7.19). There are no activities in which the unskilled manual group is most active and only four where the professional group is not the most active. The 'middle class welfare' label is perhaps even more pronounced in this sector.

Use of Computers and the Internet

Computers and the Internet are becoming an increasingly important part of people's lives.

Table 7.12. Attendance at arts events and arts participation, by gender, England, 2001.

	% of persons aged 16+ attending in last year		
	Male	Female	Total
Attendance at events			
Film at a cinema or other venue	55	55	55
Play or drama	24	30	27
Carnival, street arts or circus	23	23	23
Art, photography or sculpture exhibition	19	19	19
Craft exhibition	17	17	17
Pantomime	9	16	13
Cultural festival	10	10	10
Event connected with books or writing	8	8	8
Event including video or electronic art	7	7	7
A musical	24	24	24
Pop or rock concert	18	18	18
Classical music concert	10	10	10
Opera or operetta	6	6	6
Jazz concert	5	5	5
Folk or country and western concert	3	3	3
Other music	9	9	9
All types of live dance performance	12	12	12
Contemporary dance	3	3	3
Ballet	2	2	2
Participation			
Read for pleasure	67	79	73
Buy a novel, fiction, play or poetry for yourself	41	56	49
Write any stories or plays	3	3	3
Write any poetry	3	3	3
Clubbing	25	25	25
Other dance (but not fitness class)	8	8	8
Ballet	1	1	1
Play a musical instrument for own pleasure	11	8	9
Sing to an audience (or rehearse)	4	4	4
Play a musical instrument to an audience (or rehearse)	4	2	3
Write or compose a piece of music	2	2	2
Perform in opera or operetta	*	*	*
Perform or rehearse in a play or drama	2	2	2
Painting, drawing, print making or sculpture	12	16	14
Photography as an artistic activity	9	4	6
Buy any original works of art	6	6	6
Make any films or videos as an artistic activity	2	2	2
Textile crafts such as embroidery, sewing, etc.	1	24	14
Buy any original handmade crafts	6	17	12
Wood crafts	6	6	6
Other crafts (e.g. calligraphy, pottery, jewellery making)	–	67	4
Create original artworks or animation using computer	5	3	4
Help run an arts/cultural event or arts organization	4	4	4
Sample	2625	3417	6042

*, less than 0.5%.
Source: Arts in England – see Table 7.1.

Table 7.13. Participation in sport and physical activities by gender, Great Britain, 1996.

	% of 16+ population participating in 4 weeks prior to interview		
	Males	Females	Total
Walking	**49**	41	45
Any swimming	13	**17**	15
Swimming indoor	11	**15**	13
Swimming outdoor	3	3	3
Keep fit/yoga	7	**17**	12
Snooker/pool/billiards	**20**	4	11
Cycling	**15**	8	11
Weight training	**9**	3	6
Soccer	**10**	0	5
Golf	**8**	2	5
Running/jogging	**7**	2	5
Tenpin bowls/skittles	**4**	3	3
Badminton	**3**	2	2
Tennis	2	2	2
Bowls	**2**	1	2
Fishing	**3**	0	2
Table tennis	**2**	1	2
Squash	**2**	0	1
Horse riding	0	**1**	1
At least one activity (excluding walking)*	**54**	38	46
At least one activity*	**71**	38	64
Sample	7200	8500	15,700

*, includes those activities not separately listed. Higher numbers in bold.
Source: GHS (1996) – see Table 7.1.

Table 7.14. Participation in home-based leisure activities by age, Great Britain, 1996.

	% of 16+ population participating in 4 weeks prior to interview							
	16–19	20–24	25–29	30–44	45–59	60–69	70+	Total
Watching television	99	<u>98</u>	99	99	99	99	<u>98</u>	99
Visiting/entertaining friends or relations	**98**	**98**	**98**	97	96	95	<u>93</u>	96
Listening to radio	95	94	94	92	88	83	<u>76</u>	88
Listening to records/tapes	**98**	96	93	89	75	65	<u>46</u>	78
Reading books	63	**66**	64	**66**	65	**66**	<u>62</u>	65
Gardening	<u>15</u>	21	35	52	59	**61**	48	48
Do-it-yourself	25	34	50	**52**	48	38	<u>24</u>	42
Dressmaking/needlework/ knitting	<u>9</u>	15	14	22	26	**27**	22	22
Sample	829	1039	1441	4372	3686	2024	2305	15,700

Highest numbers in bold, lowest underlined.
Source: GHS (1996) – see Table 7.1.

Table 7.15. Attendance at arts events and arts participation, by age, England, 2001.

	% of persons aged 16+ attending in last year							
	16–24	25–34	35–44	45–54	55–64	65–74	75+	Total
Attendance at events								
Film	**88**	77	68	54	36	27	<u>12</u>	55
Play or drama	26	23	29	31	**34**	25	<u>15</u>	27
Carnival, street arts or circus	29	**30**	29	22	17	15	<u>9</u>	23
Art, photography or sculpture exhibition	17	18	20	22	**23**	19	<u>10</u>	19
Craft exhibition	<u>7</u>	14	17	20	**25**	21	13	17
Pantomime	<u>8</u>	13	**19**	12	12	13	11	13
Live dance event	**17**	14	10	13	14	10	<u>6</u>	12
Cultural festival	**15**	13	11	10	9	7	<u>5</u>	10
Event connected with books/writing	7	**9**	**9**	**9**	8	6	<u>4</u>	8
Event including video/electronic art	12	**12**	7	6	3	2	<u>0</u>	7
Opera or operetta	<u>4</u>	<u>4</u>	<u>4</u>	7	8	**9**	6	6
Classical music	<u>4</u>	6	8	12	**16**	14	12	10
Musical	27	23	23	**28**	**28**	22	<u>16</u>	24
Jazz concert	4	6	6	6	**7**	5	<u>2</u>	5
Participation								
Read for pleasure	69	75	73	**76**	75	75	<u>66</u>	73
Buy a novel, fiction, play or poetry for yourself	45	53	50	**57**	53	43	<u>34</u>	49
Write any stories or plays	**6**	4	3	<u>2</u>	4	<u>2</u>	<u>2</u>	3
Write any poetry	**6**	4	4	3	4	3	<u>1</u>	3
Clubbing	**69**	53	25	9	4	3	<u>2</u>	25
Do any other dance (not fitness class)	7	<u>6</u>	<u>6</u>	**10**	**10**	9	7	8
Do any ballet	1	1	1	*	*	*	*	1
Play a musical instrument for own pleasure	**20**	10	9	7	6	7	<u>4</u>	9
Sing to an audience (or rehearse)	**6**	<u>3</u>	<u>3</u>	4	5	4	<u>3</u>	4
Play musical instrument to audience (or rehearse)	**7**	2	2	3	3	2	<u>1</u>	3
Write or compose a piece of music	**6**	2	1	1	*	1	*	2
Perform in play/drama (or rehearse)	**8**	<u>1</u>	2	2	2	<u>1</u>	<u>1</u>	2
Painting, drawing, print making, sculpture	**30**	18	13	11	12	8	<u>6</u>	14
Photography as an artistic activity	**8**	5	5	**8**	**8**	6	<u>4</u>	6
Buy any original works of art	<u>2</u>	6	8	**10**	7	5	<u>2</u>	6
Make any films or videos as an artistic activity	**4**	1	1	1	2	1	*	2
Textile crafts such as embroidery, sewing, etc.	10	11	11	14	**20**	18	14	14
Buy any original handmade crafts	10	13	15	**17**	14	7	<u>5</u>	12
Wood crafts	**8**	<u>4</u>	5	6	6	5	<u>4</u>	6
Other crafts	3	**5**	4	4	4	<u>3</u>	<u>3</u>	4
Create original artworks/animation using computer	**8**	6	5	3	3	<u>1</u>	<u>1</u>	4
Help run arts/cultural event/arts organization	3	<u>2</u>	3	**5**	4	3	<u>2</u>	4
Sample	525	1025	1141	963	837	819	732	6042

Highest numbers in bold, lowest underlined.
Source: Arts in England – see Table 7.1.

Table 7.16. Participation in sport and physical activities by age, Great Britain, 1996.

	% of 16+ population participating in 4 weeks prior to interview							
	16–19	20–24	25–29	30–44	45–59	60–69	70+	Total
Walking	52	49	45	49	49	45	24	45
Any swimming	21	19	20	22	12	9	3	15
Keep fit/yoga	20	20	18	16	10	8	3	12
Snooker/pool/billiards	39	30	20	11	6	4	2	11
Cycling	25	17	13	15	9	6	2	11
Weight training	16	14	12	8	2	0	0	6
Soccer	25	14	9	5	1	0	0	5
Golf	5	5	4	6	6	4	1	5
Running/jogging	12	11	8	6	2	0	0	5
Tenpin bowls/skittles	12	9	6	4	2	0	0	3
Badminton	7	3	3	3	2	1	0	2
Tennis	8	3	3	2	2	1	0	2
Bowls	1	0	1	1	2	4	3	2
Fishing	2	2	2	2	2	1	0	2
Table tennis	6	2	2	2	1	1	0	2
Squash	3	2	3	2	1	0	0	1
Weight lifting	6	3	2	1	1	0	0	1
Horse riding	2	2	2	1	1	0	0	1
At least one activity (excluding walking)*	78	70	63	57	40	30	13	46
At least one activity*	86	81	77	73	63	55	31	64
Sample	829	1039	1441	4372	3686	2024	2305	15,700

*, includes those activities not separately listed. Highest numbers in bold, lowest underlined.
Source: GHS (1996) – see Table 7.1.

Table 7.17. Home-based leisure activities by socio-economic group, Great Britain, 1996.

	% participating in 4 weeks before interview, persons aged 16+						
	Professional	Employers/ managers	Intermediate/ junior non-manual	Skilled manual and self-employed	Semi-skilled/ manual and personal service	Unskilled manual	Total
Watching television	99	99	99	99	99	99	99
Visiting/entertaining friends or relations	96	97	97	95	96	94	96
Listening to radio	94	92	91	87	83	79	88
Listening to records/ tapes	86	82	81	74	72	65	78
Reading books	83	73	75	51	57	49	65
Gardening	59	61	51	50	43	41	48
Do-it-yourself	61	56	38	54	35	28	42
Dressmaking/ needlework/knitting	10	14	31	11	24	26	22
Sample	542	2187	5091	3019	2780	924	15,700

Highest numbers in bold, lowest underlined.
Source: GHS (1996) – see Table 7.1.

Table 7.18. Attendance at arts events by socio-economic group, England, 2001.

	% of persons aged 16+ attending in last year					
	Managerial, professional	Intermediate	Small employers/ self-employed	Lower supervisory/ technical	Semi-routine/ routine	Total
Film	**67**	60	47	44	<u>43</u>	55
Play or drama	**41**	29	23	<u>14</u>	15	27
Carnival/street arts/circus	24	23	**26**	23	<u>21</u>	23
Art/photo/sculpture exhibition	**33**	17	19	11	<u>8</u>	19
Craft exhibition	**24**	19	20	14	<u>11</u>	18
Pantomime	15	**16**	<u>9</u>	11	12	13
Live dance event	**15**	12	**15**	11	<u>9</u>	12
Cultural festival	**15**	9	6	<u>7</u>	<u>7</u>	10
Event connected books or writing	**13**	7	9	<u>4</u>	<u>4</u>	8
Event including video/electronic art	**10**	6	6	5	<u>4</u>	6
Opera or operetta	**11**	5	5	<u>1</u>	3	6
Classical music	**18**	10	11	<u>3</u>	5	10
Musical	**34**	27	21	<u>16</u>	<u>16</u>	24
Jazz concert	**10**	4	7	4	<u>2</u>	6
Sample	2025	862	426	596	1826	6042

Highest numbers in bold, lowest underlined.
Source: Arts in England – see Table 7.1.

Table 7.19. Sports and physical activities by socio-economic group, Great Britain, 1996.

	% participating in 4 weeks before interview, persons aged 16+						
	Professional	Employers/ managers	Intermediate/ junior non-manual	Skilled manual and self-employed	Semi-skilled/ manual and personal service	Unskilled manual	Total
Walking	**56**	48	46	44	39	<u>33</u>	45
Any swimming	**23**	19	17	11	11	<u>6</u>	15
Keep fit/yoga	14	12	**18**	7	9	<u>5</u>	12
Snooker/pool/ billiards	11	11	8	**16**	10	<u>7</u>	11
Cycling	**19**	12	9	11	10	<u>7</u>	11
Weight training	**10**	5	6	5	3	<u>2</u>	6
Soccer	5	4	<u>3</u>	**6**	<u>3</u>	<u>3</u>	5
Golf	**11**	9	4	5	3	<u>1</u>	5
Running/jogging	**9**	6	4	4	2	2	5
Tenpin bowls/ skittles	**4**	3	4	3	2	<u>1</u>	3
Badminton	3	**3**	**3**	<u>1</u>	<u>1</u>	<u>1</u>	2
Tennis	**4**	3	2	1	1	<u>0</u>	2
Bowls	<u>1</u>	**3**	2	2	2	<u>1</u>	2
Fishing	2	2	<u>1</u>	**3**	2	<u>1</u>	2
Table tennis	**5**	2	1	1	1	<u>0</u>	2

Continued

Table 7.19. *Continued*

	Professional	Employers/ managers	Intermediate/ junior non-manual	Skilled manual and self-employed	Semi-skilled/ manual and personal service	Unskilled manual	Total
			% participating in 4 weeks before interview, persons aged 16+				
Squash	5	2	1	1	1	0	1
Weight lifting	1	1	1	1	1	1	1
Horse riding	1	1	1	1	1	0	1
At least one activity (excluding walking)*	63	52	47	45	37	23	46
At least one activity*	80	69	66	63	55	45	64
Sample	542	2187	5091	3019	2780	924	15,700

*, includes those activities not separately listed. Highest numbers in bold, lowest underlined.
Source: General Household Survey, GHS (1996).

Table 7.20. Use of the Internet, by age and gender, Great Britain, 2000–2003.

	% using Internet in previous 3 months			
	October 2000	October 2001	October 2002	October 2003
Gender				
Men	47	50	60	57
Women	33	43	51	51
Age				
16–24	70	78	85	78
25–44	53	61	73	72
45–54	46	50	59	59
55–64	24	30	41	41
65+	*	*	*	16
Total	40	46	55	54

* Sample size too small for estimate.
Source: Office of National Statistics (annual) *National Statistics Omnibus Survey.* ONS, London.

Table 7.20 indicates that, by October 2003, the proportion of the British adult population who had used the Internet at least once in the previous 3 months had grown to 54%, including 78% of those aged under 25. More men use the Internet than women, but over the 3-year period indicated, the gender gap appeared to be closing.

Conclusions

As in other countries, the collection of data on leisure participation in Britain has been fragmented and inconsistent. Monitoring trends in leisure participation requires a comprehensive approach to leisure and a series of surveys over a period of time during which the survey method is not changed. On more than one occasion British leisure survey experience has highlighted the sensitivity of results to variation in survey management and design. Consequently, promising time-series of participation data have been compromised by ill-advised changes in survey design, resulting in the breaking of the time-series and the need to start with a new 'base year'. Further, fragmentation of government responsibility for leisure has led to an inconsistent approach to the totality of leisure. Only sport participation has been continuously monitored, but the arts and entertainment, informal outdoor recreation, such as visiting parks and beaches, much commercial leisure, and home-based leisure, have been neglected. Time-use research has also been spasmodic in Britain. While a new Ministry of Culture and Heritage has promoted a comprehensive approach to planning for leisure at the local level, commitment to the provision of data to monitor performance at national level has been lacking.

Note

[1] The UK covers England, Wales, Scotland and Northern Ireland; Great Britain covers England, Wales and Scotland only.

Bibliography

Aliaga, C. and Winqvist, K. (2003) How women and men spend their time: results from 13 European Countries. *Statistics in Focus: Population and Social Conditions*, (Cat. No. KS-NK-02-012-EN-N). Eurostat/European Community, Brussels. Available at: http://europa.eu.int/comm/eurostat/ (accessed July 2004).

BBC (British Broadcasting Corporation) (1965) *The People's Activities.* BBC, London.

BBC (British Broadcasting Corporation) (1978) *The People's Use of Time.* BBC, London.

British Travel Association/University of Keele (1967) *The Pilot National Recreation Survey.* BTA/University of Keele, London and Keele, UK.

ESRC (Economic and Social Research Council) Institute for Social and Economic Research and Office of National Statistics (1995) *Time Use Study.* Colchester, ISER, University of Essex, UK.

Gershuny, J. (1983) *Time-budget Research in the UK.* Science Policy Research Unit, University of Sussex, Brighton, UK.

Gershuny, J. (2000) *Changing Times: Work and Leisure in Postindustrial Society.* Oxford University Press, Oxford, UK.

Gershuny, J.I. and Fisher, K. (1999) *Leisure in the UK Across the 20th Century.* Multinational Time Use Study, University of Essex, Social Policy Research Unit. Available at: www.iser.essex.ac.uk/pubs/workpaps/pdf/1999-03.pdf (accessed February 2004).

Gratton, C. (1996) Great Britain. In: Cushman, G., Veal, A.J. and Zuzanek, J. (eds) *World Leisure Participation: Free Time in the Global Village.* CAB International, Wallingford, UK, pp. 113–130.

Gratton, C. and Tice, A. (1994) Trends in sports participation 1977–1987. *Leisure Studies* 13(1), 49–66.

Matheson, J. (1990) *General Household Survey 1987: Participation in Sport.* HMSO, London.

ONS (Office of National Statistics) (1991) *General Household Survey 1990,* HMSO, London.

ONS (Office of National Statistics) (1994) *General Household Survey 1993,* HMSO, London.

ONS (Office for National Statistics) (1996) *Living in Britain, 1996.* HMSO, London.

ONS (Office of National Statistics) (1997) *General Household Survey 1996,* HMSO, London.

ONS (Office of National Statistics) (2001) The UK 2000 Time-use Survey. ONS, London, – available at: www.statistics.gov.uk/TimeUse/default.asp (consulted July 2004).

ONS (Office of National Statistics) (annual) *National Statistics Omnibus Survey.* ONS, London.

OPCS (Office of Population Censuses and Surveys) (1974) *General Household Survey 1973,* HMSO, London.

OPCS (Office of Population Censuses and Surveys) (1978) *General Household Survey 1977,* HMSO, London.

OPCS (Office of Population Censuses and Surveys) (1981) *General Household Survey 1980,* HMSO, London.

OPCS (Office of Population Censuses and Surveys) (1984) *General Household Survey 1983,* HMSO, London.

OPCS (Office of Population Censuses and Surveys) (1985) *General Household Survey 1983.* HMSO, London.

OPCS (Office of Population Censuses and Surveys) (1987) *General Household Survey 1986,* HMSO, London.

OPCS (Office of Population Censuses and Surveys) (1988) *General Household Survey 1987,* HMSO, London.

OPCS (Office of Population Censuses and Surveys) (1989) *General Household Survey 1986.* HMSO, London.

OPCS (Office of Population Censuses and Surveys) (1990) *General Household Survey 1990.* HMSO, London.

OPCS (Office of Population Censuses and Surveys) (1993) *General Household Survey 1993.* HMSO, London.

Roberts, K. and Brodie, D. (1992) *Inner-city Sport: Who Plays and What Are the Benefits?* Giordano Bruno, Vooorthuizen, The Netherlands.

Rodgers, B. (1977) *Rationalising Sports Policies: Sport in its Social Context.* Council of Europe, Strasbourg.

Sillitoe, K.K. (1969) *Planning for Leisure*, Government Social Survey. HMSO, London.

Skelton, A., Bridgwood, A., Duckworth, K., Hutton, L., Fenn, C., Creaser, C. and Babbidge, A. (2002) *Arts in England Attendance, Participation and Attitudes in 2001 Findings of a Study Carried Out by Social Survey Division of the Office for National Statistics*. Arts Council of England, London. Available at: www. artscouncil.org. uk/information/publications. html (accessed July 2004).

Veal, A.J. (1979) *Sport and Recreation in England and Wales: an Analysis of Adult Participation Patterns in 1977*. Research Memo 74, Centre for Urban and Regional Studies, University of Birmingham, UK.

Veal, A.J. (1984) Leisure in England and Wales. *Leisure Studies* 3(2), 221–230.

Veal, A.J. (1991) National leisure surveys: the British experience 1977–86. In: Jonson, P., Cushman, G. and Veal, A.J. (eds) *Leisure and Tourism: Social and Environmental Change: World Leisure and Recreation Association Congress*, Sydney, 16–19 July.

8 Hong Kong

Atara Sivan, Bob Robertson and Sue Walker

Introduction

Analysing leisure participation in Hong Kong for the chapter in the first edition of this book revealed many similarities between leisure lifestyles in Hong Kong and Western nations, but also some striking differences. For instance, the strong role of the family in leisure decision making and the importance of social activities outside the home, such as shopping, eating out, visiting tea houses and karaoke, are reflections of Eastern culture shaping the leisure behaviour of Hong Kong's residents.

This chapter re-visits the question of East–West influences through examining findings from more recent surveys of leisure participation. It also examines the impact of technology-based leisure and mass media on the leisure lives of people in Hong Kong. It specifically examines participation trends, as well as the actual and preferred leisure activities of Hong Kong people.

Leisure Surveys in Hong Kong: an Overview

Early surveys

In comparison to many Western industrial nations, few studies have been undertaken of leisure behaviour in Hong Kong. Neither has there been a comprehensive survey of time-use. The few studies of leisure behaviour completed during the 1960s, 1970s and 1980s focused primarily on youth, generally seeking data to plan for the provision of community services for young people in the territory. Most were small-scale surveys undertaken by government and voluntary agencies to examine leisure activities undertaken in specific districts of Hong Kong or by specific age groups. The findings of these studies of leisure and recreation generally appeared in government reports on the social needs of particular districts. Seven of these earlier studies were described in the previous edition of this book and their scope and principal findings are summarized in Table 8.1.

Territory-wide surveys

The first territory-wide survey of leisure was carried out in 1993/94 for the Hong Kong Sports Development Board (SDB) by Sivan and Robertson (1993, 1995). This reflected the growing recognition of leisure as a significant domain in the lives of Hong Kong people. The results from the first phase of this survey were summarized in the previous edition. The current chapter presents the findings from the second phase of the survey in 1994, along with more recent data from surveys carried out in 1999 and 2000. The results from the 1994 and

Table 8.1. Leisure surveys, Hong Kong, 1960–1990.

Date	Author/Reference	Scope	Sample	Age range	Key findings
1965	Hong Kong Council of Social Service (1965)	Views of teenagers and young adults on leisure		15–29	Majority of respondents regarded leisure activities as important and visited community centres frequently Most leisure activities were undertaken with friends 15–19-year-olds participated more in physical recreation activities
1967	Hong Kong Baptist College (1970)	Leisure activities of workers from 23 youth centres	666	14–21	Respondents preferred outdoor leisure activities but most actually spent their leisure time at home Reading, listening to the radio and watching TV were the most common indoor activities, while social outings and going to the movies were the most popular away-from-home activities
1970	Hong Kong Baptist College	Leisure activities of young workers in two factories	390	14–21	Most frequent leisure activities: watching TV, study at evening school, playing ball games outdoors On days off and holidays, picnicking, social outings, going to the movies, window shopping and undefined physical recreation activities were the main activities Desired activities: touring, camping, attend evening schools, sewing, picnicking, social outings No statistically significant relationships between patterns of activity and age, gender, religion, occupation, income, availability of facilities, type of residence, family size, or birth order
1970	Kowloon City District (1975)	Leisure activities and attitudes towards youth service agencies	1720	School students/ youth	Leisure activities most frequently undertaken were watching TV, reading and ball games Watching TV was the most frequent activity for both sexes. For boys, ball games was the second most popular activity and reading third, while for girls reading was more popular than ball games 65% wanted to do outdoor activities, sport and ball games, but did not have the opportunity 84% participated in school-based leisure activities

1985	HK Southern District Board Social Service Committee	Leisure activities in the Southern District of Hong Kong	262	12–24	10 most frequently pursued activities were: ball games, swimming, watching TV, cycling, listening to records, watching movies, listening to the radio, camping, music and computers Desired activities: camping, overseas tours, ball games, windsurfing, watching movies, extra-mural courses, rowing, track and field sports, archery, ice skating
1984	Ng (1984)	Leisure activities undertaken by secondary school students	1400		TV watching was the dominant activity More girls than boys watched TV, and listened to the radio and records Boys were more involved in arts and crafts activities and sports Frequency of participation was age-related; older students watched less TV and used other media more and younger children participated more in physical activities
1987/88	Ng and Man (1988)	A study of leisure behaviour and life satisfaction	250	12–25	TV watching was most popular among 12–17-year-olds, while 18–25-year-olds preferred watching films, resting and sleeping Swimming and sports and out-of-home activities were more common in summer Participation in out-of-home activities increased with age

Table 8.2. Leisure surveys, Hong Kong, 1993–2000.

Year	Agency	Activities	Sample size	Age range	Timing of survey	Reference
1993; 1994	HKSDB[a]	Leisure/sport	2611; 2573	6+	1993 (summer); 1994 (winter)	Sivan and Robertson (1993, 1995)
1999	HKSDB[a]	Leisure	8079	11–18	1999	Sivan et al. (1999)
2000	HKSDB[a]	Sport	800	12+	2000 (summer)	HKSDB (2000)

[a] HKSDB, Hong Kong Sports Development Board

2000 surveys also have been compared as a first attempt to identify trends in leisure participation in Hong Kong. Details of this and other surveys conducted between 1993 and 2000 and discussed below are given in Table 8.2.

Surveys 1993–2000

The 1993/94 survey comprised two phases to cover participation in two seasons: March/April 1993 (summer) and January/February 1994 (winter). Data were collected on:

- the range of leisure, recreation and sports activities participated in during the previous month;
- frequency of participation in these activities;
- place and organizing body for the activities;
- sources of information used: level of satisfaction with facilities used;
- activities respondents wanted to participate in but had not;
- reasons for non-participation in preferred activities.

Questionnaires were distributed via educational institutions in the 19 administrative districts of Hong Kong. Selected students were given two questionnaires and asked to complete one themselves and to administer one to an adult family member. Some 3297 questionnaires were distributed and 2611 returned, a response rate of 79%. Because of the sampling method used, the resultant sample is biased towards young people, with 57% of the sample aged under 18.

Table 8.3 shows the level of participation in the top 15 leisure and sports activities by gender. The results confirm the findings of earlier surveys in terms of the most popular activities but cover a much wider range of activities and age groups.

The results from the second phase of the survey are largely consistent with those from the first phase, although seasonality affects participation rates in some sports activities; for example, the participation figure for swimming is lower in the winter survey (19%) than in the spring survey (32%).

Of the leisure activities, watching television remains the most popular, followed by shopping, going to public libraries and eating out. Males engage more in electronic and computer games, whereas females engage to a larger extent in shopping. Among the sports activities, badminton is the most popular, followed by cycling, basketball and table tennis. There are substantial differences between males and females, with the former engaging to a larger extent in basketball, table tennis and soccer, while the latter participate more in badminton, volleyball and aerobics.

For this sample of predominantly young adults, sports activities such as badminton, cycling and basketball attract participation rates similar to those for sedentary activities, such as watching television, and out-of-home activities such as shopping and going to the library.

Table 8.4 shows the top 15 activities which respondents *wanted* to do during the previous month but had not done. Many of these activities can be classified as cultural and instrumental, such as taking courses, seeing exhibitions/museums, arts and crafts and attending classical

Table 8.3. Top 15 leisure and sports activities by gender, Hong Kong, winter 1994.

	% participating in month before interview		
	Males	Females	Total
Leisure activities			
Watching TV	55.6	56.3	55.0
Shopping	30.8	52.4	42.6
Going to public library	34.8	40.6	37.7
Eating out (dinner)	35.1	33.8	34.4
Listening to radio/CDs/tapes	23.3	29.5	30.5
Reading newspapers/magazines	24.4	26.5	25.5
Playing electronic/computer games	36.6	14.1	24.1
Going to the cinema	24.1	23.6	23.7
Going to tea houses	22.1	21.5	21.9
Having a picnic/barbecue	18.0	21.5	19.9
Walking in the park	16.1	17.4	16.9
Karaoke	14.2	18.0	16.4
Reading books	14.1	15.3	14.6
Playing cards/mah-jong	16.9	10.6	13.4
Household activities	12.2	13.2	12.7
Sports			
Badminton	42.0	54.1	48.4
Cycling	40.7	41.0	40.7
Basketball	46.1	30.6	37.5
Table tennis	43.1	21.9	31.4
Jogging	25.8	30.2	27.9
Playground	20.0	29.2	24.8
Swimming	19.3	19.2	19.2
Soccer	37.7	2.3	18.3
Hiking	18.1	16.6	17.1
Volleyball	9.0	19.2	14.5
Athletics	14.8	10.9	12.7
Tennis	9.4	7.6	8.5
Aerobics	4.3	10.1	7.5
Squash	5.7	8.2	6.9
Roller skating	3.6	7.8	5.9
Sample size	1165	1408	2573

Source: Sivan and Robertson (1995).

music concerts. The data also reveal respondents' desire to take part in out-of-home activities which utilize public facilities, such as having picnics and barbecues (Hong Kong is well-supplied with picnic and barbecue sites in country and regional parks), going to the cinema, popular music concerts, going to public libraries and walking in parks.

The responses in Table 8.4 may be influenced by people mentioning what they consider to be more worthwhile ways of spending their leisure time than watching television and shopping. Nevertheless, comparing the responses in Tables 8.3 and 8.4 suggests that there is a discrepancy between people's actual use of their leisure time and their aspirations. Further research is needed to understand the reasons for this discrepancy in the Hong Kong context.

A 1999 study explored leisure participation by school students aged 11–18 (Sivan *et al.*, 1999). Using a stratified sample design (by district, type of school – primary/secondary – and by level of education), data were collected from 8079 students from 38 schools representing all the districts in Hong Kong. The sample comprised 48% males and 52% females. Students were presented with a list of 58 activities and were asked to indicate whether or not they had

Table 8.4. Top 15 leisure activities respondents wanted to do but had not done, 1994.

Desired leisure activities	%
Having a picnic/barbecue	31.2
Going to the cinema	29.5
Going to popular music concerts	27.6
Taking courses	19.4
Karaoke	18.8
Seeing exhibitions/museums	18.7
Shopping	18.0
Going to the public library	16.4
Kite flying	15.6
Playing cards/mah-jong	12.8
Walking in the park	12.3
Playing electronic/computer games	11.1
Arts/crafts	10.7
Household activities	10.5
Classical music concerts	9.8
Sample size	1912

Source: Sivan and Robertson (1995).

participated in each one in the previous month, their frequency of participation and with whom they participated.

Table 8.5 shows the prevalence of media use in the leisure time of Hong Kong youth, including information, entertainment and telecommunication technologies. Some 97%

watch television and also play electronic and computer games. Talking on the telephone is also a very popular pastime – recent market research shows that Hong Kong children have the highest level of mobile phone ownership in Asia, with 54% of 16–18-year-olds owning one (Forestier, 2000). This trend in the use of mass media among Hong Kong adolescents echoes similar trends among adolescents in other countries (Sivan, 2000a). Gender differences are also apparent from this survey, with young men engaging more in computer games and sporting and physical activities, while young women participate more in shopping, talking on the phone and aesthetic activities such as painting and drawing.

More recent information about leisure participation for adults as well as young people is presented in Table 8.6. This information was collected as part of SDB's territory-wide 2000 Sports Participation Survey. Questions about participation in leisure activities and favourite leisure activities were inserted into the summer quarter of the survey (carried out in August 2000). Over 800 people aged 12 and over were interviewed in a telephone survey carried out for SDB by the Social Sciences Research Centre of the University of Hong Kong (Hong Kong Sports Development Board, 2000).

Table 8.5. Top 15 leisure activities of Hong Kong students, aged 11–18, 1999.

	Males (%)	Females (%)	Total (%)
Watching TV, LD, CVD, DVD	97.2	97.3	97.2
Non-academic reading (e.g. plays, poetry, newspapers, magazines, comics, books)	87.8	90.9	89.4
Going to tea houses, fast food shops	84.5	88.9	86.8
Listening to radio, CD, tapes	81.5	89.9	85.9
Talking on the telephone	76.3	89.3	83.0
Playing electronic, computer or TV games	86.3	62.4	73.9
Shopping	61.4	80.8	71.5
Chat with family members	64.3	75.6	70.2
Eating out (dinner)	65.8	69.0	67.4
Ball games (e.g. football, tennis, badminton, squash, basketball, table tennis, bowling)	79.2	54.7	66.5
Going to public libraries	52.4	64.1	59.5
Playing with cards, chess	58.2	49.0	54.2
Visit friends/schoolmates and play with them	55.6	47.9	52.7
Painting, drawing, sketching	33.8	46.5	40.8
Walking (in parks, etc.)	38.6	39.8	38.9
Sample size	4116	3847	7963

Source: Sivan (2000a).

Table 8.6. Participation in leisure and sports activities by gender, Hong Kong, summer, 2000.

	% participating in last 4 weeks		
	Males	Females	Total
Leisure activities			
Watching TV	96.7	96.0	96.3
Reading newspapers/magazines	91.4	84.8	88.1
Eating out (dinner)	79.9	79.2	79.6
Shopping	75.9	82.7	79.3
Listen to radio/CDs/tapes	78.9	78.6	78.7
Reading books	69.6	64.2	66.8
Going to a tea house	61.9	55.3	58.6
Walking in the park	50.0	51.7	50.9
Surfing the web/Internet	50.6	37.7	44.1
Going to the public library	32.0	39.5	35.8
Playing electronic/computer games	43.6	26.0	34.7
Going to the cinema	32.1	32.4	32.2
Having a picnic/barbecue	25.8	25.6	25.7
Karaoke	24.4	20.0	22.2
Playground games	17.7	21.7	19.7
Sports and physical activities			
Swimming	21.5	15.5	18.5
Badminton	7.9	8.5	8.2
Basketball	12.7	2.6	7.6
Jogging	4.9	5.9	5.4
Soccer	7.8	0.2	4.0
Tennis	5.1	2.1	3.6
Hiking	2.5	3.6	3.0
Walking	2.5	2.9	2.7
Table tennis	3.9	1.2	2.5
Weight training	2.4	2.3	2.3
Exercise	1.2	2.9	2.0
Martial arts[a]	1.6	2.2	1.9
Squash	2.8	1.0	1.9
Cycling	2.5	1.0	1.7
Dancing[b]	–	2.1	1.1
Sample size	414	419	833

[a] Martial arts includes wushu, judo, qikong and taekwondo. [b] Dancing includes dance/aerobic dance.
Source: HKSDB 2000 Sports Participation Survey, summer quarter.

Table 8.6 shows the level of participation in leisure and sports activities during the previous month (i.e. July). It should be noted that not all of the sports activities included in the 2000 survey were covered in the 1994 surveys. This survey also records watching television as the most popular activity, but with a much higher participation rate than recorded in the survey by Sivan and Robertson in 1993/94: 96% compared with 55% (see Table 8.3). Indeed, with the exception of going to the library, all the participation rates from the 2000 survey are noticeably higher. This difference may be due to the different survey methods used (telephone and self-administered), as well as the different age groups included.

Other popular activities are social in nature and also involve the use of mass media, including: reading newspapers/magazines, eating out, shopping, listening to radio/CDs/tapes, reading books and going to tea houses. Substantial differences exist between males and females in their use of electronic media in their leisure time, with more males than females surfing the web, using the Internet and playing electronic and computer games.

Gender differences are also evident for sports and active leisure pursuits. For example, males record higher participation rates than females in basketball, soccer and tennis, while females are more likely than males to go hiking and to exercise.

To examine a further dimension of leisure participation, respondents were asked which were their three favourite leisure activities. Figure 8.1 shows how the activities rank in relation to participation and preference. Watching television ranks first, both in terms of participation and as the favourite leisure activity. Activities such as reading newspapers and eating out attract high levels of participation but are not 'favourites', while shopping is both a favourite activity and one which attracts a high level of participation. In contrast, reading books, surfing the web/Internet and walking in the park attract lower levels of participation than some other activities (these activities are

outside the top five) but they rank highly as favourite activities.

Tables 8.7 and 8.8 show participation in leisure activities and sports across different age groups. Watching TV is the most popular activity across all age groups, but there are differences in the use of other mass media channels between the different age groups. Those aged 55 and above engage less in reading newspapers/magazines and in listening to the radio/CDs and tapes. There is also a decrease in reading books from the age of 45 onwards. This may be more a reflection of lack of early educational opportunities than disinterest, but needs further investigation. Another striking feature of these results is the popularity of using the web/Internet, especially among those aged 12–34. Over two-thirds of people in these age groups use the web and Internet. The figure is lower (about 40%) for those aged 35–44 and drops to almost a quarter (28.6%) for those

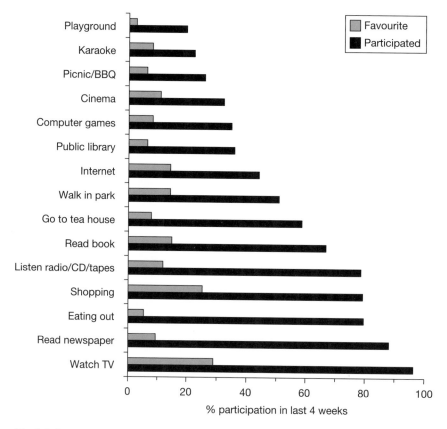

Fig. 8.1. Participation in and favourite activities, Hong Kong, 2000.

Table 8.7. Participation in leisure activities by age group, Hong Kong, summer, 2000.

	% participating in last 4 weeks								
	12–16	17–18	19–24	25–34	35–44	45–54	55–64	65+	Total
Watching TV	98.4	100.0	97.9	99.4	96.7	95.4	96.8	86.3	96.3
Reading newspapers/magazines	90.5	97.9	93.3	98.0	93.3	93.9	80.8	50.3	88.1
Eating out (dinner)	81.0	90.2	93.3	92.6	88.2	80.1	61.8	39.4	79.6
Shopping	81.8	84.2	85.6	91.1	84.6	81.3	73.1	42.2	79.3
Listen to radio/CDs/tapes	87.3	88.0	90.1	86.8	78.7	80.2	65.0	54.5	78.7
Reading books	86.8	85.9	87.9	82.0	72.3	59.0	39.4	19.8	66.8
Going to a tea house	45.3	72.6	68.9	69.3	63.9	64.4	49.1	31.9	58.6
Walking in the park	35.0	17.8	32.3	39.1	64.5	55.7	69.7	65.2	50.9
Surfing the web/Internet	69.4	66.5	78.7	64.7	41.6	28.6	11.1	–	44.1
Going to the public library	60.9	44.9	40.0	31.9	37.6	35.9	33.4	10.6	35.8
Playing electronic/computer games	74.2	69.6	64.7	47.7	25.2	18.2	6.4	–	34.7
Going to the cinema	58.1	70.7	72.3	45.0	22.5	5.3	20.7	1.5	32.2
Having a picnic/barbecue	33.8	39.8	33.7	27.5	30.8	22.8	12.6	9.0	25.7
Karaoke	29.5	53.0	54.4	32.9	13.6	13.3	8.0	1.5	22.2
Playground games	19.3	19.4	7.7	17.1	34.7	17.9	23.8	3.0	19.7
Sample size	96	34	59	182	181	105	79	97	833

Source: HKSDB 2000 Sports Participation Survey, summer quarter.

Table 8.8. Participation in sports activities by age group, Hong Kong, summer, 2000.

	% participating in past 4 weeks								
Sports activities	12–16	17–18	19–24	25–34	35–44	45–54	55–64	65+	Total
Swimming	29.2	21.4	29.0	19.0	23.2	14.0	9.3	3.0	18.5
Badminton	13.3	12.0	14.2	11.5	11.0	2.2	–	–	8.2
Basketball	27.5	32.5	21.4	4.8	2.5	–	–	–	7.6
Jogging	5.6	6.2	5.5	4.1	10.5	2.2	1.6	4.5	5.4
Soccer	8.6	13.2	17.2	3.0	2.7	–	–	–	4.0
Tennis	2.5	–	5.5	7.8	5.4	–	–	–	3.6
Hiking	1.4	–	3.4	1.2	2.2	1.6	3.1	12.0	3.0
Walking	–	–	1.2	0.6	–	4.4	11.1	7.5	2.7
Table tennis	6.6	2.1	1.2	2.7	2.5	1.4	3.1	–	2.5
Weight training	–	–	5.5	4.1	2.3	3.0	1.6	–	2.3
Exercise	–	–	1.2	1.4	1.5	1.6	4.7	6.0	2.0
Martial arts[a]	1.5	1.9	–	1.5	0.5	1.4	3.2	6.1	1.9
Squash	3.0	3.9	6.7	4.2	–	–	–	–	1.9
Cycling	3.6	3.8	3.4	0.6	2.0	1.4	–	1.5	1.7
Dancing[b]	0.9	2.1	1.2	1.5	1.0	0.8	1.6	–	1.1
Sample size	96	34	59	182	181	105	79	97	833

[a] Martial arts includes wushu, judo, qikong and taekwondo. [b] Dancing includes dance and aerobic dance.
Source: HKSDB 2000 Sports Participation Survey, summer quarter.

aged 45–54, but this is still a substantial level of involvement in this activity. Perhaps most concerning is the overwhelming predominance of sedentary behaviour – a feature of both Western and Eastern leisure.

Young adults are more likely than older ones to go to the cinema. Going to tea houses appeals to a wide age group, although teenagers 12–16 years old and older adults are less likely to participate in this activity than those aged 17 to 54.

Older adults tend to have a more limited involvement in leisure, in that participation rates for most activities are lower for those aged 55 and over than for other age groups, with the exception of walking in the park.

Not surprisingly, levels of sports participation also vary with age, with teenagers and young adults recording higher participation rates in most sports. Exceptions include tennis, weight training and squash, which attract relatively more participants from among 19–34-year-olds. Hiking and walking are more popular with older adults, as are two activities

associated with Eastern cultures – morning exercise, which includes tai chi, and martial arts.

Trends in Leisure Participation

In order to examine some recent trends in leisure participation in Hong Kong, a comparison is made between data obtained in the two territory-wide surveys (i.e. 1994 and 2000). Since the surveys employed different interview techniques and sampling methods, a comparison is made using the rank order of activities, with the activity with the highest participation rate, based on the percentage participating in each activity, ranked as one and so on.

Table 8.9 compares the rankings for the top 15 leisure activities for the two surveys. The results illustrate a number of changes in the relative popularity of leisure participation. Of the mass media activities, watching TV remains the most popular. However, reading newspapers, magazines and books were relatively

Table 8.9. Ranking of the top 15 leisure activities by gender, Hong Kong, 1994, 2000.

	Rank					
	Males		Females		Total	
Leisure activities	1994	2000	1994	2000	1994	2000
Watching TV	1	1	1	1	1	1
Reading newspapers/magazines	6	2	6	2	6	2
Eating out (dinner)	3	3	4	4	4	3
Shopping	5	5	2	3	2	4
Listen to radio/CDs/tapes	8	4	5	5	5	5
Reading books	14	6	11	6	13	6
Going to a tea house	9	7	8	7	9	7
Walking in the park	12	9	10	8	11	8
Surfing the web/Internet	*	8	*	10	*	9
Going to the public library	4	12	3	9	3	10
Playing electronic/computer games	2	10	12	12	7	11
Going to the cinema	7	11	7	11	8	12
Having a picnic/barbecue	10	13	8	13	10	13
Karaoke	13	14	9	15	12	14
Playground games	*	15	*	14	*	15
Playing cards/mah-jong	11	*	14	*	14	*
Household activities	15	*	13	*	15	*
Sample size	1165	414	1408	419	1912	833

* Activities were not included in the list.
Sources: Sivan and Robertson (1995); HKSDB 2000 Sports Participation Survey, summer quarter.

more popular in 2000 than in 1994. On the other hand, the results suggest that a number of activities involving the use of public facilities, such as public libraries and cinemas, have become relatively less popular. There is also a slight decrease in the ranking of shopping, but this activity still remains as one of the top five activities. Surfing the web and using the Internet emerges as a popular new activity. In contrast, the relative popularity of playing electronic/ computer games declined from 1994 to 2000. It may be that surfing the web has become more popular at the expense of computer games, and suggests that trade-offs are occurring in the time spent using these different electronic technologies in Hong Kong.

A closer examination of the ranking by gender reveals that the changing use of electronic technologies features more in males' than females' use of their leisure time. Reading magazines and books and listening to the radio/CDs/tapes also has become more popular for males, while going to the library has drop-

ped in ranking, from fourth in 1994 to twelfth in 2000. An increase in the popularity of reading magazines and books and a decrease in the use of the library is also a feature of the way females use their leisure time. However, comparing other activities shows fewer changes in females' than males' use of leisure time over this time period.

Table 8.10 shows the ranking of the top 15 leisure activities by age. For comparison, four age groups were established: adolescents (age 12–18), young adults (age 19–34), adults (age 35–54) and older adults (age 55 and over). The results reveal that watching TV tops the list of activities for all four age groups, both in 1994 and 2000. However, other activities are subject to varying degrees of change across the age groups. It is apparent that changes in the popularity of reading and library use described above are mostly a feature of changes in adolescents' and young adults' use of leisure time. Going to the cinema and picnicking and barbecues have also become less popular with this age group,

Table 8.10. Ranking of the top 15 leisure activities by age, Hong Kong, 1994, 2000.

	Rank							
	Adolescents		Young adults		Adults		Older adults	
	1994	2000	1994	2000	1994	2000	1994	2000
Watching TV	1	1	1	1	1	1	1	1
Reading newspapers/magazines	8	2	7	2	3	2	2	3
Eating out (dinner)	7	3	2	3	4	3	4	6
Shopping	2	4	3	4	2	4	6	5
Listen to radio/CDs/tapes	4	5	5	5	9	5	9	4
Reading books	11	6	13	6	14	6	9	8
Going to a tea house	13	7	10	7	5	7	3	7
Walking in the park	14	11	15	11	7	8	4	2
Surfing the web/Internet	*	8	*	8	*	10	*	13
Going to the public library	3	13	8	13	6	9	7	9
Playing electronic/computer games	5	9	14	9	15	13	11	14
Going to the cinema	6	10	4	10	11	14	9	12
Having a picnic/barbecue	9	14	9	14	10	12	8	11
Karaoke	10	12	6	12	13	15	10	15
Playground games	*	15	*	15	*	11	*	10
Playing cards/mah-jong	12	*	11	*	12	*	6	*
Household activities	15	*	12	*	8	*	5	*
Sample size	797	130	325	241	753	176	35	176

* Activities were not included in the list.
Sources: Sivan and Robertson (1995); HKSDB 2000 Sports Participation Survey, summer quarter.

while eating out and going to tea houses appear to have become more popular. Adults' and older adults' use of leisure time has been subject to fewer changes over this time period, although an interesting feature is the increase in listening to radio/CDs and tapes among adults and older adults, and a decrease in visiting tea houses. Walking in the park has also become more popular for older adults and this is a positive aspect, given growing concerns about the health risks associated with inactivity among ageing populations (Fiatarone, 1996; Talbot, 2001).

The data gathered from the two territory-wide surveys reveal an increase in use of mass media and communication technologies in leisure in Hong Kong. This increase is the result of the rapid uptake of new technologies and mass communication in the territory. Like other developed countries, Hong Kong has experienced a substantial increase in the range and availability of mass media and communication technologies in recent years and this is affecting people's leisure behaviour (Sivan, 2000b).

Market research indicates that people in Hong Kong are among the most eager to embrace these new technologies. Research by ACNielsen in October 2000 (ACNielsen, 2001) revealed that at that time Hong Kong was a world leader in Internet use. Out of 17 countries in Asia, the Americas and Europe, web surfers in Hong Kong spent more time on the Internet than surfers in any of the other countries (an average of 10 hours and 13 minutes a month, which was more than second-placed US surfers who averaged 10 hours and 4 minutes a month). People in Hong Kong also viewed the most pages per month and spent the longest time online (37 minutes and 49 seconds per session).

A recent report by the Telecom Association of Hong Kong (2001) also indicates that the growth of Internet traffic volume averaged 65% between 1997 and 2000. Recently, it was revealed that about 60% of adults have Internet access at home, which is a higher level of uptake than for anyone else in the Asian region (Bowman, 2001).

The number and variety of media channels offered to people as sources of entertainment and information also are increasing rapidly (Ng, 1996). Since the introduction of television in 1957, the number of technological options has grown and now includes wireless televi-sion, VCRs, laser discs and, most recently, inter-active television. The latter, introduced in 1998, offers on-demand services such as news, edu-cation, and videos, music, karaoke, horse racing, home shopping and home banking. Subscriptions to other services, allowing access to a multiplicity of different channels, has also been increasing rapidly (MDR Technology Limited, 1998). Today there are over 500,000 subscribers to pay TV services (Telecom Association of Hong Kong, 2001).

The development of advanced technology in Hong Kong may not be at the expense of more traditional leisure activities associated with Eastern cultures, as is nicely illustrated in the commentary of a media and entertainment manager at one of the consulting companies in Hong Kong. When describing the development of broadband technology, he saw the potential for broadband to give enough 'flexibility to play mah-jong with 10 close friends via computer' (Zajc, 2000, p. 29). The idea of 'virtual' mah-jong is an intriguing blend of the traditional Eastern pastime with high-tech.

Other reports highlight both positive and negative impacts of Internet use in Hong Kong. For example, ACNielsen's tracking of Internet use showed a strong interest among female web surfers aged 21 to 24 in educational and employment websites (Nairne, 2001a). Less positive is a media report by the same author of a survey by the company NetValue which found that Hong Kong's web surfers are among the most avid consumers of Internet pornog-raphy in Asia (Nairne, 2001b).

There is also concern in Hong Kong, as elsewhere in the developed world, that the increasing use of computers and mass media in leisure time is resulting in more sedentary lifestyles, with consequent increases in obesity and the risk of diseases associated with physi-cal inactivity. A recent study by Hui and Morrow (cited in Hui, 2001) found that three out of four Hong Kong adults were not suffi-ciently physically active to benefit their health. This figure puts Hong Kong on a par with the USA, placing it among the most inactive nations in the world. A study of Hong Kong's primary schoolchildren (Adab and Macfarlane, 1998) also suggests that children of this age may be among the most inactive in the world. In Hong Kong, confined living spaces and a lack of play areas and public parks close to people's homes contribute to low levels of home-based, physical activity in children (Johns and Ha, 1999).

At the other end of the spectrum, older adults in Hong Kong are one of the most active groups. This is mainly because of the popularity of morning exercise (such as tai chi), which is a traditional part of Asian cultures. It is common-place to see large numbers of adults exercising daily in parks and public places in Hong Kong. However, younger people seem less inclined to follow this tradition, raising the prospect of an increasingly sedentary population and long-term health costs for the government.

Another interesting trend revealed by the two territory-wide surveys, which can be attrib-uted to developments in technology and mass communication, is the decreasing use of public facilities, such as the public library and cinema, and increasing use of home-based facilities. This trend is evident both from the participation figures and people's preferences. Whereas the 1994 survey indicated that the activities people wanted to do most involved the use of public facilities, the activities favoured most in the 2000 survey were home-based ones. These results indicate a shift from a desire to engage in instrumental activities or those that have been classified under the category of 'serious leisure' (Stebbins, 1992) to a desire to partici-pate in activities which are expressive and casual. As noted by Ng (1996), such a trend can lead to a more individualistic pattern of leisure participation in society.

Interestingly, however, the social activities of eating out and going to tea houses, which are among the top leisure activities, retained their popularity and high participation rates. These activities are usually participated in with family and relatives, as found in the recent study on Hong Kong students (Sivan, 2000a), in which about half of the adolescents (44%) went to tea houses and the majority (67%) ate dinner out with their family members. The importance of the family in leisure decision making in Hong Kong was highlighted in the chapter in the first edition of this book. The results from recent sur-veys reported here suggest that, despite other changes in leisure participation, the family con-tinues to play a significant role in the leisure lives of people in Hong Kong.

However, while family-based leisure con-tinues to be important in Hong Kong, the grow-ing popularity of technology-based leisure suggests that more and more people are being drawn into solitary activities. More technology-based leisure also means that people's leisure lives will be shaped increasingly by outside influences. For Hong Kong, now that the terri-tory is once more part of mainland China, this begs the question of whether these influences will come predominantly from the West or the East.

References

ACNielsen (2001) Across the board, it's Hong Kong's world surfing crown. *Insights Asia Pacific* 94, January.

Adab, P. and Macfarlane, D.J. (1998) Exercise and health – new imperatives for public health policy in Hong Kong. *Hong Kong Medical Journal* 4, 389–393.

Bowman, J. (2001) Savvy Internet users prefer real things to online shopping. *South China Morning Post*, June 6, p. 3.

Fiatarone, M.A. (1996) Physical activity and func-tional independence in aging. *Research Quarterly for Exercise and Sport* 67(3), 70–80.

Forestier, K. (2000) Our spoilt children, with every-thing and nothing. *South China Morning Post*, 2 April, p. 3.

Hong Kong Baptist College (1970) *A Study of Leisure Activities of Youth Labourers in Hong Kong*. Department of Sociology and Social Work, HKBC, Hong Kong.

Hong Kong Council of Social Service (1965) *Chai Wan Social Needs Study*. HKCSS, Hong Kong.

Hong Kong Southern District Board Social Service Committee (1985) *Survey Report: How Youth Spend their Leisure Time*. Hong Kong Southern District Board, Hong Kong.

Hong Kong Sports Development Board (HKSDB) (2000) *Sports Participation Survey 2000*. HKSDB, Hong Kong.

Hui, S. (2001) *Health and Physical Activity in Hong Kong – a Review*. SDB Research Report, No. 4, March.

Johns, D.P. and Ha, A.S. (1999) Home and recess phys-ical activity of Hong Kong children. *Research Quarterly for Exercise and Sport* 70(3), 319–323.

Kowloon City District (1975) *A Study of Children and Youth*. KCD, Hong Kong.

MDR Technology Ltd (1998) *Subscription Television Survey 1998: Executive Summary*. MDR Technology Ltd, Hong Kong.

Nairne, D. (2001a) More young women surfing for jobs. *Technology Post*, 15 May.

Nairne, D. (2001b) Adult net sites a big turn-on. *South China Morning Post*, 6 February.

Ng, P.P. (1984) *Socio-demographic Patterns of Leisure Behaviour of Adolescents in Hong Kong.* Institute of Social Studies, Chinese University of Hong Kong, Shatin, Hong Kong.

Ng, P.P. (1996) Leisure and social change in Hong Kong. *Society and Leisure* 19(1), 91–115.

Ng, P.P. and Man, P.J. (1988) *Leisure Behaviour and Life Satisfaction of Youth in Eastern District, Hong Kong.* Institute of Social Studies, Chinese University of Hong Kong, Hong Kong.

Sivan, A. (2000a) Global influence and local uniqueness: the case of adolescent leisure in Hong Kong. *World Leisure* 42(4), 24–32.

Sivan, A. (2000b) Leisure in Hong Kong – perceptions and participation. *Journal of the Inter-national Council for Health, Physical Education, Recreation Sport and Dance* 36(4), 28–32.

Sivan, A. and Robertson, R.W. (1993) *The Use and Demand for Recreational and Sports Facilities and Services in Hong Kong: Phase One Report.* Report to the Hong Kong Sports Development Board, Hong Kong Polytechnic, Kowloon.

Sivan, A. and Robertson, R.W. (1995) *The Use and Demand for Recreational and Sports Facilities and Services in Hong Kong: Phase Two Report.* Report to the Hong Kong Sports Development Board, Hong Kong Polytechnic, Kowloon.

Sivan, A., Fung, A., Fung, L. and Ruskin, H. (1999) *A Study of the Physical and Psychological Dimensions of Leisure Among Hong Kong School Children.* Project supported by the Research Grants Council of Hong Kong, China (BU 2078/1997H).

Stebbins, R.A. (1992) *Amateurs, Professionals, and Serious Leisure.* McGill-Queen's University Press, Montreal, Quebec.

Talbot, L.A. (2001) Introduction: activity and aging. *Educational Gerontology* 27(3), 205–208.

Telecom Association of Hong Kong (2001) *2001 Official Guide to Telecommunication in Hong Kong.* Telecom Association of Hong Kong, Hong Kong.

Zajc, L. (2000) Bluetooth puts bite on promise. *South China Morning Post, Review 2000*, October 30, p. 29.

9 Israel

Hillel Ruskin and Atara Sivan

Introduction

This chapter considers two sources of data on leisure participation in Israel: surveys of adults (generally aged 18 and over) and surveys of children. Brief details of all the surveys discussed are presented Table 9.1.

National Leisure Participation Surveys in Israel

Survey characteristics

National leisure participation surveys in Israel have been conducted primarily by a group of researchers from the Israel Institute of Applied Social Research, led by Professor Elihu Katz. Katz and his colleagues conducted three major studies, in 1970, 1990 and 1998.

1970

The first study was conducted in 1970 (Katz and Gurevitch, 1976) and was based on nearly 4000 personal interviews with a representative sample of Jewish adults aged 18 years and over, selected at random from 56 different localities, which were themselves chosen from a stratified listing of all localities, ranging from the largest cities to the smallest villages, including different types of settlements. All cities with a population

of over 20,000 were represented in the study. Among the smaller localities, the researchers preferred to cluster more respondents in fewer settlements rather than fewer respondents in a greater number of settlements, so that the cultural life of these settlements could be represented accurately.

Three kinds of data were obtained from the study: the leisure behaviour of the population over the 24 h before the interview, including a time-budget; the attitudes of the population towards variables such as the adequacy of leisure time and of facilities available for leisure, or the relative preference for different leisure programmes; and the perceived functions of various leisure and cultural activities and institutions, ranging from the mass media to books on different subjects and traditional and secular holidays.

A pioneering aspect of this study, as compared with other studies of leisure conducted in Israel and elsewhere, was the attempt to integrate data on patterns of consumption of culture with data on the supply of cultural services. In analysing the data, the researchers chose to give primary emphasis to the variables that seemed most important to them: education and socio-economic status, age, ethnicity, city size, religiosity and gender. The object of the study was also to contribute towards policy making in the fields of leisure, culture and communication, and the study's findings did indeed have

Table 9.1. Summary of leisure surveys in Israel, 1970–2000.

Survey	Date	Sample size	Age range	Data	Reference
Adults					
Secularization of Leisure in Israel	1970	4000	18+	Time-use	Katz and Gurevitch (1976)
Culture of Leisure in Israel	1990	(1) 1442 (2) 2956 (3) 1197	18+	Time-use	Katz *et al.* (1992)
Leisure Culture in Israel	1998	1408	18+	Time-use	Haas (1999)
Young people					
Leisure and Youth	1984	384	Schoolchildren	Leisure	Sivan (1986)
Youth survey	1990/91	12,300	Schoolchildren	Leisure	Ministry of Education and Culture (1993)
Youth survey	2000	406	15–18	Leisure	This chapter

an effect on government policy-makers with regard to the provision of facilities and services and in the determination of priorities.

1990

A second national study was conducted in 1990 by the same group of researchers (Katz *et al.*, 1992). The study population had grown from 2.5 million in 1970 to 3.5 million in 1990; the mean level of education had risen from 8.8 to 11.6 years of study; and the percentage of people with a higher education (post high school) had doubled from 15% to 31%. During the period, the standard of living rose very significantly, and Israel became a typical Western-style consumer society. Time- and energy-saving devices resulted in increased free time. More discretionary income and more discretionary time affected lifestyles significantly. Television, which was introduced in 1969, exerted a major effect on patterns of leisure behaviour. Also, Israelis moved from a standard 5.5 to a 5-day working week. All of these factors, and the effects of three wars which were fought in the region between 1970 and 1990, affected patterns of leisure behaviour in Israel.

The 1990 study was conducted in three stages. In the first stage, 'cultural indicators' were determined for an annual ongoing survey of leisure behaviour. The survey investigated patterns of cultural consumption, factors affecting selection of culture, recreation and sports, factors reflecting participation in leisure

activities, attitudes towards the supply of cultural services in various localities and the effects of a shorter working week on leisure behaviour patterns. The sample for this stage included 1189 Jewish respondents in 35 localities and 253 Arab respondents in 25 localities. Data on the subjects were collected through interviews, while data on the supply of cultural services were gathered from advertisements in local newspapers.

In the second stage a comparative survey was conducted, in order to assess the change that had occurred since 1970 in patterns of leisure consumption, the content of leisure activities and values and attitudes related to cultural consumption. Data were gathered from a random, representative sample of 2956 Jewish respondents aged 18 and over. Data on the supply of cultural services were also collected through interviews.

In the third stage, a follow-up study was conducted to detect seasonal changes in cultural consumption, recreational habits and tourism behaviour in Israel and abroad. The representative sample included 1197 subjects aged 18 and over in 35 localities and the data were collected by means of interviews.

1998

A third national survey was conducted in 1998 (Haas, 1999). This study assessed patterns of leisure behaviour and aimed to assess the place and significance of Israeli cultural institutions and budgetary policy which the State should establish, and the existing and desirable attitudes towards Israel's culture. At the time of the study, Israel's population had grown to close to 6 million people.

The study sample included 1101 veteran Jewish adults aged 18 and above and new immigrants from the former USSR, who started to immigrate to Israel in large numbers (close to 1 million) from 1989. The two populations were combined into one sample, in which each of these groups was represented by its proportion in the general population. In addition, 307 subjects from the Arab population were sampled. Each sample was taken randomly from the telephone directory. Data were collected by telephone interview using a questionnaire with fixed range of responses. The questionnaire was translated into Hebrew, Russian and Arabic to be fully understood by each group of respondents.

Because of changes in survey design, it is not possible to compare the results of all three surveys directly, so the analysis below examines first the changes between 1970 and 1990 and then the changes between 1990 and 1998.

Changes in time-use, 1970–1990

In the 1970 and 1990 surveys, respondents were requested to reconstruct all of their activities in time units of 15 minutes over the 24 hours before interview. Table 9.2 indicates that in 1990 Israelis spent less time sleeping and resting than they had 20 years earlier. There was a decrease in the average amount of time devoted to paid work by those in employment, but a small increase overall, probably reflecting the growth of part-time work and the fact that many more women had entered the paid work force. There was a sharp decline in the amount of time devoted to housework, but there was no decrease in the amount of time spent caring for children. Total leisure time increased by 1 h/day as compared with 1970 and by 2 hours on Fridays, the first day of the Israeli weekend. This increase was mainly accounted for by television-watching, which, by 1990, occupied a third of all leisure time, some 2 h/day. There was a slight decrease in the amount of time spent reading newspapers, and a slight increase in

social activities. There was also a slight increase in the amount of time spent outside the home on Fridays and Saturdays, but in total, the frequency of going outside the house decreased slightly.

Table 9.3 shows that while in 1970 women in paid employment had the same amount of leisure time as men, by 1990 this had changed and working women had the least leisure time of the three employment status groups shown.

Changes in leisure activities, 1970–1990

Table 9.4 shows data on participation between 1970 and 1990. Because the data are based on time-budget data, participation refers to a 24-hour reference period. The table indicates that participation in arts activities, such as going to the movies, theatre, museums, classical music concerts, was either static or declining. At the same time, there was an increase in participation in many 'light' activities, such as social gatherings, going out to a pub or a restaurant, excursion trips in Israel and abroad, active sports, record playing and video-watching. Nevertheless, there also appeared to be a decline in participation in light entertainment, including listening to popular singers and sports spectating. Possible avenues of interpretation for these changes are associated with: (i) a general increase in hedonistic values; (ii) the search for less collective and more intimate ways of spending leisure time; (iii) the popularity of television and the slight increase in the tendency to remain at home; (iv) a search to replace television-viewing with more interactive activities; and (v) the increase in legitimacy of alternative ways of spending leisure time.

Changes in values

Along with the changes mentioned above, changes occurred in the values held by Israeli society, or more precisely, there were changes in the emphasis placed on certain areas, with direct implications for leisure. Some of the changes, which were observed when comparing the 1970 data with the 1990 data, are not presented in the tables but are discussed briefly below.

Table 9.2. Time devoted to primary activities by day of the week, Israel, 1970–1990.

| | Hours/day, adults 18 years and over | | | | | |
| | Weekday | | Friday | | Saturday | |
Activities	1970	1990	1970	1990	1970	1990
Gainful employment	4.3	4.5	3.6	2.4	0.5	0.9
Household care	2.3	1.3	2.7	2.1	1.1	0.9
Shopping	0.4	0.5	0.3	0.7	0.0	0.1
Childcare	0.5	0.7	0.6	0.7	0.6	0.5
Sleep	7.6	7.4	7.3	7.3	9.3	8.9
Rest	1.2	1.0	1.4	1.6	1.9	1.4
Eating	1.3	1.0	1.6	1.4	1.7	1.4
Personal care	0.8	0.8	1.0	0.9	0.8	0.7
Prayer	0.1	0.1	0.3	0.2	0.7	0.5
Studies	0.3	0.4	0.2	0.1	0.2	0.2
Leisure activities	4.1	5.0	4.1	6.2	6.6	7.9
Attending clubs, organizations	0.0	0.1	0.0	0.1	0.1	0.1
Reading newspapers/periodicals	0.4	0.3	0.6	0.4	0.5	0.4
Reading books	0.3	0.2	0.2	0.2	0.2	0.3
Radio	0.2	0.1	0.1	0.1	0.2	0.1
Television	0.9	1.7	0.9	2.3	0.8	2.0
Social life[a]	1.0	1.2	1.2	1.4	2.1	2.5
Conversation	0.2	0.2	0.2	0.2	0.4	0.2
Walks	0.2	0.3	0.2	0.4	0.5	0.5
Sports	0.0	0.1	0.1	0.1	0.1	0.2
Hobby, creative activity	0.1	0.2	0.0	0.1	0.1	0.1
Excursions, pleasure trips	0.6	0.4	0.4	0.6	1.3	1.1
Other non-home recreation[b]	0.2	0.2	0.2	0.3	0.3	0.4
Work trips	0.6	0.5	0.5	0.3	0.1	0.2
Other	0.5	0.8	0.4	0.1	0.5	0.4
Total	24.0	24.0	24.0	24.0	24.0	24.0
Unweighted sample size	1614	1021	320	168	267	257

[a] Includes visiting, hosting, parties, dances, games. [b] Includes movies, theatre, museums, exhibitions, concerts, light entertainment, coffee houses, night clubs, discotheques.
Source: Katz *et al.* (1992).

There appears to have been an increase in the importance of 'present-orientation', as compared with 'future-orientation'. In 1990, a higher percentage agreed with the statement: 'life is short and dangerous and one should think primarily about the present'.

There was an increase in the importance attributed to leisure time, as compared with work. In 1990, the majority of respondents (67%) attributed equal importance to leisure and work, compared with 48% in 1970. The feeling of a lack of time is felt primarily among the groups with higher education as well as among the younger age groups.

There was an increase in the value placed on the individual. An examination of the importance attributed to various needs indicated an increase in the importance attached to personal needs, both cognitive (such as 'receiving useful information on day-to-day matters', or 'the desire to study and enrich oneself') and affective (such as 'being entertained', or 'going out with friends'). On the other hand, there was a moderate decline in the importance placed on collective needs, such as 'to have faith in our leaders', or 'to feel that I am participating in actual events'. There appeared to be an increase in the importance of self-cultivation, along with a decrease in a collective orientation, which finds expression in decreased participation in public and civic activities. It should be noted, however, that the importance attributed to the

Table 9.3. Time devoted to primary activities, by gender and employment status, Israel 1970–1990.

Activity	Men employed full-time		Women employed full-time		Full-time home – childcare	
	1970	1990	1970	1990	1970	1990
Gainful employment	7.4	6.0	5.7	4.3	0.2	0.8
Household care	0.6	0.5	2.0	1.7	4.9	2.9
Shopping	0.1	0.3	0.3	0.5	0.8	0.8
Childcare	0.3	0.4	0.6	0.9	1.0	1.4
Sleep	7.2	7.1	7.4	7.4	8.0	8.1
Rest	0.9	0.9	0.9	1.0	1.5	1.4
Eating	1.4	1.0	1.1	1.0	1.5	1.4
Personal	0.9	0.8	0.9	0.8	0.8	0.7
Prayer	0.2	0.3	0.0	0.0	0.0	0.1
Studies	0.2	0.4	0.2	0.2	0.0	0.1
Leisure activities	4.0	5.1	4.0	4.6	4.4	5.2
Attend clubs, organizations	0.1	0.1	0.0	0.0	0.0	0.0
Read newspapers/periodicals	0.4	0.3	0.3	0.2	0.3	0.2
Read books	0.2	0.2	0.4	0.2	0.2	0.2
Radio	0.2	0.1	0.1	0.1	0.1	0.0
Television	1.0	1.9	0.8	1.5	1.1	2.0
Social life[a]	0.8	1.1	1.0	1.3	1.2	1.5
Conversation	0.2	0.2	0.1	0.2	0.2	0.2
Walks	0.1	0.2	0.1	0.2	0.2	0.6
Sports	0.0	0.1	0.1	0.1	0.0	0.0
Hobby, creative activity	0.0	0.1	0.1	0.1	0.2	0.1
Excursions, pleasure trips	0.4	0.6	0.5	0.5	0.8	0.3
Other non-home recreation[b]	0.2	0.2	0.3	0.2	0.1	0.1
Work trips	0.9	0.7	0.9	0.5	0.1	0.1
Other	0.3	0.5	0.2	1.1	0.8	1.0
Total	24.0	24.0	24.0	24.0	24.0	24.0
Unweighted sample size	647	248	215	252	359	119

[a] Includes visiting, hosting, parties, dances, games. [b] Includes movies, theatre, museums, exhibitions, concerts, light entertainment, coffee houses, night clubs, discotheques.
Source: Katz *et al.* (1992).

collective is still high, and the need 'to feel proud that we have a State' still received a high rating, even though the proportion attributing importance is decreased slightly.

As with the civic/collective orientation, there was a certain decrease in the importance attributed to religious tradition. A comparison of 1970 and 1990 attitudes of the public to the character of the Sabbath indicates an increasingly secular approach. Nevertheless, Israeli society continues to cling to a traditional lifestyle; the importance of family relationships is rated in first place, corresponding to the importance of taking pride in the State. A high percentage of the population observe traditional ceremonies and customs, such as lighting the Sabbath candles or holding a festive meal on the Sabbath eve, even though a considerable proportion of these view themselves as secular and do not define these customs as religious.

Changes 1990–1998

Table 9.5 presents the major findings of the 1998 study in comparison to the 1990 study. The leisure activities in which there were significant increases in participation were visits

Table 9.4. Participation in leisure activities, Israel, 1970 and 1990.

Activity	% of persons aged 18+ participating in 24 hours			Rank		
	1970	1990	Difference	1970	1990	Difference
Radio	98	96	−2	1	1	0
Television	91	94	+3	2	2	0
Social meetings	89	94	+5	3	3	0
Newspapers	86	90	+4	4	4	0
Excursions, trips in Israel	80	88	+8	5	5	0
Cinema	79	61	−18	6	11	−5
Book reading	78	77	−1	7	7	0
Prayer	74	64	−10	8	9	−1
Gambling, lottery	65	56	−9	9	13	−4
Theatre	64	49	−15	10	14	−4
Museums, exhibitions	63	63	0	11	10	+1
Hobbies	60	74	+14	12	8	+4
Lectures	56	40	−16	13	19	−6
Periodicals	53	45	−8	14	16	−2
Records	50	88	+38	15	6	+9
Singers, bands	50	49	−1	16	15	+1
Spectator sports	31	19	−12	17	22	−5
Clubs, organizations	30	18	−12	18	23	−5
Studies	28	33	+5	19	20	−1
Sports (active)	26	45	+19	20	17	+3
Pubs, night clubs	23	42	+19	21	18	+3
Trips, tourism abroad	23	57	+34	22	12	+10
Reading imported newspapers, journals	21	16	−5	23	24	−1
Concerts	19	19	0	24	21	+3

Source: Katz *et al.* (1992).

abroad, reading books, engaging in learning and studies, and visits to classical music concerts and entertainment events. Significant decreases were found in visits to museums and engagement in hobbies. Participation in several leisure activities was identified for the first time in 1998, such as: visits to shopping malls and coffee houses, Internet surfing (50% have a personal computer at home), engaging in voluntary and public activity, visiting religious sites, engaging in painting or other art activities, playing a musical instrument and visiting an operatic performance or ethnic music concert.

Overall, the activities that continued to be most popular were informal and interactive, and no significant change was noted in participation in these activities since 1990. In 1998, it seems that the decrease in participation in 'high culture' activities, such as visits to theatres, classical music concerts, reading books and studying, had stopped. Half of the population (50%) participated in at least two, and 28% in at least three, out of seven such activities.

Other findings pointed to the following.

- There has been an increase in preference for Western culture (from 69% in 1990 to 73% in 1998) and a decrease in preference for Middle-Eastern culture (from 24% to 11%), associated with an increase in the educational level of people.
- About 70% of the respondents were satisfied with the way they spent their leisure time.
- Over 50% of the respondents attributed equal significance to leisure and work.
- Only 14% of the respondents thought that leisure was the main component of life.
- The Arab population preferred a Middle-Eastern leisure culture (48%); and more

Table 9.5. Leisure participation, 1990 and 1998, Israel.

Activity	% participation in the last year		
	1990*	1998**	Difference
Cultural			
Cinema	49	41	−8
Theatre	33	41	+8
Museums	46	39	−7
Opera	−	5	−
Classic music concerts	19	25	+6
Ethnic music concerts	−	5	−
Popular culture/entertainment			
Sport spectating	19	21	+2
Pop singers and bands	38	40	+2
Entertainment events	34	42	+8
Interactive activities			
Singing and dancing events	24	22	−2
Meetings with friends	88	89	+1
Meetings with family members	−	92	−
Voluntary and public activity	−	28	−
Pubs and night clubs	33	34	+1
Excursions and trips	77	74	−3
Visits abroad[a]	−	26	−
Vacation outside home	58	56	−2
Shopping mall visits	−	59	+3
Dining out	56	56	−
Coffee house	−	85	−
Religious site visits	−	28	−
Other activities			
Book reading	77	85	+8
Play musical instrument	−	15	−
Studying	33	39	+6
Hobbies	74	60	−14
Newspaper reading	90	90	−
Internet surfing	−	18	−
Art involvement	−	23	−
Sports (active)	45	42	−3
Television	95	94	−1

[a] At least once in a lifetime. − This category was not included in the 1990 study.
Source: * Katz *et al.* (1992); ** Haas (1999).

than half (59%) of this population felt that they were, to a large extent, part of an 'Arab Nation' (59%), or 'Palestinians' (85%), rather than 'Israeli'.

Government Policy Issues

The driving force behind the 1970 leisure study was the Ministry of Education. A dialogue between researchers and policy-makers followed the presentation of its results. Two parliamentary committees (Labour, and Education and Culture) devoted several sessions to close inspection of the results, which led to policy-making in the area of a shorter working week and a policy on culture and the arts. The National Council for Culture and the Arts and other national associations, in particular areas such as adult education and sports, also examined the results. The specific issues raised by the different policy-makers included the following:

- whether there is room or need for an explicit cultural policy in a democratic society;
- how a small nation such as Israel should address the issue of shaping a national identity and blending disparate ethnic cultures into a national culture;
- how Israel should cope with the blending of old and new, religious tradition and secular modernization;
- whether the mass media can avoid coming under the overwhelming influence of the international free flow of information, which inevitably gives an advantage to the politically and culturally strong nations;
- whether Israel should become a society of European culture, arts and values, or a blend of many cultures;
- what the population should do with the increase in leisure time;
- what cultural opportunities should be offered with the increased free time and what strategies should be used for leisure education within the school and community systems;
- how cultural policy-makers might help the present less well-educated generation to overcome constraints of age; and
- how equal opportunities might be guaranteed in the provision and consumption of leisure, in educating towards it, and in the democratization of the arts and access to them.

An effort to formulate leisure policies for Israel was made in 1979, when a group of theorists, practitioners and policy-makers participated in an international seminar organized by the Israel Leisure and Recreation Association. The seminar's proceedings (Ruskin, 1984) proposed a platform of recommendations for leisure policies, based primarily on the data described above. Since then, many of the recommendations have been implemented through a long series of workshops with government practitioners, through numerous publications and through an extensive use of the media.

During the 1990s, several actions took place on a national level to implement leisure policies.

1. The Ministry of Education and Culture appointed a National Curriculum Development Commission for Leisure Education, which resulted in the publication of a comprehensive curriculum. This includes content and strategies for the education system from kindergarten to twelfth grade (Ruskin, 1995). The curriculum aims at all formal education disciplines as well as informal activities inside and outside the school, and is intended to develop in pupils the skills, knowledge, attitudes and values to be wise consumers of leisure time, and have carry-over value for their future as adults. After the publication of this important document, the Ministry appointed a Commissioner of Leisure Education in the school system, whose role is to inculcate the curriculum into the system.[1] As a result, many actions are being implemented in the development of school–community models and training of human resources (Ruskin and Spector, 2000).

2. Another significant development occurred with the development of leisure management administration within the Israel Association of Community Centres, a governmental company, which coordinates the functions of about 200 community centres in Israel. These are comprehensive institutions, which serve many needs of the community, including recreational ones. This led to the establishment of leisure policies, which follow an updated rationale of the 1979 formulated leisure policies for Israel, as mentioned above.

3. All these brought about a significant development in the training of human resources in institutions of higher learning and educational centres in areas such as leisure education consultants, community leisure leaders, leisure specialists for populations with special needs, such as handicapped youth, adults and senior adults. The whole area of leisure has gained popularity, both with the general public (the consumers) and with the professional and service community (the providers).

Young People and Leisure

In addition to the national leisure surveys, which explore the leisure patterns of the whole population, attention has been given to investigating the particular leisure behaviour and preferences of different age groups, in particular young people. Such investigations shed more light on the ways particular age groups spend their leisure, and their attitudes towards leisure activities. These studies on the leisure of youth and children in Israel are described below.

In 1984 a study was carried out to explore the ways youth in Israel spend their leisure time, their attitudes towards leisure activities and their preferences (Sivan, 1984). In order to obtain a comprehensive picture of the leisure activities, attitudes and preferences of youth, the research was based on samples of students representing the four main educational frameworks in Israel: religious and non-religious schools in the kibbutz (collective village) and religious and non-religious schools in the city. Data were collected using a questionnaire, which was submitted to 384 students of junior classes in eight schools selected randomly from a list of secondary schools supplied by the Ministry of Education. The questionnaire included a list of activities which were divided into groups, based on theoretical background and on preliminary interviews conducted with young people to elicit information on additional leisure activities engaged in by youth in Israel. The groups comprised instrumental, expressive, religious (performed alone and in group), and voluntary activities.

Results showed a strong tendency to prefer and to participate in expressive leisure activities such as watching television, listening to pop music, meeting with friends, participating in parties and travelling. The average frequency of participation in these activities was between one and three times a week. The frequency of such activities was much higher than the frequency of instrumental activities, such as taking study courses or doing voluntary work, which were performed by young people only once or twice a month. Examination of the results revealed a significant difference between youth from different educational backgrounds. There was a strong tendency among youngsters from the kibbutz to participate in social leisure activities and for youngsters from religious schools to participate more in religious activities (Sivan, 1986). Both the kibbutz and the religious environments seemed to influence the level of

participation in voluntary activities. The community life of the kibbutz, which is a unique way of life in Israel, was found to be an influential factor in the way youth spend their leisure time.

Extracurricular activities of high school students

Another survey was carried out by the Central Bureau of Statistics during the 1990/91 school year. The survey was on extracurricular activities of ninth to twelfth grade students in the Hebrew and the Arab education sectors (Ministry of Education and Culture, 1993). It was based on a sample of classes which were studied as a whole for the first time. The sample of 12,300 respondents was drawn up in two stages: in the first stage a representative sample of schools was selected according to various characteristics of the institution. In the second stage, a representative sample of classes was selected in which each of the grades participating was represented. The survey was carried out within classes, where each student was required to fill out a questionnaire.

The questionnaire included questions on activities such as activities at home, away from home and after-school activities, activity in youth movements, activity in community centres and voluntary activities. In addition the questionnaire included demographic data and a series of hypothetical questions on preferred Friday morning (weekend) activities, assuming no school studies on Friday.

Results, as indicated in Table 9.6, showed that, in both Hebrew and Arab sectors, watching TV was the most popular home activity. Watching video films was also popular among both sectors. About one-third used personal computers at least once a week and the main use was for playing games. The majority of both sectors read at least one newspaper a week and at least one book a month.

Going to the cinema was the most popular 'away from home' activity among the Hebrew sector, and attending sports competitions was the most popular among the Arab sector. Sports activities were the most popular after-school activities in both sectors. More than one-third of the students in both sectors participated in

Table 9.6. Children's participation in selected extracurricular activities, Israel, 1991.

Activity	Jewish pupils (%)	Arab pupils (%)	All pupils (%)
Leisure activity at home – weekday			
Radio	73	69	72
Records, CD, tapes	85	78	84
TV	87	85	86
Video	46	33	44
Daily newspapers	63	58	62
At least once in a month:			
Reading one periodical	73	70	72
Reading one book	58	74	61
Using a personal computer	49	39	46
Leisure activities away from home – once a month			
Theatre	21	–	–
Concert	7	–	–
Entertainment event	49	–	–
Cinema	68	26	61
Museum	24	–	–
Sporting events	31	52	35
Dining out/coffee house	82	60	79
Pub	49	19	44
Discotheque	43	15	39
Games hall	43	34	41
Art, crafts, clubs – in last month			
Drama, dance, music	21	14	20
Painting, sculpture, photography	6	13	7
Handicrafts	6	15	8
Science, technology, computer	9	17	10
Sport activity	38	44	37
Nature and geography	7	23	10
Other theory clubs (art, culture philosophy, religion)	5	9	6
Languages	4	8	5
Social activities – in last month			
Youth club	23	25	24
Community centre	21	25	21
Voluntary activity – school requirement	27	26	27
Voluntary activity – non-school requirement	22	29	23
Summer camps	31	41	33

Source: Katz *et al.* (1992).

youth movements in the course of a year. About one-third participated in voluntary activities and more than one-third participated in summer camps.

In both sectors there were differences in participation rate for activities between males and females. Males watched TV and videos and played with computers to a higher extent than females, whereas females were involved more in reading books and magazines. Overall, in the Arab sector males participated more in 'away from home' social activities, whereas in the Hebrew sector there were differences in the participation rates in different activities. There were more differences in participation rates in activities between different age groups in the Hebrew sector than in the Arab sector.

Patterns of youth and youth leisure activity during summer vacation

In 2000, a survey was conducted by the Geocartography Institute on patterns of reading

Table 9.7. Activities of youths aged 15–18 during summer vacation, Israel, 2000.

Activity	% participating at least once
Television and cinema	31
Meetings with friends	31
Summer work	25
Sporting activity	24
Pubs and discotheques	14
Computer games	11
Internet surfing	7
Reading books	6

Time-budget	Hours:min
Sleep	9:22
Meeting with friends	4:16
Watching TV	3:00
Using computers	1:45
Telephone conversations	1:52
Meals	1:41
Sport activity	1:17
Reading books	0:47

Source: Degani and Degani (2000).

books during the summer vacation among 406 15–18-year-olds, through telephone interviews. As shown in Table 9.7, 54% did not read books at all during their summer vacation; 30% read one or two books, 13% three or four, and 10% read five or more. The average number of books read during the time was 1.7. However, girls and new immigrants read more than the boys (only 41% of the girls and 33% of the new immigrants did not read at all).

Conclusions

The above surveys indicate an increasing Westernization of leisure patterns in Israel over a period of some 30 years, with a trend away from traditional and high culture activities towards popular culture. Of particular interest is the influence of leisure participation studies on public policy, facilitated partly by the relatively small population.

Note

[1] This role was assumed by the late Hillel Ruskin, one of the authors of this chapter.

Bibliography

Degani, A. and Degani, R. (2000) Survey of book reading among youth during summer vacation. *Yediot Aharonot* (daily newspaper), 1 September, p. 26 [in Hebrew].

Haas, H. (1999) Leisure culture in Israel, 1998. *PANIM: a Journal for Culture, Society and Education* 10, 107–139 [in Hebrew].

Katz, E. (1984) Problems of leisure and culture in a new nation: the Israeli experience. In: Ruskin, H. (ed.) *Leisure: Towards a Theory and Policy*. Farleigh Dickenson University Press, Teaneck, New Jersey, pp. 31–41.

Katz, E. and Gurevitch, M. (1976) *The Securalization of Leisure in Israel*. Faber and Faber, London.

Katz, E., Haas, H., Weitz, S., Adoni, H., Gurevittch, M., Schiff, M. and Goldberg-Anabi, D. (1992) *The Culture of Leisure in Israel: Changes in Patterns of Cultural Activity. 1970–1999*. Israel Institute of Applied Social Research, Open University of Israel, Jerusalem [in Hebrew].

Ministry of Education and Culture, Division for Social and Youth Education (1993) Extracurricular activities of 9th–12th grade pupils. In: *Hebrew and Arab Education 1990/91. Special Series No. 946*. Central Bureau of Statistics, Jerusalem [in Hebrew].

Ruskin, H. (ed.) (1984) *Leisure: Toward a Theory and Policy*. Fairleigh Dickenson University Press, Teaneck, New Jersey.

Ruskin, H. (ed.) (1995) *Leisure Culture Education: Comprehensive Curricula K to 12th Grades in the School System*. Ministry of Education, Culture and Sport, Jerusalem [in Hebrew].

Ruskin, H. and Spector, C. (2000) Implementation of serious leisure as part of leisure education in Israel. *European Leisure and Recreation Association Newsletter*, 1–3 June.

Sivan, A. (1984) *Leisure of High-School Youth in the Israeli Kibbutz and City*. Bar Ilan University, Ramat Gan [in Hebrew].

Sivan, A. (1986) *Influences of Beliefs and Values on Leisure of Youth*. Multi-Purpose Instructional Center, Haifa.

10   Japan[1]

Munehiko Harada

Growth and Stagnation

In the latter half of the 1970s and 1980s, high growth in the leisure market in Japan was stimulated by rapid development in the economy at large. The value of the leisure market of Japan approximately doubled between 1982 and 1992, in the period that has been referred to as the 'years of exponential growth' (Harada, 1994), meaning that the economic growth rate in a given year exceeded the preceding year's growth rate, which in turn accelerated the increase in the scale of the market. This period of growing prosperity was characterized by a substantial change in Japanese behaviour, in the form of a shift toward a more leisure-orientated lifestyle.

With the increased awareness of leisure lifestyles, the leisure market experienced changes not only in size but also in substance. The 1983 *Public Census on Lifestyles* (Prime Minister's Office, 1983) recorded for the first time that the Japanese people considered 'leisure' to be the most important aspect of daily life, while 'eating habits' and 'living habits' decreased in importance compared to previous years' polls. The proportion of respondents reporting 'leisure' in the highest importance category continued to increase into the 1990s.

With the 21st century drawing near, the government began the task, in line with public demands, of creating a leisure-orientated envi-ronment and providing more opportunities for leisure enjoyment. In the latter half of the 1980s, the issue of shortening working hours was placed on the national policy agenda, with a view to improving the working conditions of the Japanese worker. Demand for shortened working hours increased. The results came in 1992, when general annual labour time was officially reduced to 1972 hours, falling below 2000 hours for the first time. The Resorts Act was passed, which relaxed environmental regulations and provided structures for subsidy and tax breaks to promote leisure-orientated development in the private sector. This set the stage for Japan's first ever resort boom. The result of these developments was a significant increase in consumer spending, including expenditure on, and participation in, leisure.

By the early 1990s, however, the 'bubble economy' had given way to a period characterized by relative economic stagnation, with little or no growth in incomes and a reconsideration of attitudes towards wealth and lifestyles (Harada, 1998). In this chapter, data are presented which contrast the experience of leisure in Japan in these two periods.

Studying Leisure

As public interest in recreational activities grew, government organizations began to study the issue of leisure. Surveys were mounted, including the 1986 *Work and Leisure in the 1980s* survey, conducted by the Economic Planning Agency (1986a,b), and the 1991 *Public Opinion Poll on Leisure and Travel* and *Public Opinion Poll on Working Hours and the 2-Day Weekend*, conducted by the Prime Minister's Office (1991a,b). These were, however, dependent on partial polling at best, since samples were drawn from limited areas and organizations, such as businesses; they were not nationwide and did not involve any follow-up research. In 1993, a non-profit organization, the Sasagawa Sports Foundation, surveyed some 2000 persons aged 15 and over across the nation, but interviewed only those persons actively participating in sport, so failed to represent the leisure situation of the Japanese population as a whole (Sasagawa Sports Foundation, 1993).

Nationwide Study on Recreational Activities

The *Study on Recreational Activities* is a regular nationwide study on leisure in Japan, begun in 1977 by the Leisure Development Centre, an agency of the Ministry of International Trade and Industry. Using data drawn from the study, this organization publishes an annual *White Paper*, which reports on the leisure and recreational activities of the Japanese people and trends in leisure-related industries.

The study polls 4000 men and women aged 15 and over from across the nation. Initially the survey involved a sample of 3000 from urban areas only, but from 1987, each year some 3000 persons have been sampled randomly from urban areas with a population of 50,000 and over, and 1000 persons from urban and rural areas with populations of less than 50,000. The most recent poll, conducted in 2003, involved a sample of 3200 persons, 2400 of them in urban areas. The survey response rate has exceeded 80% each year, suggesting that the survey provides a fair representation of Japanese public opinion.

The survey categorizes 91 activities into four groups: (i) sports (29 activities); (ii) hobbies and entertainment (30 activities); (iii) games and amusements (21 activities); and (iv) travel

and outings (11 activities). The published results indicate levels of participation and expenditure, frequency of participation and desired activities. Some of the key data generated are:

- *percentage participation*: percentage of respondents taking part in each activity one or more times in a year;
- *frequency*: average number of times participants take part in each activity in a year;
- *expenditure*: average amount of money per capita spent in taking part in each activity in a year;
- *desired participation*: percentage of respondents wishing to take part in, or wishing to continue participating in, each activity.

Trends in Leisure Participation in the 1980s and 1990s

Table 10.1 shows participation rates and frequency of participation for the 91 activities, in 1982, 1992 and 2003. Activities are arranged in groups, in order of their 2003 popularity. Only the urban sample is included, to facilitate comparison over the two decades. Changes for 1982–1992 (referred to below as the 1980s) and for 1992–2003 (referred to as the 1990s) are shown, and those differences which are statistically significant, at least at the 5% level, are starred. It should be borne in mind that many of the differences for low-participant activities are not statistically significant.

Each activity has a different 'story' to tell. Some grew in popularity in the 1980s and declined in the 1990s, while others did the opposite. Some grew throughout the two decades, while others declined throughout. Still others showed no significant change over the whole period. These patterns are further complicated by varying changes in frequency of participation. The frequency data are not referred to in the discussion below, but are included in the table for reference purposes.

The contrast in economic conditions in Japan in the 1980s and 1990s might be expected to be reflected in trends in leisure

Table 10.1. Leisure activity participation and frequency, urban areas, Japan, 1982, 1992, 2003.

Sports	% participating at least once in year, persons aged 15+						Average annual frequency (times per annum)				
	1982	1992	2003	Change 1982–1992	Change 1992–2003		1982	1992	2003	Change 1982–1992	Change 1992–2003
Sports											
Exercise	42.2	29.5	31.6	−12.7*	2.1	>	60.4	55.6	55.5	−4.8	−0.1
Bowling	29.4	36.0	30.3	6.6*	−5.7*	○	6.4	6.5	5.2	0.1	−1.3
Jogging/marathons	28.5	23.6	25.4	−4.9*	1.8	>	39.7	38.0	39.4	−1.7	1.4
Swimming	23.2	25.5	19.9	2.3	−5.6*	○	10.4	13.6	19.3	3.2	5.7
Catch/baseball	25.5	20.2	16.0	−5.3*	−4.2*	▶	22.4	16.9	15.3	−5.5	−1.6
Fishing	18.2	17.0	15.3	−1.2	−1.7	▶	11.1	9.1	9.3	−2.0	0.2
Physical training	12.1	12.1	13.3	0.0	1.2	>	47.4	45.4	51.6	−2.0	6.2
Cycling	14.2	15.1	12.3	0.9	−2.8*	○	27.0	26.8	27.1	−0.2	0.3
Table tennis	18.9	13.6	10.9	−5.3*	−2.7*	▶	16.3	14.1	11.7	−2.2	−2.4
Golfing practice	–	18.8	10.6	–	−8.2*	–	–	18.5	18.8	–	0.3
Badminton	20.0	14.7	10.4	−5.3*	−4.3*	▶	15.0	11.8	13.2	−3.2	1.4
Skiing	11.3	17.9	10.0	6.6*	−7.9*	○	5.7	5.5	3.9	−0.2	−1.6
Golf	12.3	14.3	9.5	2.0	−4.8*	○	16.8	11.7	11.9	−5.1	0.2
Tennis	15.2	13.4	8.3	−1.8	−5.1*	▶	24.1	19.6	25.0	−4.5	5.4
Soccer	4.2	6.8	7.8	2.6*	1.0	◀	20.2	20.6	18.5	0.4	−2.1
Volleyball	14.4	11.7	7.3	−2.7	−4.4*	▶	20.5	18.7	24.6	−1.8	5.9
Softball	18.3	13.9	6.5	−4.4*	−7.4*	▶	12.6	10.4	12.7	−2.2	2.3
Aerobics/jazz dancing	4.2	4.9	5.4	0.7	0.5	◀	30.7	26.0	34.4	−4.7	8.4
Snowboarding	–	–	4.9	–	–	–	–	–	4.6	–	–
Basketball	7.6	6.9	4.2	−0.7	−2.7*	▶	22.6	26.2	18.6	3.6	−7.6
Ice skating	8.6	7.9	2.7	−0.7	−5.2*	▶	3.5	3.6	–	0.1	–
Field athletics	10.5	6.5	3.2	−4.0*	−3.3*	▶	2.7	3.3	4.2	0.6	0.9
Japanese martial arts	3.9	3.3	2.0	−0.6	−1.3*	▶	34.6	42.0	–	7.4	–
Gateball/croquet	2.4	1.4	1.3	−1.0	−0.1	▶	32.2	36.0	–	3.8	–
Skin/scuba diving	–	1.0	1.2	–	0.2	◀	–	5.8	–	–	–
Surfing/windsurfing	–	0.7	1.2	–	0.5	◀	–	10.4	–	–	–
Yachting, motorboating	–	1.4	0.7	–	−0.7	–	–	4.6	–	–	–
Riding	0.5	0.6	0.4	0.1	−0.2	○	22.0	6.5	–	−15.5	–
Hang-/para-gliding	–	0.3	0.2	–	−0.1	–	–	24.1	–	–	–

Continued

Table 10.1. *Continued*

	% participating at least once in year, persons aged 15+						Average annual frequency (times pa)				
	1982	1992	2003	Change 1982–1992	Change 1992–2003		1982	1992	2003	Change 1982–1992	Change 1992–2003
Hobbies/entertainment											
Writing (novels, poems, etc.)	8.7	6.5	3.8	−2.2	−2.7*	▶	20.6	18.9	19.9	−1.7	1.0
Photography	12.9	9.5	10.5	−3.4*	1.0	>	11.5	12.4	15.5	0.9	3.1
Making/editing video tapes	4.1	6.8	4.9	2.7*	−1.9*	○	–	11.9	16.7	–	4.8
Watching video tapes	–	43.5	43.8	–	0.3	–	9.5	22.0	22.4	12.5	0.4
Choral singing	5.0	2.8	3.3	−2.2*	0.5	>	18.3	29.3	23.6	11.0	−5.7
Playing Western music	9.0	7.7	6.4	−1.3	−1.3	▶	54.0	51.4	46.7	−2.6	−4.7
Japanese traditional music	6.3	3.2	2.2	−3.1*	−1.0	▶	44.6	45.5	–	0.9	–
Drawing/painting/sculpting	9.1	7.8	6.2	−1.3	−1.6	▶	21.8	19.3	28.1	−2.5	8.8
Ceramics	2.0	2.2	2.7	0.2	0.5	▶	8.6	17.5	–	8.9	–
Handicrafts	6.3	4.7	4.4	−1.6	−0.3	▶	15.6	22.8	14.8	7.2	−8.0
Model-building	6.8	4.5	3.0	−2.3*	−1.5*	▶	9.0	11.5	12.9	2.5	1.4
Do-it-yourself	17.1	12.0	12.0	−5.1*	0.0	▶	12.2	11.4	10.8	−0.8	−0.6
Gardening/horticulture	38.1	31.6	34.7	−6.5*	3.1	>	44.4	39.3	37.8	−5.1	−1.5
Knitting/weaving	28.7	17.4	13.5	−11.3*	−3.9*	▶	29.1	27.1	24.3	−2.0	−2.8
Sewing	21.9	12.8	8.6	−9.1*	−4.2*	▶	32.3	28.8	21.9	−3.5	−6.9
Cooking (except regular meals)	15.0	11.8	8.8	−3.2*	−3.0*	▶	20.4	15.0	20.1	−5.4	5.1
Going to athletic/sports events	20.0	22.0	18.6	2.0	−3.4*	○	6.6	5.6	5.5	−1.0	−0.1
Going to movies	34.5	31.1	37.3	−3.4	6.2*	>	5.5	5.2	5.1	−0.3	−0.1
Going to theatre	14.2	14.1	11.8	−0.1	−2.3	▶	4.0	3.7	3.7	−0.3	0.0
Going to artistic performances	6.8	5.2	5.1	−1.6	−0.1	▶	4.0	3.2	2.9	−0.8	−0.3
Going to concerts	19.9	22.9	23.6	3.0	0.7	▶	5.0	4.3	3.6	−0.7	−0.7
Listening to music	35.0	42.0	40.6	7.0*	−1.4	○	72.1	69.6	69.9	−2.5	0.3
Going to art exhibitions	13.7	16.8	14.6	3.1	−2.2	○	7.0	5.8	5.0	−1.2	−0.8
Calligraphy	7.1	7.3	4.2	0.2	−3.1*	○	36.9	33.6	30.9	−3.3	−2.7
Tea ceremony	5.5	4.3	2.5	−1.2	−1.8*	▶	28.2	22.5	–	−5.7	–
Flower arranging	8.1	6.8	3.4	−1.3	−3.4*	▶	31.5	30.3	23.5	−1.2	−6.8
Traditional Japanese dance	2.2	1.4	1.2	−0.8	−0.2	▶	42.4	38.0	–	−4.4	–

Western dance (e.g. ballroom)	3.6	1.9	2.1	-1.7	0.2	v	21.7	29.9	-	8.2	-
Personal computer networking	-	1.7	38.7	-	37.0*		-	46.0	75.3	-	29.3
Non-work study and research	12.9	14.2	15.3	1.3	1.1		39.4	39.9	51.2	0.5	11.3
Games and amusements											
Go	12.3	4.9	4.4	-7.4*	-0.5	◄	22.5	28.4	21.9	5.9	-6.5
Shogi	24.7	12.0	8.3	-12.7*	-3.7*	◄	19.4	15.6	13.6	-3.8	-2.0
Board and card games	50.9	36.5	28.3	-14.4*	-8.2*	►	13.5	12.5	10.6	-1.0	-1.9
Karaoke	30.1	51.5	45.2	21.4*	-6.3*	►	14.8	11.4	9.7	-3.4	-1.7
Video games	27.1	27.1	28.2	0.0	1.1	►	20.4	38.6	44.6	18.2	6.0
Video arcade games	22.0	22.7	22.4	0.7	-0.3	○	14.9	13.8	12.0	-1.1	-1.8
Mah-jong	23.3	13.3	9.7	-10.0*	-3.6*	►	20.8	13.2	10.6	-7.6	-2.6
Billiards	4.9	6.8	6.3	1.9	-0.5	○	6.8	6.0	7.8	-0.8	1.8
Pachinko	34.0	27.7	19.8	-6.3*	-7.9*	►	20.5	25.7	25.5	5.2	-0.2
Lotteries	-	38.0	41.1	-	3.1	-	-	5.4	8.1	-	2.7
Lotteries (soccer)	-	-	4.9	-	4.9	○	-	-	10.2	-	-
Horse races (JRA)	8.8	11.5	8.6	2.7*	-2.9*	○	13.6	13.4	17.3	-0.2	3.9
Horse races (NAR)	-	3.2	1.4	-	-1.8*	-	-	12.1	-	-	-
Bicycle races (spectator)	2.1	1.5	1.2	-0.6	-0.3	►	11.1	7.5	-	-3.6	-
Boat races (spectator)	2.4	1.7	1.0	-0.7	-0.7	►	11.8	21.7	-	9.9	-
Auto races (spectator)	0.8	0.4	0.3	-0.4	-0.1	►	7.8	20.8	-	13.0	-
Eating out (not regular meals)	61.1	68.8	70.8	7.7*	2.0	◄	18.8	17.4	17.5	-1.4	0.1
Visit bars/pubs	42.4	44.1	34.6	1.7	-9.5*	○	18.0	16.6	14.9	-1.4	-1.7
Club or cabaret	10.6	5.6	2.6	-5.0*	-3.0*	►	11.2	7.7	-	-3.5	-
Discotheque	7.5	3.6	0.4	-3.9*	-3.2*	►	8.1	8.9	-	0.8	-
Public sauna	8.8	10.9	8.5	2.1	-2.4*	○	10.4	13.6	11.8	3.2	-1.8
Travel and tourism											
Amusement parks	37.6	39.9	32.4	2.3	-7.5*	○	4.1	3.6	3.2	-0.5	-0.4
Going for drives	52.3	56.3	54.3	4.0*	-2.0	○	10.6	12.5	12.5	1.9	0.0
Picnics, hikes, nature walks	39.2	36.4	31.2	-2.8	-5.2*	►	-	9.1	10.3	-	1.2
Mountain climbing	-	8.5	8.0	-	-0.5	-	-	3.9	3.5	-	-0.4
Camping	-	5.1	6.2	-	1.1	-	8.7	2.3	2.3	-6.4	0.0
Going to the beach	38.6	31.0	21.7	-7.6*	-9.3*	►	2.7	2.8	2.7	0.1	-0.1

Continued

Table 10.1. Continued

	% participating at least once in year, persons aged 15+						Average annual frequency (times pa)				
	1982	1992	2003	Change 1982–1992	Change 1992–2003		1982	1992	2003	Change 1982–1992	Change 1992–2003
Zoos, bot. gardens, aquaria, museums	38.4	44.0	39.0	5.6*	−5.0*	○	3.3	3.3	3.5	0.0	0.2
Exhibitions and events	26.1	26.3	21.1	0.2	−5.2*	○	4.0	3.9	3.7	−0.1	−0.2
Family reunions	24.4	23.6	21.0	−0.8	−2.6	▼	3.6	3.5	3.3	−0.1	−0.2
Domestic tourism	54.4	60.6	57.7	6.2*	−2.9	○	3.0	3.1	3.4	0.1	0.3
Overseas trips	6.1	10.8	11.3	4.7*	0.5	▲	1.4	1.4	1.8	0.0	0.4
Sample size	1606	2414	2425								

Samples from urban areas with populations of 50,000 or more.

* Difference significant at 5% level; −, information not collected and/or participation level too small to register; JRA, Japanese Racing Association; NAR, National Association of Racing; v, decreasing in the 1980s, increasing in the 1990s; ▲ increasing throughout; ○, increasing in 1980s, decreasing in 1990s; ▼ decreasing throughout.

Source: Leisure Development Centre (1995); Prime Minister's Office (1991a); Japan Productivity Centre for Socio-Economic Development (2004).

activities in the two periods. In the table, the following symbols are used to indicate the characteristic trend in participation levels for each activity:

▲   increasing throughout – 8 activities
▼   declining/stagnant throughout – 42 activities
○   increasing in the 1980s, declining/stagnant in the 1990s – 22 activities
v   declining/stagnant in the 1980s, increasing in the 1990s – 8 activities
–   limited information – 11 activities

Of the 91 activities listed, only 8 showed consistent growth throughout the two decades: including four sporting activities; two activities in the hobbies/entertainment group; and one each among the games and amusements and travel and tourism activities. Information on personal computer use was not collected in 1982, but showed a massive increase in the 1990s, from less than 2% to 37%, so it can be assumed to have been growing throughout the period. Given that the growth in participation levels took place in both decades, it is reasonable to conclude that they reflect long-term changes in tastes, rather than temporary fads or fashions or economically influenced shifts, although, in most cases, there was a slowing down in the rate of growth over the period, with the increase in the 1990s being less than in the 1980s, perhaps reflecting the changed economic conditions of the 1990s. It is not possible to explain the presence of all activities in this group, but some can be seen to reflect worldwide trends (soccer, aerobics, computer use) and some growing affluence, even in a period of low economic growth (eating out, travel).

However, the largest group comprises the 42 activities which declined in popularity throughout the period. They are spread throughout the leisure activity groups, with 12 sports; 17 hobbies/entertainment activities; 10 games and amusements; and four travel and tourism activities. As with the previous group, the consistent pattern suggests a long-term, rather than short-term or cyclical, trend. A quarter of the activities are sports. It might be speculated that this represents a shift in sporting taste, rather than necessarily an overall

decline in sport participation, but when participation rates are multiplied by the frequency of participation to obtain a measure of the volume of activity per 100 population, a decline of 25% in overall sport participation is indicated. Most of this took place in the 1980s, suggesting an inverse relationship between economic growth and sport participation. This is contrary to expectations, but such expectations have generally been built on cross-sectional studies of the relationship between income and participation rather than time-series data. Among the 17 declining hobbies/entertainment activities, there is a predominance of the more traditional Japanese activities, although this is not counteracted by strong increases in other activities, with the exception of computer use. Television-watching, which is the largest single absorber of leisure time in Japan, as elsewhere in developed economies, is not included. Among the 10 declining games and amusements, there is a mixture of traditional and Western activities. With the exception of overseas trips, travel and tourism activities showed a decline across the board in the 1990s, arguably a clear reflection of the economic situation.

A total of 22 activities show an increase in participation in the 1980s, followed by a decline in the 1990s: six sports; five hobbies/entertainment activities; six games/amusements; and five travel and tourism. In about half of the activities, the final levels of participation are lower than the first, representing an overall decline over the two decades – in the other half there is still an overall increase in participation. This pattern would seem to reflect the economic environment, with boom conditions in the 1980s and stagnation in the 1990s. This is only partially reflected in the nature of the activities; for example, among the sports, relatively expensive activities, such as skiing, golf and horse riding, are included, but so also are bowling, swimming and cycling. Most of the other activities do involve spending money and so they may have been the victim of 1990s economic conditions.

Finally, eight activities went against the trend, showing a fall in participation the 1980s and an increase in the 1990s. The two sport activities, exercise and jogging/marathons, could be seen as a shift towards relatively cheap alternatives, but may also reflect a trend towards instrumental fitness activities as opposed to sport participation for enjoyment and camaraderie. Two of the five hobbies/entertainment activities, choral singing and gardening, also reflect relatively cheap alternatives.

The mixed picture presented by the data in Table 10.1 provides a cautionary tale, suggesting that prediction of trends in leisure participation based on short-term trends is risky. Long-term trends may well exist, but they can be hidden behind contradictory short-term fluctuations.

Government Policy Aimed at the Private Sector and Increased Recreation Participation

The period from the latter half of the 1960s, into the 1970s, while Japan was experiencing high economic growth, saw a growth in facilities that provided opportunities for people to take part in leisure activities. In particular, large-scale development of golf courses and resort hotels became profitable enterprises because of governmental privatization of land and a general willingness among businesses to invest capital in the so-called 'bubble economy'. However, the results of this government and business activity were not reflected in increased participation levels, as shown by the official surveys. In later surveys, the range of activities was increased to include technologically based activities, such as watching videos and computer-based activities, new activities, such as hang-gliding and para-gliding, and additional recreational activities, such as camping. Surfing, sailing and skin-diving were listed separately, rather than as one activity category as before. This increase in activity categories is believed to be linked directly to the increase in the range of recreational opportunities available.

Shortened Working Hours and Greater Diversification in Recreational Behaviour

In the 1960s and 1970s Japanese workers were working an average of 2300 h/year and the two-day weekend was practically non-existent in

the business sector. Thus few had time for much leisure, and recreational behaviour was limited. It has been noted that the Japanese government took steps to reduce normal working hours from 2111 hours a year in 1988 to 1972 hours in 1992. The expressed need for, and effects of, shortened working hours and greater free time can be read from the results of the surveys. In the 1980s, personal preferences shifted away from materialistic concerns to embrace more humanistic values and a desire for a better quality of life. If we examine data on desired leisure participation, we discover that, in 1992, the most desired activities were overseas travel (37%), domestic sight-seeing and vacationing (16%) and camping (13%). Moreover, a change could be seen in leisure in general, as greater numbers of people were taking part in a more extensive array of activities.

Leisure and Social Inequality

The Japanese are, basically, extremely homogeneous in their characteristics. Unfortunately, the surveys examined in this chapter were not designed to ascertain respondents' socio-economic characteristics, such as culture, religion, income or class. However, according to a 1991 survey by the Prime Minister's Office (1991a), 90% of Japanese working people considered themselves to be part of the 'middle class'. For this reason, the issue of social class and leisure participation is difficult to assess in Japan. In the Edo (1603–1867) and Meiji (1868–1911) eras, leisure was reserved for the privileged classes of *samurai* and the nobility, but the leisure boom phenomenon of modern-day Japan seems to involve the entire nation being drawn to the golf course or karaoke lounge. Social inequality with regard to leisure seems to be related more to availability or lack of free time than to level of income. However, it is clear that the 'leisure repertoire' has expanded for the mass of the people compared with the situation in the past.

Despite the official reduction in working hours, the free time of the average working male, aged 30–50, living in an urban area, is greatly limited by long working hours and the great amount of time spent commuting to and from work. Some 60% of such individuals spend 1 hour or more each way, in commuting to work, often returning home after 20.00 hours. Although the majority of Japanese view themselves as belonging to the 'middle class', in reality, some, because of their low incomes, belong to the 'lower class'. The lower-class workers inevitably have to work longer hours to make up for lower income levels, while others, either because of their higher occupational position or simply out of habit or custom, sacrifice their free time to put in more working hours. These circumstances create a different situation from that described by Schor (1991) who, in describing *The Overworked American*, wrote that 'inequality of income creates inequality of time'. She speaks of American workers having sufficient money to enjoy themselves, but not having the leisure time in which to spend it, making it totally impossible to describe them as a 'leisure class'.

A Problem of Methodology

The problems of a nationwide survey on leisure participation, as Kelly (1980) pointed out, are that: (i) studies aimed at formulating theory are generally lacking; (ii) the highs and lows of participation are partly related to the supply of facilities; and (iii) the uncertainty of reported 'desired' activities demands the formulation of theory relating to 'substitution' and 'socialization', rather than just measuring participation. This is one issue that must be confronted in regard to the future of such surveys.

Participation rates reported here relate to the percentage of persons taking part in a given recreational activity one or more times during the past year, but do not identify 'regular' participants who take part in the activity frequently. The frequency of participation data are presented in aggregate terms only and are not used to distinguish between regular and infrequent participants. It has been shown (Chase and Harada, 1984) that, using a 1-year reference period, people tend to overestimate the number of times they take part in an activity. As such, the results of surveys using such a reference period may be useful in determining trends in participation in leisure activities, but should be used with caution when formulating theory. Furthermore, as Veal (1984) has pointed

out, it would be best to improve the validity of the data by conducting such surveys four times a year to obtain a view of seasonal variations in participation.

Conclusions

The survey on leisure participation that the Ministry of International Trade and Industry has conducted regularly over the past 16 years has provided a database on Japanese leisure activity which has been an effective source of information for policy-making, particularly industry-directed policy. The survey has also provided evidence of the leisure and recreation needs of the general population when government decisions were being made on such matters as resort development and shorter working hours.

As we move into the 21st century, participation by Japanese people in leisure activities is predicted to rise, in the long term, since the general opinion in the nation continues to support reform of basic social and economic structures. Outdoor recreation activities, particularly highly desired activities such as short-break vacations and longer holidays, are expected to grow in popularity. Also, as the 'leisure-able' generation ages, the need to accommodate the demands of the elderly for recreation will become more pressing. The advantage of the surveys reported here is that they take place every year. Taking advantage of this feature of the surveys, personal leisure and socialization processes can be analysed, enabling accurate conclusions to be drawn concerning the ageing of society and recreational demand. If applied in this sense, the survey would be useful in assisting the formulation of theory in relation to such topics as *substitution* and *resocialization*, rather than just measuring levels of participation. This is one issue to be discussed in regard to the future of leisure research.

Note

[1] It has not been possible to fully update this chapter since the first edition of the book, but Table 10.1 has been updated with 2003 data and the commentary related to the table has been

appropriately modified. I am grateful to Tony Veal for undertaking the modifications to the text. – M.H.

References

Chase, D. and Harada, M. (1984) Response error in self-reported recreation participation. *Journal of Leisure Research* 16(4), 322–329.

Economic Planning Agency (1986a) *Educating the Importance of Leisure*. Government Printing Office, Tokyo.

Economic Planning Agency (1986b) *Work and Leisure in the 1980s*. Government Printing Office, Tokyo.

Harada, M. (1994) Towards a renaissance of leisure in Japan. *Leisure Studies* 13(4), 277–287.

Harada, M. (1998) Changing relationships between work and leisure in the 'bubble economy' in Japan. *Society and Leisure* 21(1), 195–212.

Japan Productivity Centre for Socio-Economic Development (2004) *Leisure White Paper, 2003*. JPCSD, Tokyo.

Kelly, J.R. (1980) Leisure and quality: beyond the quantitative barrier. In: Goodale, T.L. and Witt, P.A. (eds) *Recreation and Leisure: Issues in an Era of Change*. Venture, State College, Pennsylvania, pp. 300–314.

Leisure Development Centre (1995) *Leisure White Paper '95* [in Japanese]. LDC, Tokyo.

Prime Minister's Office (1983) *The Public Census on Lifestyle*. Government Printing Office, Tokyo.

Prime Minister's Office (1991a) *Public Opinion Poll on Leisure and Travel*. Government Printing Office, Tokyo.

Prime Minister's Office (1991b) *Public Opinion Poll on Working Hours and the 2-day Weekend*. Government Printing Office, Tokyo.

Sasagawa Sports Foundation (1993) *Sports Life Data*, Vol. 3. SSF, Tokyo.

Schor, J.B. (1991) *The Overworked American*. Basic Books, New York.

Veal, A.J. (1984) Leisure in England and Wales. *Leisure Studies* 3(2), 221–229.

11 The Netherlands

Wim Knulst and Hugo van der Poel

Introduction: a Concise History of Dutch Leisure Research

Blonk *et al.*'s early (1936) study, *The Use of Free Time by Labourers*, asked labourers directly about the ways they spent their spare time. At the time, this was very modern: for the first time in The Netherlands researchers used questionnaires and a 14-day diary. Admittedly, the 621 members of the Social-democratic Party and Union who were asked to fill in the questionnaires were among the more highly skilled workers, and were not fully representative of the labouring classes, let alone the Dutch population as a whole. The results of the study were disappointing for those who had hoped that the working class would use its newly acquired free time for education, social and political work, and thus for the establishment of a new 'socialist' society. But they were reassuring for those who had feared drunkenness and licentiousness. All-in-all it appeared that most of these workers had copied the manners of the lower middle class, and enjoyed rather innocent pastimes, such as listening to the radio, practising sports, reading newspapers and going to the cinema (Beckers, 1991).

The first nationwide and representative survey of free-time activities was reported in 1955/56 (brief details of the surveys discussed in the chapter are provided in Table 11.1). The study was conducted by the Central Bureau for Statistics (CBS) and involved a sample of 7200 respondents, supplemented with 3300 interviews and 250 in-depth interviews, the latter also including observations of homes and social relations. The project resulted in 10 reports, dealing with topics such as: the spending of evenings and weekends; visiting cinemas; religious affiliation and free time; and age and free time. Particularly, the introduction of television in the late 1950s and the introduction of the free Saturday in the early 1960s suggested the need for a repetition of this survey in 1962/63 (Beckers and Mommaas, 1991).

In 1973, during the heyday of the Dutch welfare state, the Social and Cultural Planning Bureau (SCP) was established and started the two most important sources of time-series data on leisure participation and time-use: the Facility Use Survey (AVO) and the Time-budget Survey (TBO) (Knulst, 1991).

The TBO was carried out for the first time in 1975, and has since been repeated at 5-year intervals, always in the first half of October. Originally, the initiative came from media organizations, wanting to know when people watched television and listened to the radio. Wanting to repeat the CBS investigation, other (media-oriented) parties became interested, and the idea emerged to model the investigation on the framework of the time-budget analyses of Szalai *et al.* (1972), and extend it to include a whole-week diary. At this time the SCP decided

Table 11.1. Leisure surveys and time-budget surveys in The Netherlands, 1970–2000.

Year	Survey	Organization/author	Type	Sample size	Age range
1955/56 +1962/63	Survey of Free Time Activities	Central Bureau of Statistics	QS	7200	Workers
1962	People on Sunday	Hessels (1962)	QS	4 towns × 4000	
1968	Social Determinants of Free Time	Wippler (1968, 1970)	QS	880 (Groningen)	16–65
1975, 1980, 1985, 1990, 1995, 2000	Time-budget Research (TBO)	Social and Cultural Planning Bureau	TBO	1975: 1309 1990: 3451 1995: 3277 2000: 1813	12+
1979, 1983, 1987, 1991, 1995, 1999	Facility Use Survey (AVO)	Social and Cultural Planning Bureau	QS	–	6+
1987– Annual	Continuous Holiday Survey	Central Bureau of Statistics, NRIT, NBT	QS	5200 panel	2–75

QS, questionnaire survey; TBO, time-budget survey; NRIT, Dutch Research Institute for Tourism and Recreation; NBT, Dutch Tourism Board.

to participate in this 'multi-client' project and to publish the outcomes in the bi-annual *Social and Cultural Report*, in monographs on time-use (Knulst, 1977; Knulst and Schoonderwoerd, 1983; Knulst and van Beek, 1990; Hart, 1995; Broek *et al.*, 1999) and a multitude of reports on more specific topics, ranging from mobility (Batenburg and Knulst, 1993) to performing arts (Knulst, 1995), and from volunteer work (Hart, 1999) to sport (Haan and Breedveld, 2000). In most of these publications the authors also used data taken from the Facility Use Survey (AVO), which focuses more particularly on the use of a broad range of (subsidized) facilities, including leisure facilities.

Most of the SCP publications are policy orientated, including those dealing with leisure topics. Traditionally, much attention has been given to the differentiation in participation in leisure activities and use made of public leisure facilities related to the backgrounds of respondents. A second important emphasis has been on the roots and development of governmental policies in the field of leisure, more particularly cultural policies (Knulst, 1991).

Another 'root' of contemporary leisure studies is to be found in the field of studies of recreational behaviour commissioned by departments or agencies dealing with physical planning. An early and typical example of

this type of research was *Mensen op Zondag* (People on Sunday), which included a survey of weekend activities in four towns in the western area of The Netherlands, in each of which approximately 4000 people were interviewed (Hessels, 1962). The author of this report later wrote one of the first doctoral dissertations in the field of leisure, focusing on the development of holidays in The Netherlands since early 1900 (Hessels, 1973). In a similar vein, Wippler studied recreational patterns in the province of Groningen, in order to determine the need for recreational facilities and the factors determining this need. The sociological approach and conviction that this question could be solved by the (relatively new) statistical instrument of factor analysis is clearly conveyed by the title of his doctoral dissertation: *Sociale determinanten van vrijetijdsgedrag* (The social determinants of free time behaviour) (Wippler, 1968, 1970).

During the 1960s and 1970s individual academics from various disciplinary and institutional backgrounds began to take an interest in leisure topics (for an overview, see Mommaas, 1996). These researchers came to meet each other in an inter-university working group on leisure (IWV) which, in 1990, merged into the Vereniging voor de VrijetijdSector (VVS, Association for the Leisure Sector). The foundation of this association had a variety of bases, but among the most relevant was the desire to intensify the exchange of information, research questions and results among academics and practitioners, and to professionalize the leisure sector. Also stimulating interest was the growth of leisure studies courses at polytechnic level followed, in 1986, by the establishment of the first Dutch degree course in leisure studies at Tilburg University (Beckers and Mommaas, 1991).

Developments in Obligatory Time and Free Time

While restrictions on labour time for women and children had been in place for some time, the Labour Law of 1919 brought – at least formally – an 8-hour working day and 45-hour working week for industrial labourers. However, it did not embrace labourers in such sectors as agriculture and domestic service, which at that time still employed large segments of the labour force (Karsten, 1990). And, of course, in many factories actual working hours differed from contractual working hours, due to overtime work. The 1930s saw high rates of unemployment, but those who were able to keep their jobs worked longer hours. Proposals to redistribute the available labour among all the workforce by reducing the working week were generally ignored (Beckers, 1983, p. 117 ff). Few people had more than 1 week's annual holiday before the Second World War.

After the reconstruction of the country in the immediate post-war period, the 1960s brought high rates of economic growth, fuelled by very high birth rates, the expanding world economy, low wages and long working hours. In 1958 Dutch industrial labourers worked 49 h/week, 10 h more than comparable workers in the USA and Canada, and 4 h more than those in France, West Germany or the UK. However, increasing labour shortages led to a 'wage explosion', but also the introduction of the free Saturday in 1960–1963 and paid holidays. A 'leisure society' truly appeared to be arriving. The CBS studies on time-use referred to above gave ample support for this idea: the amount of free time for male labourers had increased from 48 h/week in 1954/55 to 53 h in 1962/63, and for managers from 42 h to 46 h (Beckers, 1983, p. 390).

The first of the new series of time-budget studies in 1975, using a slightly different definition of leisure from earlier studies, showed an average of almost 48 h of free time per week for the population aged 12 years and older (Table 11.2). This average peaked at 49 h in 1985, then fell again to approximately 47 h/week in 1990 and 1995 (not shown in the table) and then rapidly fell further, to less than 45 h/week, in 2000. Compared to 1995, when the picture was still quite similar to that in 1990, in 2000 all age groups, with the sole exception of the 65-plus group, experienced a considerable loss in free time per week. Both men and women lost leisure time and the loss was greater the higher the educational level.

Not only is the amount of free time decreasing, people are also tending to spend less time on sleep, eating and personal care. The hours of leisure appear to be vulnerable, while obligatory time is increasing (Peters, 2000). Compared to 1975, people spend 9% more time on paid work, household chores and childcare, and/or education, as shown in Table 11.3. The single most important development appears to be the doubling of the proportion of women who undertake paid work, resulting in an increase of 93% in the time spent on paid work by women. In 1997, women filled 42% of the 6.4 million jobs available. Of total jobs, 12% were flexible and 30% were part-time, most of these held by women. Of all female jobs, only a third involve 35 or more hours a week (compared to 84% of all male jobs), another third involve 20–35 h and a third less than 20 h (CBS, 1999). The Dutch household has thus developed into a one-and-a-half income-earner household, in which, on average, men spend two-thirds of their obligatory time in paid work and one-third on household tasks and childcare, while women spend one-third of their obligatory time on paid work and two-thirds on childcare and household tasks. The increasing participation in paid labour by women is not evenly spread among the female population, but mainly concentrated among the younger generations. Today, people also tend to live in smaller households: the strong increase in one-person and two-person households creating a loss in efficiency in household tasks – there are fewer members

Table 11.2. Free time and diversity of leisure activities by gender, age and educational level, The Netherlands, 1975, 1990, 2000.

	Free time per week (hours)				% of free time per week out of home				Number of leisure activities per week[a]			
	1975	1990	2000	Trend 1975–2002	1975	1990	2000	Trend 1975–2000	1975	1990	2000	Trend 1975–2000
Whole sample	47.9	47.2	44.3	−7%	36	37	36	0%	11.9	12.5	12.7	+6%
Gender												
Men	49.6	48.2	45.2	−9%	37	37	35	−6%	11.5	11.7	11.9	+4%
Women	46.2	46.2	43.5	−6%	35	37	37	+6%	12.4	13.3	13.3	+8%
Age												
12–19	44.2	39.6	37.4	−15%	45	42	42	−8%	12.5	12.5	12.5	0%
20–34	44.8	43.1	38.9	−13%	41	42	41	+2%	12.5	13.2	13.9	+11%
35–49	46.9	44.3	40.1	−14%	32	35	35	+8%	12.1	13.5	13.7	+13%
50–64	50.5	55.3	49.7	−2%	30	34	33	+10%	11.8	11.5	11.9	+1%
65 and over	57.0	59.2	58.2	+2%	27	28	29	+6%	10.1	10.2	9.9	−2%
Level of education[b]												
Primary education	50.0	54.4	52.2	+4%	30	30	26	−15%	11.5	10.7	10.1	−12%
Secondary education, low	48.1	48.5	47.4	−2%	36	35	32	−10%	11.8	12.3	11.8	0%
Secondary education, high	49.8	45.6	42.5	−15%	39	38	37	−6%	12.2	13.0	13.1	+7%
Professional, academic	47.6	47.0	43.7	−8%	40	41	40	+1%	12.6	13.1	13.8	1%

[a] Recorded number of different activities per 47 free hours (average level per week). [b] Educational level: 18 years and above.

Source: SCP (2000) (see Table 11.1).

Table 11.3. Obligatory time-use, October, by gender, age and educational level[a], The Netherlands, 1975, 1985 and 2000.

	Paid work (hours/week)				Domestic tasks and childcare (hours/week)				All obligations: paid work, household and/or education (hours/week)			
	1975	1985	2000	Trend 1975 = 100	1975	1985	2000	Trend 1975 = 100	1975	1985	2000	Trend 1975 = 100
Whole sample	14.8	16.6	19.3	+31%	19.1	18.5	19.9	+4%	40.7	42.1	44.4	+9%
Gender												
Men	23.7	24.5	27.4	+15%	8.6	10.4	12.2	+43%	39.9	42.0	44.9	+13%
Women	6.1	8.8	11.7	+93%	29.5	26.5	27.2	−8%	41.4	42.0	43.9	+6%
Age												
12–19	8.2	6.3	7.3	−11%	6.0	5.5	4.7	−22%	42.5	46.9	46.8	+10%
20–34	23.2	24.2	26.1	+13%	21.2	17.9	22.7	+7%	47.9	47.9	51.5	+8%
35–49	18.9	23.4	28.3	+50%	22.4	22.7	22.2	−1%	42.6	48.1	51.6	+21%
50–64	15.1	11.8	19.5	+30%	21.9	20.0	18.5	−15%	37.4	32.7	39.0	+4%
65 and over	1.3	0.7	1.6	+18%	24.3	22.4	24.1	−1%	25.8	23.6	26.2	+1%
Level of education												
Primary education	11.2	5.4	6.6	−41%	23.6	23.7	26.8	+14%	35.9	30.0	33.7	−6%
Secondary education, low	19.0	16.5	15.8	−17%	22.3	23.0	24.3	+9%	42.4	40.5	40.9	−4%
Secondary education, high	17.1	21.9	24.4	+43%	15.2	17.8	20.9	+37%	41.0	44.9	47.2	+15%
Professional, academic	21.5	21.1	25.8	+20%	16.6	15.3	17.8	7%	43.5	44.6	46.9	+8%

[a] Educational level: 18 years and above.
Source: SCP (2000) (see Table 11.1).

of a household to profit from the household tasks performed.

Leisure Activities During the Week

The combined effects of less free time and more discretionary income are, to some extent, similar to those hypothesized by Linder in his book, *The Harried Leisure Class* (1970). Time-consuming activities with low costs tend to be squeezed out of the leisure pattern, whereas more consumption-intensive activities that cost relatively little in terms of time are becoming increasingly popular. For a growing proportion of the population, time is becoming a more scarce resource than money. For them, the lack of time to realize all their ambitions is stressful, as is the coordination of all the obligatory and leisure activities of the various members of the household and networks of relatives and friends. On the other hand, the growing wage gap between well-off and less well-off households causes stress among pensioners, the unemployed, the handicapped and other dependent low-income groups, who witness a growing disparity between their spending opportunities and those of the affluent middle class.

In 1995, compared to 1975, the amount of money spent on leisure rose by 51%. Free time spent out of the home increased by 10%, and the time spent on travelling for leisure purposes by 21% (SCP, 2000, p. 507). However, Table 11.2 makes it clear that the percentage of free time spent out of the home has decreased since 1990, particularly due to changes in leisure behaviour of men, youth and those with lower education. These unexpected developments still demand a satisfactory explanation.

Figure 11.1 provides an overview of the trends in the time spent on various leisure activities during the week from 1975 to 2000. The 'Linder effect' is visible in some of the changes in the overall leisure pattern, but this does not explain all developments, such as, for example, the relatively high growth in time spent watching television among the younger generations, compared to older generations. An additional explanation for some of the changes might be sought in the changing composition of the population. With an increasing number of one-person and two-person households,

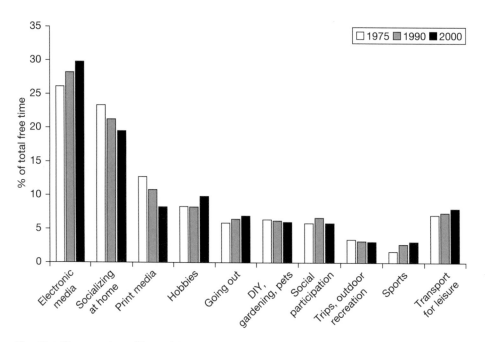

Fig. 11.1. Time spent on different leisure activities, The Netherlands, 1975, 1990, 2000.

particularly among the growing group of the elderly, it should be no surprise that the time spent on the use of electronic media (i.e. mostly watching television) rises and socializing at home is in decline. However, Knulst (1999), using TBO data, could find no corroboration for this plausible hypothesis.

Similar trends can be seen in changes in particular leisure activities, such as sport or cultural activities. Table 11.4 presents an overview of changes in sport participation over the past 20 years. 'Losers' are relatively cheap team sports, such as handball and volleyball, and 'winners' are the more expensive solo sports, particularly golf, fitness and motor sports. The table also makes it abundantly clear that demographic and economic changes have a much greater impact on trends in sport behaviour than elite sport performances, such as the winning of Olympic gold medals. On the contrary, the Dutch Olympic gold medals for field hockey and volleyball in Atlanta and the first Dutch champion at Wimbledon (Krajicek), all in 1996, seem to have had a negative effect, if any, on participation levels in these sports (see also Bottenburg, 1994).

Table 11.5 and Fig. 11.2 show a decrease in participation in forms of 'conventional' culture for a range of age groups, comparable to a similar trend in reading and watching public television (see Fig. 11.4). Time-budget analyses make the Dutch appear 'cultural omnivores'. No one appears to be solely involved in 'high culture', or to be spending all their free time on popular culture. Nonetheless differences still exist with respect to the quantities of conventional and popular forms of culture in overall leisure patterns, along the traditional dividing lines of age, gender, educational level, income level and ethnic background.

Holidays

The first national survey of holiday patterns was carried out in 1947, commissioned by the *Rijksdienst voor het Nationale Plan* (Agency for National Planning) and the Ministry for Education, Arts and Sciences. At that time most holidays were domestic, which explains why knowing how the Dutch spent their holidays was important for the agency responsible for

the planning of water-sport areas, cycle paths, camping sites and the like (Beckers, 1983, p. 194). New surveys followed at irregular intervals, but in 1968 the Central Bureau for Statistics started a yearly holiday survey and periodic studies of supply-side developments. From 1987 onwards CBS has participated in the *Continu Vakantie Onderzoek* (CVO, Continuous Holiday Survey). Important partners in the CVO are the NRIT (Dutch Research Institute for Tourism and Recreation) and the NBT (Dutch Tourism Board). The fieldwork is conducted by GfK, a commercial research bureau (Bargeman, 2001).

The CVO includes a representative panel of 5200 people aged up to 75 years. Members of this panel complete questionnaires four times a year, answering questions about short and long holidays in the previous 3 months. About 3500 respondents appear to fill in all four questionnaires. Weighting factors are used to maintain representativeness. The yearly published tourism trend report provides an overall view of the most relevant trends in holiday behaviour of the Dutch population (Bargeman, 2001).

The Dutch are among the most active pleasure travellers in the world, with three out of four (12 million) taking a short or long holiday at least once a year, as shown in Fig. 11.3. This figure clearly reflects the travel patterns of a small, densely populated, basically middle-class society, where most people enjoy roughly 40 days' holiday per year (see Richards, 1998) and there is one private car for every 2.5 inhabitants. The trends are towards more holidays per year (on average almost two per year), more holidays abroad (particularly long holidays), as shown in Table 11.6, and more expensive holidays. In 1999 the Dutch spent 22 billion guilders on holidaying, of which 18 billion was spent abroad. The higher spending abroad is the result of longer holidays (on average 14 days) and three times the level of expenditure per day.

Linking up with the World Wide Web: the Use of New Media

The use of new media, by definition, cannot be traced back very far. An interesting question is how and when to decide that a new phenomenon is not just a passing fad, but a new way of

Table 11.4. Sport participation, The Netherlands, 1979–1999.

	% participating in year before interview						Index (1995 = 100)						NOC*NSF[a]
	1979	1983	1987	1991	1995	1999	1979	1983	1987	1991	1995	1999	1999/1995
All sports	51.6	57.4	57.0	61.2	62.2	63.5	83	92	92	98	100	102	–
Team sports	19.2	19.7	18.7	18.6	18.0	17.4	107	109	104	103	100	97	–
Duo sports	19.0	18.7	18.2	19.2	19.7	18.3	96	95	92	97	100	93	–
Solo sports[b]	42.3	47.2	44.1	49.7	51.1	51.5	83	92	86	97	100	101	–
Team sports													
Basketball	1.8	1.6	1.5	1.4	1.5	1.5	120	107	100	93	100	100	94
Handball	1.6	1.3	1.2	0.9	0.9	0.9	178	144	133	100	100	100	92
Field hockey	1.4	1.7	1.9	1.8	1.6	1.2	88	106	119	113	100	75	102
Korfball	1.2	1.1	1.2	0.9	1.0	1.2	120	110	120	90	100	120	101
Softball/baseball	–	–	–	0.9	0.7	0.6	–	–	–	129	100	86	95
Soccer	12.1	11.5	10.3	9.5	9.8	9.5	123	117	105	97	100	97	100
Volleyball	5.1	5.2	5.1	5.5	4.6	4.4	111	113	111	120	100	96	90
Indoor soccer	3.2	4.1	3.9	3.6	3.7	3.9	86	111	105	97	100	105	–
Duo sports													
Badminton	7.7	6.8	6.4	6.6	5.1	5.0	151	133	125	129	100	98	77
Squash	–	–	–	–	3.2	3.2	–	–	–	–	100	100	162
Table tennis	6.9	5.4	4.0	3.1	3.1	3.3	223	174	129	100	100	106	93
Tennis	8.1	8.3	9.5	10.2	10.4	8.6	78	80	91	98	100	83	96
Martial arts	2.2	2.1	2.1	2.4	2.5	2.6	88	84	84	96	100	104	–

Solo sports[b]													
Athletics	1.0	1.1	1.3	8.0	1.0	8.0	100	110	130	80	100	80	108
Auto/motor sport	8.0	9.0	8.0	1.0	1.3	1.5	62	69	62	77	100	115	129
Fitness/aerobics	–	–	–	9.1	11.4	12.8	–	–	–	80	100	112	–
Golf	–	–	–	1.2	1.3	1.5	–	–	–	92	100	115	179
Gymnastics	9.1	9.0	8.2	6.7	5.6	5.9	163	161	146	120	100	105	96
Equestrian sports	2.5	3.5	2.5	2.7	3.4	3.1	74	103	74	79	100	91	118
Ice skating	14.6	11.0	15.4	13.0	7.0	5.5	209	157	220	186	100	79	105
Inline skating	–	–	–	–	–	11.0	–	–	–	–	–	–	–
Cycling[c]	25.9	28.2	24.4	14.4	15.3	14.8	169	184	159	94	100	97	125
Jogging	8.1	9.6	9.1	10.5	9.5	8.1	85	101	96	111	100	85	–
Walking/hiking[c]	22.4	22.1	23.1	7.6	8.2	10.7	273	270	282	93	100	130	89
Water sports[d]	6.1	10.5	7.7	7.4	7.6	5.7	80	138	101	97	100	75	–
Swimming	31.8	35.5	30.7	33.0	35.6	32.3	89	100	86	93	100	91	95
Other	4.7	8.8	12.0	10.1	7.8	11.5	60	113	154	129	100	147	–

[a] Development membership of NOC*NSF sport unions, index 1995 = 100. [b] Excluding cycling and walking/hiking. Participation including cycling and walking/hiking 55.5% in 1999. [c] Change in definition in 1991 makes numbers for 1979–1987 incomparable to those of 1991–1999. [d] Sailing/rowing/canoeing/surfing.

Source: SCP (AVO 1979–1999) and NOC*NSF, adapted from Haan and Breedveld (2000, p. 28).

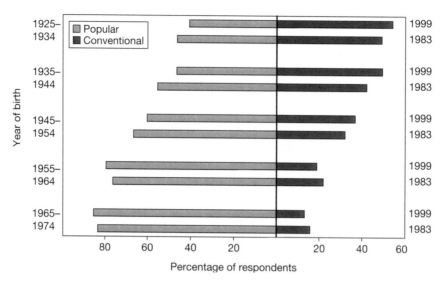

Fig. 11.2. Percentage of those surveyed whose culture package included predominantly popular items or conventional items, by year of birth, The Netherlands, 1983 and 1999.

Table 11.5. Participation in popular and conventional culture, The Netherlands, 1979–1999.

	% participating in year before interview					
	1979	1983	1987	1991	1995	1999
Popular culture						
Theme park	44	47	48	51	49	50
Cinema	43	43	41	41	43	46
Cinema films on TV	–	83	82	78	76	74
Pop music, jazz, musical	12	17	20	23	24	25
Cabaret	12	11	11	11	11	14
Conventional culture						
Ancient architecture, monumental sights	40	43	44	48	43	41
Museum	25	29	33	34	30	32
Art gallery	17	17	19	20	19	17
Theatre	21	22	21	22	22	23
Concerts of classical music, opera	12	13	14	15	17	15
Classical music listened to at home	–	57	63	62	55	51
Ballet, mime	3	4	5	5	4	4

Source: AVO (1979, 1983, 1987, 1991, 1995, 1999) (Haan and Breedveld, 2000).

spending free time that is here to stay. Table 11.7 gives insight in the use of 'new media' over the past 10 years, on the basis of data from the TBO. A quarter of the population appears to have been surfing the Internet during their free time in the survey week in October 2000, spending, on average, 2 hours on the activity.

Use of a personal computer and the Internet started as an activity of younger, higher edu-

cated males, but has since spread among other groups of the population. The diffusion and use of information and communication technology (ICT) devices among the Dutch population is lower than average for persons in low-income households; the unemployed; people with a lower (secondary) education; the elderly; and (single) women. However, Dijk et al. (2000) do not conclude that there is a clear-cut division

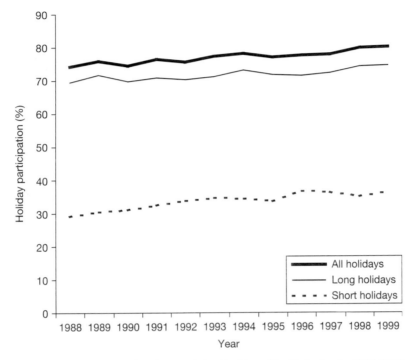

Fig. 11.3. Holiday participation, long and short holidays, The Netherlands, 1988–1999.

Table 11.6. Number of holidays (millions) by destination and duration, The Netherlands, 1990–1999.

	1990	1991	1992	1993	1994	1995	1996	1997	1998	1999
Total number of holidays (millions)	25.4	26.7	26.4	27.7	29.0	27.8	29.9	29.2	29.6	30.5
Domestic holidays										
Short	7.3	7.8	7.8	8.1	8.7	8.5	8.8	8.7	8.3	8.7
Long	7.3	7.4	7.2	7.5	7.2	7.8	8.3	7.6	7.7	7.6
Foreign holidays										
Short	1.8	2.1	2.0	2.1	2.3	2.2	2.4	2.4	2.3	2.5
Long	9.0	9.4	9.4	10.0	10.8	10.1	10.4	10.5	11.3	11.7

Source: CVO, adapted from Bargeman (2001, p. 3).

between 'haves' and 'have-nots' in the information society. First, the differences are relatively small and there are no groups that do not possess or use ICT devices at all. Secondly, the possession and use of ICT devices is still spreading. Thirdly, the structure of the diffusion pattern – that is, the background characteristics of 'early adopters' and 'late adopters' – resembles the diffusion pattern of other advanced and luxury consumer durables.

Figure 11.4 illustrates the impact of age on the use of media. The post-Second World War generations show a strong increase in time spent on the new media between 1990 and 2000. In this figure 'new media' include personal computers and the Internet, but also commercial television – made possible only since the early 1990s, due to the single European market ending the monopoly of public broadcasting in The Netherlands. The

Table 11.7. Use of IT or new media, The Netherlands, 1990, 1995 and 2000.

	1990	1995	2000
VCR			
% using at least once a week	27	28	24
Time spent by users, hours per week	2.5	2.3	2.0
Teletext, cable TV information service			
% using at least once a week	16	15	19
Time spent by users, hours per week	0.8	0.9	0.9
Computer			
% using in free time per week	58	61	60
Time spent by users, hours per week	2.0	2.1	2.1
Internet			
% using in free time per week	–	–	25
Time spent by users, hours per week	–	–	2.0

Source: SCP (2000) (see Table 11.1).

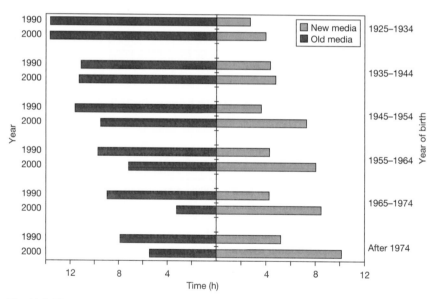

Fig. 11.4. Time spent on older media and on newer media in 1990 and 2000 by year of birth, The Netherlands, 1990 and 2000. New media = commercial TV channels, personal computer, World Wide Web; old media = printed media, public TV channels.

increase of the time spent on the new media clearly coincides with a decline in the time spent on the older media (reading books, newspapers and so on, and watching public television). Among the pre-war generations, however, we see a slight increase in time spent on both the older and the new media, and in total more time spent on the old media compared to the new media.

In 1996 there was one television set for every two inhabitants in The Netherlands, and almost 95% of households had access to a cable network, and used this network for radio and television and, increasingly, to access the Internet. The number of personal computers was 200 per 1000 inhabitants. On all of these indicators, The Netherlands scores slightly above the European average, except for access to cable networks, which is double the European average (SCP, 2000, p. 535).

Conclusion

Compared to other European nations, the Dutch attach a relatively high value to leisure, and have relatively few complaints about the availability of leisure and/or opportunities to enjoy their spare time (SCP, 2000, pp. 521–522). In an attempt to cluster the leisure patterns of 14 European countries, the Social and Cultural Planning Bureau places The Netherlands on the fringe of the group of Scandinavian countries (between these countries and the UK) which attaches relatively high value to leisure, is relatively content about the way leisure is or can be spent, pays more frequent visits to museums, buys more compact discs and has a higher holiday participation rate. The SCP suggests that the relatively high level of satisfaction with leisure in The Netherlands may have to do with the high levels of holiday and sport participation, and perhaps also with the high level of provision of facilities – not so much in terms of provision per inhabitant, but in terms of distance: there is a high density of facilities due to the high number of inhabitants per square kilometre (SCP, 2000, pp. 544–545).

Although the amount of free time in Holland is still high compared to that of other industrialized countries, it has become clear that during the 1990s there was a change from a pattern of growth in free time to an overall loss. The most important reason for this new trend has been the sharp increase in the number of women entering the labour market, even though mostly as part-timers. Average hours worked by men have also started to increase, due to more overtime working and less unemployment. With less free time and more financial resources to spend on leisure, there is an overall shift from low-cost and time-intensive leisure activities to much more consumption-intensive forms of leisure.

Gender differences in the availability and patterns of use of free time seem to be diminishing. Differences by age and educational level (and thus by socio-economic status), on the other hand, seem to be increasing. This seems particularly true in regard to older age groups, who, besides being older have, on average, lower levels of education. The differences are clear, and increasing, in the pattern of use of new media, but also in levels of sport and holiday participation and, on a more general level, in the availability of leisure or the diversity of leisure activities per week.

Historically, The Netherlands has been a relatively 'open' country, and highly involved in the global economy right from its inception. Scrutinizing Dutch leisure practices, reveals a highly eclectic and diverse 'melting pot' of activities, goods and services from all over the world. Even typical 'Dutch' icons, such as the tulip (from Turkey), 'rijsttafel' (from Indonesia) or the orange colour which is unavoidable when meeting Dutch supporters (from the city of Orange in southern France), come from elsewhere. In terms of its contents then, 'Dutch' leisure is no more, and no less, than an historically grown local amalgam of globally available activities, goods and services. Perhaps the Dutch are so satisfied with their leisure because they feel they live in a very well stocked supermarket of leisure opportunities.

References

Bargeman, B. (2001) *Kieskeurig Nederland. Routines in de Vakantiekeuze van Nederlandse Toeristen.* KUB/VTW, Tilburg.

Batenburg, R.S. and Knulst, W.P. (1993) *Sociaal-culturele Beweegredenen. Onderzoek Naar de Invloed van Veranderende Leefpatronen op de Mobiliteitsgroei Sinds de Jaren Zeventig.* SCP, Rijswijk.

Beckers, T.A.M. (1983) *Planning Voor Vrijheid. Een Historisch-sociologische Studie van de Overheidsinterventie in Recreatie en Vrijetijd.* Pudoc, Wageningen.

Beckers, T. (1991) Vrijetijdsonderzoek en arbeidersemancipatie. In: Beckers, T. and Mommaas, H. (eds) *Het Vraagstuk Van Den Vrijen Tijd. 60 Jaar Onderzoek Naar Vrijetijd.* Stenfert Kroese, Leiden/Antwerp, pp. 12–24.

Beckers, T. and Mommaas, H. (eds) (1991) *Het Vraagstuk Van Den Vrijen Tijd. 60 Jaar Onderzoek Naar Vrijetijd.* Stenfert Kroese, Leiden/Antwerp.

Blonk, A., Kruijt, J.P. and Hofstee, E.W. (1936) *Het Gebruik Van Den Vrijen Tijd Door De Arbeiders.* Nutsuitgeverij, Amsterdam.

Bottenburg, M. van (1994) *Verborgen Competitie. Over de Uiteenlopende Populariteit van Sporten.* Bert Bakker, Amsterdam.

Broek, A. van der, Knulst, W., and Breedveld, K. (1999) *Naar Andere Tijden? Tijdsbesteding en Tijdsordening in Nederland, 1975–1995.* SCP, The Hague.

CBS (Centraal Bureau voor de Statistiek) (1999) *Statistisch Zakboek 1999.* CBS, Voorburg/ Heerlen.

Dijk, L. van, Haan, J. de and Rijken, S. (2000) *Digitalisering van de Leefwereld. Een Onderzoek Naar Informatie- en Communicatietechnologie en Sociale Ongelijkheid.* SCP, The Hague.

Haan, J. de and Breedveld, K. (2000) *Trends en Determinanten in de Sport. Eerste Resultaten uit het AVO 1999.* SCP, The Hague.

Hart, J. de (1995) *Tijdopnamen. Een Onderzoek Naar Verschillen en Veranderingen in de Dagelijkse Bezigheden van Nederlanders op Basis van Tijdbudgetgegevens.* SCP, Rijswijk.

Hart, J. de (1999) Vrijwilligerswerk Vanuit Tijdbudgetperspectief. In: Dekker, P. (ed.) *Vrijwilligerswerk Vergeleken. Civil Society en Vrijwilligerswerk III.* SCP, The Hague, pp. 143–179.

Hessels, A. (1962) *Mensen op Zondag.* Staatsdrukkerij en Uitgeverijbedrijf, The Hague.

Hessels, A. (1973) *Vakantie en Vakantiebesteding Sinds De Eeuwwisseling.* Van Gorcum, Assen.

Karsten, L. (1990) *De Achturendag. Arbeidstijdverkorting in Historisch Perspectief, 1817–1919.* Stichting beheer IISG, Amsterdam.

Knulst, W.P. (1977) *Een Week Tijd. Rapport van een Onderzoek Naar de Tijdsbesteding van de Nederlandse Bevolking in Oktober 1975.* SCP, The Hague.

Knulst, W. (1991) Vrijetijd en verzorgingsstaat. In: Beckers, T. and Mommaas, H. (eds) *Het Vraagstuk Van Den Vrijen Tijd. 60 Jaar Onderzoek Naar Vrijetijd.* Stenfert Kroese, Leiden/Antwerp, pp. 234–244.

Knulst, W. (1995) *Podia in en Tijdperk van Afstandsbediening. Onderzoek Naar Achtergronden van Veranderingen in de Omvang en Samenstelling van het Podiumpubliek Sinds de Jaren Vijftig.* SCP, Rijswijk.

Knulst, W. (1999) *Werk, Rust en Sociaal Leven op Zondagen Sinds de Jaren Zeventig.* KUB/VTW, Tilburg.

Knulst, W. and Schoonderwoerd, L. (1983) *Waar Blijft de Tijd. Onderzoek Naar de Tijdsbesteding van Nederlanders.* Staatsuitgeverij, Gravenhage.

Knulst, W.P. and van Beek, P. (1990) *Tijd Komt met de Jaren. Onderzoek Naar Tegenstellingen en Veranderingen in Dagelijkse Bezigheden van Nederlanders op Basis van Tijdbudgetonderzoek.* SCP, Rijswijk.

Linder, S.B. (1970) *The Harried Leisure Class.* Columbia University Press, New York.

Mommaas, H. (1996) The study of free time and pleasure in the Netherlands: the end of the legislator. In: Mommaas, H., van der Poel, H., Bramham, P. and Henry, I.P. (eds) *Leisure Research in Europe: Methods and Traditions.* CAB International, Wallingford, UK, pp. 63–106.

Peters, P. (2000) *The Vulnerable Hours of Leisure. New Patterns of Work and Free Time in the Netherlands, 1975–95.* Thela-Thesis, Amsterdam.

Richards, G. (1998) Time for a holiday? Social rights and international tourism consumption. *Time and Society* 7(1), 145–160.

SCP (Social and Cultural Planning Bureau) (2000) *Social and Cultural Report 2000.* SCP, The Hague.

Szalai, A. (ed) (1972) *The Use of Time. Daily Activities of Urban and Suburban Populations in Twelve Countries.* Mouton, The Hague.

Wippler, R. (1968) *Sociale Determinanten van het Vrijetijdsgedrag.* Van Gorcum, Assen.

Wippler, R. (1970) Leisure Behavior: a Multivariate Approach. *Sociologica Neerlandica* 6(1), 51–65.

12   New Zealand

Sue Walker, Mary Donn and Allan Laidler

Introduction

This chapter updates and broadens the picture of leisure participation in New Zealand that was presented in the first edition of this book (Laidler and Cushman, 1996). Detail is drawn from more recent and wide-ranging research in order to show New Zealanders' leisure behaviour and time-use in a new perspective and to highlight a number of relevant influences and changes over the closing years of the 20th century. The chapter also re-visits some of the problems associated with national participation surveys, particularly comprehensiveness, continuity and comparability. The aim is to locate New Zealand in the international context created by the book as a whole, without obscuring the local distinctiveness and the unique bicultural forces that have shaped it.

Leisure Participation in the 1990s

Leisure, sport and the arts

The short history of systematic research into leisure participation in New Zealand was outlined in the New Zealand chapter in the first edition of the book. Data-gathering on a national scale began as late as the mid-1970s, although by the early 1990s the *Life in New Zealand* (LINZ) survey (Russell and Wilson, 1991) had provided a wide-angled view of leisure in the lives of teenagers and adults. The survey was initiated by the Hillary Commission for Sport, Fitness and Leisure and, although an immediate interpretation of the results in the media was that New Zealand was 'not a sporting nation' but one that preferred to watch television and read, more analysis was subsequently directed at sport and 'active leisure' than at leisure more broadly. The Hillary Commission conducted further surveys during the 1990s but they have been conducted in accordance with the 1992 Sport, Fitness and Leisure Amendment Act, under which the Commission was to focus more specifically on sport and physical activity. Table 12.1 provides details of these and the earlier surveys discussed in the earlier edition.

At the same time, the 'recreational arts' were moved into the Arts Council's realm of responsibility, a change endorsed in the 1994 Arts Council of New Zealand/Toi Aotearoa Act. The Act required the Council (with its trading name 'Creative New Zealand') to attend to the whole arts spectrum, from the professional to the community and recreational, in order to encourage, support and promote the arts 'for the benefit of all New Zealanders'. Since participation and access were to be guiding principles, the Act provided the rationale for a comprehensive survey of national involvement in the arts and cultural leisure activities. *Arts Every Day* (Creative New Zealand, 1999a),

© CAB International 2005. *Free Time and Leisure Participation: International Perspectives* (eds G. Cushman *et al.*)

Table 12.1. National leisure surveys, New Zealand, 1975–1999.

Name	Year	Agency	Survey type	Activities	Reference period	Sample size	Age range	Reference
NZ Recreation Survey	1975	NZ Council for Recreation & Sport	QS	Recreation	Year	4011	10+	Robb and Haworth (1977)
Social Indicators Survey	1980/81	Dept of Statistics	QS	Recreation	Year	6891	15+	Dept of Statistics (1984)
Life in New Zealand Survey	1989/90	Hillary Commission	QS	Recreation	4 weeks	4373	15+	Cushman et al. (1991)
New Zealand Time Use Survey	1998/99	Statistics New Zealand	TUS	Time	48 hrs	8535	12+	Dept of Statistics (1991)
Sport and Physical Activity Survey	1997, 1998	Hillary Commission	QS	Sport, physical	Year	5470, 4051	5+[a]	Hillary Commission (undated a and b)
Arts Every Day	1997	Creative New Zealand	QS	Arts/cultural	Year	5846	18+	Creative New Zealand (1999a)

[a] For young people aged 5–17, information was collected by proxy interview with an adult respondent in the household. QS, questionnaire survey; TUS, time-use survey.

and New Zealand's first time-use survey (see Table 12.1) compensated in no small measure for the narrowed research focus of the Hillary Commission.

In addition to these large-scale quantitative surveys, several other studies have added to the knowledge about New Zealand's leisure sector. These include qualitative research investigating barriers to participation in physical activity (Hillary Commission, 1994), sector-specific surveys, such as the New Zealand Artists Survey (Creative New Zealand, 2003), social and economic impact studies (Business and Economic Research Limited, 1997; Hillary Commission, 1998a,b) and the analysis of cultural spending (Statistics New Zealand and the Ministry of Cultural Affairs, 1996; Statistics New Zealand and the Ministry of Culture and Heritage, 2000). Leisure activity has also been researched as part of consumer lifestyle studies (Consumer Research Group, 1996, currently being updated). Some commercial market research companies also monitor participation in leisure activities through omnibus surveys, although the results are not usually published or made freely available.

All of these studies provide insights into New Zealanders' use of leisure time in the 1990s and, although the following section is confined to the results of enquiries into time-use and leisure participation, findings from the other studies are referred to thereafter.

Time-use

The first attempt to gather comprehensive data on how New Zealanders use their time was sponsored by the Ministry of Women's Affairs and nine other government agencies in 1990 (Department of Statistics, 1991) but, after the pilot survey, several years passed before sufficient funding was available for the full project to be conducted in 1999. The time-use survey (TUS) was carried out by the government agency, Statistics New Zealand, under contract to the Ministry of Women's Affairs. Extensive information about its background, objectives and implementation can be found in the *Users' Guide* (Statistics New Zealand, 1999a).

As the initial impetus came from Women's Affairs, a primary aim was to improve gender analysis for mainstream policy. A second aim was a better understanding of time-use inside New Zealand's two main cultural streams: Mäori and non-Mäori. To this end, the survey 'oversampled' Mäori in order to create a statistical base large enough to permit inferences to be drawn about the minority group (15%) who identified themselves as Mäori in the 1996 national census. Summaries of time-use in relation to the labour market, education, health and welfare have been released. A more detailed report presents the main findings (Ministry of Women's Affairs and Statistics New Zealand, 2001) and 50 tables of data (Time Use Statistics, 1999) are accessible through Statistics New Zealand's website.

The survey findings sketch in free time and leisure as elements in the day-to-day life of the nation. As indicated in Table 12.2, one-fifth of the average day (just over 4½ hours) can be classified as 'free', based on analysis of 'primary' activities. In reality, of course, people often engage in more than one activity at a time and, when these are aggregated, free time activity virtually doubles. The category 'free time' comprises 34 activities clustered in groups to include social, cultural and civic involvement, sports, hobbies and other unobligated interests. The question of how much of this free time is leisure cannot be answered without further analysis of the disaggregated data, but this is lower in the priorities of the main sponsoring agency than questions relevant to policy issues such as unpaid work, paid employment, education and health.

The proportions of 'free' time vary little across gender or culture, although some differences emerge. On average, Mäori men and women spend more time daily than non-Mäori on caregiving to household members, on unpaid work outside the home and on cultural and religious pursuits (Ministry of Women's Affairs and Government Statistician, 1999). Differences between the way males and females spend their time are also apparent. The findings tend to confirm the stereotype of girls and women as homemakers and caregivers, and point to their greater involvement in unpaid work. In contrast, boys and men spend more time on 'contracted' activities, such as paid work, education or training.

As might be expected, it is on weekend days that people have most free time: an average over

Table 12.2. Daily time-use, persons aged 12 and over, by gender and ethnic group, New Zealand, 1998/99.

Type of time	Total			Females			Males			Māori[a]		Non-Māori	
	Primary		All	Primary		All	Primary		All	Primary		Primary	
	min	%	min	min	%	min	min	%	min	min	%	min	%
Necessary time	696	48	699	704	49	708	687	48	690	698	49	696	48
Contracted time	237	16	240	177	12	180	300	21	303	220	15	240	17
Committed time	228	16	558	286	20	703	166	12	406	229	16	228	16
Free time	278	19	554	271	19	575	286	20	532	291	20	276	19
Total	1440	100		1440	100		1440	100		1440	100	1440	100

[a] Time spent on all activities by Māori/non-Māori has not been published.

Source: Statistics New Zealand (1999) (Tables 1 and 29 of preliminary tables); Ministry of Women's Affairs and Government Statistician (2000).

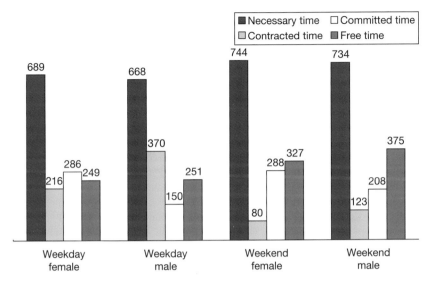

Fig. 12.1. Time-use during weekdays and weekends by gender, New Zealand, 1998/99 (min/day, 12+ years). Source: Statistics New Zealand (1999a; Table 16 of preliminary tables).

5½ hours compared with just over 4 hours on weekdays. Again, these figures are based on primary activities. More time is also spent on 'necessary' and 'committed' activities on weekend days and these gains are at the expense of 'contracted' time. Men and boys enjoy about 45 minutes more 'free time' at weekends than women and girls, as shown in Fig. 12.1, but the averages for weekdays are almost identical.

Predictably, 'mass media and free time' activities again predominate (almost 2.5 h/day), followed by social entertainment (around 1.5 h/day) and sports and hobbies (40 min/day, of which 20 min is spent on sport and exercise). In all households, watching television and/or videos is the most common free-time activity (averaging 1.4 h/day).

The TUS offers the potential for a much closer look at the way New Zealanders spend their leisure time, but, until this analysis is carried out, the main sources of activity-specific information are surveys commissioned by sports and arts agencies.

The Hillary Commission's *Sport and Physical Activity Survey* and Creative New Zealand's *Arts Every Day* survey were carried out in 1997 as a joint data collection exercise. This collaboration was pragmatic, producing cost savings for both organizations and avoiding

separate, contemporaneous surveys on related topics, and followed a precedent: the two agencies had joined forces previously to make joint submissions to government on issues of mutual concern, particularly gaming and gambling (The Queen Elizabeth II Arts Council and The Hillary Commission for Recreation and Sport, 1990; Hillary Commission and Creative New Zealand, 1995), and to produce guidance on legislation for local government (Hillary Commission and Creative New Zealand, 1997).

Together, the two surveys collected information on over 200 arts, sporting and other popular leisure activities. Each survey used a prompt list of around 40 activities, but others mentioned by respondents were also recorded. In addition to the arts and sports activities usually associated with European-based cultures, the survey elicited information on participation in traditional Māori activities and, in the arts section, in Pacific Island activities.

Table 12.3 shows the participation rates for selected at-home and out-of-home activities across the arts and sports spectrum. Judging by the results given in the earlier edition of this book, little has changed in leisure patterns: watching television, listening to the radio and music, and reading are still the three activities with the highest participation rates. Likewise,

Table 12.3. Participation in selected leisure activities, New Zealand, 1997/98, by gender and ethnic group.

	% aged 18+ participating in past 4 weeks		
	Women	Men	Total
Arts, cultural and sporting activities			
At least one arts or cultural activity	94	86	90
At least one arts or cultural activity, excluding reading	83	72	78
At least one sport/active recreation activity, excluding gardening/walking	60	72	66
In-home activities			
Watched television	96	95	95
Listened to the radio	90	91	90
Watched sport on television	71	88	79
Listened to music (CD, tape, other pre-recorded format)	76	73	75
Read a book for pleasure	77	64	71
Did some gardening	56	44	50
Played computer games/'surfed the net'	25	36	30
Listened to recorded pop/rock music	26	30	28
Did some craft work	38	10	24
Out-of-home activities			
Went for a walk	73	55	64
Watched a live sports event	28	38	33
Went to the movies	32	33	32
Went to a pop/rock music concert	18	25	22
Went to a museum or gallery	18	14	16
Played computer games/'surfed the net'	12	18	15
Went to a live theatre performance	17	8	13
Went to a classical music concert	7	6	7
Top five Mäori sports and arts activities[a]			
Karakia (prayer-chant)	29(6)	17(3)	24(5)
Waiata (singing)	28(6)	17(4)	23(5)
Te reo (Mäori language)	28(5)	14(3)	22(4)
Kapa haka (performance involving song, dance, martial arts)	14(2)	7(1)	11(2)
Poi (ball attached to string manipulated to a rhythmic beat)	13(2)	1(1)	8(1)
Top five Pacific Islands arts activities[a]			
Choir/group singing	29(2)	19(1)	24(1)
Dance	25(2)	12(1)	18(1)
Storytelling	8(1)	8(1)	8(1)
Performance	5(<1)	4(<1)	5(<1)
Chants	2(<1)	6(<1)	4(<1)

[a] Figures in brackets show the participation rates for all New Zealanders.
Sources: 1996 and 1998 Sport and Physical Activity Survey; 1997 Arts Every Day Survey (see Table 12.1).

the Hillary Commission's analysis of the sports data shows similar levels of sport and active leisure participation in 1990 and 1996. This is true for both the overall level of adult participation and most of the individual activities common to both surveys (Hillary Commission, undated a).

However, some changes are evident, with two activities showing noticeable increases in participation. Going to the movies was twice as popular in 1997 as in 1990, and playing computer games was five times more popular. Other changes have occurred in the popularity of individual activities. For example, touch rugby (a game based on rugby league) emerged as the most popular team sport, enjoyed by one in ten adult New Zealanders, in the second half of the 1990s, as indicated in Table 12.4. By

Table 12.4. Participation in top ten arts and sports activities, by gender, New Zealand, 1997/98.

	% 18+ participating in the last 4 weeks		
	Women	Men	Total
Arts activities			
1. Reading	77	64	71
2. Pop/rock music	39	41	40
3. Chamber/classical music	19	15	17
4. Country/folk music	11	13	12
5. Storytelling	16	8	12
6. Singing	13	8	11
7. Knitting	19	<1	10
8. Design arts	10	8	9
9. Band music	6	8	7
10. Photography	5	7	6
Sports activities			
1. Golf	5	15	10
2. Tennis	3	6	5
3. Touch rugby	2	6	4
4. Cricket – outdoors	1	5	3
5. Soccer	1	5	3
6. Netball	4	1	3
7. Shooting	1	5	3
8. Motor sports	1	4	3
9. Horse riding	3	2	3
10. Rugby Union	>1	5	3

Sources: 1998 Sport and Physical Activity Survey; 1997 Arts Every Day Survey (see Table 12.1).

1998, some 7% of New Zealanders reported participation in mountain biking, although it had not been identified as a separate activity in the LINZ survey.

Comparing adults who are physically active with those who are sedentary (in a preceding 4-week period) demonstrates that active adults are also more likely to participate in passive activities such as reading a newspaper, watching sport on television, going to the movies, playing computer games and going to museums/exhibitions, than adults who are sedentary. This suggests that there is one group of people who participate in a wide range of leisure activities and another with a limited range of, mostly passive, activities in their 'leisure portfolio'. Whether constraints, such as restricted income, or personal preferences give rise to these differences is not evident from this survey.

The distinction between 'active' and 'passive' participation in the arts is probably not as clear-cut as it is for sport and physical activity: *Arts Everyday* shows that people 'participate' in a variety of ways and settings. While most involvement is as a member of an audience, it has been argued that both the producer and the audience of art engage actively in it: 'the artistic transaction remains incomplete until the alert perceiver has done his or her bit' (Volkerling, 1998, p. 311).

The figures in Table 12.3 confirm the leisure preferences of men and women outlined in the first edition: men are more likely to participate in sport, as players and spectators, and women are more likely to engage in home-based and informal activities such as reading and walking. Women have higher participation rates in arts activities and lower in sport. *Arts Everyday* also reveals that women take part in a wider range of arts activities than men, and have higher participation in areas such as reading, classical music, storytelling and singing (Table 12.4). Notable exceptions to this are the markedly higher levels of participation of men in jazz, film and video making and photography. Some of these gender differences can be attributed to culturally assigned roles, especially in Mäori and Pacific Islands arts. Men and women's preferences for individual sporting activities also vary, as the 'top ten' sports for the two sexes clearly show.

A gender imbalance in participation in 'technological leisure activities' is evident in New Zealand, with males almost one and a half times more likely than females to play computer games and/or access the Internet. Cultural differences in participation are also apparent. By international standards, New Zealand is a 'well-wired' nation; in a recent report New Zealand was rated seventh out of OECD countries in terms of connections to the Internet (Porter, 1999). However, it is estimated that only 6% of New Zealand's Internet users are Mäori (Maharey and Swain, 2000) and, while more Mäori content is appearing on the web, it is being accessed mostly by non-Mäori people. Disparities in levels of Internet access, therefore, as well as different levels of participation in other technological leisure activities, suggest that technology impacts differently on New Zealanders' leisure lives across social, economic and cultural dimensions.

New Insights

Several trends – some of them new – are suggested by the recent surveys reported in this chapter. The relatively high levels of participation in a large number of arts and cultural activities dispel the myth that the arts are the preserve of the 'privileged few'. Past studies have focused on a small range of often 'elite' arts activities, giving the impression that the arts thrive only in the realm of the wealthy. *Arts Every Day* asked about a broad range of activities and showed that overall participation in the arts is not correlated with income, even though income influences the types of activities that people participate in. For instance, those with high incomes are more likely to take an interest in ballet, contemporary dance, opera and theatre than people in the lower income groups. The latter are more likely to knit and participate in country and folk music or band music. The survey also revealed that education level is a better indicator of commitment to the arts than income.

New Zealanders' participation in sport or the arts is not mutually exclusive; many participate enthusiastically in both.

The home is an increasingly important venue for sports and arts activities. While much arts activity occurs outside the home, the arts are overwhelmingly a leisure activity pursued in it. People's homes are also the venue for a great deal of physically active leisure pursuits. Over 60% of adults take part in home-based activities, such as gardening and exercising by playing sports such as cricket, tennis and soccer, probably as family games (Hillary Commission, undated b). The importance of the home as a venue for leisure activities reflects the fact that most New Zealanders have grown up in relatively spacious homes with sizeable gardens but, as discussed below, this may be changing.

Evidence that participation in sport, active leisure and the arts brings benefits to both the individual and society continues to grow (Hillary Commission, 1998b; Creative New Zealand, 1999a).

A better understanding of participation by Māori and Pacific peoples is emerging as a result of recent surveys, which also allow bench-marking and will facilitate future tracking. Some Māori activities, such as kapa haka (which includes choreographed dance and singing, as well as forms of martial arts), were included in both the arts and sports surveys (Creative New Zealand, 2000b). This reflects the Māori view that these activities are part of both cultural and active lifestyles, and is a reminder of the need to examine arts and sports participation in a more holistic perspective. As Matunga (1995) points out, while contact with European society has seen Māori adopt many of its recreational activities and behaviour patterns, the fundamentally inseparable nature of work and leisure in Māori culture is still strong today. In line with earlier analysis (McGregor and McMath, 1993), the surveys are reminders that people's cultural background influences choice of leisure venue. For Pacific peoples living in New Zealand, the church, community venues and festivals are pivotal. For Māori, the marae (the traditional meeting-place for iwi (tribe) and whanau (family)) is the hub of much leisure activity.

The reasons why people do not participate in sports and arts activities are becoming clearer. For the arts generally, time and lack of interest are the reasons given, but men are more likely to say they are not interested, while women tend to say that cost is a barrier. Lack of time is also a barrier to physical activity, but emotional and attitudinal barriers seem even more influential (Hillary Commission, 2000). *Arts Every Day* shows that age is also a factor, with 25–44-year-olds either more interested in playing sport than taking part in arts activities, or saying they do not have the time. People over 60 years were often limited by a disability, an observation with increasingly important implications for sport and arts delivery organizations as, in common with other developed countries, the New Zealand population 'greys'. By 2051 the elderly will probably outnumber children by over 65%.[1]

More comprehensive information can now be found on how and where young people participate in sport and active leisure (Walker *et al.*, 1999), and on how participation rates change over the life cycle. The survey findings show high participation levels among 5–12-year-olds, a decline during the teenage years, an increase in young adulthood, followed by a gradual decline from the mid-thirties onwards.[2] Looking at the activities that people give up and take up also shows that the transition from school to young adulthood is characterized by many people, particularly women, switching from traditional team sports to other pursuits, such as walking, swimming, exercise and aerobics classes. The latest survey also serves as a reminder that, while New Zealand is often portrayed as a 'rugby-mad' nation, golf is the sport most men and women play (Table 12.4) and soccer is now played by more young people than rugby or the other 'national' sport, netball.

Holiday-taking and Domestic Tourism

While in-bound tourism has been monitored annually since 1995 by the New Zealand Tourism Board's *International Visitor Survey*, surveys of domestic tourism – that is, trips by New Zealanders within New Zealand – have been more sporadic. National surveys of overnight domestic trips were conducted from 1986 to 1990 but were discontinued until 1999, when the *Domestic Tourism Survey* was carried out to measure overnight and, for the first time, day trips.

As Table 12.5 indicates, the 1999 survey estimated that New Zealanders made 16.6 million domestic overnight tourism trips and 44.3 million day trips in 1 year. Almost one-half

(46%) of overnight trips and day trips (44%) were holiday or leisure. Visiting friends and relatives was recorded as the other main purpose of both.

Holiday-taking tends to be measured in terms of the number of trips made, and it is difficult to find out what proportion of New Zealand residents take a holiday or make leisure day trips away from home. An Otago University study (Lawson *et al.*, 1997) found that 17% of respondents usually travelled overseas for their holidays, but holiday-taking by New Zealand residents within New Zealand was not recorded. New Zealanders on overnight trips tend to stay with friends or relatives (56% of nights away) or in low-cost accommodation: holiday homes, or 'baches' and 'cribs' as they are often called in New Zealand (10%), and camping grounds (9%). A study of consumer lifestyles (Consumer Research Group, 1996) suggested that this choice of accommodation may reflect the fact that many people see simplicity as an attractive goal. For them, the high value placed on career, convenience and variety makes this goal difficult to achieve, and so they travel in search of simplicity. This study also suggested that families value holidays that offer them the opportunity to spend more time together. At home widespread use of products like microwaves, computers and video recorders encourages them to function more as a group of individuals than as a family unit.

Table 12.5. Domestic tourism in New Zealand, 1999.[a]

	Overnight trips[b]	Day trips[c]
Number of trips, millions	16.6	44.3
% of all nights/trips that are for holiday/leisure	46	44
Number of nights away from home, millions	52.9	–
Average number of nights away – all trips	3.2	–
Average number of nights away – holiday trips	3.8	–
Total expenditure, NZ$ billions	4.1	2.8
Sample size (population aged 15+)	17,037	

[a] Travel (recreational or business) made in New Zealand outside the area in which the respondent usually works or lives.
[b] Overnight trips = at least one night away from home in the last 4 weeks.
[c] Day trip = trips taken in the past 7 days of at least 40 km, one way, from home or travel by aeroplane or ferry.
Source: 1999 Travel Survey undertaken by Forsyte Research and funded by Foundation for Research Science and Technology (FRST) (Forsyte Research, 2000).

The consumer lifestyles study segmented the New Zealand domestic holiday market into six groups:

- *outdoor adventurers* (13%) – who seek new challenging experiences and wilderness or nature experiences;
- *sports devotees* (21%) – who travel for the principal purpose of watching or participating in sports events;
- *fun-loving holiday-makers* (14%) – who seek fun, shopping, entertainment, and safety, in destinations where people speak the same language;
- *education-seekers* (17%) – who are interested in learning, knowledge, a sense of history, experience cultural differences, authentic experiences, and nature experiences;
- *people celebrating special family occasions* (21%) – who visit friends or relatives and visit the place from which their family originated;
- *family holiday-makers* (14%) – who travel with immediate family to favourite and familiar places and are influenced by availability of children's attractions and opportunities for rest and relaxation.

The *Domestic Tourism Survey* found that people who do not travel say it is because they have no reason to, are too busy or cannot afford to. Demographic analysis shows that age and income influence holiday-taking more than they influence day trips. Overnight trip-taking is inversely related to age, with teenagers and young adults (15–24 years) most likely to make trips, and positively related to income; people with household incomes over NZ$100,000 are more than twice as likely to make overnight trips as those whose income is below NZ$20,000. A comparison of overnight trips in 1999 with those 10 years earlier shows that New Zealanders are travelling more often but for shorter periods.

Domestic tourism expenditure totalled NZ$6.9 billion in 1999. This exceeded spending by international visitors, which that year was just under NZ$4 billion, excluding international air fares.

Research has also investigated the impact of tourism on host communities. Studies are under way to monitor the social and environmental consequences of tourism growth in popular holiday destinations and, in areas where the ratio of hosts to visitors can exceed 1:300, this is providing indications of communities' ability to absorb and adapt to tourism.[3] For residents as well as visitors, the choice of holiday destination is affected by perception of scale: significant numbers said they would avoid areas such as Queenstown, Rotorua and Auckland as holiday destinations because they were seen as expensive and crowded (Consumer Research Group, 1996).

Limitations of National Surveys

New Zealand's national surveys provide valuable insights into the way New Zealanders use their free and leisure time, but they have their limitations. As this chapter illustrates, while some gains have been made in the past decade, many of the limitations common to large-scale surveys that were pinpointed in the first edition still hinder thorough analysis. These limitations can be discussed under three headings: comprehensiveness, continuity and comparability.

Comprehensiveness

None of the individual surveys described here is as comprehensive as the 1990 LINZ survey. While the arts, sports and time-use surveys provide information about a wide range of free- and leisure-time activities, they cannot provide a total picture. Understanding the 'big picture' is unlikely to be a priority for individual sponsoring agencies and for leisure researchers seeking specific patterns of trends and behaviour. Moreover, activities that are not of primary interest to funding agencies continue to 'fall through the cracks'. For example, none of the most recent surveys throws much light on 'leisure shopping', but the growing number of shopping centres and malls makes it obvious that, as in other countries, this activity now occupies a considerable amount of New Zealanders' discretionary time. Likewise, the 'café culture' is obvious in the streets, if not in the questionnaires. The café industry has grown by over 50% in real terms in the past 5 years (The Heart of the Nation Strategic Working Group, 2000) and cafés are undoubtedly the venue for social leisure activity not detected in national surveys. Less structured and/or antisocial activities (for example, 'hanging-out' with friends, or drug-related activities) are also omitted from the sector-specific surveys or subsumed in broader categories in time-use surveys.

National surveys can rarely afford sample sizes large enough to track minority or new interests, for example variations on existing activities, like underwater hockey and canoe polo, or new 'extreme sports' such as bungy jumping and river boarding. In consequence, while there is some evidence that individual, rather than team sports, and less conventional leisure activities are growing in popularity in New Zealand (Thomson, 2000), this is not mirrored in the survey results.

The growth in national and regional festivals based around arts, wine, food or all three has also gone uncharted by the New Zealand national surveys. Yet these are now prominent leisure events. As one example, the New Zealand International Festival of the Arts sold 228,000 tickets in 2000 and 245,000 people were attracted to free events; striking numbers in a region with a population of around 430,000. The festival contributed an estimated NZ$23.5 million to the economy of its host town, Wellington. All major wine regions now have festivals and the wineries attract many domestic and overseas holiday-makers: recent estimates indicate that New Zealanders made 2.5 million visits per annum out of a total of about 3 million visits (Mitchell *et al.*, 2001).

Continuity

Changes during the time gap between LINZ and the later national surveys led to problems with continuity in both methodology and coverage, and thus also affected comparability. LINZ used a mail survey and the electoral roll as the primary sampling frame but, by 1996, changes in electoral legislation precluded repetition of this method and the more recent surveys have adopted the geographic areas defined by Statistics New Zealand as the primary frame, and favoured face-to-face interviews over mailed questionnaires. It is well

known that an individual's responses to mail and face-to-face interviews will differ, but it is difficult to quantify the impact of this factor on the comparability of the results from the LINZ and the later arts and sports participation surveys. Telephone interviews were considered, but rejected as they tend to produce response rates below 50% and unacceptable levels of non-response bias.

Changes in leisure activities, or possibly terminology, in the 5-year gap between the surveys also posed problems for continuity in coverage. As one example, 'jazzercise', which was sufficiently popular to be included in the activity list used in the 1990 LINZ survey, was no longer in vogue by 1996 and was not included, or mentioned, in either the arts or sports surveys. The question arises, however, as to whether it has 'disappeared' or been transformed into more contemporary forms of dance/exercise.

Comparability

Comparability is often affected by changes in the agendas of the agencies commissioning the surveys, which in consequence can change the way aspects of leisure behaviour are defined and measured. As an example, the publication of the US Surgeon General's report on *Physical Activity and Health* (US Department of Health and Human Services, 1996) and the message that 30 min of frequent moderate-intensity physical activity can deliver real health benefits had an immediate and profound impact on the Hillary Commission's promotion of physical activity. In consequence a lower threshold was adopted in defining 'inactive' than was used in the analysis of the LINZ data.

The *Sport and Physical Activity* surveys have generated what has been nicknamed the 'couch potato index' (CPI). Results showed that, even though almost all New Zealanders take part in some form of sport or active leisure, around one-third (a CPI of 32) fell into the inactive category; that is, below a 2.5 h/week threshold. In response, the Commission launched a *Push Play* campaign in 1999 to promote the '30 minutes a day' message (Hillary Commission, 1999a, 2000). This advocates less formal activities such as walking and cycling, has resulted in new initiatives like *KiwiWalks*, a network of short, accessible walkways throughout New Zealand,[4] and has fostered the development of active leisure strategies at the local government level (Christchurch City Council, 2000). The Commission set itself the target of reducing the CPI by 10% by the end of 2000, a target also adopted by the health sector (Ministry of Health, 1998).

A requirement that all government agencies and departments pay closer attention to the cultural (and especially bicultural) foundations of New Zealand society has led to changes in survey content designed to generate more information about activities and interests specific to ethnic groups. This does not necessarily affect the comparability of surveys, but additions have to be considered with regard to interview length and, inevitably, as a result of the changes, some activities lose prominence and others are dropped.

In recognition of earlier problems, the sport and arts surveys were designed to facilitate comparisons across sectors, between countries and over time. This included using comparable recall periods and wording. Creative New Zealand crossed sector boundaries in *Know Your Audience* (Creative New Zealand, 2000a). This report contained profiles of audience involvement in 19 arts but also listed the respondents' main sports and active leisure pursuits. The findings thus illuminated both sectors:

> . . . it would be wrong to assume that an interest in sport and an interest in the arts are mutually exclusive. The survey found that 79% of all Kiwi adults watch sport on television within a four-week period. The findings in *Know Your Audience* show that on average, arts audiences show a similar level of interest in watching sport on television. Does this mean that advertising and promotion at sports events should be a promotional option for arts events?
>
> (Creative New Zealand, 2000a, p. 3)

Various recall periods – last year, last month, last 2 weeks – have been used to facilitate comparisons of sports and arts participation in New Zealand and in other countries, but the work required to assemble and analyse comparable data sets has still to be done. Relatively sophisticated analysis of sampling errors (Creative New Zealand, 1999b; Hillary Commission, 1999b; Gray, 2000) has also been

undertaken to facilitate comparisons over several national surveys, including those relating to leisure and health (Ministry of Health, 1999).

International comparability was an additional concern for the designers of the New Zealand Time Use Survey. The activity classification adopted was designed not only to identify separately the activities of particular interest to the TUS sponsors, but also to be consistent with the broad-level classifications used in overseas surveys. Methodological choices were made after a review of 13 other similar time-use surveys, as described by Fleming and Spellerberg (1999), who also provide a useful discussion of how such data, including leisure data, are commonly used. The TUS allows for broad comparisons with the sector surveys, although the activity classifications are not exactly matched.

Achieving comprehensiveness, continuity and comparability

The New Zealand experience leads to the conclusion that achieving comprehensive coverage, continuity and comparability in national leisure surveys will continue to be difficult until leisure becomes part of the official national statistical framework. Although a framework that encompasses most leisure activities has been developed in New Zealand (Statistics New Zealand and Ministry of Cultural Affairs, 1995), leisure is not yet being included in the ongoing surveys conducted by the government's statistical agency, and neither the sport and recreation section nor the natural environment section is well drawn in this framework. The tourism sector may fare better in future, with the publication of the governments' core tourism statistics and information[5] and the publication of the inaugural Tourism Satellite Account (Statistics New Zealand, 1999b), although how well domestic tourism will be served by these initiatives remains to be seen.

Influences on New Zealanders' Leisure Time

The national participation surveys reveal relatively few signs of change over the past decade in the main ways New Zealanders use their leisure time. However, social, economic and political changes are occurring that affect patterns of leisure behaviour.

Social and economic influences

There is a widely held perception that New Zealanders traditionally 'work hard and play hard'. If accurate, the tradition is under threat: those in full-time work have fewer hours for play, as indicated in Fig. 12.2, while increasing numbers can find no paid employment at all. For many people the weekend is no longer a 'work-free zone' and more and more 'leisure time' is being devoted to further education and training in attempts to keep pace with technological change and switches in career path (Ansley, 1999).

Leisure activities are also tending to place competing demands on discretionary time, and there are signs that 'value for time' is becoming more important than 'value for money'. This is affecting not only choice of leisure activities but also volunteer participation which, for many decades, has provided the backbone of sport, arts and other cultural organizations. In the sports infrastructure, for example, while the number of volunteers increased between 1991 and 1996, the total number of volunteer hours

declined from 95 million per year to 74 million (Hillary Commission, 1998a).

Other social and economic pressures are changing lifestyles and leisure. Increasing urbanization[6] and a reduction in living space, as more people move from houses to urban apartments, or suburban residential sites are subdivided for 'infill' housing, mean that the space available for both individual and community leisure activities is being reduced. The drift to urban areas has also meant a growth in numbers moving north in New Zealand, increasing the demand for leisure facilities and services in North Island cities. At the same time, the declining population in non-urban areas and the South Island makes it harder to sustain the range of leisure facilities and services that rural communities have come to expect. A high rate of internal migration is also breaking down traditional communities in general, eroding the base of many of the organizations providing leisure activities at the local level.

The dominance of 'mass media and free time activities' and the growing popularity of 'technological leisure activities' both conspire to make New Zealanders more sedentary. The revolution in mobile computing devices may, however, make this a short-lived phenomenon: it will soon be a simple matter to take a walk around the block while answering an e-mail or tuning into a favourite television programme.

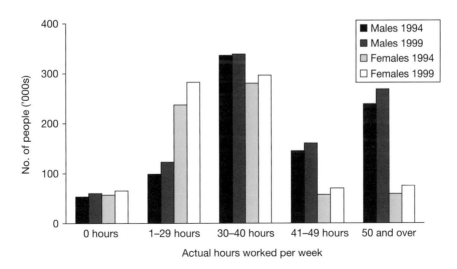

Fig. 12.2. Hours worked, employed persons, by gender, New Zealand, 1994 and 1999.
Source: Statistics New Zealand.

Some social commentators (e.g. Geering, 1999) see the current social and economic changes in New Zealand resulting in a move from a collective to an individualistic outlook on life. People are focused on their own families and careers and spend more time on individual than collective activities, and this is influencing their choice of leisure activities and involvement in volunteerism. This change is not restricted to New Zealand but the consequences may be different, and a source of tension, in a country where Māori and Pacific Island communities still subscribe more to a collective ethos than the majority of the population. For Māori, as Prentice (1992) points out, this collective ethos is evident in their view of leisure and recreation, in which higher priority is placed on people involvement and cooperation in the whanau, than on competitiveness and individual pursuits.

Economic pressures have increased for many New Zealanders, particularly those in the middle-income bands, and this has limited their choices in the leisure marketplace. Free market policies that characterized government policy in the 1990s have widened the gap between the 'haves' and 'have-nots'. In 1996, over 25% of after-tax income went to the top 10% of households, compared with 20% in 1982. In general terms, those at the top are getting more, those in the middle are getting less and those at the bottom are staying the same. Māori are over-represented in the lowest 25% of incomes, although the gap is narrowing.[6] While leisure spending increased through the 1990s,[7] the top income earners were responsible for a disproportionate amount of this expenditure. In the sport and active leisure sector, for example, household spending on goods and services increased by 26% between 1991 and 1996 and, although spending increased on almost all sports goods and services, most of the increase was due to the purchase of 'big-ticket' items such as recreational vehicles and pleasure craft (Hillary Commission, 1998a). Likewise, in 1995–96 the 10% of households with the highest gross annual income spent NZ$76 per week on arts and culture, which was five times as much as the sum spent by the 20% of households with the lowest income (Statistics New Zealand and Ministry of Cultural Affairs, 1996).

Government reforms

The free market ethos also encouraged new 'managerialist' approaches to government that led to the overriding of 'social criteria of organizational effectiveness by goals of economic efficiency' (Henry and Theodoraki, 2000, p. 501). In the leisure sector this has had both positive and negative repercussions. On the one hand, it has fostered more professional management in many sports, arts and leisure organizations, and improved services for members. On the other, the pressure to become more economically efficient and professional has meant some organizations, including even prominent and longstanding bodies have struggled to survive. In the arts, the drive for economic efficiency, in line with stringent contemporary requirements of the public sector, was implied both in the Arts Council Act 1994 and in comments from the Chair of the Council about demands for lean and effective service delivery and accountability (Arts Council, 1994, 1995). Dramatic changes in policy and organizational structure followed.

Local government legislation (Local Government Amendment Act 1997) similarly obliged local authorities, who are the biggest provider of many leisure facilities and services in New Zealand, to clarify whether they were delivering public or private goods, and to charge accordingly. In some cases this has led to increases in user charges, but in others, councils have worked with clubs and organizations to improve the community benefits. All councils have been forced to consider how to evaluate benefits (Manukau City Council, Creative New Zealand, and Hillary Commission, 1997). The Labour Government elected in 1999 has reviewed the Local Government Act once again, and further changes that affect the provision of leisure facilities and services can be anticipated.

Globalization

New Zealanders' leisure is affected by global as well as local influences. The 'death of distance', resulting from falling transport and communication costs and rising import penetration, mean that New Zealand is no longer geographically isolated.[6] New Zealanders are faced with an expanding range of goods, services and ideas from overseas. Many of these are American; indeed, with reference to activities (e.g. hip hop, rap, gridiron), products (e.g. Starbucks coffee, Nike clothing) and media coverage of sport, Americanization may be a more relevant term than globalization (Bernstein, 2000). As a small country, evidenced by the fact that the top 25 *Fortune* 500 companies all have annual revenues in excess of its gross domestic product, New Zealand has no simple task if it is to maintain an independence distinguishable from larger regional and global identities.

The media

The mass media, particularly television, the Internet and new technologies like VCDs and DVDs, play a key role in spreading global products and associated fashions. For most of the media, however: leisure = entertainment = profit. They seek to mould leisure activities to maximize entertainment value and profit. Sports such as rugby and cricket have already changed their rules to make them more appealing to spectators and television viewers (Hillary Commission, 1998c). Phillips (2000) charts the growth of mass media influence and professionalism in sport and, with reference mainly to Australia and New Zealand, accentuates such developments as: the timing of games to fit television schedules; emphasis on brand names; reduction in rough play, in part to protect valuable players from injury; and the promotion of women's sport, ranging from netball to rugby, as new sources of revenue. For the players, he sees the lure of money replacing local and patriotic sentiment, and sport becoming 'just a job'. Mass participation becomes secondary to spectatorship. Phillips' conclusion, that 'the presentation of sport and the sports which people choose to enjoy as either participants or spectators will be determined by the discretionary entertainment dollar' (Phillips, 2000, p. 332) seems pertinent to leisure generally.

The domestication of news and events through focusing on matters of local interest can, however, act as a counter to globalizing forces (Bernstein, 2000) and the global media themselves can bring benefits by offering more and faster access to information about leisure opportunities, both in New Zealand and overseas. They also allow New Zealand to broadcast its own culture and leisure attractions to the rest of the world. Initiatives are under way to help organizations make better use of relevant technology to this end.

While global influences appear to be gaining strength, New Zealanders are making renewed efforts to re-assert their identity. The issues have been brought to the fore by the current New Zealand prime minister who has assumed the portfolio of Minister of Arts and Culture and is strong in her support. A 'Cultural Recovery Package' announced in 2000 led to an extra NZ$87 million being invested in the cultural sector by central government. The government has also supported a new Film Production Unit and a Music Commission intended to 'support the expression of creative talent . . . and have significant economic development spin-offs'.[8] However, while the rescue package will stabilize some sections of the sector, it is questionable whether it will compensate for 'the fragility of the whole' (The Heart of the Nation Strategic Working Group, 2000, p. v).

The *Heart of the Nation* report, presented to government in 2000, collated a wealth of information on the cultural sector, including: its contribution to employment and GDP; its intersection with other sectors, such as tourism and the knowledge-based industries; and the likely impact of demographic changes on the demand for cultural goods and services. It estimated government's investment in the sector to be NZ$500 million annually with local government's contribution to be in the vicinity of NZ$300 million. However, this investment is not guaranteed in the long term, being subject to changes in policy and government legislation. While renewed support for the cultural sector is to be welcomed, it is apparent that it is no longer being viewed primarily as a producer of goods and services that the wider public enjoy when they have the time and the money. Rather, it is being positioned though government policy as a potential major contributor to GDP.

The government also sees the arts as a principal contributor to the development of a national identity, in the face of globalization. Government investment in the music and film industries is accompanied by a drive to establish quotas for local content on television and radio[9] 'so that we New Zealanders are able to see and hear more of our stories, music and perspectives . . . broadcast [through] local programming of quality which reflects the diversity of New Zealand life'.

The wider contribution of the arts to society also is acknowledged in *The Arts in the New Zealand Curriculum*, introduced in primary and secondary schools in August 2000. This replaced syllabus statements for each subject area developed in the 1980s. In his foreword, the Secretary for Education emphasized the role of the arts in encouraging and providing opportunities for 'imaginative and innovative thought and action, emotional growth, and for deeper understanding of the cultural practices and traditions of New Zealand and overseas. Such opportunities are integral to young people achieving their potential as learners and participating in their communities and society' (Ministry of Education, 2000).

The new Labour Government has increased spending for the sports sector too, with NZ$16 million (over 4 years) being committed to the New Zealand Academy of Sport, a national network of high performance sports centres. In spite of these increases, the sports sector in New Zealand argues that it is still severely underfunded. The wider benefits of sport to the individual and society are also receiving increasing recognition in government circles, as exemplified in the briefing paper from the Office of Tourism and Sport (OTSP) to the incoming Minister for Sport, Fitness and Leisure. Sport, fitness and leisure are seen as contributing positive outcomes to the economy, health, education, social welfare and justice, Māori development, community building, national identity and international profile and reputation (OTSP, 1999).

Some features of the New Zealand leisure sector have not changed over the past decade. For example, organization and administration continue to be fragmented. This is despite a number of past reviews (such as the review of the structure and funding of high performance sport),[10] a review of Māori sport (Hillary Commission, 1998d) and more recent ones.[11] Even so, moves have been made to put cultural 'icons' on a more secure financial footing. The Royal New Zealand Ballet, and the Aotearoa Traditional Māori Performing Arts Society, both

now receive direct-line funding from government. Furthermore, although there is no comprehensive leisure policy in New Zealand, some progress has been made. There is now a physical activity policy (OTSP and Ministry of Health, 1999) and more coordinated policy advice is available for the tourism and sport sectors through the creation of the OTSP.[12]

Calls for a more integrated approach to the leisure sector, or components of it, were a recurring theme in briefing papers submitted to the new government in 1999 (OTSP, 1999; Local Government New Zealand[13]). The next edition of this book may be able to report that government has responded to these calls.

Conclusion

Participation and time-use surveys provide valuable insights into how New Zealanders use their leisure time. Such surveys can also provide 'hard facts' that help put leisure, or at least some components of it, more firmly on the government's agenda. National surveys also enable national targets to be set to monitor the performance of leisure policy-makers and providers.

However, as the New Zealand experience suggests, these large-scale surveys are less useful in charting the broader influences that are changing New Zealanders' leisure lives. Future research will require instruments better able to monitor changes that may be subtle and rapid. In New Zealand, where both global and local influences seem set to shape the leisure future, new approaches will have to be sensitive to external pressures, creating uniformity, and internal forces creating diversity and distinctiveness. As elsewhere, leisure behaviour might best be explained in the future in terms of the 'balance and blend between diminishing contrasts and increasing varieties' (Maguire, 2000, p. 358).

Notes

[1] Information about demographic changes in New Zealand's population is available online at: www.stats.govt.nz

[2] Although the results show that people in their fifties and early sixties are more active than people

in their late thirties and forties (unpublished Hillary Commission data).

[3] Details of the research by Dr David Simmons at Lincoln University are available online at: www.lincoln.ac.nz/trrec/trrecpub.htm

[4] KiwiWalks can be located through the website, available online at: www.sport.org.nz/kiwiwalks

[5] See www.trncz.govt.nz/Tourismframe.htm

[6] See *Changes in Society*, available online on Statistics New Zealand's website at: http://www.stats.govt.nz/domino/external/web/ nzstories.nsf/Response/The+big+shifts+now+in+ train:+Changes+in+society

[7] Total spending on leisure in 1998 was NZ$10.8 billion (20% of the total household expenditure). From 1993 to 1998 leisure spending increased by 13% in real terms (total household spending increased by 8.5% over this period). Spending on cultural goods and services was NZ$2.2billion in 1998 (an 8.3% increase in real terms). Spending on leisure market goods and services is projected to increase by 15% (NZ$1.6 billion) between 1998 and 2010 (*Heart of the Nation* p. 35).

[8] Quoted from 'Arts, Culture and Public Policy' a speech by the Rt Hon. Helen Clark, Prime Minister. Available online at: http://www.beehive.govt.nz/ PrintDocument.cfm?DocumentID=8266

[9] Quoted from Rt Hon. Helen Clark's speech.

[10] The Winning Way Review was conducted in 1995, resulting in a contract for joint public/private sector funding for sport.

[11] A ministerial Taskforce was set up in June 2000 and is reported to the Minister of Sport, Fitness and Leisure in 2001. Details are available online at: http://www.sparc.org.nz/aboutus/reports.php

[12] The Office of Tourism and Sport was established in 1998 and inherited policy functions previously performed by groups within the Ministry of Commerce and Department of Internal Affairs. The tourism functions are now the responsibility of the Ministry of Tourism and the sport functions the responsibility of Sport and Recreation New Zealand (SPARC).

[13] See Local Government New Zealand's briefing paper to the Rt Hon. Helen Clark, Prime Minister and Minister for Arts, Culture and Heritage, April 2000, available online at: www.lgnz.co.nz (see archived publications).

References

Ansley, B. (1999) The future of work. *The Listener* 4 September, 14–19.

Arts Council of New Zealand (1994a) *Toi Aotearoa Act 1994*. ACNZ, Wellington.

Arts Council of New Zealand (1994b) *Annual Report of the Queen Elizabeth II Arts Council of New Zealand for the Year Ended 30 June 1994*. ACNZ, Wellington.

Arts Council of New Zealand (1995) *Annual Report of the Arts Council of New Zealand/Toi Aotearoa for the Year Ended 30 June 1995*. ACNZ, Wellington.

Bernstein, A. (2000) 'Things you can see from there you can't see from here'. Globalisation, media and the Olympics. *Journal of Sport and Social Issues* 24(4), 351–369.

Business and Economic Research Ltd (1997) *Economic Growth of the Copyright Industries. A report for the Copyright Council of New Zealand*. Wellington. (Updates reports from 1990 and 1992.) Copyright Council of New Zealand Inc., Wellington.

Christchurch City Council (2000) *Recreation and Sport Strategy, Discussion Document*. Christchurch City Council, Christchurch.

Consumer Research Group (1996) *New Zealand Towards 2000*. Consumer Research Group, University of Otago, Dunedin.

Creative New Zealand (1999a) *Arts Every Day*. Creative New Zealand, Wellington.

Creative New Zealand (1999b) *Technical Report*. Creative New Zealand, Wellington.

Creative New Zealand (2000a) *Know Your Audience*. Creative New Zealand, Wellington.

Creative New Zealand (2000b) *Māori Arts Participation*. Creative New Zealand, Wellington.

Creative New Zealand (2003) *Portrait of the Artist: a Survey of Professional Practising Artists in New Zealand*. Creative New Zealand, Wellington.

Department of Statistics (1991) *Testing Time: Report of the 1990 Time Use Survey*. Department of Statistics, Wellington.

Fleming, R. and Spellerberg, A. (1999) *Using Time Use Data. A History of Time Use Surveys and Uses of Time Use Data*. Statistics New Zealand, Wellington.

Forsyte Research (2000) *New Zealand Domestic Travel Study 1999*. Forsyte Research, Auckland, New Zealand.

Geering, L. (1999) Community ethics. In: New Zealand Futures Trust, *Our Country: Our Choices*. NZ Futures Trust, Wellington.

Gray, A.G. (2000) *Hillary Commission Sport and Physical Activity Survey: Comparison of Design Effects for the 97/98 and 98/99 data*. Report for the Hillary Commission, Wellington.

Heart of the Nation Strategic Working Group (2000) *The Heart of the Nation: a Cultural Strategy for Aotearoa, New Zealand*. Report to the Prime Minister and Minister of Culture and Heritage, Wellington.

Henry, I. and Theodoraki, E. (2000) Management, organizations and theory in the governance of sport. In: Coakley, J. and Dunning, E. (eds) *Handbook of Sports Studies*. Sage, London, pp. 490–503.

Hillary Commission (undated a) *Sport Facts* (issue 1) *Participation in Sport and Physical Activity by New Zealand Adults*. Hillary Commission, Wellington.

Hillary Commission (undated b) *Sport Facts* (issue 2): *Sport and Physical Activity – How and Where Adults Play*. Hillary Commission, Wellington.

Hillary Commission (1994) *Solving the Mystery of Inactivity*. Hillary Commission, Wellington.

Hillary Commission (1998a) *The Growing Business of Sport and Leisure – Economic Impact*. A report for the Hillary Commission by Business and Economic Research Ltd. Hillary Commission, Wellington.

Hillary Commission (1998b) *The Growing Business of Sport and Leisure – Social Impact*. A report for the Hillary Commission by Business Research Centre (BRC). Hillary Commission, Wellington.

Hillary Commission (1998c) *Sports Entertainment Television*. A report for the Hillary Commission by Carrad and Fitzgerald Ltd. Hillary Commission, Wellington.

Hillary Commission (1998d) *1998 Task Force Report on Māori Sport*. Hillary Commission, Wellington.

Hillary Commission (1999a) *Push Play facts*. Hillary Commission, Wellington.

Hillary Commission (1999b) *1997 Sport and Physical Activity Survey – Technical Report*. Hillary Commission, Wellington.

Hillary Commission (2000) *Pushing Play: Active Leisure in New Zealand in 2010: a Discussion Paper*. Hillary Commission, Wellington.

Hillary Commission and Creative New Zealand (1995) *Community Funding for the Arts, Sport and Physical Leisure in New Zealand*. A submission by the Hillary Commission and Creative New Zealand to the Review of Gaming 1995. Hillary Commission, Wellington.

Hillary Commission and Creative New Zealand (1997) *Arts and Recreation: a Guide to the Local Government Act*. A report to the Hillary Commission and Creative New Zealand by McKinlay Douglas. Hillary Commission, Wellington.

Laidler, A. and Cushman, G. (1996) New Zealand. In: Cushman, G., Veal, A.J. and Zuzanek, J. (eds) *World Leisure Participation: Free Time in the Global Village*. CAB International, Wallingford, UK, pp. 165–182.

Lawson, R., Thyne, M. and Young, T. (1997) *New Zealand Holidays: a Travel Lifestyles Study*. Marketing Department, University of Otago, Dunedin.

Maguire, J. (2000) Sport and globalization. In: Coakley, J. and Dunning, E. (eds) *Handbook of Sports Studies*. Sage, London, pp. 356–369.

Maharey, S. and Swain, P. (2000) Closing the digital divide – what do we know about the digital divide in New Zealand? http://www.executive.govt.nz/minister/maharey/divide/01-02.htm

Manukau City Council, Creative New Zealand, and Hillary Commission (1997) *Valuing the Benefits of Recreation, Arts and Parks*. Report by McKinlay Douglas Ltd, Manukau City Council, Wellington.

Matunga, H. (1995) Māori participation in outdoor recreation: an exploration of the issues. In: Devlin, P.J., Corbett, R.A. and Peebles, C.J. (eds) *Outdoor Recreation in New Zealand, Vol 1: a Review and Synthesis of the Literature*. Department of Conservation and Lincoln University, Canterbury, pp. 17–30.

McGregor, H. and McMath, M. (1993) Leisure – a Māori and Mangaiian perspective. In: Perkins, H. and Cushman, G. (eds) *Leisure, Recreation and Tourism*. Longman Paul, Auckland, pp. 44–57.

Ministry of Education (2000) *The Arts in the New Zealand Curriculum*. Ministry of Education, Wellington. (Background papers available online at: www.minedu.govt.nz/curriculum/thearts/artscont.htm).

Ministry of Health (1998) *Progress on Health Outcome Targets 1998*. Ministry of Health, Wellington.

Ministry of Health (1999) *Taking the Pulse: the 1996/97 New Zealand Health Survey*. Ministry of Health, Wellington.

Ministry of Women's Affairs and Government Statistician (1999) *Time Use Survey (1999) – Media Release*, 14 December, Ministry of Women's Affairs and Government Statistician, Wellington.

Ministry of Women's Affairs and Government Statistician (2000) *Time Use Survey: Health and Welfare Results (1999) – Media Release, 11 May 2000*. Ministry of Women's Affairs and Government Statistician, Wellington.

Ministry of Women's Affairs and Statistics New Zealand (2001) *Around the Clock: Findings From the New Zealand Time Use Survey 1998–99*. Statistics New Zealand, Wellington.

Mitchell, R., Hall, M. and Johnson, G. (2001) *Case Study 7.2: Wine Tourism in New Zealand*. In: Hall, C.M. and Kearsley, G. (eds) *Tourism in New Zealand: an Introduction*. Oxford University Press, Melbourne.

Office of Tourism and Sport (OTSP) (1999) *Portfolio Briefing, Minister of Sport, Fitness and Leisure*. OTSP, Wellington.

Office of Tourism and Sport (OTSP) and Ministry of Health (1999) *Physical Activity. A Joint Policy Statement by the Minister of Sport, Fitness and Leisure and the Minister of Health.* OTSP and Ministry of Health, Wellington.

Phillips, J. (2000) Epilogue: sport and future Australasian culture. In: Mangan, J.A. and Nauright, J. (eds) *Sport in Australian Society Past and Present.* Frank Cass, London, pp. 323–332.

Porter, M. (1999) *The Global Competitiveness Report 1999.* World Economic Forum, Geneva, Switzerland.

Prentice, N. (1992) Engaging Māori leisure time. *Leisure Management,* Spring, 21–22.

Queen Elizabeth II Arts Council of New Zealand and the Hillary Commission for Recreation and Sport (1990) *Review of Gambling in New Zealand.* Hillary Commission, Wellington.

Russell, D.G. and Wilson, N.C. (1991) *Life in New Zealand Commission Report Vol 1: Executive Overview.* University of Otago, Dunedin.

Statistics New Zealand (1999a) *New Zealand Time Use Survey: Users' Guide.* Report for the Ministry of Women's Affairs. Statistics New Zealand, Wellington.

Statistics New Zealand (1999b) *Tourism Satellite Account, March 1995.* Statistics New Zealand, Wellington.

Statistics New Zealand and the Ministry of Cultural Affairs (1995) *New Zealand Framework for Cultural Statistics.* Statistics New Zealand, Wellington.

Statistics New Zealand and the Ministry of Cultural Affairs (1996) *Household Spending on Culture.* Statistics New Zealand, Wellington.

Statistics New Zealand and the Ministry of Culture and Heritage (2000) *Government Spending on Culture.* Statistics New Zealand, Wellington.

Thomson, R. (2000) Physical activity through sport and leisure: traditional versus non-competitive activities. *Journal of Physical Education New Zealand* 33(1), 34–39.

Time Use Statistics (1999) Statistics New Zealand. http://www.stats.govt.nz/domino/external/web/Prod_Serv.nsf/3153e23ac69cb3d84c25680800821fa4/ed5677fc1db05458cc256b260010cc9c?OpenDocument

US Department of Health and Human Services (1996) *Physical Activity and Health: a Report of the Surgeon General.* US Dept of Health and Human Services, Centers for Disease Control and Prevention, National Center for Chronic Disease Prevention and Health Promotion, Atlanta, Georgia.

Volkerling, M. (1998) The arts and optimal experience: theory, practice and policy. In: Perkins, H.C. and Cushman, G. (eds) *Time Out: Leisure, Recreation and Tourism in New Zealand.* Longman, Auckland, pp. 310–326.

Walker, S., Ross, J. and Gray, A. (1999) Participation in sport and active leisure by New Zealand children and adolescents. *Journal of Physical Education New Zealand* 32(1), 4–8.

13 Poland

Bohdan Jung

Introduction

This chapter concentrates on changes that took place in Polish leisure after 1989, when the communist system collapsed. The changes are also compared to the situation that existed in the 1970s and 1980s, to trace the roots of the processes which shaped the 1990s, using mainly publicly available statistics. The structure of the chapter follows the categorizations used for statistical purposes, namely: time-use; household spending; household equipment, including leisure durables; cultural and sports participation; and tourism. The analysis begins with a review of the statistical sources available for the study of leisure in Poland.

Availability of Leisure Statistics in Poland

In the post-Second World War period, the knowledge on leisure participation in Poland came primarily from official statistics routinely gathered by state institutions and firms and processed and published by the Central Statistical Office (GUS). This process was financed and organized by the state, and resulted in a situation which was, in many ways, comfortable for leisure scholars. Large-scale statistical studies were carried out at regular intervals, providing a body of data to be analysed and compared.

These studies included: time-budget surveys conducted in 1969, 1976 and 1984, with samples of over 49,000 representative households; annual household budget surveys (with similar sample sizes); cultural participation studies, involving data from both institutions and population surveys conducted in 1969, 1971, 1973, 1975, 1982 and 1989, with samples of some 25,000; surveys of participation in holidays and tourism; and annual statistical series on culture, sports, recreation and tourism published in the country's statistical yearbooks.

Following the breakdown of the communist system in Poland in 1989, a number of austerity programmes were instituted to curb government spending and generally reduce the scope of the state's presence in economic and social life. With a few exceptions described below, the collection of state statistics on leisure participation did not suffer substantially from these cutbacks. The most notable casualty to date has been the time-budget survey, originally scheduled for 1992 but delayed until 1996. Given their relevance to marketing strategies and social policy, household spending surveys continued to be compiled on an annual basis (this applied also to the data on ownership of household consumer durables, many of which are leisure-related). Interest in the economic dimension of tourism also prompted frequent and exhaustive collection of data, whereas culture and sport were less fortunate in this respect.

© CAB International 2005. *Free Time and Leisure Participation: International Perspectives* (eds G. Cushman *et al.*)

From the perspective of late 2000, statistics from large-scale studies on leisure participation in Poland in 1991/92 were still a valuable, albeit historical, source of data, but the key evidence on the way Polish leisure evolved in the 1990s came from the latest time-budget study, carried out in 1996. Even though it was carried out using a much smaller sample than the two previous studies, and the scope of leisure activities featured in the questionnaire was narrower and not always compatible with the earlier studies, this study forms the basis of the discussion in this chapter. Other statistics quoted below originate from smaller, more specialized, studies carried out by market analysts, public opinion pollsters, research commissioned by government departments, international (mainly EU) assistance programmes and work of academic and policy-oriented institutes. It can also be assumed that there was an important body of knowledge gathered on commercially vital aspects of leisure participation by consultancy firms and market analysts: this knowledge has not, however, been made publicly available and one may only speculate as to its likely impact.

On the whole, it can be said that the breakdown of the communist system has not affected the availability of leisure statistics in Poland, but has made the statistical sources more varied and, predictably, more geared to the potential market value of the gathered information. The wealth of government statistics on various aspects of leisure (culture, tourism, sports, recreation, household budgets, time-use) continued to be made available at regular intervals. The reduction in the mammoth size of the representative samples was most felt in the time-use surveys, especially for activities involving a small percentage of participants, for example theatre, opera, museum and similar activities traditionally related to high culture. On the other hand, very large samples became less important when there was no need for them to be representative of the country's 49 departments, these having been reduced to 16.

A summary of leisure statistics gathered by the Central Statistical Office (GUS) is presented in Table 13.1. This list is not exhaustive but it gives an idea of the interest that government still had in the leisure area.

The Use of Time

The changing dynamics of time-use

Nationwide time-use surveys were conducted in Poland in 1976, 1984 and in 1996. Smaller studies were carried out in 1966 and 1969, but were more restricted in character in terms of representative sampling and activity categories used, and are not drawn on here. The fundamental factor that shaped Polish leisure at the end of the 1990s was the continuing growth in the amount of leisure time available both to the average Pole and to all those that had free time, as depicted by data from the successive time-budget surveys. Data from these studies are presented in the traditional forms: time devoted to a given activity by those engaged in it (further referred to as *time per participant*); the proportion of persons from the whole study engaged in a given activity (*% participating* or *participation rates*); and average time spent on a given activity per person taking part in the study (*average time*). The relation between these measures can be presented for a single activity as:

average time = % participating × time per participant

As shown in Table 13.2, from 1976 to 1996 the total amount of time available for leisure per person increased on average by 46 min/day. This was taking place at the expense of time spent on work, which fell by as much as 1 hour 43 minutes over 20 years, with over half of the reduction taking place in the second half of the period. After a steady increase during the economic, political and social crisis in Poland in the 1980s (rationing of food, queues for everyday products, mass shortages, etc.), the time devoted to household obligations decreased by nearly half an hour between 1984 and 1996. In this period, the time for education, travel to all activities and physiological obligations (mainly for sleep) all increased.

In terms of averages, this seems to paint a rosy picture of the changes that took place after 1996. However, a different picture emerges when the same phenomenon is studied from the perspective of participation rates and the time

Table 13.1. Public leisure statistics in Poland.

Type of survey	Sample unit	Sample size	Representative sample	Years conducted	Survey institution
Time-budget study	Persons	2480–49,990	Yes	1976, 1984, 1996	GUS
Household budgets	Households	29,140–31,780	Yes	Annual	GUS
Participation in culture	Persons	2500–11,630	Yes	1972, 1979, 1985, 1988, 1999	GUS
Consumer durables	Households	3900	Yes	1995	GUS
Yearbook of culture	Institutions, participants	–	Complete	Annual	GUS
Participation in tourism	Persons	24,000	Yes	1986	GUS
Recreation of the population	Persons	69,360	Yes	1984	GUS
Participation in tourism in 1986	Persons	10,800	Yes	1986	GUS
Physical culture in 1990–1998		n/a	Complete	1990–1998	GUS
Tourism in 1999		n/a	Complete	1999	GUS
Participation of Poles in sports and physical recreation	Households	3750	Yes	1998/99	GUS
Tourism and recreation	Households	3850	Yes	1997/98	GUS
Participation in tourism and culture	Households	3910	Yes	1994/95	GUS

n/a, not applicable; GUS, Central Statistical Office.

per participant. While leisure time per participant in each of the periods between time-budget surveys grew by 17 min and the proportion of those having leisure increased from 93% in 1976 to nearly 98% in 1996, the percentage of those in paid work fell from 66% in 1976 to 43% in 1996. Part of this very significant drop was explained by the ageing of Polish society and the increasing proportion of retired people and of pensioners, but over half of those not working were unemployed. Whereas at the end of the 1980s the country had no unemployment, by the end of the next decade the rate of unemployment increased to 13–15%. In the early 1990s unemployment was initially restricted to traditional industrial sectors in decline and manual jobs requiring low skills, but by the mid-1990s it was spreading to new, hitherto untouched, socio-professional groups, including young university graduates (Roberts and Jung, 2000).

For those 'gainfully employed', work time was also reduced, albeit in a less spectacular way, decreasing from 7 hours 10 minutes in 1976 to 6 hours 55 minutes in 1996, despite there being no change in duration of the working week between 1984 and 1996.[1] These data run very much against the public feeling of a big 'time-squeeze' after 1989, but this feeling might be related to the increased productivity of employment, rather than the nominal time spent working. Time-use surveys also pointed to an increase in the time spent on work by those engaged in additional jobs, where increases of nearly 2 h were noted between 1984 and 1996, although the proportion of those engaged in such jobs fell from 3% to 0.6% in the period.

While the statistical image of 'less work, more leisure' would be hotly contested by most Poles, in terms of *time per participant*, changes in the other 'social time' were more convergent with the logic of changes taking place under market reforms. Less working time for those in work resulted in more time spent sleeping, while the unemployed spent more time on household obligations. Unemployed men took up household

Table 13.2. Changes in the use of time, Poland, 1976–1996.

	Period	Time per participant (hours:min per day)			% participating			Average time: whole population (hours:min)		
		Total	Men	Women	Total	Men	Women	Total	Men	Women
Physiological needs	1996	10:50	10:48	10:53	99.9	99.9	99.9	10:50	10:47	10:52
Change	1984–1996	00:35	00:37	00:35	-0.1	-0.1	-0.1	00:35	00:36	00:34
Change	1976–1996	00:47	00:49	00:47	-0.1	-0.1	-0.1	00:47	00:48	00:46
Work	1996	06:55	07:40	06:00	43.5	53.1	35.6	03:01	04:04	02:08
Change	1984–1996	-00:17	-00:17	-00:21	-10.8	-11.6	-10.4	-00:54	-01:05	-00:47
Change	1976–1996	-00:15	-00:28	-00:12	-22.7	-22.8	-23.1	-01:43	-02:06	-01:30
Travel to all activities	1996	01:15	01:19	01:12	84.7	87.3	82.5	01:04	01:04	01:00
Change	1984–1996	00:03	00:02	00:04	23.5	19.1	27.0	00:20	00:16	00:22
Change	1976–1996	00:00	-00:01	00:02	15.9	12	18.8	00:13	00:09	00:15
Education	1996	04:45	05:13	04:25	4.5	4.1	4.9	00:13	00:13	00:13
Change	1984–1996	-00:24	-00:10	-00:33	1.3	1	1.6	00:03	00:03	00:03
Change	1976–1996	-01:10	-00:48	-01:24	-2.4	-3.3	-1.7	-00:12	-00:12	-00:10
Household obligations[a]	1996	04:19	02:47	05:24	91.5	83.5	98.1	03:57	02:19	05:18
Change	1984–1996	00:12	00:37	00:15	9.6	19.8	1.5	-00:29	00:55	-00:48
Change	1976–1996	00:13	00:39	00:24	13.0	26.7	2.9	00:06	00:40	-00.13
Free time (leisure)	1996	04:59	05:31	04:33	97.7	97.7	97.6	04:52	05:52	04:26
Change	1984–1996	00:17	00:09	00:24	2.1	0.2	3.6	00:22	00:10	00:32
Change	1976–1996	00:34	00:34	00:34	4.6	1.6	6.9	00:46	00:39	00:49

a Both in and out of the home.
Source: Calculations based on data from *Time Use Survey 1996* (GUS, 1998).

chores, which for the first time resulted in a statistically significant restructuring of social time between the two sexes. Time spent on education was significantly lower than in 1976 (down by 1 hour 10 minutes), but from 1984 the percentage of those in education was growing again.

Between 1976 and 1996 leisure time per participant grew by 34 minutes for both sexes. It should be noted that between the last two time budget surveys, however, women's leisure grew by 24 minutes, while that of men grew by only 9 minutes. In terms of the proportion of the population having free time, women have caught up with men. While at the outset of the period one in ten women claimed to have no leisure, compared with one in 20 for men, by 1996 the proportions were less than 1% for both sexes. In addition to the decrease in the average time spent on work, this may be considered as one of the most significant developments in Polish leisure in the 1990s.

Structure of leisure time and levels of participation

Between 1976 and 1996 leisure time in the daily time-budget of the average Pole increased by 34 minutes. As Table 13.3 indicates, the share of time spent watching television also increased, from 34.6% of leisure time (1h 35min) to 47.0% of leisure time (2h 20min), an increase of 45 minutes, which suggests that more than the entire growth in Polish leisure time was consumed by this medium. Closer examination of the data from successive time-use surveys shows that this was indeed the case. The share of television in leisure time progressed steadily from 36% in 1976 through 40% in 1984 to nearly 49% in 1996. This was taking place at the expense of nearly all other forms of leisure, with the exception of religious practice, categorized by some as a semi-leisure/semi-obligation.

Table 13.3. The structure of leisure time by gender, Poland 1976, 1984, 1996.

| Activity | Year | % of leisure time | | |
		Total	Men	Women
Reading papers and periodicals	1976	6.1	7.4	4.6
	1984	5.6	7.0	3.8
	1996	4.5	4.9	4.1
Reading books	1976	4.1	3.2	4.6
	1984	3.3	2.9	3.8
	1996	2.7	2.2	3.4
Watching TV	1976	35.8	37.5	34.6
	1984	40.0	40.4	40.2
	1996	48.6	50.0	47.0
Listening to the radio	1976	2.0	2.5	3.7
	1984	2.2	2.9	1.7
	1996	1.0	1.2	1.1
Theatre, ballet, concerts	1976	0.4	0.4	0.5
	1984	–	0.3	–
	1996	–	–	–
Cinema	1976	1.2	1.1	0.9
	1984	0.7	0.6	0.4
	1996	–	0.3	–
Passive resting	1976	11.8	11.9	12.0
	1984	11.5	11.8	11.1
	1996	7.5	7.7	7.9
Religious practice	1976	3.7	2.1	4.6
	1984	4.1	2.9	5.6
	1996	6.2	4.3	7.9

–, Not available.
Source: Calculations based on data from *Time Use Survey 1996* (GUS, 1998).

Noteworthy is the absence (or level below statistical significance) of activities associated with high culture (now also including the cinema, which was a popular mass culture activity of the 1960s and the 1970s). In addition, there was an increase in the average time spent on religious practice: after the downfall of communism the percentage of those engaging in religious activities increased on the average by nine percentage points, but despite the stereotypical image, the level of religious participation in Poland in 1996 was only approximately 25%. The share of time spent on passive resting, an indirect indicator of the general attractiveness of leisure time, also decreased sharply between the last two time-budget studies, which suggests that there were opportunities to spend time more actively.

The time-budget study of 1996 introduced some categories which were not comparable with previous surveys. Taking into account the full range of leisure activities analysed in 1996, the predominance of the mass media was also pronounced, with all media taking up to 60% of all leisure time. Television alone accounted for 49% of this time, while 7% went to various forms of reading. The second most time-consuming form of leisure was socializing and entertainment (especially meeting with family and relatives), but this took up only half of the amount of time spent on watching television (25% of leisure time). Sports and recreation took on the average 9% of leisure time, while personal hobbies, followed by civic and religious activities took just 6%, and games only 2.4%.

Television- and video-watching engaged nearly 90% of the Polish population (with a slight predominance of men) devoting 2:23 to 2:58 hrs of their time to this activity out of 2:46 to 3:22 hrs devoted to all mass media. There was no other leisure activity comparable to television- and video-watching in terms of its nearly universal reach. The next group of activities – socializing and entertainment – was recorded by two-thirds of Poles, while sports/recreation and civic activities attracted a quarter of the population.

The changes that took place in Poland after 1989 did not result in significant changes in the ranking of leisure activities. Perhaps the only statistical manifestations of these changes could be found in the even stronger position of the electronic media and reduced participation in high culture, art and hobbyist activities. However, those that engaged in these latter activities showed high levels of time commitment, comparable to that made by the entire population with respect to mass media. The data also confirm the increasingly marginalized character of cinema as a pastime. According to cultural participation statistics, in 1972 the cinema was attended by over 50% of the Polish population, while in 1990 it still attracted over 30% and was among the most popular pastimes. By 1996 only 0.5% of respondents taking part in the time-budget study declared they went to the cinema – a very low figure, but nevertheless five times the percentage going to the theatre and over twice the percentage going to the museum.

Passive resting was practised by over one-third of Poles, which made it one of the most popular activities, but it did not compare with media use, especially watching television and video, as well as with socializing/visiting friends and family. Passive resting was not stigmatized by the much publicized 'active resting', promoted by advertising, health organizations and sports organizations.

The level of sports participation, both active and passive (watching), has traditionally remained at a modest level throughout the post-Second World War years, and the reforms of 1989 brought no change to this pattern. There was no single form of sport which involved more than 20–25% of the Polish population, with 75% never engaging in any form of physical recreation other than walking. As shown in Table 13.4, the participation rates from time-budget studies are consistent with findings from cultural and sports participation surveys which asked about Poles' favourite leisure pursuits.

Differentiation in the use of leisure

While the market reforms of 1989 were successful in establishing a fast-growing entrepreneurial capitalism, they were also effectively producing new types of inequality, including unemployment, income polarization and marginalization, at a pace and on a scale unprece-

Table 13.4. Favourite leisure pursuits (%), Poland, 1998.

Passive resting	40
Reading	33.8
Listening to radio, music, watching TV	74.8
Socializing	34.6
Going to coffee shops, restaurants	4.1
Sports, physical exercise	17.2
Watching sports events	12.1
Museums, exhibitions, monuments	4.6
Cinema, theatre, cultural events	8.8
Religious practice	11.3
Hobby, studying to enhance knowledge	9.7
Work on allotment gardens	15
Shopping for pleasure	5.0
Other	2.8

n = 10,975. First-choice activity, multiple answers allowed.
Source: GUS (1999), 38.

dented in the post-war communist era (Kleer, 1994).

The data show that even though access to leisure had become more differentiated, the heavy predominance of mass media in general, and of television in particular, made these disparities less evident from the perspective of leisure-time use and participation rates. Simplifying this problem somewhat, age group, gender and level of education still seem to have more impact on the practice of leisure than the level of income, the influence of which seems to be strongest in relation to weekend practices and holiday patterns – elements which are not essential in the construction of daily leisure time-budgets in Poland, since they are followed by only a small part of the population (*Time Use Survey 1996*. GUS, 1998).

A different picture emerges when one looks at the other categories used in time-use surveys: socio-professional status of the household, place of dwelling, number of children in the household, days of the week (Łagodziński, 1992).

In the 1970s and 1980s, in working households, Saturdays were clearly a time to catch up on household obligations neglected throughout the working week. Despite an overall significant decrease, by 29 min, in the average amount of time devoted to household obligations, this pattern did not change in the 1990s,

but on Saturdays more time was also spent on leisure activities (but not on reading, technical hobbies, arts or listening to the radio). Sunday continued to have its distinct pattern of time-use, dominated by home-centred leisure. The level of engagement with the media continued to be high throughout the week, but activities involving religious participation, visiting friends and family, sport and recreation were significantly higher during weekends.

The categories used to describe socio-economic status of the household in Polish time-survey statistics in 1996 included the following: gainfully employed; hired farm workers; self-employed farmers; other self-employed; retired/pensioners; living from non-earned sources (stipends, dependants, unemployment benefits, etc.).[2] Households of the retired and those living from unearned sources spent more time on religious participation and use of mass media (both audiovisual and printed) than any other socio-economic groups. The self-employed had by far the highest time commitments to entertainment, visiting museums and exhibitions, arts and technical hobbies, and spent the least time on passive resting. Among all the socio-economic groups it was farmers and hired farm labour who spent most time visiting friends. Those gainfully employed were too large an aggregate to be distinct from the other groups; however, it was in this group that highest time commitments for theatre and cinema were to be found in 1996. With respect to participation rates, the retired and the self-employed were most likely to read, watch and listen to the media; together with the gainfully employed they were also heavily engaged in visiting friends and family (lowest participation rates were recorded for farmers, who also had very low rates for reading – 13%). Highest participation rates for recreation (32%) were recorded among the retired, and the lowest among the farmers. Participation in high culture was noted only in households of the self-employed, gainfully employed and the retired, but this participation was under 1% of the respondents in each of the groups. Religious practice drew roughly one-third of the farmers, hired farm labour, retired and those living from unearned sources, but dropped to one-fifth for all other groups.

When leisure time and participation rates

are analysed from the perspective of the place of dwelling, the most obvious disparity in leisure patterns is between large cities and rural areas, but only with respect to such forms of free time use as high culture activities, sports and recreation, hobbies, reading newspapers and magazines and listening to music, whereas, in terms of time per participant, much more time commitment was found in the large cities than in the rural areas. Those living in villages spent more time watching sports events, passive resting, watching television and video, and visiting friends and family. There was no clear relationship between the size of the city and the use of leisure time. Probably the explaining factor would be the geographic proximity of the smaller cities to larger cities and associated leisure infrastructure. When participation rates are analysed, there is a very pronounced disparity in readership levels and in sports participation between large cities and villages; those living in rural areas also have a much higher level of religious participation and are less likely to visit friends and family, but otherwise there is no clear pattern of differentiation.

Finally, in families with numerous children and in single-parent families the time available for various leisure activities outside of home and the percentage of participants was significantly lower than among those with no children. This was the only group where even the time spent on the media, traditionally high in Poland, was much lower (generally by one-third) than the average.

Leisure Spending and Equipment

Spending from household budgets

Despite large representative samples, the categories of household spending related to leisure have not been consistent throughout the analysed period, resulting in a fragmented picture of leisure spending. Different aggregations of spending categories and different socio-economic groups were used in the available studies (including the introduction of the self-employed group after 1991). There were also important variations in the structure of cost and pricing of leisure goods and services, many of which ceased to be the object of public provision[3] (Danecki, 1993).

Bearing in mind the reservations raised above, it can nevertheless be argued that after an initial fall in leisure spending accounting for 10% of the household budget in the years 1988–1991,[4] from around 1993 the share of this expenditure stabilized at around 5–6% of household spending, as shown in Table 13.5, with the self-employed and white-collar workers being top spenders (the former on tourism and the latter on high culture).

Unlike the late 1980s, when Polish leisure spending was dominated by electronic equipment (replacement of black-and-white television with colour sets in the lower-income groups and purchase of a VCR in rural areas), in the late 1990s, for white-collar workers and the self-employed, holidays and tourism were the area of fastest growth in expenditure. The rising prices of books and magazines, which were subsidized by the state in the 1980s, has also helped to push up spending on these items, while electronic equipment became relatively cheaper (Cieloch *et al.*, 1992).

If more disaggregated data were available, they would probably point to the fact that in the 1980s there was little disparity between the structure of leisure spending of blue- and white-collar workers, but in the late 1990s the spending patterns of blue-collar workers were distinctive. They were still directing more of their leisure discretionary spending to catch up with the electronic equipment found in the other socio-economic groups, spending relatively more of their modest leisure funds on television licences, and with only very limited spending on tourism.

The data from household budgets thus suggests far greater stratification of leisure spending than the analysis of time-use against income groups, as discussed earlier in the chapter. The pattern of leisure spending of the self-employed is also more distinct from that of the white-collar workers than might be expected from the analysis of time-use and participation rates. White-collar workers seem to spend more in the domain of high culture, while the self-employed spend more on tourism, especially vacationing abroad.

Table 13.5. Leisure spending by households, Poland, 1988–1999.

						% of household expenditure					
	1988	1991	1993			1996			1999		
	National average	National average	Blue collar	White collar	Self-employed	Blue collar	White collar	Self-employed	Blue collar	White collar	Self-employed
Culture and recreation	10.5	9.8	3.6	5.0	5.3	3.2	4.6	5.1	4.7	6.2	6.0
Culture:	6.2	6.3	2.7	3.4	3.3	2.3	2.9	2.9	1.2	1.3	1.3
Newspapers, magazines, books, stationery	0.52	0.5	0.4	0.5	0.5	0.3	0.4	0.5	1.2	1.3	1.3
Books			0.1	0.3	0.2	0.1	0.3	0.2			
Electronic equipment	2.7	2.6	0.6	0.6	0.6	0.5	0.6	0.5	–	–	–
of which TV	–	–	0.3	0.3	0.2	0.2	0.2	0.1	–	–	–
Cultural services	1.1	1.3	0.8	0.9	0.7	0.7	0.7	0.8	1.0	1.3	1.1
of which TV licence and cable fee	0.3	0.5	0.5	0.4	0.3	0.5	0.4	0.4	0.5	0.5	0.4
Sports, tourism and holidays (mass tourism for 1999)	3.3	2.3	0.9	1.7	1.9	0.9	1.7	2.2	0.7	1.5	1.6
in Poland	0.3	0.2	0.5	0.9	1.0	0.5	0.9	1.2	–	–	–
abroad			0.1	0.4	0.5	0.1	0.4	0.5	–	–	–

–, Not available.
Source: Calculations based on household budget surveys, GUS (1988, 1991, 1993, 1996, 1999) (see Table 13.1).

Leisure equipment

Access to leisure equipment in Polish house-holds is quite important to the country's leisure patterns, since many activities, by choice or as a result of climatic conditions, are home-based, and media consumption plays such a crucial role at home. Some of the most spectacular changes which took place in Polish leisure in the 1980s and in the 1990s are related to a very substantial increase in the proportion of households equipped with leisure durables, as well as improvements in the quality of this equipment, as measured by its age, techno-logical level, functionality, etc. As indicated in Table 13.6, by 1999 the presence of these goods in Polish households was comparable to levels found in much richer countries in the EU. This was particularly true of colour television sets, hi-fi sets, VCRs and cable or satellite tele-vision. With respect to more advanced elec-tronic equipment (CD players and recorders, PCs, printers) this level was still much lower and subject to steep social stratification, with highest levels found in households of the self-employed and lowest among farmers, hired farm workers, blue-collar workers and retirees. Access to the Internet is discussed in more detail in a later section of the chapter.

More interesting than the absolute level of saturation of Polish households with leisure-related durables has been the dynamics of this process. While important differences exist between the different social strata, the general level of leisure-related household equipment is steadily rising throughout Polish society. This is particularly true of home electronics. It must also be added that the proportion of Polish households in possession of sports and recre-ation infrastructure, such as skis, tennis equip-ment, tents, boats and home fitness equipment, is much lower than in other developed coun-tries. Sledges, sports bicycles, soccer and basket balls are the only type of recreational equipment available in over 25% of Polish households.

Price relations

It is difficult to judge leisure consumption in Poland without considering the change in the purchasing power of the average wage in rela-tion to the price of leisure goods and services. This information is available only for the public sector, but is considered representative of the whole economy. Public statistics offer data on price growth in aggregate spending groups (such as 'articles of cultural usage', as well as on chosen leisure items) which are part of the 'basket' used to analyse inflation data. While by 1998 the general index of growth in prices of all goods (for 1990 = 100) had reached 734, that for articles of cultural usage was slightly lower – 709 (*Rocznik Statystyczny*, GUS, 1999, pp. 344–345). However, prices of publications increased by 1214 and those of sports and tourism equip-ment by 974. Prices for consumer electronics only rose by one-third as much as the general price index, which probably further strength-ened the attractiveness of the media in the trade-off against all other forms of leisure (*Rocznik Statystyczny*, GUS, 1999). While from 1990 to 1998 the growth in the price index for all services in Poland – at 1545 – was much higher than for goods, prices for culture, sports and recreation services grew at a slower pace of 1114, prices for cinema, the-atre and museum tickets grew by 1950 and licence fees for television increased in pro-portion to inflation.

A vivid picture of the differentiated, and sometimes unexpected, character of changing price relations for leisure in Poland can be obtained by calculating how much of a given good or service an average wage could buy in a given year. Such annual comparisons are available since 1983 and are presented in Table 13.7. Expressed in US dollars at market ('black market' up to 1989) prices, the average wage in Poland increased roughly 18-fold in the period 1983–1998. Even though still low by Western European standards, by 1998 it could buy a far greater range of imported goods. In terms of what it could buy domesti-cally, there is a great disparity between its increased (relative) purchasing power versus various leisure goods and services. The most interesting examples once again come from home electronics, where the increase in pur-chasing power is most spectacular. On the other hand, the average wage in 1989 could buy only one-fifth or one-quarter of the high

Table 13.6. Leisure-related consumer durables in homes by type of household, Poland, 1976–1999.

	% of households								
	1976	1985		1988		1990		1999	
	All employed	I	II	I	II	I	II	I	II
Radios	75.3	82.2	81.9	90.5	88.0	96.9	91.5	53.0	50.8
TV sets	95.2	116.4	111.9	127.7	120.8	138.0	130.2	99.3	99.8
Colour	–	30.3	18.9	54.5	34.4	79.8	59.1	98.8	98.2
VCRs	–	–	–	3.2	1.2	25.1	16.9	79.0	70.0
Hi-fi sets	–	–	–	26.9	17.0	44.3	32.4	63.8	64.9
Bicycles	57.9	77.1	83.2	88.2	96.0	91.2	94.2	58.6	64.3
Cars	10.3	38.4	20.6	41.8	23.6	44.8	25.8	61.7	44.9

I, White-collar households; II, Blue-collar households; –, not available.
Source: *Rocznik Statystyczny* (GUS, 1978, 1986, 1991, 1999).

culture, press or cinema attendances, that it could buy in 1983. It can be surmised that changes in price relations played an important role in strengthening the position of the media in Polish leisure after the reforms, and probably also explain why the levels of cultural consumption (high culture, cinema, publications, etc.) fell so dramatically, as depicted by cultural participation surveys.

Cultural Participation and Leisure Provision

Cultural participation

The data from statistics on cultural participation suggest far greater changes to Polish leisure patterns than might be expected from time surveys and household budgets. Since 1972 participation rates in nearly all leisure activities (other than watching television) have been dropping steadily. Comparing data from cultural participation surveys with participation rates recorded from the latest time-use survey, suggests that, for most activities, this drop has reached catastrophic proportions (Łagodziński, 1992).

All activities related to readership decreased dramatically by the end of the 1990s. Even reading newspapers involved less than one-fifth of the population. Books were read by barely one-tenth of respondents. Cinema attendance (over half of the population in the 1970s and one-third at the beginning of the 1990s) was

close to statistical insignificance (0.5%), while all high-culture activities were already statistically insignificant. In the 1970s and 1980s sports events were attended by one-quarter of the respondents, while in the late 1990s by 0.5% of them.

The comparison of cultural participation surveys with time-use data paints a particularly grim picture. When other statistical sources are used (surveys asking whether respondents engaged in a given activity in the last week, month, year), readership levels increase to 30% for newspapers, 20% for books and cinema attendance, 2% for high-culture activities, but, regardless of the type of survey, they all point to lower levels of participation than in the 1970s and in the 1980s.[5]

Cultural output and institutionalized leisure provision

Yet another picture emerges when comparing the data on institutionalized leisure provision (cultural and sports institutions) with the number of persons taking advantage of these forms of leisure. With the exception of the cinema, where cinemas have been practically wiped out from the Polish cultural landscape in rural areas and smaller cities, the institutionalized providers of culture and recreation seem to have survived the changes in 1989, at least in numbers, and could even boast of a modest expansion in their facilities and output. An important expansion took place in tourist

Table 13.7. Wage/price relations for selected goods and services, Poland, 1983–1998.[a]

Product/service		Ratio of average monthly wage to price of item									
	1983	1989	1990	1991	1992	1993	1994	1995	1996	1997	1998
Holiday in Zakopane,[b] 14 days	1.2	1.7	1.5	1.1	1.1	1.1	1.2	1	1.3	1.1	1.3
Warszawa-Zakopane II class Intercity train ticket	–	94	31	21	19	17	23	25	27	31	27
Admission to theatre (tickets)	207	239	161	70	44	43	61	75	61	58	51
Cinema tickets	290	518	193	84	124	117	122	125	115	116	107
Music CDs	–	18	18	22	26	27	37	33	36	36	31
Polityka (influential weekly)	725	1777	967	700	620	513	508	395	459	466	515
Colour TV 21-inch	0.1	0.1	0.4	0.5	0.6	0.5	0.7	0.8	1	1.1	1.7
PC with monitor	–	–	–	0.1	0.1	0.1	0.2	0.2	0.3	0.4	0.5
Average wage expressed in US$	22	69	149	179	195	195	250	304	320	329	368

[a] Prices as at December, Warsaw. [b] Popular major ski resort in the south of Poland.
Source: Koszyk (1999).

infrastructure, as depicted by a rapid increase in the number of beds available in hotels and other tourist accommodation. The other area of rapid growth was media broadcasting.[6]

On the whole, it would seem that the Polish leisure consumer now has much more choice and variety. There were more published book and magazine titles to choose from, seating capacity in theatres and concert halls increased, and the number of museums and exhibitions, as well as sports clubs, was also growing. Yet, this improvement in the cultural infrastructure did not stop Poles from massively withdrawing from most institutionalized forms of leisure provision. On the positive side, as indicated in Table 13.8, in the period 1995 to 1998, it seems that the dynamics of this process of mass retreat from most leisure activities stabilized and that leisure participation found its new equilibrium after nearly a decade of adjustment to a new reality.

Globalization

Poland's relative openness during the communist days

In the post-Second World War years, compared to the other communist countries, Poland was less isolated from the Western world. This could be attributed to a number of factors of a political, cultural and economic nature. The communist political regimes in the country were less orthodox and more open in their travel and passport policies. Some 50 million Poles live abroad, many of them in the USA. They maintained close ties with their relatives in the home country, visiting them, hosting their stays abroad, sending them money and involving them in their economic activities. These contacts resulted in a relatively good understanding of the Western world (Jawłowska *et al.*, 1993; Roberts and Jung, 1995).

Many Poles also took advantage of more liberal government policies to work in the West (usually in the shadow economy). This casual or seasonal employment also brought them closer to the Western realities (including knowledge of global brands, fashions, etc.). While the communist system was clearly disintegrating in the 1980s, many 'suitcase importers' regularly

supplied the domestic market with Western goods not found in state retail outlets.

Polish culture was traditionally receptive to Western ideas and the country's cultural identity was clearly in the West. Despite censorship and the communist party's ideological grip over culture, the country was quick to import Western films, music and art trends and to translate popular authors, etc. These imports were mainly those of high-quality Western culture. Local artists and intellectuals were also able to maintain a dialogue with these trends, and the quality of Polish avant-garde and high culture rose to unprecedented standards. Its output was readily consumed by growing strata of culture connoisseurs, the intelligentsia, which, for a number of years, managed to promote 'high culture' as a very fashionable pastime (Babiuch-Luxmoore, 1994).

A relatively good quality of general education, a taste for keeping abreast of world events, even a certain idealization of the West, also helped to keep Polish society relatively less 'fenced-off' from the non-communist world than its neighbours.

Tourism

When the changes of 1989/90 took place, Poland was thus seemingly better prepared to cope with the opening to the West and the resulting mix of 'Westernization' and globalization. If we were to follow Robertson's (1987) understanding of the process, in which globalization is seen as the shrinking of the world, one of the earliest symptoms of this shrinking was an explosion in the movement of people across borders, as depicted in Fig. 13.1. Over 20 years (1980–1999) the number of visitors to Poland rose tenfold, from 9 million to 90 million, while the number of Poles travelling abroad rose by eight times, from 7 million to 55 million. Nearly all of that growth took place after 1989. Surveys of travellers suggest that about 44% of these numbers are genuine tourists (conforming to the WTO of the duration of stay abroad and purpose of visit), while about one-third travel for business reasons. Regardless of this distinction, such significant movements of people to and from Poland was an essential element of globalization. In 2000

Table 13.8. Cultural output, leisure infrastructure and participation, Poland, 1980–1998.

	1980	1985	1990	1995	1998	1999
Books published (titles)	11,919	9649	10,242	11,925	16,462	19,192
Books (circulation '000s)	147,138	246,321	175,562	115,634	84,999	78,078
Newspapers (titles)	88	97	130	108	81	74
Newspapers (circulation, millions)	2627	2467	1390	1434	1269	1190
Magazines (titles)	2482	2846	3007	4340	5297	5518
Magazines (circulation, millions)	869	1024	679	1777	1632	1527
Public libraries	9315	9899	10,269	9505	9167	9046
Readers in libraries ('000s)	7388	7514	7423	7023	7314	7332
Museums	427	528	563	589	612	623
Visits to museums and exhibitions ('000s)	20,079	19,857	19,282	17,060	18,582	–
Art galleries			174	209	218[a]	215
Visits to art galleries ('000s)			5036	2318	2262[a]	2361
Theatres and concert halls	134	139	143	181	186	190
Seating capacity of theatres and concert halls	63,517	62,845	58,697	62,478	65,619	66,070
Visits to theatres and concert halls ('000s)	17,803	17,032	12,873	10,198	10,784	10,667
Cinema halls	2228	2057	1435	721	686	695
Seating capacity of cinema halls ('000s)	502	473	373	213	201	211
Cinema attendance ('000s)	97,540	107,080	32,798	22,613	20,318	27,475
Production of feature films	37	43	37	23	14	24
Radio broadcasters of			63[b]	169	173	175
which public				17	17	17
TV broadcasters of			31[b]	24	25	28
which public				11	12	12
Hours of radio broadcasting	48,408	52,420[d]	71,584			
Radio subscribers ('000s)[c]	8666	10,077	10,944	10,193	9577	9461
TV subscribers ('000s)[c]	7954	9468	9919	9677	9266	9187
Hours of TV programming	8976	9161	13,931	–	46,351[e]	–
Hours of films shown on TV	2938	3150	4139	–	24,881[e]	–
No. of beds available year-round ('000s)	305	255	245	263	337	341
No. of beds in hotels ('000s)	50	51	57	75	90	92
Sports organizations	35,333	33,384	29,557	11,537	12,649	11,898
Sports clubs	1815	1866	1846	2901	2875	3638
Membership in sports organizations ('000s)	2989	2422	2295	709	756	713
Membership in sports clubs ('000s)	1394	951	641	443	407	372

[a] In 1997; [b] in 1992; [c] i.e. paying a licence fee; [d] in 1988; [e] in 1999.
Source: Based on data from: *Rocznik Statystyczny 1995* (GUS, 1995, pp. 276–290); *Rocznik Statystyczny 1999* (GUS, 1999, pp. 299–305); *Culture in 1998* (GUS, 1999); *Kultura Fizyczna W Latach 1990–98* (GUS, 1999, pp. 20–21); *Rocznik Statystyczny Kultury 1989* (GUS, 1989, p. 188); *Informacja o Podstawowych Problemach Radiofonii i Telewizji* (KRRiTV, 2000).

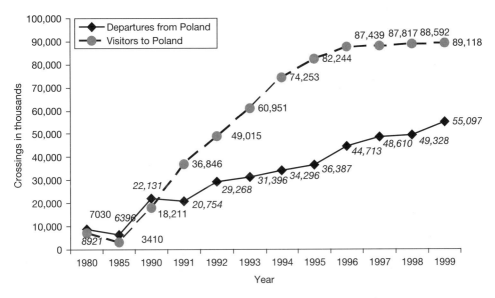

Fig. 13.1. Travel to and from Poland, 1980–1999 (border crossings in thousands).
Source: compiled from *Rocznik Statystyczny,* GUS, 1985, 1990, 1995, 1996, 1997, 1998, 1999.

3.2 million Poles (about 8% of the population) spent holidays abroad, 0.8 million more than in 1999. The globalizing effect of these holidays in the home country can be seen in the form of such things as exotic restaurants, drink and food outlets and imports of music.

Internet

A similar globalizing effect could be expected from the recent rapid growth of the Internet, although the mass character of this phenomenon in Poland dates back to the mid-1990s. An important breakthrough in the development of the Internet in Poland at that time was the provision of public access to the World Wide Web by what was then the state's telecom monopolist. For the price of a local telephone call, web access was provided to all households equipped with a telephone and PC with a modem. By the end of the 1990s, this form of web access was still predominant, but the number of Internet providers, diversification of services and – most important of all – the number of users, reflected the dynamics of the phenomenon. By mid-2000 there were 5 million Internet users in Poland (16% of the population), a tenfold increase from 1997. At the

end of 2000 some 77% of households equipped with a computer had access to the Internet. Some 46% of users had access to the Internet at home, 36% at work and 14% at school/university.[7]

About one-third of those with access surfed the net every day; over 30% surfed more than once a day. Nearly 60% of interviewed 'Internauts' declared that they were using the web regularly to have access to information related to their hobbies – a leisure orientation. Nearly 38% declared that the Internet was their main way of spending leisure time, and 59% pointed to the entertainment function of the web. The need to communicate with others (primarily via e-mail) was declared by 75% of the Internauts (multiple answers were allowed). Every week they were spending on the average 2 h 20 min on e-mail communication.[8] Some 42% of the Polish 'Internauts' interviewed frequently visited the websites of popular Polish newspapers and magazines. The bulk of 'consumption' of the Internet took place at times known as 'prime time' for television and, in consequence 47% of respondents stated that they were spending less time watching television, while 42% rated their television time as 'about the same' and only 2% as 'greater' since they started using the web. Nearly 70% had been using the Internet since 1997 or later, while only 10% had been doing so from 1995 and 4% from before 1993. In many ways Polish Internet users were similar to the profile of US surfers around 1995 – male-dominated, with a predominance of young (high school and university students) and middle-aged users, relative newcomers to the area, with higher levels of education, coming from large urban areas, with nearly half of the users with access to the web only from work or school.

When the last time-use survey was conducted in Poland in 1996, the time spent online was probably not significant and, in any case, it was not featured in the study. However, by the end of 2000 some 5 million 'online' Poles were spending less time watching television, but online reading by a relatively well-educated Internet population was compensating for the falling levels of traditional 'hard-copy' reading, as shown in the cultural participation statistics.

Opening of the Polish economy

After the market reforms were introduced in 1989, the Polish economy opened itself to the West, especially to Western imports, and the structure of its trade was drastically re-oriented. The turnover with the former COMECON (communist equivalent of the EU), which was predominant in Poland's foreign trade until the late 1980s, shrank, and the country's trade re-aligned itself mainly to the EU countries, especially Germany. While at the end of 2000 Poland was negotiating its EU membership and hoping to become a full member early in the next decade, by virtue of its economic linkages with the EU, its economy was already integrated with this grouping.

The opening up of the Polish economy, convertibility of its currency and liberalization of trade, resulted in huge imports of Western consumer goods, services and advertising, with all the consumer imagery they entailed. While this meant unprecedented choice for the Polish leisure consumer, it had severe consequences for the Polish economy, which could not stand up to foreign competition. In consequence, many companies went bankrupt or were taken over by foreign firms. To illustrate

Table 13.9. Production of selected cultural goods, Poland, 1980–1991.

	1980	1985	1990	1991
Radio and stereo sets, '000s	2700	2700	1400	600
Colour TV sets, '000s	147	158	338	304
Tape recorders, '000s	806	384	299	108
VCRs, '000s	–	–	2014	6172
Cameras, '000s	83	43	–	–
Photographic paper (m²)	6190	6539	1995	1104

Source: *Kultura 1992* (GUS, 1992, p. 23).

this phenomenon, which is one aspect of the globalization of Polish leisure, we can use the example of the collapse or takeover of the country's electronic industries. As can be seen from the Table 13.9, those of Poland's electronic companies which were producing television sets and VCRs, and which were taken over by foreign investors, managed to expand or keep their pre-1990 level of output, but others saw a drastic drop and, in consequence, went bankrupt under the pressure of cheap imports from South-east Asia.

Another example comes from the Polish music market. By the mid-1990s, this market was dominated by five global music companies (or 'majors'): Pomaton-EMI, PolyGram, BMG, Warner and Sony. All of these companies were set up in the early 1990s through buy-outs of existing Polish independent music producers (Jaros and Pźczak, 1996, p. 4). In terms of the number of CDs and cassettes sold, the majors had between them 49% of the musical output, the independents had 39% and pirates 12% (Podziały wœród liderów, 1997, p. 25). Sales of Polish music in these companies' turnover (in terms of the number of cassettes and CDs sold, as well as the volume of sales), fell to under 25% (in the communist days the share of Polish music was kept artificially high at some 90%); see Table 13.10.

Yet another set of examples comes from the Polish film industry. Table 13.11 contains data on the fall in domestic film production, as well as the drastic shrinking of the cinema audience. With the opening up of the Polish film market to

Table13.10. Music market leaders and sales, Poland, 1996.

Producer	Share of Polish music market (%)	Sale of cassettes and CDs (millions)	Of which sales of Polish music (millions)	Estimated total value of sales (US$ millions)	Estimated value of sales of Polish music (US$ millions)
Pomaton-EMI	21	4.5	1.7	16.5	4.9
PolyGram Polska	18	3.9	2.1	13.9	5.7
BMG Ariola	9	2.0	0.0	7.4	n.a.
Warner Music Poland	9	1.8	n.a.	7.2	0.5
Sony Music PL	8	1.7	0.2	6.6	n.a.

n.a., not available. Source: Calculations based on data from *Rzeczpospolita*, No. 46, 24.II.1997, p. 25.

Table 13.11. Premiere films and percentage of revenues, selected countries, 1989, 1994/95.

Country	No. of premieres 1989	1995	% of revenues 1989	1994
USA	35	93	63	75
Poland	37	15	21	9
France	7	12	4	0
UK	5	14	1	0
Germany	–	4	0	0
Former USSR	14	1	1	0
Total	134	151	100	100

Source: *Film Business* (1996) No. 4/5, p. 22.

international competition, by the mid-1990s it was clearly under the domination (as elsewhere in the world) of American imports, both in terms of the number of premieres and revenues. When looking at the box office receipts for 1990–1995, all the top ten hits were American. The situation changed for the first time in 1999 and 2000, when Polish cinematography produced two domestic 'mega-hits', which were adaptations of Polish classics and which outsold all foreign imports, boosting cinema attendances and revenues for the first time in the decade; but in the long run the domination of American film production in Poland is likely to prevail.

Many other examples of foreign incursions can be found in the Polish mass media. The daily press is largely owned by German and Scandinavian publishers. Polish magazines, the circulation of which is quickly expanding, are for the most part Polish versions of global titles – this is especially true of women's magazines. The largest commercial radio stations are

foreign-owned, just like private television stations (legislation sets a limit to foreign capital participation to 33%, but through a series of mixed capital subsidiaries, control of the foreign investor is assured).

This dominance is also evident in television programming. According to a recent report of the State Radio and Television Council (official body overseeing the media sector), in 2000 American film programming accounted for 56% of all films shown by television broadcasters (both public and private), while Polish films took up 10% and all other European films accounted for 15% (KRRiTV, 2000).

Another dimension of the globalization of Polish leisure lies in the fact that, as suggested by data on the availability of satellite/cable television in households, at least 50% of the television audience watches foreign channels. Data from other sources confirms this phenomenon. The ESRC study, 'Young People and Economic Change', showed that, in 1993, in the 2 weeks prior to the survey, some 61% of young people in two age groups (18–19 and 22–24) watched MTV or video clips, 81% watched commercials on television, and 56% watched foreign (satellite or cable) television (Roberts and Jung, 1995).

Yet another aspect of globalization connected with foreign capital, media consumption and leisure is the commercialization of both public and private media through advertising, including advertisements for global products and brands, some directly serving leisure needs (home electronics, sports equipment, etc.). The analysis of advertising expenditure in Polish television shows that the top spenders are the same global companies that dominate the

Table 13.12. McDonald's outlets in Eastern Europe, 1995.

Country	Restaurants
Poland	44
Hungary	38
Czech Rep.	23
Russia	7
Serbia	7
Slovenia	5
Romania	4
Croatia	3
Estonia	3
Latvia	2
Bulgaria	2
Slovakia	2
Lithuania	1

Source: Central and East European Economic Review (Jul–Aug 1996), p. 7.

market in North America and the EU (KRRiTV, 2000).

Similar conclusions can be drawn from another celebrated index of globalization, the level of 'McDonaldization' (Ritzer, 1996): by the mid-1990s the company was well established in Central and eastern Europe and growing rapidly. The data for mid-1990s roughly points to a correlation between the number of McDonalds and the economic success of the Central and Eastern European countries, as indicated in Table 13.12.

Conclusions

The relative abundance of leisure statistics in Poland throughout the post-Second World War years did not enable an easy interpretation of the new phenomena which emerged in the 1990s. Part of the difficulty lies in the statistics themselves, but much of the untold story of Polish leisure is contextual, rooted in wider changes taking place in the country's social, cultural and economic life.

While the volume of statistical information pertinent to culture, recreation, sports participation, time-use, household expenditure and price indices did not decline after 1989, the sample sizes and (above all) descriptive categories used in the various studies changed. The most striking example of this was seen in the time-use survey of 1996, when the size of the sample was reduced from nearly 50,000 to just under 2500 respondents. This meant that, for most 'high-culture' activities reported by 0.1–0.3% of respondents, it was the answers of single respondents that formed the basis of the national average. The range of leisure activities was narrowed (only eight activity categories were available for comparisons with 1976 and 1984, compared with 54 categories in the original 1969 study patterned after Szalai, and 17 categories in the 1976 GUS survey) and did not identify new pastimes such as Internet usage. No data were available on secondary activities, which are important for media usage. The level of unemployed in the sample, non-existent in previous studies, was a significant feature of the 1996 data, making reliable comparisons even more hazardous.

In the area of household expenditure and equipment, two groups of statistical problems with wider social or economic implications should be mentioned. First, reporting of expenditure of households by category based on socio-economic status, without referring to income groups is a serious omission which obscures the basic factor of affordability of the various leisure goods and services, so important for consumers in emerging economies. The introduction of a new socio-economic group – the self-employed – reflected the statisticians' eagerness to report on the emerging capitalists, but this group is very heterogeneous and ranges from petty traders to multi-millionaires, from agriculture to Internet providers, with very different sets of spending patterns, levels of education, etc. The meaning behind socio-economic categories used in household spending surveys was changed in the course of the 1990s. It was originally designed to reflect the status of manual and clerical employment in the state sector (then virtually the totality of the economy), private farmers, workers employed in the state farms, students and the retired (all benefiting from state assistance). Given the changes that took place in Poland in the 1990s, such a structure is no longer representative of the society (Adamski, 1993).

The second point relates to the complete disruption in the structure of prices after the downfall of communism, as suggested for leisure goods and services in Table 13.7. Price movements have been erratic, without any clear pattern other than the relative cheapening of home electronics. This reflected the irrationality of the pricing pattern under communism, which was not reflective of production cost or world prices, as well as the level of state subsidies for some products deemed 'socially important'. Prices for goods and services essential to the functioning of the household (in particular food, housing and medical care) evolved unpredictably, making it difficult for individuals and whole households to rationally plan their leisure budgets. To these difficulties must be added the problems of changes in spending categories, such as the belated introduction of new spending items such as game consoles or web-enabled computers, and the fact that no attempt was made to assess the value of free collective leisure services provided to the public under the previous system, but which became increasingly commercialized throughout the 1990s (Golinowska, 1992).

Apart from the problems presented by the methodology and practice of leisure statistics, evaluation of leisure patterns in Poland was made more difficult after 1990 because of the completely different social, cultural and economic context in which leisure was enjoyed. The statistical data point to the increasing amount of time available for leisure, the growing percentage of those acknowledging that they have leisure (nearly universal for the population), and more egalitarian distribution of leisure time among sexes. The proportion of household budgets devoted to leisure remained fairly constant, with expenditure on the media and tourism growing steadily. The proportion of households equipped with various leisure-related consumer durables quickly increased to levels comparable to those found in the EU. Does that mean that all is well with Polish leisure?

If we leave aside the methodological doubts raised above, related to the drastic reduction in the sample size of the last time-use study, the data on growing availability of leisure time is most probably inflated by time-use patterns of the unemployed and the growing proportion of the retired in the whole society. The latter reflects current demographic trends, but also the pressure to implement early retirement schemes in some decaying traditional sectors of industry (such as mining and steel manufacture) to alleviate the problem of unemployment. The availability of leisure time among the unemployed is hardly to be envied, even though there is empirical evidence that young people, nominally unemployed but still supported by their families, were having a 'good time' (Roberts and Jung, 1997). The growing proportion of women with leisure time, and a more equitable distribution of household chores among the sexes that made this possible, may also reflect a forced new division of labour in the households of the unemployed, rather than deeper changes in attitudes. Increases in leisure spending may be interpreted as a defensive measure to preserve some basic leisure (usually media) at a time when many forms of leisure became commercialized and no longer freely available from public institutions.

Even more significant are the changes in the social structure within Poland. The overview of available leisure statistics points to two new elements pertinent to changes in social structure: the emergence of the self-employed and of the unemployed. However, the story not told by these statistics is, on the one hand, the decline in the status of the intelligentsia, a powerful role model and consumer of high culture during the communist days, and, on the other, the rise of the *nouveau riche* entrepreneurs or young professionals, typically employed in advertising, media, consultancy or financial services.

In the former communist countries the position of the intelligentsia was unique (Ryszard and Federowicz, 1993). Its existence and prominence was made possible by a combination of factors which could not be reproduced under new market conditions. The intelligentsia was high in cultural and educational capital but, as typical wage earners, its members were low in economic capital. But the latter did not matter because free education, nearly free access to culture, and secure and prestigious position in society compensated for comparatively lower material wealth. The intelligentsia acted not only as producers and consumers of high-quality culture, but also as cultural brokers, similar to the 'new service class' in the West (Hall and Jacques, 1989). The intelligentsia generally hoped that the downfall of communism, to which it actively contributed by playing a key role in the dissident movement, would facilitate development of creativity and wider diffusion of the values of high culture (Jawłowska et al., 1993; Venturelli, 1994), but when high levels of cultural activity ceased to be a mark of social distinction, the position of the intelligentsia, with its traditional humanist rhetoric, was undermined (Kurczewska, 1993). The post-communist societies' social imagination was increasingly captured by the mythology of the market and material wealth. The glamour and quality of high culture, the traditional bastion of the leisure of the intelligentsia, lost its allure, while the novelty effect of Western mass culture, now readily available throughout the region, was still strong.

The decline in the position of the intelligentsia, occasionally linked to its material pauperization (McCauley, 1993), was accompanied by the emergence of new elites, whose fortunes were often made overnight in shady circumstances. These elites had no clear social origin; their norms of behaviour, status symbols and ways of passing free time were *in statu nascendi*. The media made considerable efforts to glorify the 'new entrepreneurs', presenting them as 'workaholics', with no spare time, but in rare moments of leisure enjoying exclusive and sophisticated material luxury (Mierzejewska, 1995). Their ostentatious *nouveau riche* lifestyle was more reminiscent of Veblen's descriptions of the 'new capitalists' from the beginning of the 20th century than that of playful and sophisticated post-modern jugglers of symbols. Despite their low levels of educational or cultural capital, their lifestyles, inevitably an object of interest for the tabloid press, were highly visible and created a demonstration effect, which was perhaps strongest among the Central and Eastern European youth. The latter were not uncritical of the *nouveau riches* but, under conditions of a general cultural vacuum and disorder which followed the end of the communist system, they lacked other positive role models (Vladimorov, 1992). Anxious to break away from the communist past, Poles adopted a 'presentist' attitude, cutting themselves off from their past (Tarkowska, 1992). Many Poles lost the ability to pass leisure time in non-material pursuits not involving the use of commercial outlets or involving low levels of expenditure. The frame of reference also changed: in the days when material means and commercial outlets for leisure were both scarce, the demonstration

effect of high-spenders was not widespread and aspirations were kept at a modest level (Jung, 1999).

The relative social status of the different socio-economic groups also changed greatly. Under communism, certain traditional industrial professions – miners, shipyard workers, workers in the metal industries, car manufacture, textiles – rose to prominence, and their lobbying strength with the ruling elites was high, partly because their power of industrial action, including the threat of their strikes, could provoke power struggles and changes in the political leadership. The expression of these professional groups' privileged position was not only reflected in their wages, but also in the collective industrial agreements they were able to negotiate, the strength and wealth of their trade unions, and the additional 'perks' they were able to obtain, including access to such services as state-subsidized holiday centres, sports facilities and youth clubs. The decline in these groups' political and material status, which followed the collapse of traditional industrial production in Poland in the 1990s, not only reflected economic and political realities of the market reforms, but also reflected the loss of free or heavily subsidized leisure provision.

The withdrawal of the state from public life had a number of implications for leisure, but they were not those one would mostly expect, such as the curtailment of public funding available for culture or sports (Golinowska, 1992). As can be seen from Table 13.7, most of the providers survived and even managed to modestly increase their output, even though their position remains fragile. Where the withdrawal of the state was most felt was (paradoxically) in the areas where the civil society was to take over. When the communist state in Poland was running 'official trade unions', these were generously subsidized from public funds. For example, the official unions were the owners of holiday centres and hotels which were the backbone of the country's holiday industry. Packaged full-board domestic holidays (usually 2 weeks) offered various levels of quality, but were certainly affordable. Trade unions also frequently organized excursions from the workplace.

The communist system also offered a measure of stability with respect to job security, retirement pensions, health care and free education, which formed the framework within which leisure could be enjoyed. The increasing scope of uncertainty, a specific Central and Eastern European reflection of the 'risk society', must be taken into account when considering the conditions in which the statistically measured free time, participation rates or leisure spending are manifested. The insecurity of the 'new times' is underlined by economic uncertainty, including high bankruptcy rates among private firms, the collapse of the public sector, fraudulent business practices, the uncertainty of employment in the informal economy, informal pressure not to form trade unions in the private sector, and difficulty in extracting contractual obligations with respect to timely pay, right to paid holidays, etc. from private employers. In addition there are increased crime rates and eruptions of violence (both much publicized by the media, especially by the tabloids). There is also a genuine time squeeze felt by all those in employment, but not reflected by time-budget surveys. After decades of rather slack work discipline and low productivity levels, the changes in the Polish economy transformed the style of work both in the private and public sector. Work has become much more intense and stressful, yet carried out in conditions of competitive pressure and insecurity. There is no research on how these changed conditions of work were reflected in leisure.

In the 1990s Poland was the region's leader in attracting foreign direct investment. The establishment of American and EU companies in the country introduced their corporate and work cultures and lifestyle changes. Among the fastest developing sectors of the Polish economy one could find fast food chains and supermarkets, resulting in changed eating and shopping patterns of Poles. The creation of shopping centres and Sunday trading introduced 'shopping for pleasure' as a popular leisure activity on weekends – again a development not taken into account by official leisure statistics.

The impact of globalization on Polish lifestyles and leisure patterns also brought about a counter-reaction reminiscent of the 'Jihad vs. McWorld' debate of late 1980s (Barber, 1995). The position of conservative, nationalist groups, often related or claiming affiliation with the Catholic Church, strengthened in Polish politics. With respect to leisure, they succeeded in banning some cultural events, which they deemed as offensive to their religious or national feelings. They were also busy organizing cultural alternatives, such as Catholic 'family' media and concerts, which opposed what, in their opinion, was the growing glorification of violence, sex, secularization, materialism, cosmopolitism, egoism and normlessness associated with the 'excesses of liberalism'.

Given the role that the media plays in Polish leisure, any changes in this area are bound to have a profound impact. After 1989 the country's media experienced both expansion and restructuring. The press came under the control of Western media groups. Commercial radio flourished, private national television networks sprung up, public television was greatly transformed and the condition of local film industry became fragile, but global film distributors were prospering and a wave of multiplex cinemas was constructed in the country's major cities. The number of new book titles published every year nearly doubled between 1990 and 1999. The music market was taken over by five majors, but local musicians were not driven out of the market, as many expected. The number of Internet users grew as dynamically as elsewhere in the world. Consumer durables relative to media consumption became much more affordable and time, participation rates and expenditure on the media grew or retained their high levels (Jung, 1997).

As with the general evolution of leisure in Poland after 1989, this positive picture should be considered against the lack of certain background information from leisure statistics. While under the reign of the communist dogma all media were under political control, and in this sense were extremely politicized. After the downfall of the old system they shifted to the other extreme and became very commercialized. This also applies to public audiovisual media, which were now allowed to carry advertising and changed much of their programming to meet the needs of specified target audiences and joined the 'ratings war'. Despite the fact that the premier public television channel still draws the largest audience, by the end of 2000 it had a much smaller advertising revenue than the second most popular private national network

(KRRiTV, 2000). While not as successful as private operators in attracting advertising revenue, public television has suffered from many of the known drawbacks of commercialization of the media – the quest for sensation, trivialization of content, search for a low common denominator often offered by 'B'-rated American films, sitcoms, *telenovelas*, and the rescheduling of high-culture programmes to hours outside of prime time. A similar 'dumbing down' can be seen in the Polish print media. Much of the development in the Polish press has been towards tabloid-like publications. Fast growth took place in magazines, which were exact replicas of 'global' titles, especially women's magazines with expanded gossip columns – yet another manifestation of globalization.

It is difficult, if not impossible, to weigh up all the merits and drawbacks of the changes which took place in Poland after 1989 and their implications for leisure. While the context presented above seeks to offset the unidimensional optimism flowing from quantitative analysis of leisure statistics, it perhaps needs to be reappraised in the context of increased personal freedom, unprecedented choice, individualization of life patterns and opportunities offered by the 'new times', but available to those who have the means, skills and interest to take advantage of them. Activities which were very time consuming under communism's widespread shortages (such as queuing for food) disappeared, but they were replaced by the need to take additional jobs to meet newly created wants and, more often, simply to make ends meet. Many of the unemployed were spending what was equivalent to a full-time working-week in job seeking and work in the informal economy. New phenomena such as homelessness, long-term joblessness, marginalization and relative impoverishment of entire social strata and professional groups have to be contrasted with abundance of leisure equipment in homes, high proportions of the population with access to modern media, including the Internet, relatively good levels of education, the growing number of university graduates (which doubled between 1989 and 2000) and (potentially) high levels of cultural capital and leisure skills. Other than a narrow managerial, capitalist or skilled professional elite (2–5% by most estimates), who thrive on the changes, but at a price of total

commitment to their work, it is not clear how the balance of advantages and disadvantages of the changes which have taken place in Poland have been distributed within society. The roots of the capitalist elite cannot be traced to a single social class or strata; also, the losers are not a homogeneous group.

There seems to be no clear answer to the question on whether the reforms in Poland created conditions for better enjoyment of leisure. The ambivalence of such an answer seems to reflect the growing complexity of societies, cultures and economies emerging from the decades of communism, as well as the (postmodern) difficulty in making valid generalizations. If such a question had been posed in the 1980s, and even in the early 1990s, the answer would have been easier. The communist system was then disintegrating and old forms of institutionalized, collective and subsidized leisure provision were gradually disappearing, while the market had not yet stepped in. While longing for many missing material goods associated with 'modernity' and with the West, deep in the social psyche the belief that 'being' is more important than 'having' continued to be very strong. When market forces stepped in, consumption become primary and experience (or enjoyment) secondary in the leisure activity of Poles. This was a complete reversal of the trends of the 1980s, when Polish society was increasingly turning towards home-based leisure and alternative (clandestine) circuits of culture to offset the dwindling of decent leisure provision or strengthened political grip over culture after the period of martial law in 1981/82. But the question of whether experience without consumption, or consumption without experience, is preferable is a personal choice, decided in private by Polish households in the 1990s. The available body of leisure-related statistical information does not enable us to generalize as to whether the decisions taken were ultimately to everyone's satisfaction.

Notes

[1] By 1976 the working week was 46 h (with one Saturday per month off). Starting in 1981, three Saturdays per month were free from work as result of pressure from 'Solidarnoœę', bringing the working

week down to 42 h. This lasted until November 2000, when new proposed legislation called for rearrangement of the work load throughout the week so that all Saturdays would be free, but without shortening the working week.

[2] In the earlier time-budget studies, the gainfully employed group was restricted to those employed in the public sector (at that time the main employer for the bulk of the population), but it was split into white-collar and blue-collar occupations. Self-employed did not feature in the previous studies (see *Analiza Budæetu Czasu Ludnoœci Polski W Latach 1976 and 1984*, GUS, 1987).

[3] It should be noted that between 1988 and 1999 Poland went through a period of hyperinflation, in 1988–1990, when prices increased by 500–900% in 2 years. This reflected the move from state-administered pricing during the period of widespread shortages of consumer goods and services during the communist era, to market prices reflecting real production cost and supply–demand relationships in the market. The convertibility of the Polish currency and the opening of the Polish economy also meant competition from foreign suppliers. The problem of changing price relations for leisure goods is discussed further in this chapter.

[4] Compared to previous periods, this spending at this time was unusually high, since people were protecting themselves from hyperinflation by investing in the purchase of consumer durables, many of which were leisure-oriented, such as television sets.

[5] See OBOP's (Unit for the Study of Public Opinion) study of leisure-time activities, October 1999, quoted in Czubaj and Pćzak (2000, p. 25); 'O stylach æycia Polaków', CBOS (Centre for the Study of Public Opinion) 1997, quoted in Polityka (1997, p. 20); and CBOS 1998, quoted in GazetaWyborcza, 3.I.99 p. 2.

[6] The recorded drop in the number of radio and television subscribers is relatively easy to explain. In the period in question, it resulted from an increasing number of people not paying for their licence, rather than giving up radio and television. After 1990 the number of private radio and television stations, both local and national networks, established themselves on the Polish market, hitherto dominated by state broadcasters. The 'ratings war' which followed, was generally lost by public broadcasters, whose programming strategies and quest for advertising revenues (public media are allowed to sell advertising time) have, in the process, become very similar to commercial ones, and the sense of their 'public mission' is now widely questioned.

[7] See www.badanie.ae.kraków.pl

[8] According to the 'Net Track' study for the third quarter of 2000, 35% were spending between 1 and 4 hours online every week (web.reporter.pl/2000/06/w0903.html).

Bibliography

Adamski, W. (ed.) (1993) *Societal Conflict and Systemic Change. The Case of Poland 1980–1992.* IFiS Publishers, Warsaw.

Babiuch-Luxmoore, J. (1994) Portrety inteligencji w oczach robotników. In: Morawski, W. (ed.) *Zmierzch Socjalizmu państwowego. Szkice z Socjologii Ekonomicznej.* PWN, Warsaw.

Barber, B. (1995) *Jihad vs McWorld.* Random House, New York.

Bourdieu, P. (1984) *Distinction: a Social Critique of the Judgement of Taste.* Routledge and Kegan Paul, London.

Cieloch, G., Kuczyński, J. and Rogoziński, K. (1992) *Czas Wolny – Czas Konsumpcji?* PWE, Warsaw.

Czubaj, M. and Pćzak, M. (2000) Po fajrancie. *Polityka* 14(10).

Danecki, J. (1993) Social costs of system transformation in Poland. In: Ringer, S. and Wallace, C. (eds) *Societies in Transition: East-Central Europe Today. Prague Papers on Social Responses to Transformation*, Vol. 1. CEU, Prague.

Golinowska, S. (ed.) (1992) *Komercjalizacja w Kulturze. Szanse I Zagroæenia.* Instytut Kultury, Warsaw.

Hall, S. and Jacques, M. (eds) (1989) *New Times. The Changing Face of Politics in the 1990s.* London.

Jaros, M. and Pćzak, M. (1996) Szpony Wielkiej Pitki. *Polityka* 50 (14 December).

Jawłowska, A., Kempny, M. and Tarkowska, E. (eds) (1993) *Kulturowy Wymiar Przemian Spoecznych.* IFiS PAN, Warsaw.

Jung, B. (1992) Economic, social and political conditions for enjoyment of leisure in central and eastern europe of 1992 – the Polish perspective. *World Leisure and Recreation* 34(4).

Jung, B. (1994) *Young Unemployed and Self-employed in Poland.* Working Paper No. 199, World Economy Research Institute, Warsaw School of Economics.

Jung, B. (1997) *Selected Audio-visual Media Markets in Poland in 1996 (TV, Cable, Film and Multimedia Markets).* Working Paper, No. 174, World Economy Research Institute, Warsaw School of Economics, Warsaw.

Kleer, J. (1994) Druga kategoria. *Polityka* 7(16).

Koszyk, (1999) Polityki. *Polityka* 2(2175), 9 January.

KRRiTV (2000) *Informacja o Podstawowych*

Problemach Radiofonii i Telewizji. KRRiTV, Warsaw.

Kurczewska, J. (1993) Kulturowe tradycje realnego socjalizmu. In: Jawłowska, A., Kempny, M. and Torkowska, E. (eds) Kulturowy Wymiar Przemian Spoecznych. IFiS PAN, Warsaw.

McCauley, A. (1993) Economic justice in Eastern Europe. In: Ringer, S. and Wallace, C. (eds) *Societies in Transition: East-Central Europe Today. Prague Papers on Social Responses to Transformation,* Vol. 1. CEU, Prague.

Mierzejewska, B. (1995) Portrayal of businessmen in the Polish press. M.A. dissertation, SGH, Warsaw.

Podziały wœród liderów (1997) *Rzeczpospolita* 46 (February).

Ritzer, G. (1996) *The McDonaldisation of Society.* Sage, New York.

Roberts, K. and Jung, B. (1995) *Poland's First Post-Communist Generation.* Avebury, Aldershot, UK.

Roberts, K. and Jung, B. (1997) Leisure and lifestyles of the young unemployed and self-employed in four Central and East European countries. *World Leisure and Recreation* 39(4).

Roberts, K. and Jung, B. (2000) The New East's new businesses: heart of the labor market problem and/or part of the solution. *Journal of East European Management Studies* 5(1).

Robertson, R. (1995) Globalization: time–space and homogeneity–heterogeneity. In: Featherstone, M., Lash, S. and Robertson, R. (eds) *Global Modernities.* Sage, London, pp. 25–44.

Ryszard, A. and Federowicz, M. (eds) (1993) *Społeczeństwo w Transformacji.* IFiS PAN, Warsaw.

Szalai, A. et al. (eds) (1972) *The Use of Time.* Mouton, The Hague.

Tarkowska, E. (1992) *Czas w Æyciu Polaków. Wyniki Badań, Hipotezy, Impresje.* IFiS PAN, Warsaw.

Venturelli, S. (1994) Reinventing culture of 'humanism' in post-socialist society: New social thought on civic community. In: Jawłowska, A. and Kempny, M. (eds) *Cultural Dilemmas of Post-communist Societies.* IFIS Publishers, Warsaw.

Vladimorov, J. (1992) *Le Vide Culturel 'Postsocialiste' ou Les Nouvelles Orientations Culturelles en Europe de L'Est.* EDES, Neuchâtel.

Statistical sources

Analiza Budæetu Czasu Ludnocœci Polski W Latach 1976 and 1984. GUS, Warsaw 1987.

Badania Budæetów Gospodarstw Domowych [Household Budget Surveys]. GUS, Warsaw, 1985, 1988, 1989, 1990, 1991, 1992, 1993, 1995, 1996, 1997, 1998, 1999.

Culture in 1998. GUS, Warsaw, 1999.

Film Business, 1996, no. 4/5.

Kultura 1992 [Yearbook of cultural statistics]. GUS, Warsaw, 1992.

Kultura w 1993 r. GUS, Warsaw, 1994.

Kultura Fizyczna W Latach 1990–98. GUS, Warsaw, 1999.

Łagodziński, W. *Uczestnictwo W Kulturze. Podstawowe Wyniki Badań Reprezentacyjnych Z Lat 1972, 1979, 1985, 1988 and 1990.* GUS, Warsaw, 1992.

Rocznik Statystyczny [Statistical Yearbooks]. GUS, Warsaw, 1978, 1985, 1986, 1990, 1991, 1995, 1996, 1997, 1998, 1999.

Rocznik Statystyczny Kultury 1989. GUS, Warsaw, 1989.

Time Use Survey 1996. GUS, Warsaw, 1998.

Turystyka i Wypoczynek (W Okresie 1.x.97–30.ix.1998), Studia I Analizy Statystyczne 88. GUS, Warsaw, 1999.

Uczestnictwo w Kulturze. GUS, Warsaw, 1992.

Wyposaæenie Gospodarstw Domowych w Dobra Trwa³ego Uæytkowania w 1995. GUS, Warsaw, 1995.

Internet sources

www.badanie.ae.kraków.pl

http://web.reporter.pl/2000/06/w0903.html

14 Russia

I.A. Butenko

Introduction

Time-budget studies were first conducted in Russia in 1922/23 by the prominent economist and statistician S.G. Stroumilin. For political reasons, no further empirical research on the leisure, time-use and lifestyles of the population was conducted until the 1970s. The Institute for Sociological Studies was established in 1974 and included a special division devoted to time-budget research, directed by V. Patroushev. The prevailing concept was that free time was a broader concept than leisure. Leisure, in the sense of pure recreation engaged in for its own sake, lacked recognition in the USSR, which claimed to be the 'state of working people'. The book titles of the period reflect this view, for example *Man After Work: Social Problems of Everyday Life* (Gordon and Klopov, 1972), *Trends and Changes in the Time Budgets of Working People* (Patroushev, 1979), *Work and Free Time under Developed Socialism* (Maximov, 1981) and *Labour and Free Time* (Shmarov, 1987). Activities not related to work were believed to be unimportant; recreation was considered to be necessary only as recovery time after and for work; fun and pleasure were seen as almost disgraceful[1] and, hence, not a suitable topic for scholarly examination. Published research on free time contained non-comparable indicators and a variety of measurement devices, which made comparisons very difficult.

In the late 1980s political change in the Soviet Union brought major social and economic transformations to the country, and their impact on the lifestyle of the whole population was substantial. Under socialism, culture was subsidized and public leisure facilities grew in ideological importance. After 1990, while cultural activity was no longer subject to political and ideological constraints, government subsidies for facilities decreased sharply and many institutions were forced to close. At the same time, private enterprise was on the rise, although many of the services it offered were available only to the affluent few. The economic crisis of 1998 accelerated these processes. In this chapter, therefore, while information about the Soviet era is presented as necessary background, the 1990s are the subject of the most detailed examination.

Political and social changes of the 1990s led to an abrupt reduction of state funding for research, and no institution has conducted a nationwide study of time-use since 1990. Academics have indicated varying levels of interest in the subject of free time, conducting sporadic surveys with small samples in certain cities and/or towns, such as Moscow (Patroushev *et al.*, 1992), St Petersburg (Ille, 1996, 2000) and Pskov (Patroushev *et al.*, 1996), or among certain social groups

Table 14.1. Data sources, Russian time-use and leisure surveys, 1990–.

Name	Organization	Year	Sample size	Area sampled	Reference
Time-budget study	State Statistics Committee	1990	47,000	National	State Statistics Committee (1992, 2000)
Parts of omnibus surveys	WCIOM (All-Russia Public Opinion Service)	1990s	1500	National	FOM-INFO Bulletins
Free time in Moscow	Academic	1992	1500	Moscow	Patroushev et al. (1992)
Cultural life in St Petersburg	Academic	1996	1000	St Petersburg	Ille (1996, 2000)
Way of life of the citizens of Pskov	Academic	1995	1000	Pskov	Patroushev et al. (1996)

Table 14.2. Work days and days off (% of all days), Russia, 1950–1990.

	1950	1960	1970	1980	1990
Holidays/days off	15.2	16.2	25.9	26.5	27.9
Paid work days	75.0	79.8	64.9	62.4	67.5
Other (sickness, strikes, etc.)	9.8	4.0	9.2	11.1	4.6
Total	100.0	100.0	100.0	100.0	100.0

Source: State Statistics Committee (1991, p. 57).

(Butenko, 1998, 2000; Patroushev, 1998). These studies have partially bridged the gap in the information on leisure activities over recent years. The main findings of these studies were that: passive leisure has become more pervasive (Orlov, 1989); the higher a person's education level and the more complicated their work, the more leisure time is needed and the more intense is its use (Prokofiev, 1989); leisure skills of the urban population are very low and the major share of free time is spent at home (Yampolskaya, 1994).

Since the late 1990s a number of major sociological agencies, including the All Russia Public Opinion Service (WCIOM), the 'Public Opinion' Foundation (FOM) and 'Romir' have conducted several surveys among representative samples covering the adult (over 16 years old) population of Russia.

This chapter therefore draws on a wide range of sources. The lack of recent data has meant that, to make the situation in Russia clear, it has been necessary to use not only time-budget and leisure participation surveys, but also information from a number of other sources. Information about the main surveys which are drawn on in the chapter is provided in Table 14.1.

Amount of Free Time

In the past 40 years, there has been a reduction in time spent at work in Russia. The average duration of the working week in the manufacturing sector in the period 1965–1987 was 40 hours, while for the total economy it was 39 hours (State Statistics Committee, 1988). The transition to the 5-day working week in the mid-1960s markedly changed the use made of work-free days, which now accounted for more than half of weekly free time. In addition, the number of official holidays increased, as shown in Table 14.2.

Table 14.3. Structure of time-use for workers in large cities (% of daily time), Russia, 1963–1990.

	1963	1977	1986	1988	1990
Paid work	24.0	25.4	25.5	24.8	25.5
Paid work-related activities	5.4	2.3	4.5	5.5	3.9
Housekeeping	15.4	14.3	12.3	15.6	14.2
Total work load	44.8	42.1	42.3	45.9	43.6
Personal needs	38.6	39.2	36.8	34.4	38.2
Leisure activities	14.8	16.0	20.0	19.7	18.2
Other	0.8	2.8	0.9	–	–
Total	100.0	100.0	100.0	100.0	100.0

Source: Patroushev (1991, p. 6).

For workers, net free time increased by 3 hours/week and the share of leisure in the daily time-budget increased from 15% in 1963 to 18% in 1990, as shown in Table 14.3. In the 1970s, the annual amount of free time reached, and for some groups exceeded, the annual amount of work time (Patroushev, 1979).

Although not reflected in the official statistics, from the early 1960s, *moonlighting* became more widespread, particularly from the late 1980s, when restrictions on holding second jobs were abolished. For example, in the regional centre of Pskov, in 1995, some 9% of adult persons had a second job on a regular basis and 14% on an occasional basis (Patroushev *et al.*, 1996). On average, 14 hours/week were spent on moonlighting. Countrywide the proportion of those holding two jobs grew from 14% in 1989 to 40% in 1994 (State Statistics Committee, 2000). In 2000, according to WCIOM data, 11–15% of the adult population in various social groups moonlighted (WCIOM, 2002).

Unpaid work, when employees were not paid for months at a time, and latent unemployment grew in the 1990s. It has been estimated that, in 1996, over a third of industrial workers in Russia were, in fact, unemployed (Routkevich, 1997).

The reduction of work time experienced by some population groups did not result in a growth in leisure time because of the increase in the time spent on household tasks. This became more and more time-consuming, given the shortage of consumer goods during the socialist period, making the 'home-based economy' a reality. Thus, for many people, gardening, which generally featured as a 'free time activity' in official statistics, was not engaged in primarily for pleasure but for survival and to provide basic needs.[2] In addition, in 1999, across all income groups, between 36% and 42% undertook major household tasks during their vacations, and 56% undertook additional paid work (FOM-INFO, 1999b).

So, while official figures indicate decreases in paid work time in the late 1990s, most free time left over after everyday maintenance requirements had been attended to were not spent in active pursuit of cultural interests but in passive relaxation. Even the amount of time devoted to sleeping increased (WCIOM, 2002). So it is clear that the 'golden age' of leisure had not yet arrived in Russia.

Use of Free Time

From the mid-1970s, opportunities to satisfy cultural aspirations at home began growing, as a result of improvements in housing conditions and the spread of television and audio-equipment and, later, the advent of video. The main location for spending leisure time was the home. On workdays, 70–80% of free time was spent in the home and on days off it was 50% (Patroushev, 1988). The most popular leisure activities in the 1960s were reading books and newspapers, then watching television, then participation in sport and physical recreation and, finally, just relaxing. From 1985 on, television-watching rose to first place, ahead of reading, walking and sports and physical recreation, as shown in Table 14.4.

From 1965 to 1985, the average time spent on television-viewing increased threefold.

Table 14.4. Free time-use, by type of settlement and gender, Russia, 1985 and 1990.

| | 1985 | | | | 1990 | | | |
| | Urban | | Rural | | Urban | | Rural | |
	M	F	M	F	M	F	M	F
Free time, min/day	275	187	267	148	227	126	169	83
% of free time								
TV and radio	48	47	44	61	51	46	59	61
Reading	17	13	16	12	13	17	17	13
Movies, concerts, theatres	5	7	5	6	4	7	4	4
Walking and playing sports	13	13	5	6	7	8	6	3
Hobbies	2	3	10	2	2	1	3	2
Other	17	12	11	11	8	12	7	8

Source: State Statistics Committee (1991, p. 226).

Initially, this was a result of growing number of households with TV sets, but after 1985 it was due to increased viewing time. Selected results from two surveys conducted by WCIOM in 1990 and 1994 are presented in Table 14.5.

However, other survey evidence suggests that the population was not satisfied with opportunities for leisure participation. In 1997, when asked to name activities in which their participation declined following the major social and economic changes, 29% of those polled by the Public Opinion Foundation mentioned socializing with friends, 27% attending cinema, 24% shopping, 22% attending theatre, museums and concerts, and 20% travelling. But when asked about preferred activities, respondents rated socializing first, then going to museums, theatres and concerts, then hobbies and physical activities. Material security and consumption concerns took precedence over leisure (FOM-INFO, 1998a).

Table 14.5. Time spent on selected activities by gender (min/day), Russia, 1990 and 1994.

| | Males | | Females | |
	1990	1994	1990	1994
Watch TV	220	224	224	225
Listen to radio	183	188	213	185
Read newspapers	200	109	167	95
Read books	65	68	62	75
Read magazines	81	22	75	19

Source: WCIOM (1994, p. 29).

In 1997, respondents reported that they had started to work more on their garden plots and watched television more often, while going to the cinema, going on outings, attending museums and galleries, visiting friends and eating out were done less often (FOM-INFO, 1998b). 'Work in the garden plot' rated the second (56% did it 'often' or 'very often'), after television-viewing (74%) (FOM-INFO, 1998c). It appears that the economic crisis of 1998 had little effect on the rating of free-time activities, as shown in Table 14.6.

Reading deserves a special note. Reading books was one of the most widespread leisure-time activities before the 1990s, in many cases being used as a kind of escape from everyday life. In the 1980s, some 19% of adult Russians read 'regularly', 25% read two or more books a month, 35% read one or two books a year, and 21% did not read at all (Butenko and Razlogov, 1997). In urban areas, eight out of ten families had large collections of books at home that were both prestigious and considered a good investment. Since the early 1990s, however, reading newspapers has become less and less popular, especially with females, who read more books. In the late 1990s, reading became either more pragmatic or more entertaining, with interest in serious literature almost disappearing.

Although access to electronic information is increasing rapidly, new technologies have a significant impact on only a small part of the Russian population. The Internet audience (those who have access and use it at least twice a month) was booming in the late 1990s,

Table 14.6. Leisure activities, Russia, 1997–1999.

	% of 'regular' activities		
	1997	1998	1999
Watch TV	65	50	74
Household tasks	57	45	59
Socializing with friends	45	38	46
Reading newspapers, magazines	30	31	36
Reading books	21	25	28
Walking, being outdoors	16	18	21
Listening to music	14	17	21
Caring for pets	12	14	15
Amateur activity/hobby	10	9	12
Watch video	12	8	10
Play sport, physical recreation	4	6	8
Go to club, restaurant, bar, discotheque	4	5	5
Education-related	4	4	4
Go to theatre, museum, concert	3	3	3
Computer activities	2	2	3
Other activities	3	1	2

Source: FOM-INFO (1999a).

although from a small base, involving almost 3 million people, or 5% of the adult population. The majority were professionals, followed by students and businessmen. In a 2000 survey, in response to a question about what the Internet was, the majority said it was a means of information, with only one-tenth saying it was a means of socializing, and very few calling it a means of entertainment (FOM-INFO, 2000).

The ratio between leisure time spent in public institutions and social organizations, and leisure time spent privately or individually was 1:25, and this ratio did not change for many years (Patroushev, 1988). The mandatory participation in public associations and voluntary organizations, which had been required under socialist rule, was generally replaced by private activity. In 2000, when asked what they might do instead of television-viewing, 27% of Muscovites mentioned reading and doing household tasks, 21% listening to the radio, 13% sports and walking, 12% socializing, 11% watching video, 9% moonlighting and 3% using the computer and Internet (FOM-INFO, 2000).

In the 1990s, with the commercialization of the recreation sphere, new types of facilities, such as nightclubs and golf clubs, were introduced. Nevertheless, in 1997 some 65% of

Muscovites, the most affluent group of Russians, reported that they had not been to a restaurant that year and in 1999 the figure was 71%. Only 5% of survey respondents reported that they socialized in clubs and public associations on a weekly basis, while just 4% did so once or twice a month, 8% several times a year and 78% never; the corresponding levels of participation in religious and community associations were 2%, 4%, 15% and 66%, respectively (FOM-INFO, 1999b).

It can be seen therefore that, in contemporary Russia, leisure activity is dominated by passive, home-based pastimes.

Cultural Activity

Under socialism, the leisure institutions available to the Russian population, while heavily subsidized, were neither numerous nor varied. The ideological inspiration and educational orientation of these state-subsidized institutions, and centralized supervision of the programming and management of their activities, resulted in declining public interest. Before the 1980s, individuals spent an average of 65 min/week at performances, movie theatres, sporting events and concerts (Shmarov, 1987), but by 1985 this had fallen to an average of just 16 min (State Statistics Committee, 1991). The new economic situation in the 1990s resulted in the closure of many of these Soviet-era institutions or their privatization, and dramatic changes in services offered.

Average annual per capita movie attendance decreased from 22 visits in 1970 to nine in the 1990s. The audience partly returned to the cinema in the late 1990s, but only in some of the large cities, where old-fashioned one-screen 1000-seat cinemas have been transformed into multi-screen, air-conditioned facilities with modern equipment and the smell of popcorn – even though the price for a cinema ticket in such centres may exceed the price for a theatre ticket. Table 14.7 provides information on attendance at cultural activities in 1998.

Significant trends related to cultural activities from the 1980s to the 1990s include the following:

- Attendance at theatres and concerts gradually grew, peaking in the mid-1980s, but then went into decline, from 50 million visits in 1990 to 28 million in 1997, in spite of an increase in the number of theatres. Only 30% of the population attend theatres at all; the regular audience was therefore very small.
- Between 1978 and 1990, the annual audience for concerts dropped from 67 million to 54 million and the number of concerts almost halved.
- Museum attendance increased from 1960 to 1990, but in the first year of the reforms,

Table 14.7. Last attendance at selected cultural institutions, Russia, 1998.

	Cinema (%)	Museum (%)	Library (%)
This week	0	1	3
This month	1	2	4
This half a year	3	7	7
This year	4	6	5
More than a year ago, do not remember	67	59	57
Difficult to answer	25	25	24
Total	100	100	100

Source: FOM-INFO (1999b).

the number of visits to museums dropped by almost half (from 114 million in 1991 to 58 million in 1992), recovering to 70 million in 1995, due mainly to lower prices and price reductions for students and the elderly; but in 1998, even with these incentives still in place, it fell back to 67 million.

- Library attendance peaked in the mid-1980s (due mainly to 'glasnost' and readership interest in periodicals that bridged numerous gaps in history and provided up-to-date overviews of various domestic and foreign economic and social issues), then decreased, and then peaked again in the late 1990s, due mainly to educational needs and rapidly increasing magazine subscription prices. Students form the majority of library users.

Sport and Fitness

After 1960, there was a significant increase in the number of people engaged in different types of sport. Government concern with shaping the health of the population resulted in the construction of numerous stadiums and other sports facilities from 1960 to 1980. However, this led eventually to a growth of passive attendance at sports events and a corresponding decrease in both outdoor and institutionalized sporting activities. The number of people engaged regularly in different kinds of organized physical recreation decreased from 24 million in 1983 to 10 million in 1992[3] (Kzdorovoi, 1994). The proportion of Russian adults indicating that they did not engage in any sporting activity was 75% in 1997, 68% in 1998 and 80% in 1999 (FOM-INFO, 1999b).

The most popular types of organized sports were those not requiring any special equipment or infrastructure. However, from 1987 to 1991, growing interest in more personalized forms of physical activity led some people, particularly women, to spend more time in activities such as aerobics, body building and karate. Physical training for body shaping was the most popular sport activity, followed by team games, such as football, volleyball and hockey, then skiing, skating, athletics and martial arts (Bychovskaya, 1997).

Like many other societies, the level of sport spectating in Russia constantly exceeds the level of active involvement. But, unlike in most industrial countries, a significant part of the Russian population feels that work in their garden is the most valuable and useful form of physical activity. In the 1990s the development of out-of-the-city gardening cooperatives with individual cottages was booming. From 1985 to 1992 the number of people who owned a plot for kitchen-gardening (normally with a live-in house) increased almost threefold (State Statistics Committee, 1992).

Holidays

From the mid-1960s, the minimum duration of paid annual vacation was 15 working days. More then 80% of workers and employees had longer vacations, the average reaching 23 working days.[4] Between 1960 and the late 1980s the number of holiday-takers grew, facilitated by the growth in the number of hotels and vacation resorts. In 1987, 27% of the population spent their vacations in resort hotels, camping, on tourist excursions and in sanatoriums; 19% had recourse to health care in convalescent homes; and 3% went on excursions lasting 1 or 2 days (State Statistics Committee, 1988).

In the 1990s the actual duration of vacations decreased. In 1995 some workers, in urban and rural areas, reported that they had to work during their vacation in order to earn additional income. The number of people working during their vacation increased considerably and reached 44% in 1997, and 46% in 1998. In 1999, after the economic crisis, some 39% of workers reported that they had no vacation or had not used their vacation time for its intended purpose in the current year. Among vacationers, 58% said they did not go out; 55% also reported doing the chores, 8% referred to earning additional money and only 23% mentioned some form of relaxation (FOM-INFO, 1999b).

Traditionally, a considerable number of urban families, particularly those with children, spent most of the summer in the country, living in their own or rented cottages (*dachas*). Another traditional vacation type among urban dwellers (especially those with children) is vis-

iting relatives – mostly older relatives – in the countryside. However, the decrease in the proportion of first-generation urban dwellers limited this trend in the 1990s.

Under socialism, holidays in state- or enterprise-subsidized resort hotels and health-care centres were the most popular types of vacation, with many families drawn to the numerous Black Sea resorts. Until the 1980s, health resorts and resort hotels were however virtually unavailable for many working people due to a shortage of rooms and facilities, while in the 1990s their accessibility was restricted by high prices.

The variety of sites and facilities available for summer vacations expanded in the mid-1990s, as did the opportunities to travel abroad. Before the 1990s the overwhelming majority of tourist trips were within the USSR, limited by the lack of bus routes and train, aviation and hotel services. Under socialism, the ability to travel abroad as a tourist was not a function of income but was a privilege granted to the most loyal citizens. Tourist destinations were limited mainly to other socialist countries. After 1991 travel destinations became more varied and trips were used not only for recreation and tourism, but also for in-service and language training, and other purposes related to self-improvement and work. Access to this travel was now determined mainly by income.

In the late 1990s, resort hotels in Turkey, Bulgaria or Algeria became cheaper for Muscovites than those in the Moscow region. In 1987, only 0.5% of the population travelled abroad: some 800,000 went to eastern Europe, 63,000 to Western Europe and other developed countries, and 23,000 to other countries. In the 1990s, the number of Russians holidaying abroad grew, from 1.2 million in 1990 to 3.3 million in 1998 (State Statistics Committee, 2000).

Social Differences and Inequalities

Gender

Gender differences are persistent in leisure patterns of Russians, as indicated in Tables 14.4 and 14.5. The difference between the amount of free time available to men and women has fluctuated, but never disappeared. In 1924, men had twice as much free time as women; in 1959, 1.5 times as much; when paid working hours were reduced by 1 hour/day in 1959–1963, free time increased by 7%, but most of this accrued to men (Orlov, 1989). In 1965 men had 65% more free time than women; in 1985, 30% more; in 1990, about 50% more (Patroushev, 1988). From 1972 to 1980, there was some reduction in work time, particularly in the service sector, where most women were employed, but the amount of free time enjoyed by women grew only slowly, if at all, because undertaking domestic duties with a limited family budget became more time-consuming.

Between 1965 and 1985, men's leisure time increased by 4 hours/week, although the total amount of disposable time remained almost constant. This happened because of a sharp (4 hours) drop in time spent on education. For women, the decrease in time spent on education was only 1.3 hours (Yampolskaya, 1994).

Regardless of the lesser amount of free time, 1999 data indicate that females were more active in a number of leisure activities, as shown in Fig. 14.1. Other surveys indicate that in the 1990s, men spent three times as much time participating in sports as women, and sports clubs and beer parlours were attended by men more frequently than by women (Bychovskaya, 1997). This explains, in part, the fact that the ratio between leisure time spent in public places as opposed to individually was one to 21 for men and one to 30 for women (Patroushev, 1988).

Age

As indicated in Fig. 14.2, age differences are most evident in socializing, which is most popular among the youngest age groups, while listening to music, watching videos, visiting clubs and restaurants are popular among those aged 35–50. The elderly are most active in walking and caring for pets. Other research indicates that the middle-aged are the most numerous group among visitors to cultural events. Young people are interested in popular music concerts, while the elderly prefer classical music concerts and attending museums, exhibitions and art galleries (Ille, 1996).

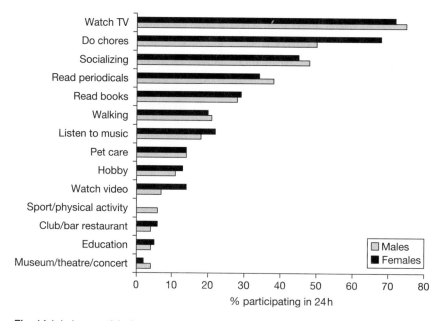

Fig. 14.1. Leisure activity by gender, Russia, 1999. Source: FOM-INFO (1999a).

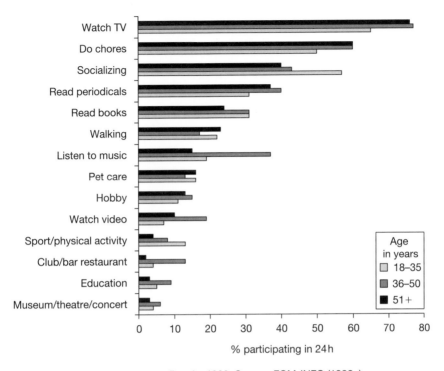

Fig. 14.2. Leisure activity by age, Russia, 1999. Source: FOM-INFO (1999a).

Type of settlement

Sharp differences in the availability of goods and services for rural and urban populations were a permanent feature of Russian life under socialism. The rural population, especially females, had less free time, shorter vacations, and more often stayed at home during holidays and vacation periods (see Table 14.4). From 1985 to 1990, free time for those employed dropped by more than a third: but while the decline was 18% for urban men and 33% for urban women, it was 37% for rural men and 44% for rural women (Artemov, 1990; State Statistics Committee, 1991). In 1990, urban dwellers spent twice as much money on theatre, movies and museum visits as rural dwellers (State Statistics Committee, 1992). Some 50% of rural families had books in the home, but their collections were only one-third the size of collections of urban families (Butenko, 1997). This urban/rural inequality remains long after the collapse of socialist rule.

Education

The level of education also reflects certain inequalities in leisure participation. The higher the level of education, the more likely the individual is to be involved in reading, listening to music, hobbies, physical activity, additional educational activities and attending cultural events, as indicated in Fig. 14.3.

Conclusions

Certain trends in leisure participation in Russian society over the past 40 years are similar to those in Western societies, including shorter working hours, longer vacations, higher levels of mobility in vacations and weekend trips, more time spent watching television, growth in sport spectating, greater variety in free-time activities, more time spent in family or individual activities and less in institutionalized social activity. But the extent and timing of these trends is not the same. Some of these changes came

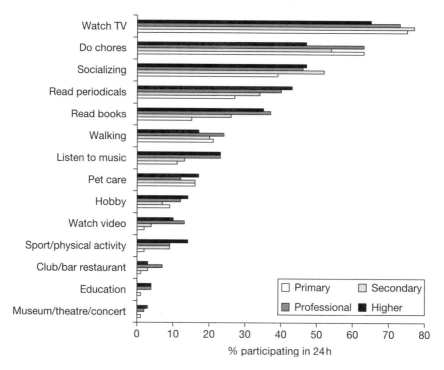

Fig. 14.3. Leisure activity by level of education, Russia, 1999. Source: FOM-INFO (1999a).

comparatively late to Russia – particularly in the 1990s, with the late and accelerated process of modernization that took place in that period. In a few cases, such as increased working hours, trends went into reverse in this period.

Thus it would appear that the 'golden age of leisure' had not arrived, either quantitatively or qualitatively, in Russia by the end of the 1990s.

Inequality among social groups persists in the amount of free time available and in the pattern of leisure activities, and is most obvious between males and females and between urban and rural populations. These inequalities reflect the situation that previously existed in the Soviet era, with urban males having the largest access to free-time activities. Sharp income inequalities were not yet clearly reflected in patterns of leisure activity. Behavioural patterns were formed in an era when most people were neither very poor nor very rich and most appeared to keep doing mainly the same things as they did before the social and economic changes, regardless of their current economic situation. Nevertheless, both rich and poor are less

satisfied with their leisure than with their work, health, circle of friends or 'life in general' (Butenko, 1998).

This situation is not just a Russian one, it is widespread in eastern Europe, for instance, in Bulgaria (Genov and Krasteva, 1999). This leads to a broader conclusion: that people in the post-socialist societies are experiencing exclusion from many contemporary leisure opportunities. This is believed to be a temporary trend which might eventually be mitigated by growing stability in these societies, increasing levels of economic well-being and further Westernization of lifestyles. The latter is becoming directly available to the affluent few and only indirectly, via the mass media, to the general public. On the other hand, a kind of 'backward trend' towards a more work-orientated lifestyle is currently affecting the younger age groups, because of the growing demands of the new economy and time required for improving skills and (re)education. The most affluent as well as the career-oriented youth are therefore the two groups who seem to be the most adaptable to leisure-style changes.

Further research will be needed to assess the degree to which emerging 'Russian leisure styles' increasingly reflect the leisure styles of the Western world.

Notes

[1] This belief remains strong: in a 1998 survey of adult population 67% of respondents considered work to be more important than leisure, although 12% of the young and educated among the sample found it difficult to answer this question (FOM-INFO, 1998b).
[2] In 1998, over 62% of urban families had garden or kitchen plots, 98% of them for cultivating fruit and vegetables, including 4% for sale (FOM-INFO, 1998c). In 1999, 27% of Russian families produced almost half of their own food requirements and 30% even more than half (www.romir.ru).
[3] These figures include school and university students, who were required to take part in sports once or twice a week as part of their curricula.
[4] Before the 1980s, these vacations were actually 2–3 days shorter, mainly due to monetary compensation received for unused vacation time when changing jobs. Workers and employees younger than 18 were given a 1-month annual vacation. There were other types of paid vacations: for studying or medical treatment, to compensate for overtime, and for maternity leave. In 1956, the length of paid maternity leave increased from 77 to 112 days. In 1981a 1-year partly paid maternity leave was introduced. In the late 1990s some of these regulations were not followed, especially by private enterprises.

References

Artemov, V.A. (1990) Dinamika obraza zhizni sel-skogo naselenia. Sotsiologicheskie issledovania [Dynamics of the rural population's lifestyle]. *Sociological Studies* No. 4.

Butenko, I.A. (1997) *Chitateli i Chtenie na Rubezhe XX Veka* [Readership and Reading at the End of XXth Century]. Nauka, Moscow.

Butenko, I.A. (1998) Kachestvo dosuga bogatykh i bednykh. Sotsiologicheskie issledovania [Quality of leisure of rich and poor]. *Sociological Studies* No. 7.

Butenko, I.A. (2000) Razlichia v dosugovoi deiatel-nosti muzhshchin i zhenshchin [On gender differences in leisure activity]. *Informkultura* No. 6.

Butenko, I.A. and Razlogov, K.E. (1997) *Cultural Policies in the Russian Federation*. Council of Europe, Strasbourg.

Bychovskaya, I.M. (1997) Athletics and sports. In: Boutenko, I.A. and Razlogov, K.E. (eds) *Recent Social Trends in Russia. 1960–1995*. McGill-Queen's University Press, Montreal.

FOM-INFO (1998a) *Informatsionnyi biulleten Fonda 'Obshestvennoe mnenie'* [Information Bulletin of 'Public Opinion' Foundation], No. 1 (196).

FOM-INFO (1998b) *Information Bulletin of 'Public Opinion' Foundation*, No. 17 (212).

FOM-INFO (1998c) *Information Bulletin of 'Public Opinion' Foundation*, No. 53 (374).

FOM-INFO (1999a) *Information Bulletin of 'Public Opinion' Foundation*, No. 22 (447).

FOM-INFO (1999b) *Information Bulletin of 'Public Opinion' Foundation*, No. 35 (460).

FOM-INFO (2000) *Information Bulletin of 'Public Opinion' Foundation*, No. 46 (471).

Genov, N. and Krasteva, A. (1999) *Bulgaria 1960–1995*. National and Global Development, Sofia.

Gordon, L.A. and Klopov, E.V. (1972) *Chelovek Posle Raboty. Sotsialnye Problemy Povsednevnoi Zhizni i Vnerabochego Vremeni* [Man After Work. Social Problems of Everyday Life and Out of Work Time]. Nauka, Moscow.

Ille, M.E. (1996) Monitoring kulturnoi aktivnosti zhitelei Sankt-Peterburga. Sotsiologicheskii zhurnal [Monitoring cultural activities of St Petersburg's citizens]. *Sociological Journal* 1–2, 176–181.

Ille, M. (2000) Kulnurnaia zhizn' zhitelei Sankt-Peterburga: 10 let nabliudenii. [Cultural life of the St Petersburg citizen: 10 years of observa-tion]. *Telescope* No. 5.

Kzdorovoi, R. (1994) *Doklad Gos. Centra Profilakticheskoi Meditsiny* [Towards a Healthy Russia. A Report of the State Centre for Prophylactic Medicine]. Vodoley, Moscow.

Maximov, A.L. (1981) *Rabochee i Svobodnoe Vremia v Usloviakh Razvitogo Sotsializma* [Work and Free Time Under Developed Socialism]. Nauka, Moscow.

Orlov, G.P. (1989) *Svobodnoe Vremia – Uslovie Razvitia Cheloveka i Mera Obshchestvennogo Bogatstva* [Free Time as a Precondition for Human Development and the Measure of Public Good]. Ural GU, Sverdlovsk.

Patroushev, V.D. (1979) *Tendentsii Izmenenia Biudzheta Vremeni Rabotaiushchikh* [Trends in Time Budgets of Working People]. Institute for Sociological Research, Moscow.

Patroushev, V.D. (1987) *Kak i s Kem Provodim my Svobodnoe Vremia?* [How and with Whom are We Spending Free Time?]. Institute Sotsiologi-cheskikh Issledovanii, Moscow.

Patroushev, V.D. (ed.) (1988) *Vremia i Ego Ispolzovanie* [Time and Its Use]. Institut Sotsiologicheskikh Issledovanii, Moscow.

Patroushev, V.D. (1998) Izmenenia v obraze zhizni i biudzhetakh vremeni pensionerov. Sotsiologicheskie issledovania [Changes in way of life and time-budgets of retirees]. *Sociological Journal* No. 3-4, pp. 242–245.

Patroushev, V.D., Karachanova, T.M. and Koushnareva, O.N. (1992) Svobodnoe vremia zhitelei Moskvy i Moscovskoi oblasti. Sotsiologicheskie issledovania [Free time of the Moscow and Moscow region population]. *Sociological Studies* No. 6.

Patroushev, V.S., Karachanova, T.V. and Temnitsky, A.L. (1996) Stil' zhizni gorozhan: panelnoe issledovanie zhitelei Pskova v 1986 i 1995 godakh. Sotsiologicheskii zhurnal [Way of life of the citizens: the panel survey of Pskov's residents in 1986 and 1995]. *Sociological Journal* No. 1–2.

Prokofiev, V.V. (1989) Svobodnoe vremia promyshlennykh rabochikh. Sotsiologicheskie issledovania [Free time of industrial workers]. *Sociological Studies* No. 1.

Routkevich, V.I. (1997) Transromatsia sotsialnoi structury Rossii. Sotsiologicheskie issledovania [Transformation of the social structure of the Russian society]. *Sociological Studies* No. 7.

Shmarov, A.I. (1987) Trud i Svobodnoe Vremia [Labour and Free Time]. Ekomonika, Moscow.

State Statistics Committee (1988) *Narodnoe Khoziaistvo Rossiiskoi Sovetskoi Federativnoi Sotsialisticheskoi Respubliki za 70 let* [National Economy of the Russian Soviet Federative Socialist Republic over 70 Years]. State Statistics Committee, Moscow.

State Statistics Committee (1990) *Narodnoe Khoziaistvo Rossiiiskoi Sovetskoi Federativnoi Sotsialisticheskoi Respubliki v 1989 Godu* [National Economy of the Russian Soviet Federative Socialist Republic in 1989]. State Statistics Committee, Moscow.

State Statistics Committee (1991) *Narodnoe Khoziaistvo Rossiiskoi Sovetskoi Federativnoi Sotsialisticheskoi Respubliki v 1990 Godu* [National Economy of the Russian Soviet Federative Socialist Republic in 1990]. State Statistics Committee, Moscow.

State Statistics Committee (1992) *Narodnoe Khoziaistvo Rossiiskoi Federatsii v 1991* [National Economy of the Russian Federation in 1991]. Republic Publishing Centre, Moscow.

State Statistics Committee (2000) *Rossia v Tsifrakh v 1999 Godu* [Russia in Figures in 1999]. State Statistics Committee, Moscow.

WCIOM (1994) Ekonomicheskie is sotsialnye peremeny. Monitoring obshestvennogo mnenia [Economic and social change. Monitoring of public opinion]. *WCIOM Bulletin* No. 5.

WCIOM (2002) Ekonomicheskie is sotsialnye peremeny. Monitoring obshestvennogo mnenia [Economic and social change. Monitoring of public opinion]. *WCIOM Bulletin* No. 3.

Yampolskaya, S.M. (1994) Dinamika dosugovogo obshchenia. Sotsiologicheskie issledovania [Dynamics of leisure socialising]. *Sociological Studies* No. 3.

15 Spain

Concepción Maiztegui Oñate

Background

With the accepted contribution of leisure to quality of life and life satisfaction, traditionally Spanish scholars have thought of leisure as a context for the development of self-esteem as well as personal and social skills. Even though this hypothesis has been widely accepted theoretically and pragmatically, few empirical research studies have addressed this issue. The chapter on Spain in the first edition of this book (Maiztegui Oñate, 1996), which outlined the historical background to the development of leisure research in Spain, noted that research on participation in leisure activities at the national level was scarce, with the last broad study having been published in 1994 by the Foundation for the Development of Social Studies and Applied Sociology (Fundación para el Desarrollo de Estudios Sociales y Sociología Aplicada; FOESSA). To draw a fuller and more contemporary picture of leisure participation in Spain it is necessary to draw on a number of different surveys. Most of the available data come from three different sources:

1. *Studies from closely related fields.* Certain types of leisure activity have received attention from specialist researchers and institutions, providing extensive data on activity groups such as sport, cultural activities and tourism (e.g. Centro de Investigaciones Sociológicas, Turespaña).

2. *Studies focused on particular social groups (e.g. young people) in which leisure is one domain of the investigation.* These data are available in studies supported by a number of public ministries and foundations (e.g. Emakunde, Fundación Santamaría, Ministry of Culture, Ministry of Social Affairs). Both the Fundación Santamaría and several ministries have funded various projects on the social conditions and lifestyles of young people, and the reports invariably include a chapter on leisure (Gil Calvo, 1985b; Zarraga, 1988; Gonzalez Blasco *et al.*, 1989; Elzo, 1990; Elzo *et al.*, 1999).

3. *General social surveys of the population with a section devoted to leisure.* Certain publications, such as those of the National Institute of Statistics (Instituto Nacional de Estadísticas; INE) have included a section devoted to *culture and leisure*. General social studies at the national level have typically focused on demand and supply, mainly from an economic perspective.

The social survey conducted by FOESSA in 1993, has provided an important database on Spanish leisure activity patterns. The study was a general social survey involving a sample of 8500 individuals aged 18 years and over (details of this and other surveys mentioned are presented in Table 15.1). The leisure participation results of this survey were reported in a chapter entitled 'Leisure and lifestyles', which interpreted and analysed leisure broadly to embrace the idea of *lifestyles* (Ruiz Olabuenaga, 1993). The study covered a total of 24 different leisure practices, which were grouped into the following fourfold leisure typology using time and space categories: (i) *daily, home leisure* – free time activities such as television-watching, chatting and playing cards; (ii) *non-daily, home leisure* – family gatherings and celebrations, anniversaries and the like; (iii) *daily, out-of-home leisure* – activities performed out of the home but on a daily or regular basis, e.g. sports, outings with friends; and (iv) *non-daily, out-of-home leisure* – such as vacations and holidays.

In the period 1978–1991 the Ministerio de Cultura conducted a series of studies on the cultural practices of Spaniards, considering a range of activities directly related to leisure and free time (Ministerio de Cultura, 1978, 1985, 1991), but did not continue after 1991. The regular studies on time-use and cultural consumption carried out by Diez Nicolas and published by the Centre for Social Research (Centro de Estudios de la Realidad Social, CIRES) during the 1990s ceased with the closure of CIRES. These changes created considerable difficulty in studying change in patterns of leisure participation over time.

From the standpoint of research conducted on specific areas of leisure, however, the situation changes. Systematic and regular studies have been conducted on participation in sport (Centro de Investigaciones Sociales, 1995a,b, 1997) and tourism patterns (Turespaña, 2000).

A recent survey published by Sociedad General de Autores (SGAE, 2000) which analyses all cultural sectors from a sample of 24,000 personal interviews, provides a rich source of relevant data. Using a questionnaire with more than 100 questions on interests, satisfactions, frequency of participation and consumption of activities and cultural products, the survey provides insight into the cultural, recreational and educational activities that Spaniards prefer, activities engaged in during the last year and frequency of participation in

each activity. The result is an extensive map of Spanish cultural life.

Profile of Leisure Participation

The aim of this section is to analyse the major leisure activities of the Spanish population, drawing on the sources discussed above. First of all, the availability of free time is discussed, and this is followed by an outline of leisure activities engaged in during that time. Leisure activities are classified into six groups: family and social relations; mass media; membership in organizations; sport activities; cultural activities; and holiday-taking.

Time-budgets

Working time, paid and unpaid, occupies Spaniards, on average, for 7.7 hours a day on weekdays, for 6.4 hours on Saturdays and 4.2 hours on Sundays (CIRES, 1993, 1997; Ruiz Olabuénaga, 1994). However, the averages hide considerable differences in the allocation of free time between men and women, and employed and non-employed persons. One of the most relevant features concerning time-budgets is the increasing presence of women in the labour market, and continuation of their unpaid family roles, resulting in a broadening of responsibilities to include paid and unpaid work. Table 15.2 shows that employed women work an average of 3.5 hours more than employed men, and this difference is maintained during the weekend. Family schedules are reported as the main factor influencing the organization of women's time: 65% mention the family as a factor but only 23% mention paid work schedules, whereas 61% of men mention paid work schedules and only 25% mention family commitments (CIRES, 1993). So it is not an overstatement to say that: 'their paid job and other public commitments do not affect the amount of care and time that women devote to their families or their workloads in the house' (Setien, 1996, p. 114).

Indeed, as Table 15.2 indicates, the differences between men and women in hours worked per day increases considerably among

Table 15.1. Surveys of leisure and related topics, Spain, 1978–2000.

Name of study	Agency	Date	Sample size	Age range	Activities/topic	Reference
FOESSA Social Survey	Fundación FOESSA	1993	8500	18+	All leisure (24 activities)	Ruiz Olabuénaga (1994)
Surveys of Cultural activities	Ministerio de Cultura	1991, 1985, 1978	12,000 15,010 31,385	18+ 18+ 18+	Cultural activities	Ministerio de Cultura (1978, 1985, 1991)
Cultural Consumption	Centro de Estudios de la Realidad Social (CIRES)	1990/91, 1991/92, 1992/93, 1995/96	12,000 10,800 10,800 7800	18+ 18+ 18+ 18+	Cultural activities and recreation	CIRES (1992, 1993, 1994, 1997)
Sport Participation	Centro de Investigaciones Sociales (CIS)	1995	2493	18+	Sport	CIS (1995a)
Tourism	Turespaña, Centro de Investigaciones Sociales (CIS)	2000 1995	10,800 10,800	18+ 18+	Trips, tourism Holidays	Turespaña (2000) CIS (1995a)
Cultural Activity	Sociedad General de Autores (SGAE)	2000	24,000	18+	Cultural, recreation and education activities	SGAE (2000)

Table 15.2. Working time, Spain, 1993.

	Paid and unpaid work, hours/day, adults aged 18+				
	Employed			Non-employed	
	Women	Men	Total	Women	Men
Weekdays	12.4	8.8	7.7	7.7	2.6
Saturday	9.9	5.4	6.4	8.1	2.1
Sunday	6.8	2.6	4.2	5.9	1.3

Source: FOESSA (1993).

the non-employed. Being older and being married seems to increase the male privileges in this (fewer hours worked) respect. Except for the very young (aged 14–18) and the oldest group (over 64), the differences in time devoted to household chores by male and female increase during the weekend. Given this pattern of inequality, it is not surprising to find that there are two groups of women who report being extremely dissatisfied with their free time. The first group are married women with double workdays, comprising a small group of married women, aged 30–49, with low incomes. The second group are traditional housewives, aged between 50 and 64, with low levels of education, from low or lower-middle class backgrounds (Setien, 1996).

Leisure Activities: Family and Social Relations

Family life and use of the mass media are the most popular leisure activities among the Spanish population, as shown in Table 15.3. The relationship between these two activities is clear, given that the majority of people (97%) watch television with the family (CIRES, 1992). As in other countries, the family in Spain has changed in recent years and become more complex, but it continues to be one of the main reference groups for most individuals. The family has reduced in size and its forms have diversified, but it still shows strong evidence of continuing a traditional role in fostering social relationships, involving daily contact between parents and children, which combine enjoyment and provision of essential support (Iglesias de Ussel, 1994). That sharing free time with the family continues as the major leisure activity

reflects a society where satisfaction with family life has increased since 1981, both in terms of the proportion of satisfied individuals and the measure of general satisfaction (Elzo et al., 1999). In sum, watching television with the family constitutes one of the most important activities of daily, home-based social leisure, and is much more widespread than any other home-based individual leisure activity, including reading (Ruiz Olabuénaga, 1994, p. 1932).

Out-of-home leisure patterns present a more complex and diversified situation and, as Table 15.3 indicates, are characterized by informal interaction and sociability, for example, 'being with friends'. Playing sports, attending the cinema or shows, or watching or playing sport are less significant in the national picture of leisure participation. This pattern is similar for men and women and for young and old, and regardless of level of education, although the older age groups and those with less education are considerably less active overall. Whereas the family situation has a great influence on leisure behaviour, there is little difference in leisure participation between employed and non-employed populations (Ruiz Olabuénaga, 1994, p. 1936).

For young people, most of them unmarried, the role of peers is important as the primary identification group with which they spend most of their free time. From the last survey on young people (Elzo et al., 1999) a picture of a high positive assessment of other leisure options emerges, such as travelling, going to the cinema and listening to music, as indicated by the 'would like to' column in Table 15.4. Laespada and Salazar (1999, p. 365) observe a tendency for girls to have higher levels of participation, particularly in cultural activities. Girls appear to be more concerned with 'adult activities', while

Table 15.3. Leisure participation by gender, age and educational level, Spain, 1992.

| | % participating[a] in last 3 months, adults aged 18+ | | | | | | | | | |
| | Home-based | | | | | Out-of-home | | | | |
	Family activity	Television- watching	Read magazines, books	Listen to radio	Listen to music	Go to cinema	Be with friends	Watch sports	Play sports	Go to shows
Gender										
Men	77.3	66.9	20.9	19.6	16.1	6.3	56.1	17.2	13.8	2.4
Women	84.4	70.3	25.8	28.1	15.2	7.0	45.7	2.5	4.6	1.9
Age										
18–21	62.6	53.2	20.3	15.3	36.2	15.5	79.0	12.8	22.9	2.7
22–25	64.9	49.1	22.1	14.7	31.5	15.4	74.0	10.0	21.6	5.3
26–35	78.0	58.4	27.9	17.8	20.8	10.3	59.8	10.8	12.1	3.3
36–45	86.9	65.2	27.3	19.8	13.6	6.3	46.2	8.9	8.2	2.5
46–60	89.0	78.5	19.7	28.7	7.8	2.3	39.6	9.3	2.9	0.7
60+	85.5	85.8	21.8	36.0	5.0	0.5	35.3	7.9	1.8	0.5
Education										
No qualifi- cation	86.8	87.0	12.2	30.6	4.7	0.6	38.2	6.5	1.2	0.3
Primary school	87.2	84.6	15.4	31.6	7.5	1.1	39.0	7.5	2.4	0.9
Secondary school	73.6	53.1	28.3	15.9	25.3	11.7	64.0	12.8	16.9	3.3
University	66.6	41.5	50.5	14.3	24.8	15.4	60.7	8.3	15.9	6.8

[a] Three activities selected.
Source: FOESSA (1993).

Table 15.4. Leisure participation by youth, Spain, 1998.

| | % of young people aged 18–24 participating frequently | | | | |
	Total participation	Would like to participate	Difference	Male	Female
Going out with friends	97.2	98.7	1.5	97.0	97.4
Listening to music (CD, tapes)	95.4	97.3	1.9	95.1	95.7
Travel	80.0	95.3	15.3	78.7	81.4
Going to the cinema	86.2	94.1	7.9	84.6	87.9
Watching television	89.8	92.5	2.7	92.4	91.9
Live music concert	77.3	91.9	14.6	75.3	79.3
Playing sport	70.1	85.0	14.9	81.8	58.8
Going to disco	77.2	81.3	4.1	76.8	77.6
Visiting museums, exhibitions	43.0	65.4	22.4	39.2	46.9
Computers	47.6	64.1	16.5	51.5	43.5
Eventual work	35.6	59.3	23.7	37.2	34.0
Join organizations	9.3	57.2	47.9	9.7	8.9
Going to conferences	25.0	35.7	10.7	23.2	27.0
Join a religious association	8.3	19.1	10.8	6.3	10.3

Source: Laespada and Salazar (1999).

boys lean towards 'teenage activities' (Laespada and Salazar, 1999). However, participation in sport and use of computers, and interest in these areas, are much higher among boys than girls.

While elderly people tend to drop out of out-of-home leisure activities as home-based activities increase in popularity (see Table 15.3), it has been found that when good health prevails some leisure activities, such as sport, travel and educational activities, are increasingly incorporated into older people's lifestyles, playing an important role in maintaining social interaction (Maiztegui Oñate, 1997; Medina Tornero and Ruiz Luna, 2000).

Mass Media

In Western societies, including Spain, every single individual is a consumer, directly or indirectly, of the mass media. The most common cultural resources are those that serve as vehicles for conveying messages to the masses, especially television, radio and recorded media. They are followed at some distance by Toffler's (1984) so-called 'demassed' mass media, such as print. Due to the fact that 98.9% of Spanish households have at least one television set (SGAE, 2000), it can be said that the mass media reach everybody. This situation was observed as early as 1991, when the report of the Ministry of Culture, noting a television ownership level of 97.8%, concluded: 'lack of equipment is an almost residual situation, . . . and can be explained by the critical situation of the household or is directly related to the location of the residence – rural or urban – of the families' (Ministerio de Cultura, 1991, p. 39).

Several investigations (CIRES, 1997; INE, 2000; SGAE, 2000) show that the Spanish population has frequent and direct contact with radio and television. Both have committed audiences that follow their programmes on a daily basis. Among all mass media, television is the preferred medium by all social groups, ages and levels of education. Time spent watching television occupies a significant proportion of all free time available to virtually all citizens – nearly all Spanish people (90.7%) watch television every day and the average daily time devoted to watching television is approximately 2 hours. Nevertheless important

differences appear: 18% report watching television less that 45 minutes daily; and 13% watch for more that 3 hours a day (CIRES, 1993). The key variables seem to be age and social status. Young people (under 19), older people (over 65) and people with lower levels of education have the highest rates of daily television-watching (SGAE, 2000). On the other hand, time spent on watching television decreases with increasing socio-economic status and size of residence (CIRES, 1993, 1994; SGAE, 2000).

Most of the time (78%), people watch television with someone else, mainly family members, and report having conversations about what is being viewed (CIRES, 1994). As Dumazedier (1989) pointed out, it is possible for television to be a catalyst for new relationship patterns, and to facilitate familial conversations and discussion regarding the programmes being viewed. Spaniards prefer informative programmes and films, although half of them report watching television as a secondary activity while they do something else, such as chatting (24%), eating (47%), doing household chores (15%) or reading (6%). Even though there are no differences between men and women in time spent watching television, it is much more common for women to simultaneously perform household chores while watching television (CIRES, 1994).

As Table 15.5 shows, other mass media, except for the radio, are not so popular. Listening to the radio every day and the weekly reading of magazines reaches just over a half of the population. There is a lower preference for reading newspapers, with only 49% of the Spanish population reporting doing so. Patterns of reading of print media vary greatly among social groups: people over 65 and those with low socio-economic status comprise more than the 40% of those who never read the daily press (CIRES, 1993). The majority of press readers are males. Women are the main consumers of the most popular magazines, that is women's magazines and 'sentimental' stories.

Finally, the results of recent SGAE studies show there is a striking development in listening to music on the radio or CDs, with 31% claiming to listen to music every day in 1997, compared with just 19% in 1991 (SGAE, 2000).

Table 15.5. Use of the mass media, Spain, 1990–1997.

	% of population aged 14+							
	1990	1991	1992	1993	1994	1995	1996	1997
Newspapers (daily)	31.9	32.4	33.6	36.4	36.8	38.0	38.2	37.7
Magazine (weekly)	35.3	36.9	36.6	37.9	36.1	33.8	32.9	32.4
N & M	56.8	58.2	57.9	56.2	54.0	54.7	55.6	54.7
Radio (every day)	50.5	52.2	52.4	52.9	55.4	56.5	56.6	55.0
Television (every day)	87.4	89.5	89.5	90.1	90.4	91.1	91.3	90.7
Cinema (weekly)	6.7	6.3	6.9	7.6	7.8	8.3	9.3	8.8

Source: Estudio General de Medios (1998) and INE (2000).

Memberships of Organizations

Membership of organizations does not reach the level seen in other European countries, perhaps due to a certain resistance on the part of Spaniards to associate. Basically, this aspect of leisure involvement might be characterized as a small but growing interest. In 1994, some 40% of Spaniards were members of at least one association, compared with 37% in 1978 (Ministerio de Cultura, 1978; Ruiz Olabuénaga, 1994, 2000). However, younger generations (under 24), run counter to this trend, with 28% belonging to an association in 1981; increasing to 46% in 1994 (Mota, 1999).

Many of the persons recorded as belonging to at least one association could be members of several at the same time. A study referred to by FOESSA (1993) found that 23% of the population were members of just one association, 10% belonged to two and some

8% were members of three or more. It should be noted that, while these data refer to all types of organizations, leisure-orientated associations (e.g. sport, culture, gastronomic) are the most popular (58%).

Sport

The main result of a number of leisure surveys relating to sport lead to the conclusion that there has been an overall increase in participation during the 1980s and 1990s, with both quantitative and qualitative features. Thus, participation levels in 1995 were substantially higher than those recorded previously, both in terms of participation rates and frequency of participation per week. The overall level of sports participation per week was 42%; this is double the level recorded 10 years earlier (García Ferrando *et al.*, 1998) (Table 15.6).

Table 15.6. Participation in top ten sports by gender, Spain, 1995.

Men	% participating per week	Women	% participating per week
1. Football	56	1. Swimming	42
2. Cycling	30	2. Aerobics	27
3. Swimming	28	3. Gymnastics	25
4. Basketball	14	4. Cycling	22
5. Jogging	13	5. Jogging	13
6. Tennis	13	6. Tennis	11
7. Athletics	11	7. Basketball	10
8. Excursions	10	8. Athletics	9
9. Jai-Alai (Pelota frontón)	9	9. Volleyball	7
10. Fishing	8	10. Skiing	5

Source: García Fernando *et al.* (1998).

Table 15.7. Frequent sport participation – over three times a week, by gender and age, Spain, 1995.

	% of population aged 16+ participating in previous week
Gender	
Men	41
Women	44
Age	
16–24	45
25–34	37
35–44	37
45–54	42
55–65	56

Source: García Ferrando et al. (1998).

In general, the level of participation in sport increased from 15% of the population in 1975 to 23% in 1995. Nearly a quarter of the population participated in one sport, 16% in two sports or more, with 35% having no active involvement in sport at all. The most popular activities were football (36%), recreational swimming (33%), cycling (27%), gymnastics (16%), basketball (14%), jogging (13%), tennis (12%) and aerobics (12%). All other sports achieved participation rates of under 10%.

Sports participation varies by gender, age, education levels and marital status (Table 15.7). But according to García Ferrando et al. (1998, p. 51) the increase in regular sport participation (three times or more a week) is spread across different groups of population and is not peculiar to any one of them.

Cultural Activities

Participation in a number of cultural activities is limited to a restricted part of the population and participation rates remain stable. There have not been significant changes for example, in attendance at the theatre over the past 10 years (INE, 2000; SGAE, 2000). At present some 75% of the Spanish population does not attend theatre performances, and audiences mainly comprise women and people with high levels of education. Geographically, Madrid and Cataluña, with historical traditions in the arts, have the most active populations, culturally. Demand is focused on comedy, music hall and contemporary drama.

Visiting museums and galleries and going to classical music concerts, dance performances and opera all attract under 10% of population at least once a year (CIRES, 1997; SGAE, 2000). Participation is clearly influenced by social status and educational level, with important cultural and social barriers faced by broad social groups.

Another feature of the cultural sector is that sightseeing has increased in popularity, turning cultural heritage facilities into major tourist attractions. During their holidays, for example, 31% of the population report visiting heritage sites, 23% visit museums and 15% visit national parks, which are considered by the state to be part of the cultural heritage (Turespaña, 2000). As Bauer (1996) has observed, major exhibitions form the boundary between urban cultural activities and cultural tourism, attracting local residents and domestic and foreign tourists alike.

In popular culture, pop and rock concerts increased their audiences during the 1990s, with 10% attending in the last 3 months in 1991 and 19% in 1999 (SGAE, 2000).

Since 1990 the average frequency of cinema attendance increased by 2.9 times a year, compared with the European average of 2.2 times a year (SGAE, 2000). Spanish and American films are rated equally on value by audiences, even though American films are more popular at the box office (SGAE, 2000). Younger people, aged under 35 years, are the most devoted film-goers, reflecting not just an interest in cinema itself, but also the need for young people to socialize and meet friends (SGAE, 2000).

Much culture is now distributed via new communication technologies, and nearly one-third of Spanish homes have a VCR, with this linked directly to higher socio-economic levels (SGAE, 2000). The group of people who report that they go to the cinema at least twice a month are also the main group of video-buyers, along with parents of children under 14 years old (SGAE, 2000). Available data indicate that 7% of the population aged over 14 years have used the Internet at least once in the past month (INE, 2000), with the proportion of men (10%) more than double that of women (4%).

Reading as a leisure activity is experiencing a gradual decline, with just a small group of regular readers (around 20%), and 49% declaring that they never read in 1999, an increase from 42% in 1991. Available data from a SGAE study indicates that reading habits – particularly of infrequent readers – have been affected by audiovisual technologies, such as video, television and the Internet (SGAE, 2000).

Geographical location seems to affect people's cultural interests. Madrid, Cataluña and northern Spain stand out for their apparent dynamism and cultural interest. Their populations are more acquainted with book shows, music festivals, theatre and art visits. This reflects historical tradition in these areas, stemming from early urban and economic development, even though the current economic global situation particularly affects the northern regions of the country, with their economies based on mining and iron and steel industries. Inhabitants of urban areas seem to prefer cultural trips and reading, although education level and age also account for the high levels of participation in these activities (Ministerio de Cultura, 1991).

Holiday-taking

In 1999, half of the Spanish population (of a total of 40 million) took a holiday away from home – defined as a leisure trip involving at least one night away from home. The average number of such trips taken in 1999 was six. Focusing on households, some 61% made a trip (seven per household). However, if visits to second homes are excluded, this percentage goes down to 58% and the frequency to three. However, behind the averages there is considerable variation. According to Turespaña (2000), the profile of a Spanish tourist is an employed person, 35–44 years old, with a high level of education.

As far as domestic tourism is concerned, the majority of trips (92%) are to the Mediterranean coast. Loyalty is a notable characteristic of domestic tourism, with some 94% returning to the same location in the following year. Only 8% had a holiday abroad, the favourite destinations being the neighbouring countries of France, Portugal and Andorra. Leisure and 'holidays' are mentioned as the primary motivation for travelling (70%), followed by visiting friends and relatives (18%) (Turespaña, 2000).

Discussion

Based on frequency of participation in leisure activities, the Fundación FOESSA (1993) report establishes seven types of 'leisure lifestyle', each style being focused on a different group of activities, namely: hunting; sporting activities; play; home activities; television-watching, etc.; and social activities. As Ruiz Olabuénaga (1994) argues, these groups of activities can be considered as indicators of lifestyles because they are practiced frequently, in a regular (daily or weekly) and 'normal' fashion, and cannot be considered as exceptional behaviour. The remaining important role of familial and social relations is worth mentioning and the decrease of some traditional activities, such as crafts, playing cards, reading and making collections have been replaced by new computer games, video-watching, sport and open-air activities. These new types of leisure activities are close to some of the above-mentioned leisure lifestyles (based on sports, play, home activities), but other leisure lifestyles are linked to more 'traditional' leisure activities, such as hunting or social activities.

To conclude, leisure has been accepted as an important part of new patterns of social life, and recent surveys show the emergence of a number of new trends in travel, cultural and sport participation. These trends should be closely monitored in order to understand the use of time and, therefore, the changing way of life of the Spanish population.

Although surveys of household consumption are undertaken in Spain, and there are signs that people increasingly utilize their consumption power to shape their leisure identities, there has been little effort to develop specific leisure participation surveys, at the national level. Specific empirical research on leisure participation is of relatively recent origin in Spain. Numerous institutional obstacles, arising from academia and the public and private sectors of leisure, have mitigated against the conduct of national surveys, and thus local research still tends to predominate. Further, there is no tradition of leisure research in Spain as a significant field of academic knowledge, university leisure departments are very few, and scholars continue working within their original disciplinary fields and publish in their specialist journals. There is a need, therefore, to develop leisure fora at which research can be presented and discussed – the hosting of the World Leisure Conference in Bilbao in July 2000 was one step in this direction. Global perspectives presented at such gatherings will be of interest not only to researchers but also to planners and managers, both public and commercial, and to the leisure services sector which is one of the fastest-growing sectors of the Spanish economy.

Bibliography

Bauer, M. (1996) Cultural tourism in France. In: Richards, G. (ed.) *Cultural Tourism in Europe*. CAB International, Wallingford, UK, pp. 147–164.

Centro de Investigaciones Sociales (1995a) *Comportamiento de los Españoles ante las Vacaciones*. CIS: Catálogo del Banco de Datos, Madrid.

Centro de Investigaciones Sociales (1995b) *Los Hábitos Deportivos de los Españoles*. CIS: Catálogo del Banco de Datos, Madrid.

Centro de Investigaciones Sociales (1997) *Tiempo Libre y Deportes*. CIS: Catálogo del Banco de Datos, Madrid.

CIRES (Centro de Estudios de la Realidad Social) (1992) *La Realidad Social en España 1990–91*. Ediciones B, Barcelona.

CIRES (Centro de Estudios de la Realidad Social) (1993) *La Realidad Social en España 1991–92*. Ediciones B, Barcelona.

CIRES (Centro de Estudios de la Realidad Social) (1994) *La Realidad Social en España 1992–93*. Ediciones B, Barcelona.

CIRES (Centro de Estudios de la Realidad Social) (1997) *La Realidad Social en España 1995–96*. Fundación BBV, BBK and Caja Madrid, Madrid.

Dumazedier, J. (1989) *Révolution Culturelle du Temps Libre*. Méridiens Klinscksieck, Paris.

Elzo, J. (1987) *Una Lectura de la Juventud Vasca*. Servicio Central de Publicaciones del Gobierno Vasco, Vitoria-Gazteiz.

Elzo, J. (1990) *Jóvenes Vascos 1990: Informe Sociológico*. Servicio Central de Publicaciones del Gobierno Vasco, Vitoria-Gazteiz.

Elzo, J., Orizo, A., González-Anleo, J., González Blasco, P., Laespada, Mª.T. and Salazar, L. (1999) *Los Jóvenes Españoles 99*. Fundación Santamaría, Madrid.

Estudio General de Medios (1998) see www.aimc.es/02egm/24.html

Fundación FOESSA (1976) *Informe Sociológico Sobre la Situación Social en España*. Euroamérica, Madrid.

Fundación FOESSA (1993) *Informe Sociológico Sobre la Situación Social en España. Sociedad Para Todos en el 2000*. Fundación FOESSA, Madrid.

García Ferrando, M. (1990) *Aspectos Sociales del Deporte: Una Reflexión Socilógica*. Alianza, Madrid.

García Ferrando, M. (1993) *Tiempo Libre y Actividades Deportivas*. Instituto de la Juventud, Madrid.

García Ferrando, M., Martín Morales, J.R. and Acuña Delgado, D. (1996) *Ocio y Deporte en España: ensayos Sociológicos Sobre el Cambio*. Tirant Lo Blanc, Valencia.

García Ferrando, M., Puig Barata, N. and Lagardera Otero, F. (eds) (1998) *Sociología del Deporte*. Alianza, Madrid.

Gil Calvo, E. (1985a) *Los Depredadores Audiovisuales*. Tecnos, Madrid.

Gil Calvo, E. (1985b) *Ocio y Prácticas Culturales de los Jóvenes*. Ministerio de Cultura, Madrid.

Gonzalez Blasco, J., Orizo, F.A., Toharia, J.J. and Elzo, F.J. (1989) *Jóvenes Españoles 89*. Fundación Santamaría, Madrid.

Iglesias de Ussel, J. (1994) *Informe Sociológico Sobre la Situación Social en España. Sociedad Para Todos en el Año 2000*. Fundación FOESSA, Madrid, pp. 415–548.

INE (2000) *Indicadores Sociales*. Instituto Nacional de Estadística, Madrid (www.ine.es/).

Laespada, Mª.T. and Salazar, L. (1999) Las actividades no formalizadas de los jóvens. In: Elzo, J., Orizo, A., González-Anleo, J., González Blasco, P., Laespada, Mª.T. and Salazar, L. (eds) *Los Jóvenes Españoles 99*. Fundación Santamaría, Madrid, pp. 355–400.

Maiztegui Oñate, C. (1996) Spain. In: Cushman, G., Veal, A.J. and Zuzanek, J. (eds) *World Leisure Participation: Free Time in the Global Village*. CAB International, Wallingford, UK, pp. 199–214.

Maiztegui Oñate, C. (1997) *Modelos de Representación de Las Personas Mayores en Los Medios de Comunicación*. Universidad de Deusto, Bilbao [duplicated typescript].

Medina Tornero, M.E. and Ruiz Luna, Mª.J. (eds) (2000) *Políticas Sociales Para las Personas Mayores en el Próximo Siglo*. Universidad de Murcia & Caja de Ahorros del Mediterráneo, Murcia.

Ministerio de Cultura (1978) *Demanda Cultural de los Españoles*. Ministerio de Cultura, Madrid.

Ministerio de Cultura (1985) *Encuesta del Comportamiento Cultural de los Españoles*. Ministerio de Cultura, Madrid.

Ministerio de Cultura (1991) *Encuesta de Equipamiento, Prácticas y Consumos Culturales*. Ministerio de Cultura, Madrid.

Mota, F. (1999) La realidad asociativa en España. In: Subirats, J. (ed.) *Existe Sociedad Civil en España? Responsabilidades Colectivas y Valores Públicos.* Fundación Encuentro. Madrid, pp. 37–64.

Ruiz Olabuénaga, J.I. (1994) Ocio y estilos de vida. In: Fundación FOESSA (ed.) *Informe Sociológico Sobre la Situación Social en España. Sociedad Para Todos en el Año 2000.* FOESSA, Madrid, pp. 1881–2074.

Ruiz Olabuénaga, J.I. (Dir.) (2000) *El Sector no Lucrativo en España.* Fundación BBV, Madrid.

Setien, M.L. (1996) Spanish women: between family and autonomous leisure. In: Samuel, N. (ed.) *Women, Leisure and the Family in Contemporary Society: a Multinational Perspective.* CAB International, Wallingford, UK, pp. 111–141.

SGAE (Sociedad General de Autores) (2000) *Informe SGAE Sobre Hábitos de Consumo Cultural.* SGAE, Madrid.

Toffler, A. (1984) *Previews and Premises.* Pan, London.

Turespaña (2000) *Movimientos Turísticos de los Españoles (Familitur) Año 1999.* www.iet.tourspain.es/new/eye/familitur/1999

Vazquez, B. (1993) *Actitudes y Prácticas Deportivas de las Mujeres Españolas.* Instituto de la Mujer, Madrid.

Zarraga, J.L. (1988) *Informe Juventud en España.* Ministerio de Asuntos Sociales, Madrid.

16 United States of America: Outdoor Recreation

H.K. Cordell, G.T. Green, V.R. Leeworthy, R. Stephens, M.J. Fly and C.J. Betz

Introduction

The first nationwide survey of outdoor recreation in the USA was conducted in 1960 for the Outdoor Recreation Resources Review Commission (ORRRC, 1962; Cordell *et al.*, 1996). Since that time, seven additional national surveys have been conducted, in 1965, 1970, 1972, 1977, 1983, 1995 and 2000/01 – summary details are presented in Table 16.1.

Table 16.1. National Recreation Surveys, USA, 1960–2001.

Survey	Date	Managing agency	Sample size	Age range	Ref. period	Ref.
National Recreation Survey (NRS)	1960	ORRRC	6000	12+	Year	ORRRC (1962)
NRS	1965	BOR	7190	12+	Summer	Bureau of the Census (1965)
NRS	1970	BOR	16,770	12+	Year	Bureau of the Census (1970)
NRS	1972	HCRS	3770	12+	Summer	Audits and Surveys (1972)
NRS	1977	HCRS	4030	12+	Year	US Dept of the Interior/ HCRS (1979)
NRS	1982/83	NPS	5760	12+	Year	US Dept of the Interior, National Park Service (1986)
National Survey on Recreation and the Environment (NSRE)	1994/95	USFS + NOAA	17,000	16+	Year	Cordell *et al.* (1996, 1999)
NSRE	2000/01	USFS + NOAA	47,000	16+	Year	This chapter

ORRRC, US Outdoor Recreation Resources Review Commission; USFS, US Forest Service; NOAA, National Oceanic and Atmospheric Administration; BOR, Bureau of Outdoor Recreation; HCRS, Heritage Conservation and Recreation Service; NPS, National Park Service.

© CAB International 2005. *Free Time and Leisure Participation: International Perspectives* (eds G. Cushman *et al.*)

245

The surveys conducted in the 1970s were found to be problematic for a number of reasons and are not often referenced. In working with the other surveys of 1965, 1982/83, 1994/95 and 2000/01, the focus has been on comparability.

Comparability between surveys is a challenge each time this US national survey is conducted. But comparability and consistency in question phrasing are essential if long-term and short-term trends are to be tracked. The approach is to include, each time as nearly as possible, an identical set of core questions, cast in comparable contexts, and also to repeat the survey as close to a 5-year cycle as possible, so that recent as well as long-term trends can be identified. Renamed the National Survey on Recreation and the Environment (NSRE) for its 1994/95 application, the survey has expanded beyond the former National Recreation Survey's singular focus on recreation participation to include questions on topics such as the environment, public land policy and lifestyles. The latest survey, NSRE 2000/01, was the eighth national survey in the series, and it has run virtually continuously from late 1999 to the writing of this chapter in May 2004. Over 80,000 interviews were collected during this time, making the NSRE the largest federal recreation survey ever conducted in the USA. In this chapter we focus on the 42,868 completed interviews collected between November 1999 and July 2001. The next NSRE is planned for 2005.

Since the late 1980s, the NSRE has been under the management of the US Forest Service and the National Oceanic and Atmospheric Administration (NOAA). Day-to-day operations are housed within the Outdoor Recreation, Wilderness and Demographic Trends Assessment Group, a research unit of the Forest Service Research and Development Branch located in Athens, Georgia. To raise funds for the survey and to attract a wide range of expertize, the Forest Service and NOAA seek additional sponsors, including other federal and state government agencies and private organizations. The NSRE sponsoring agencies from the federal government have included the USDA Forest Service (FS), the National Oceanic and Atmospheric Administration (NOAA), the Bureau of Land Management (BLM), the National Park Service (NPS), the US Environmental Protection Agency (EPA) and the Economic Research Service (ERS).

The name change from National Recreation Survey to the National Survey on Recreation and the Environment reflects not only continuing interest in outdoor recreation, but also a growing interest in the natural environment and the management of public lands. So, in addition to questions about recreation participation, constraints and demographics, the survey now includes many more questions dealing with topics such as knowledge of natural land issues, environmental attitudes, preferences for public land objectives and values of wilderness. In addition, each sponsor has specific information needs beyond recreation. This characteristic of NSRE sponsorship adds considerable complexity to the survey's design. However, this broader array of subject matter adds possibilities for exploring a wider range of relationships between recreation behaviour, demographics, environmental attitudes, lifestyles, public land management preferences, and other aspects of people's lives. In this chapter we describe the NSRE, its operational design and how that design is implemented.

Design

Principal objectives and intended uses

A core purpose of the NSRE is to describe current patterns and recent trends in participation in a wide range of outdoor recreation activities by the people of the USA as a whole. Central to this core purpose is estimation of proportions and numbers of the population participating in the outdoor activities listed for them. A second major purpose is to estimate the distribution of participation by region, state, metropolitan area and other geographic locations in the USA. Of particular interest to NOAA is estimating participation within coastal states around the country. Thirdly, the NSRE seeks to describe, among other things, responding individuals' uses and values in relation to public lands, and attitudes regarding natural resource policy issues, lifestyles and demographic characteristics. It is also designed to provide periodically updated information on public opinions and values with regard to the natural environment, public land management, and changing uses of protected systems of public lands, such as the National Wilderness Preservation System.

The US Forest Service uses data from the NSRE in a number of ways, but the principal one is to examine trends in support of the *National Assessment of Outdoor Recreation and Wilderness*, which is completed every 10 years, with updates in the intervening 5 years. This assessment is required by the federal Forest and Rangeland Renewable Resources Planning Act, 1974. Data from the NSRE are also used to assist National Forest recreation planners and managers, as well as operations in other federal and state agencies, in evaluating recreation-related land and water management issues. Other uses of the data include the assessment of the emerging recreation demands on local, state, federal, and private providers of outdoor recreation, and evaluation of alternative methods for financing the provision of outdoor recreation services and facilities.

The NSRE also provides broad-scale information about market trends and futures for outdoor recreation, regionally and nationally. University researchers and graduate students use the data to develop and test theoretically grounded hypotheses. Specialized sets of questions and analyses address specific needs as they are identified, including those of secondary sponsors seeking results only from their own questions. Results of the 1995 NSRE were published in 1999 in *Outdoor in American Life* (Cordell *et al.*, 1999). Comprehensive results from NSRE 2000/01 are published in *Outdoor Recreation for 21st Century America* (Cordell *et al.*, 2004).

Organization of the survey

The NSRE is an in-the-home telephone survey. For the surveying done in 2000–2004, over 80,000 people, aged 16 or over, across all ethnic groups throughout the USA were interviewed. The NSRE actually consists of a number of different survey versions made up of different mixes of question sets or modules, each version being administered to approximately 5000 people. Throughout the administration of different versions of the NSRE, questions on activity participation and demographics are included as the core of the survey. Where appropriate, ques-tions are asked about special issues, such as disabled persons' recreation participation and access to recreation opportunities.

Modules include sets of questions covering: environmental attitudes; objectives for public land management; attitudes toward and values gained from protected wilderness; appropriateness of charging access fees; knowledge of public lands; lifestyle indicators; leisure; rural land ownership; interest in farm-based recreation; and other more specific questions. Of specific interest to the EPA, for example, were questions dealing with child and adult bicycle helmets for safety. Of specific interest to the cooperative Scenic Byways Research Program, were questions on use and values associated with state-designated scenic highways. Of specific interest to the Forest Service (among a number of other question sets) were questions dealing with fees charged for admission to recreate in National Forests.

Participation questions

In its most recent application, the NSRE included 74 outdoor recreation activities, as listed in Table 16.2. Not all of these activities were asked in every version of the survey, although the majority of them were. For each activity included in a particular version, respondents were asked whether or not they participated at least once during the past 12 months. In some versions, questioning about activities in which a respondent had participated went further, including the number of different days on which they had participated and the number of holidays or trips they took where the activity was the primary reason for taking a trip. The trip questioning included both single- and multiple-day trips. For a randomly selected activity, identified as involving primary purpose trips, more detailed data were collected. The focus was on the last trip of 15 or more minutes taken from home, where the activity was the primary purpose for that trip. The information asked for included a description of the destination, other activities engaged in, travelling companions, mode of travel and other trip characteristics. This detail has been used primarily in modelling activity demand.

Table 16.2. Activities[a] examined in the US National Survey on Recreation and the Environment (NSRE), 2000/01.

Running/jogging	Caving
Golf	Bird watching
Tennis outdoors	Wildlife viewing
Baseball	Fish viewing
Volleyball	Viewing natural vegetation, flowers
Basketball	Nature study/photography
Softball	Small game hunting
American football	Big game hunting
Soccer	Migratory bird hunting
Handball/racquetball/squash outdoors	Gathering mushrooms, berries, firewood or other natural products
Yard games/horseshoes, croquet	Downhill skiing
Bicycling	Snowboarding
Mountain biking	Cross-country skiing
Horse riding	Ice skating
Equestrian activities	Snowmobiling
Picnicking	Sledding
Family gathering	Snowshoeing
Inline skating or rollerblading	Off-road vehicle use
Visiting a historic site, building, monuments	Sightseeing
Nature museums, nature trails, visitor centres, zoos	Visit beach/waterside
Outdoor concerts/plays	Nature tours in an ocean bay or inlet
Outdoor sports events	Driving for pleasure on country roads
Prehistoric/archaeological site	Riding motorcycles for pleasure on highways
Visiting a farm or agricultural setting	Fishing: anadromous
Walking	Cold and warm water fishing
Visit a wilderness or other roadless area	Fishing: freshwater
Home gardening or landscaping	Fishing: saltwater
Day hiking	Ice fishing
Orienteering	Sailing
Backpacking	Rowing
Camping/primitive and developed	Rafting/tubing/other floating
Mountain climbing	Motor boating
Rock climbing	Water-skiing
Swimming/non-pool	Canoeing/kayaking
Swimming in an outdoor pool	Surfing
Personal water craft such as jet skis	Sailboarding/windsurfing
Scuba diving	Snorkelling

[a] Activities are shown in the order asked during the phone interview. Activity ordering is kept consistent from survey to survey.

Issue-specific questions

Short descriptions of some of the questions covered in the NSRE are provided below.

Persons with disabilities

A very significant issue in the USA, as elsewhere, is whether persons with challenging conditions are inappropriately restricted or constrained from participating in outdoor recreation. In addition to concerns about participation, the NSRE includes a section asking about the nature of disabilities and opinions on adequacy of access. Access questions address both legislatively mandated and policy-driven programmes, which seek to improve access for all US citizens. Because disabled respondents were asked the same full-breadth of NSRE questions as everyone else, the data developed provide an in-depth national profile of persons with disabilities that goes well beyond data that are typically available.

Wilderness

Despite numerous studies of wilderness users, the general American public has been little studied with regard to its values, opinions and awareness of protected wilderness. In the NSRE, perhaps the most comprehensive coverage ever assembled about wilderness in the eyes of the public has been completed. Coupled with data from other sections of the NSRE, specifically tailored questions about wilderness can be examined in the full social context in which opinions about wilderness are formed and held.

Trip profiles and valuation objectives

Resource economics literature dating back a number of decades describes a method generally referred to as travel-cost modelling (Clawson and Knetsch, 1966). This methodology focuses on recreational trips taken to different types and qualities of destination sites. Greatly refined over the years by other economists, the basic premise put forward by Clawson and Knetsch was that persons taking recreation trips incur, and are willing to pay, costs for travel and access and, in so doing, provide the researcher an opportunity to observe a relationship between costs incurred and number of trips taken. From this relationship, a formal trip demand function can be estimated, as can the amount the trip-taker is willing to pay for that recreational trip over and above what they actually do pay. This 'over-and-above' willingness to pay is the economist's way of deriving an estimate of the economic value of the trip and of the place visited during that trip. This travel-cost method is firmly grounded in theory and provides a reliable measure of recreation benefits (Walsh, 1986; Bergstrom, 1990). The NSRE provides the necessary trip profile data to support travel cost demand modelling.

Favourite activities

Because individuals vary in what they enjoy and commit themselves to in outdoor recreation, a section of the survey asks about favourite activities. Included is a measure of commitment and the preferred 'setting' or environment for the identified favourite activity(ies). Asking respondents about favourite activities serves a number of purposes. One is to enable tracking trends in most favoured activities from generation to generation and from decade to decade. Often participation data alone are not sufficient to identify activities favoured most, even though participation levels may point to popularity. A second purpose is to set up the respondent for the constraints module (explained below). In preceding national surveys, it has been found that asking about constraints to participation has more meaning to respondents if asked in the context of favourite outdoor pursuits. A third purpose in asking about favourite activities is to identify differences in preferences between different groups in American society, by age, gender, race and other characteristics.

Barriers and constraints

Reasons for non-participation in outdoor recreation are of particular interest to outdoor recreation managers. The NSRE replicates and adds to the list of barriers and constraints considered in previous national surveys and allows open-ended responses to capture new or previously unidentified barriers and constraints. Questions in this section were asked in one of two situations: (i) for respondents who reported that they did not participate in any outdoor recreation; and (ii) for respondents who reported that they did not participate in their favourite activity as often as they would have liked.

Environmental issues

Within political and public arenas, information on how the public uses and values the environment and natural lands is useful in forming or reforming environmental policy, particularly where public lands are the focus. Often, organized interests, natural resource professionals, political interests, commodity interests and local communities are at the decision-making 'table' and their voices are heard. But, the 'voice of the public' is often not at the table and is not heard. The emphasis that people place on different environmental resources and services is growing in importance in the USA and elsewhere in the world. A number of tailored scales have been developed for the NSRE to help describe how people across American society view and value natural lands and other environmental resources.

Lifestyles

New in the 2000/01 NSRE was a scale of 36 'lifestyle indicators'. The intention was to identify 'lifestyle' activities which respondents participated in regularly. The dimensions in this lifestyle scale included: hobbies, chores, family activities, sports spectatorship, community and church activities, vacations and travel, self-learning, health and exercise, environmental involvement, fads, socializing and going out. Together with recreation participation, environmental attitudes and demographics, information regarding lifestyles adds enormously to the breadth of profiling that can be undertaken for any particular group or interest in American society. Adding lifestyles data provides a new level of opportunity for cluster analysis and other approaches for grouping people by interests, behaviours and/or attitudes. These segmentation results will be used to help make more effective programmes for outreach, education and involvement aimed at the American people.

Bicycle safety

With the signing of Executive Order 13045, *Protection of Children from Environmental Health Risks and Safety Risks*, in April 1997, the protection of children's health and safety has become a priority for federal agencies and programmes. To assess many of the regulations that affect children's health and safety, policymakers need estimates of the monetary value of reducing risks to children. While some research and literature have provided first-round estimates of the value of reducing health and safety risks, especially for adult populations, it has provided none for school-age children. The 'bicycle helmet' module of NSRE is a highly specialized interest of the EPA aimed at providing data for evaluating reduction of risks in bicycle riding to both child- and adult-age riders through increased emphasis on wearing helmets.

Survey Implementation and Bias Control

The computer-assisted telephone interview system

As with NSRE 1995, telephone interviews for the 2000/01 survey were facilitated using a computer-assisted telephone interview (CATI) system. The CATI system has three primary functions: (i) it facilitates dialling and interviewing; (ii) it manages the administrative functions associated with interviewing; and (iii) it organizes and stores the data for later processing. As quickly as one interview is completed, the CATI system randomly selects another telephone number for the interviewer. Delays are minimal. If the next number proves successful in reaching an eligible person, and they are willing to continue with an interview (an increasingly difficult thing to accomplish), the interviewer reads the survey questions as they appear on the computer screen and records responses directly into the computer as prompted.

The CATI system assures that 'skip' and 'branching' patterns in the interview are executed flawlessly, that responses are within range, that there are no unintended missing data, and that data entry occurs in real time as the survey is administered. If the CATI system and the interviewer are not able to establish contact with a potential interviewee, then a code is entered (e.g. busy, no answer). If the timing of the call is inconvenient, a call back is scheduled for another date and time. Overall, the CATI system is of great assistance to interviewers executing telephone surveys such as the NSRE. In this era of exponentially expanding phone numbers, and voice mail, caller ID, call screening, and many other innovations in telephone communications, CATI might even be viewed as essential to large-scale telephone survey research.

Sampling

Because the NSRE serves many different needs, its sampling framework must be designed to accommodate a variety of needs. For example, the planned modelling and valuation work conducted by EPA and ERS using NSRE 2000/01 activity participation data for agricultural land and farms, requires participation data reflecting rural recreation trip destinations. Sampling allocations, therefore, require oversampling in rural areas to assure adequate numbers of responses in rural recreation destinations throughout the country, especially in sparsely populated areas.

Another example of a special need is the interest of the NOAA in coastal activity participation. To obtain a sample in the 2000/01 NSRE sufficient to cover activities with low participation rates (less than 5%), a large overall sample was needed to assure sufficient coverage of participation in each coastal state. For this use, a large sample spatially distributed as the population is distributed would have been adequate, but because rural intensification was needed by the ERS and EPA, a compromise sampling design was agreed to by the sponsoring agencies. This first set a quota of a minimum of 400 completed interviews per state, spatially distributed as the population within each state was then distributed. This accounted for 20,000 (50 states × 400) of the targeted 50,000 interviews. The remaining 30,000 of the targeted interviews were distributed by a formula to assure adequate sampling in rural counties. The allocation employed for these 30,000 was 65% urban, 25% near urban and 10% rural. The strategy of setting a minimum state quota along with proportionate population sampling provided data adequate for separate reports on participation for each state and region in the USA, as well as reliable estimates of days of participation in states along the coast.

Table 16.3 provides a breakdown of sample sizes attained for the entire USA by the nine Census Divisions. All data are post-weighted before analysis to compensate for the deliberate, as well as chance, disproportionate sampling with respect to social strata and geographic regions.

Potential for estimation bias

There are many potential sources of bias in any large survey of human subjects, such as the NSRE. The principal categories are response bias and non-response bias. Response biases include recall bias and 'digit preference'. Sources of non-response bias include: avidity, incomplete telephone listings, language barriers and refusals (Vaske *et al.*, 1996; Steeh *et al.*, 2001). These sources of bias are discussed in turn below.

Recall bias is simply the inability of a respondent to recall accurately, or to recall at all, whether they participated in particular recreational activities and, if they participated, how often and where that participation occurred. Social scientists often disagree over the optimum recall period (1 week, 1 month, 6 months, etc.) and the best way to account for any recall bias that does occur. In any survey, it must be assumed that some recall bias will occur. For example, one form of recall bias is referred to as 'telescoping' – uncertainty on the part of the respondent as to when participation occurred,

Table 16.3. Regional distribution of sample, NSRE, 2000/01.

Census division	% of population	% of sample	Sample size[a]
East North Central	16.1	13.9	5962
East South Central	6.0	7.6	3254
Middle Atlantic	14.1	10.6	4511
Mountain	6.5	9.6	4118
New England	4.9	7.5	3214
Pacific	16.0	12.6	5365
South Atlantic	18.4	17.7	7568
West North Central	6.8	10.9	4634
West South Central	11.2	9.6	4114
Total	100.0	100.0	

[a] Regional sample sizes sum to 42,740; 128 respondents did not provide their place of residence.

but certainty that they did participate some time in the past. The problem arises when that participation actually occurred outside the time period specified in the interview.

Digit preference is a form of recall bias which involves the common tendency for respondents to round off reported numbers of times they have participated in an activity. Typically, the rounding is upward. For example, for activities of frequent participation, such as walking or running/jogging, respondents often round upward to the nearest 5 or 10, such as 25, 30 or 40, rather than the actual number of occasions, such as 28 times during the past 12 months.

Avidity bias is the tendency of persons who do not participate in outdoor recreation activities, or who participate only infrequently, to refuse to take part in the survey because they feel it is does not apply to them. Avidity bias can result in over-representation of persons who participate and are interested in outdoor recreation. Left unaccounted for, avidity bias can result in seriously inflated estimates of participation rates and biased estimates of participation differences by social group.

Incomplete telephone listings, like any other incomplete sampling frame, can occur for many reasons. More frequently encountered reasons include institutionalization, simply not having a telephone, and access only to pay phones or other non-individualistic arrangements.

Bias comes from language barriers and the resulting, inadvertent exclusion of non-English speaking residents. According to the 2000 Census, 12.5% of the US population is Hispanic. For the non-English-speaking segment of the Hispanic population, the NSRE was conducted in Spanish. The most difficult part of this process was making the translation 'generic' enough for overall comprehension by all the various Hispanic dialects.

Of all sources of bias it is perhaps the non-response bias potentially caused by some households and individuals simply refusing to participate in an interview that is of greatest concern. Increasingly, in today's fast-moving, high-technology world, it is difficult to make contact to set up and complete telephone interviews. First, the expansion of telephone numbers that has been occurring over the past two decades makes it much more difficult to identify a potential individual interviewee in a private household. Cellular telephones, pagers, fax machines, and the growing number of businesses and households are creating more and more demands for new telephone numbers.

But more numbers is only a part of the growing challenge. Once a legitimate phone number is obtained and a candidate household is identified, the process then must focus on making voice contact and on gaining the responding person's confidence and cooperation. Technology is placing a greater burden on attempts to reach and talk with persons in a typical household. Just a few years ago, interviewers only had to deal with answering machines. Before that, 'no answer' or a 'busy' signal were the only issues. Current technology now includes caller ID, call blocking, and other privacy managers. Households using any or all of these devices can easily choose whether to accept a call without the caller knowing such screening is occurring. With these kinds of screeners in place, and with people's often busy schedules, it can take up to 15 to 20 attempts to get a person in the household to answer the telephone.

Much of today's society is fast-paced and time-conscious. In this environment, keeping a respondent on the phone to complete an interview is more and more difficult. Competition with telemarketers, charitable organizations, political pollsters, and other solicitors affect the likelihood that a respondent will stay on the phone and complete an interview. Usually, unless the survey is viewed promptly as interesting or important to respondents, they will not be willing to give the 15–20 minutes needed to complete an interview. In the USA, willingness to cooperate tends to vary by state. It also varies by urban or rural part of the country. For the NSRE, in general, households in urban areas of the country were more easily contacted, but they were less likely to complete the interview process. On the other hand, people in rural areas were more likely to cooperate, but they were more difficult to contact.

For the NSRE, a concerted effort to estimate avidity, listing, and refusal biases was made by asking two key questions of persons who refused to participate in the survey. These were: age and whether or not the respondent participated in outdoor recreation in the past 12 months. The gender of the respondent was also recorded when recognizable. The estimated proportions of non-respondents, relative to respondents, was combined with weights derived from the 2000 Census of the US population to weight each response to correct for over-representation or under-representation by that respondent's social group in the sample. As with any survey, regardless of scope or complexity, bias is a reality that must be dealt with early on, to the extent that it is recognizable and correction measures are affordable. Often this is addressed through sample design, questionnaire order and content, and weighting the data.

Patterns of Participation Based on the 2000/01 NSRE

Overall participation

The estimates of participation presented here are based on the 42,868 completed NSRE interviews that were conducted between November 1999 and July 2001. This period is defined as the base period for statistical reporting from the NSRE, even though interviewing has continued well beyond that time. The final column of Table 16.4 shows the overall, weighted proportion of total respondents, aged 16 or older, who participated in a selection of the more popular outdoor recreation activities in the past 12 months. First listed is overall 'Outdoor recreation participation', indicating the percentage of the population that participated in at least one activity during the base period. An individual is defined as an 'outdoor recreation participant' if he or she participated in at least one activity.

Almost all (97%) Americans aged 16 or older had taken part in at least one activity in the previous 12 months. Activities with the highest levels of participation include: walking for pleasure (83%); attending family gatherings outdoors (73%); viewing natural scenery (60%); visiting nature centres (57%); picnicking (55%); sightseeing (52%); and driving for pleasure (51%).

Table 16.4. Outdoor recreation participation in the past 12 months by gender, USA, 2000/01.

	% of persons aged 16+ participating in year		
Activity	Males	Females	Total
Outdoor recreation participation (at least one activity)	97.5	96.6	97.0
Walking	79.8	85.9	83.0
Family gatherings	72.7	74.1	73.4
View natural scenery	59.5	61.1	60.3
Nature museums/nature centres	57.9	56.6	57.2
Picnicking	51.9	57.1	54.6
Driving for pleasure	51.4	51.4	51.4
Sightseeing	50.1	53.7	52.0
Historic areas/sites/buildings/memorials	47.9	44.3	46.0
Wildlife viewing	45.6	43.8	44.7
Swimming/other than pool	44.6	39.7	42.0
Bicycle	44.2	35.6	39.7
Visit beach	41.2	39.4	40.3
Boating	41.5	31.8	36.4
Fishing	44.2	25.1	34.2
Visit a wilderness area	39.7	26.4	32.7
Bird watching	30.1	34.6	32.5
Hiking	37.0	29.6	33.1
Visit waterside	27.7	24.7	26.1
Snow and ice activities	29.6	23.4	26.3
Developed camping	27.9	24.5	26.2
Motor boating	29.1	20.5	24.5
Outdoor team sports	30.7	15.8	22.9
Mountain biking	25.9	17.3	21.4

Continued

Table 16.4. *Continued*

| | % of persons aged 16+ participating in year | | |
Activity	Males	Females	Total
Prehistoric structure/archaeological sites	21.9	19.9	20.9
Off-road driving	22.1	13.3	17.5
Primitive camping	21.0	11.2	15.9
Hunting	19.9	3.6	11.4
Backpacking	14.0	7.6	10.7
Horse riding	8.2	7.6	7.9
Canoeing	11.7	7.9	9.7
Snorkelling	8.2	5.3	6.7
N	18,694	24,096	42,790[a]

[a] The total NSRE 2000/01 sample size was 42,868, but gender was missing for 78 respondents.

Participation profiles by social characteristic

Gender

Participation rates for many activities vary considerably by gender, as shown in Table 16.4. Activities exhibiting the greatest participation difference by gender include team sports, mountain biking, visiting wilderness areas, hunting, off-road driving, fishing and boating. These tend to be male-dominated activities, in that males reported participation more frequently than females. Higher percentages of females than males participated in walking, picnicking, bird watching, viewing natural scenery and sightseeing. However, across the years that the USA has been conducting national recreation surveys, participation rates have risen faster for females than for males in many activities.

Age

Participation rates for almost all of the more active outdoor pursuits (such as bicycling, hiking, primitive camping, snow and ice activities, swimming, snorkelling and canoeing) vary considerably by age, as shown in Table 16.5. The pattern is as seen in previous surveys, that is, the participation rate declines with increasing age. Activities with the least differences by age include walking, picnicking, family gatherings, visiting historic sites, wildlife viewing, viewing natural scenery and sightseeing. Activities with the greatest difference by age comprise mainly

the more physically active pursuits: team sports, mountain biking, hiking, off-road driving, snow and ice activities and canoeing.

Ethnic group

Table 16.6 shows participation rate by ethnic group. Generally, larger percentages of Caucasians and Hispanics participate in outdoor activities than do African Americans. Activities most attracting African Americans include walking, family gatherings, sightseeing, picnicking and visiting nature centres. Overall, Caucasians tend to participate in higher percentages than Hispanics. Exceptions where the Hispanic participation rate is higher are limited to outdoor team sports and hiking. Caucasian participation rates are higher than the other ethnic groups across most activities and are especially higher for visiting historic sites, camping, bird watching, wildlife viewing, viewing natural scenery, hunting, snow and ice activities and several more. These differences in participation rate by ethnicity hold for most of the other activities included in the NSRE, but not shown in Table 16.6.

Region

Not shown in a table is a comparison of participation rates by region. Historically, participation percentages have been lowest in the South (south-eastern quarter of the USA). The NSRE shows this difference continuing into the beginning of the 21st century. For most activities,

Table 16.5. Outdoor recreation participation in the last 12 months by age, USA, 2000/01.

Activity	% of age group participating in year					
	16–24	25–34	35–44	45–54	55–64	65+
Outdoor recreation participation (at least one activity)	98.9	98.2	97.6	97.7	95.6	93.1
Walking	83.8	84.1	84.9	84.4	81.6	78.0
Family gatherings	77.9	78.4	77.5	73.2	67.9	62.5
View natural scenery	57.0	61.8	67.1	66.0	61.5	47.8
Nature museum/nature centres	58.3	67.4	65.9	59.5	52.1	36.9
Picnicking	47.7	59.3	63.4	59.7	52.8	44.5
Driving for pleasure	49.9	54.2	54.9	55.8	51.8	41.8
Sightseeing	46.9	54.2	55.9	57.3	52.9	45.4
Historic areas/sites/buildings/memorials	46.9	47.9	51.0	50.6	46.1	32.5
Wildlife viewing	43.6	45.7	50.5	48.8	44.8	33.8
Swimming/other than pool	57.5	50.5	50.4	41.1	28.5	15.5
Bicycle	56.0	45.9	48.2	35.2	26.4	17.2
Visit beach	50.3	46.9	46.5	40.2	30.8	21.1
Boating	49.5	41.6	41.3	35.5	27.2	17.3
Fishing	42.3	36.6	39.1	33.6	29.6	20.6
Visit a wilderness area	41.9	36.7	37.7	31.5	25.7	17.9
Bird watching	22.2	27.7	36.3	37.5	39.0	34.9
Hiking	36.3	39.7	40.8	34.1	26.1	17.7
Visit waterside	34.3	30.5	31.0	24.9	18.7	12.4
Snow and ice activities	47.8	33.4	31.6	19.8	11.0	4.3
Developed camping	32.1	31.2	32.2	25.4	19.8	12.4
Motor boating	30.5	28.1	28.4	23.8	20.2	13.3
Outdoor team sports	48.3	28.9	24.1	14.2	6.9	3.9
Mountain biking	33.7	29.3	26.5	17.6	10.7	4.0
Prehistoric structures/archaeological sites	22.5	21.6	24.2	22.8	20.0	12.9
Off-road driving	29.3	22.9	18.2	14.3	10.5	5.3
Primitive camping	25.1	19.2	17.7	14.9	10.7	4.5
Hunting	15.2	12.1	12.7	11.2	9.9	6.1
Backpacking	17.6	14.6	12.2	9.5	4.9	1.9
Horse riding	16.2	11.7	11.2	9.4	5.5	2.3
Canoeing	15.7	10.7	11.3	9.2	5.4	3.1
Snorkelling	9.6	8.4	8.1	7.0	3.7	1.6
N	5981	7672	8868	8289	5341	5974

Table 16.6. Outdoor recreation participation by ethnicity, USA, 2000/01.

	% of persons aged 16+ participating		
	Caucasian	African American	Hispanic
Outdoor recreation participation (at least one activity)	97.9	96.1	93.5
Walking	85.6	83.0	71.3
Family gatherings	74.4	73.8	68.4
Viewing natural scenery	66.7	39.3	46.2
Nature museum/nature centre	61.2	42.3	52.7
Picnicking	57.2	47.4	49.1
Driving for pleasure	58.0	40.6	33.6
Sightseeing	57.8	44.9	32.9
Historic areas/sites/buildings/memorials	50.9	37.4	30.9
Wildlife viewing	51.7	26.9	28.3

Continued

Table 16.6. *Continued*

	% of persons aged 16+ participating		
	Caucasian	African American	Hispanic
Swimming/other than pool	49.3	19.9	28.6
Bicycle	41.2	35.4	36.2
Visit beach	43.6	33.6	29.3
Boating	43.9	15.9	21.1
Fishing	38.5	25.9	23.6
Visit a wilderness area	37.7	16.9	23.7
Bird watching	36.8	20.1	22.6
Hiking	34.3	10.8	47.1
Visit waterside	30.3	16.9	15.4
Snow and ice activities	31.3	13.3	15.1
Developed camping	29.9	13.1	20.7
Motor boating	30.8	8.6	12.4
Outdoor team sports	21.3	26.4	26.5
Mountain biking	23.3	14.4	19.3
Prehistoric structure/archaeological sites	21.8	17.6	19.3
Off-road driving	20.1	11.1	12.1
Primitive camping	19.3	5.2	10.0
Hunting	14.2	4.9	5.7
Backpacking	12.1	3.5	9.9
Horse riding	11.3	5.1	8.5
Canoeing	12.3	2.9	3.7
Snorkelling	7.7	2.9	3.8
N	34,577	3115	2791

participation levels of Southerners are less than those for the other three regions (Northeast, Midwest and West), with the exception of hunting, off-road driving, fishing and motor boating. The Northeast participation rate tends to be high relative to other regions in snow and ice activities, visiting historic sites, visiting the beach and swimming in natural water. The West tends to have higher percentages associated with nature-based activities ('The great outdoors'), while the Midwest tends to have relatively high participation for bicycling, visiting nature centres, bird watching, sightseeing and boating.

Income

Table 16.7 indicates that income appears to have a very strong effect on participation across almost all activities. Those with the strongest positive correlation include golf, tennis, visiting prehistoric and archaeological sites, hiking, rock climbing, studying nature near water and snorkelling. Those activities for which partici-

pation rates remain relatively steady across most income groups include primitive camping, hunting, off-road motor vehicle driving and fishing. Overall, however, participation in any kind of outdoor recreation was strongly and positively correlated with income, rising from 93% among those earning less than US$10,000 to more than 99% among those earning over US$100,000.

Trends

Long-term trends

National recreation surveys have been conducted in the USA since 1960. Figures 16.1 and 16.2 and Table 16.8 show long-term trends in the eight activities that can be tracked back to the first survey in 1960. In the USA, population and incomes have both risen significantly in the more than 40 years since the first national survey. As shown in Table 16.8, the population aged 12 years and older grew from 131 million in 1960

Table 16.7. Outdoor recreation participation by income, USA, 2000/01.

	Annual total family income, US$'000s					
	<US$15	US$15–24	US$25–49	US$50–74	US$75–99	US$100+
	% of persons aged 16+ participating in year					
Outdoor recreation participation (at least one activity)	93.4	96.9	98.5	99.2	99.0	99.3
Walking	76.4	81.6	85.4	89.2	90.8	89.0
Family gatherings	65.0	74.6	77.8	78.6	80.1	77.5
View natural scenery	45.4	57.7	66.4	73.9	76.1	75.8
Nature museum/nature centre	42.6	51.7	62.5	69.5	75.1	72.1
Picnicking	46.8	54.8	61.1	66.1	64.3	62.5
Driving for pleasure	38.5	48.8	58.8	63.2	63.6	61.9
Sightseeing	38.7	48.6	57.9	64.5	66.3	64.2
Historic areas/sites/buildings/ memorials	30.8	37.8	49.9	59.1	64.4	67.3
Wildlife viewing	33.9	43.3	49.9	56.8	56.9	57.5
Swimming/other than pool	26.9	33.5	46.6	54.1	57.6	62.0
Bicycle	29.7	31.2	40.2	45.5	52.1	52.9
Visit beach	26.5	32.2	43.9	51.1	56.2	59.6
Boating	21.4	26.5	38.3	45.9	52.3	58.8
Fishing	26.5	30.9	37.8	40.2	41.5	40.7
Visit a wilderness area	25.1	28.6	36.6	41.1	41.9	44.1
Bird watching	27.5	30.8	34.7	40.3	40.2	42.6
Hiking	28.5	31.2	33.9	37.4	39.2	43.1
Visit waterside	16.5	20.6	29.5	35.7	35.5	37.8
Snow and ice activities	13.1	17.8	25.7	32.1	38.9	43.9
Developed camping	18.5	22.1	30.9	33.5	34.0	29.5
Motor boating	13.8	17.2	26.4	32.7	35.4	41.9
Outdoor team sports	14.0	19.3	21.1	24.2	26.4	29.4
Mountain biking	14.9	15.5	22.6	25.7	29.4	30.8
Prehistoric structure/ archaeological sites	16.3	17.5	22.4	25.9	29.0	30.1
Off-road driving	9.9	14.4	18.9	21.5	22.9	24.4
Primitive camping	13.1	14.9	18.3	19.9	19.9	19.0
Hunting	6.8	9.4	14.3	14.6	13.3	13.3
Backpacking	8.8	7.9	11.3	12.9	14.5	16.9
Horse riding	7.4	6.6	9.8	11.9	12.8	15.4
Canoeing	4.8	6.5	10.1	12.9	14.4	16.4
Snorkelling	2.7	2.6	5.6	8.6	12.9	19.2
N[a]	5981	7672	8868	8289	5341	5974

[a] Because of refusals and respondents who said 'Don't know', the sample size for the income variable was 26,685.

to 229 million in 2001 – an increase of 75%. During this period real household incomes rose 53% for the lowest-earning 20% of households and by 112% for the highest-earning 5%.

Trends in participation rates for land-based activities show mixed results, with bicycling and camping rising at relatively steady rates, as shown in Fig. 16.1. The level of participation in horse riding has, however, been flat, while the participation rate in hunting has dropped. Because of the growth of population, the number of participants has increased for all activities since 1960. Change in the number of participants has been highest for bicycling, next highest for camping, moderate for horse riding, and lowest for hunting.

A similar mixed story can be seen for water-based activities (Fig. 16.2). The participation

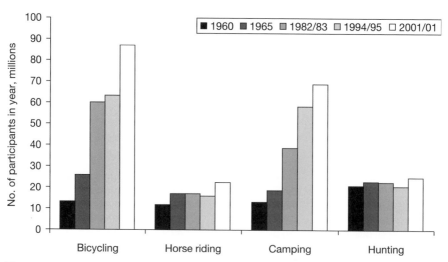

Fig. 16.1. Long-term trends in participation in land-based outdoor activities, USA, 1960–2001. The 1960, 1965 and 1982/83 data refer to populations aged 12+, and the 1994/95 and 2000/01 data to populations aged 16+. Sources: see Table 16.1.

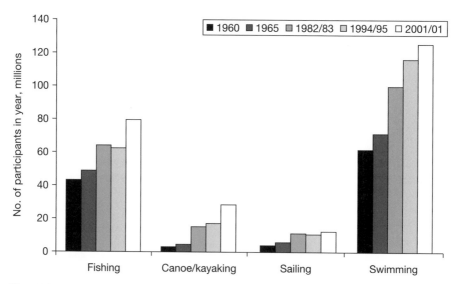

Fig. 16.2. Long-term trends in participation in water-based outdoor activities, USA, 1960–2001. The 1960, 1965 and 1982/83 data refer to populations aged 12+, and the 1994/95 and 2000/01 data to populations aged 16+. Sources: see Table 16.1.

rates for fishing and sailing were near constant over the 41-year period, but due mostly to population growth, the numbers of participants grew substantially for the first half of the period. Trends for canoeing/kayaking and swimming have shown substantial growth in both percentage and numbers participating.

Recent trends

Participation trends can be plotted for a wider range of activities over the period 1982/83 to 2000/01, as shown in Table 16.9. Activities are listed in order of level of growth in the number of participants. The

Table 16.8. Long-term trends in participation in selected outdoor activities, USA, 1960 to 2000/01.

	% participating in year				
	1960[a]	1965[a]	1982/83[a]	1994/95[b]	2000/01[b]
Bicycling	13	18	32	32	41
Horse riding	9	12	9	8	10
Camping	10	13	21	29	37
Hunting	16	16	12	10	12
Fishing	33	34	34	30	35
Canoe/kayaking	2	3	8	8	12
Sailing	3	4	6	5	5
Swimming	47	50	53	55	55
US population, millions	131	144	188	216	229

[a] Population aged 12+; [b] population aged 16+.
Sources: see Table 16.1.

Table 16.9. Trends in participation in selected outdoor activities, USA, 1982/83 to 2000/01.

	Persons aged 16+	
	Percent growth, 1982/83 to 2000/01	Millions of participants in 2000/01
Bird watching	231	73
Hiking	194	76
Backpacking	182	25
Snow-mobiling	125	14
Primitive camping	111	38
Off-road driving	110	42
Walking	91	191
Developed camping	86	62
Downhill skiing	73	21
Swimming/river, lake or ocean	66	98
Motor boating	62	57
Bicycling	53	93
Cross-country skiing	50	9
Sightseeing	37	118
Picnicking	37	124
Horse riding	37	23
Driving for pleasure	30	117
Outdoor team sports	25	56
Fishing	24	80
Hunting	21	27
Water skiing	19	20
Sailing	10	12

fastest growing activity, among those listed in the NSRE, is bird watching, with 231% growth in the number of participants since 1982/83. Other rapidly growing activities include: hiking, backpacking, snow-mobiling, primitive camping, off-road driving and walking. Slowly growing activities include: outdoor team sports, fishing, hunting, water skiing and sailing. The lists of most popular activities in 1960, 1982/83 and 2000/01 differ, partly as a result of changing tastes and incomes and changing patterns of availability of outdoor recreation facilities, and partly because of advances in the design of outdoor equipment, clothing and transport. For example, water skiing, which was a growth activity for many years in the USA, is today growing slowly and may eventually decline due to the popularity of personal water craft as a substitute.

A Much Expanded NSRE

Analysis of data describing leisure, holiday-taking, and a number of other dimensions of the most recent NSRE has yet to be completed. Summarized below, however, are the results from three of several dimensions employed within the NSRE between 2000 and 2001 that were not in previous US surveys, namely lifestyle indicators, segmentation and exploring diversity.

Lifestyle indicators

Table 16.10 presents information on 20 lifestyle indicators for five regions of the USA. Across the five regions listed, there are many similarities and

only a few differences, notably running one's own business, eating out in restaurants, attending church and recycling. Much greater variation is shown across other variables, such as gender and income strata. Added to recreation activity participation and demographics, lifestyle indicators such as these give a much deeper set of variables for describing particular groups of interest.

Segmentation

The adult American public has been segmented by means of cluster analysis of a range of variables representing recreation activity participation. The eight 'outdoor recreation personalities' identified, the names assigned to them and the percentage of the population each represents is shown in Table 16.11. Each of these segments clustered tightly around their respective participation characteristics, while the demographic characteristics for each were quite different. For example; the 'Nature lovers' are older, most are white females and they are predominantly from rural areas. The 'Outdoor avids' are mostly younger to middle-aged white males with

Table 16.10. Percentage participation in activities defining lifestyles by region, USA, 2000/01.

Activity	% of persons aged 16+				
	North	South	Great Plains	Rocky Mountains	Pacific Coast
Belong to environmental group	7.3	9.0	8.6	8.9	8.0
Run own business	14.5	17.5	15.4	23.6	21.0
Have a vacation home	15.1	15.1	11.3	15.3	15.5
Commute >45 min	16.1	16.6	12.6	11.8	14.9
Raise kids	44.6	47.0	46.2	42.2	44.3
Youth volunteer	19.9	20.4	20.2	19.8	17.3
Playing stock market	24.2	23.0	20.1	20.4	21.8
Read nature magazines	25.1	27.1	27.6	23.6	26.1
Collect things	26.1	29.8	26.7	24.3	25.6
Creative arts	27.2	23.9	23.9	25.6	29.0
Crafts	27.2	27.3	27.8	32.3	30.4
Grow a garden	32.8	30.6	34.5	30.4	33.6
Eat out	37.9	50.6	43.0	44.7	44.6
Exercise	40.6	41.2	39.4	45.4	46.7
Follow sports	44.3	48.9	43.5	43.5	45.3
Attend church	46.5	57.3	49.7	44.1	36.0
Use computer at home	56.0	51.8	50.5	55.6	58.7
Care for pets	56.7	59.5	60.3	62.0	60.3
Recycle	75.9	52.4	64.7	54.3	77.1
Cook at home	79.9	76.9	80.4	84.0	84.5
N	18,335	12,774	2148	4118	5365

Table 16.11. Outdoor recreation personalities, USA, 2000/01.

Group description	% of population aged 16+ in group
Inactives	23.9
Passives	15.0
Non-consumptive moderates	11.7
Nature lovers	12.5
Water bugs	13.3
Backcountry actives	8.6
Outdoor avids	7.5
Motorized consumptives	7.5

reasonably high incomes. The 'Motorized consumptives' are younger white males primarily in middle income categories. There are many more characteristics attached to these eight segments, and these are described in greater detail in *Outdoor Recreation for 21st Century America* (Cordell *et al.,* 2004).

The results of this segmentation analysis will be used in a number of public land management programmes. Wilderness education is one such programme. The USA established the National Wilderness Preservation System in 1964, but in recent years there has been growing concern that the public has little access to information about this protected system of lands and thus has limited awareness of its existence and the issues surrounding it. An educational programme to provide the American people with information about wilderness is under way, in part using NSRE data to identify segments and communication pathways that will improve the efficiency of educational delivery and better permit monitoring of learning results.

Segmentation of the public will also assist in meeting objectives such as improving delivery of conservation education, improving responsiveness to differing recreation demands, enhancing the effectiveness of public involvement and ensuring that outreach in public land management is better operated.

Differences in opinions

A major purpose for many of the question modules in the NSRE is to examine the issue of differences related to outdoor recreation participation and land management opinions. Whether these differences are viewed through the lens of environmental justice, social justice or simply equity in service delivery, they are important to track and describe. The NSRE includes demographic questions that match the format used by the United States Census Bureau. This enables us to compare responses to questions dealing with such topics as participation, constraints, opinions, values and access, even though the groups compared may not have been proportionately represented in the final sampling.

One example of exploring differences through the NSRE is a study of how different groups within American society perceive federal lands. A series of questions was designed to solicit opinions on the most important objectives for management of these lands. Figure 16.3 presents differences found between five ethnic groups regarding the level of importance attached to various land management options, including: conserving and protecting sources of water; designating more wilderness areas, restricting trail systems to non-motorized recreation; and expanding access for motorized vehicles. Some clear differences between groups are revealed. Compared with other groups, a smaller proportion of Native Americans see conservation of water as important. Asian Americans see designation of wilderness areas as important, but do not see expanded access for motorized vehicles as important. These results help to identify and explore environmental justice issues related to management of public lands.

Overview

The 2000/01 NSRE has explored outdoor recreation participation by the people of the USA in ways consistent with the seven preceding national recreation surveys conducted between 1960 and 1995. But, it also explored many other aspects of Americans' views on and use of the outdoor environment. Much more emphasis has been placed on environmental topics, to seek an understanding of the public's opinions and values with regard to the natural environment, public lands generally,

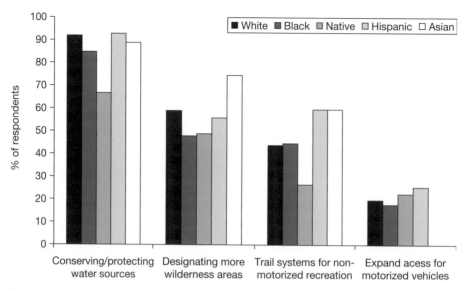

Fig. 16.3. Percentage indicating land-management options important, by race, USA, 2000/01.

and protected public lands. In addition, greater emphasis has been placed on more fully describing respondents' characteristics. Questions have been included on the uses and values of wilderness and other public lands, attitudes regarding natural resource policy issues, lifestyle indicators and demographic characteristics.

Across American society, outdoor recreation continues to be enormously popular, with 97% of Americans aged 16 or older reporting participation to some extent in outdoor recreation during any given year. Traditional activities popular in the 1960s are still popular, but many new forms of activity have been added as technology improves access, comfort and, indeed, what is known and possible. People want to experience nature by viewing it, learning about it, travelling through it and living in it.

Most in demand by Americans are recreation settings and services for passive activities, such as walking, family gatherings, sightseeing, picnicking, and places to visit and learn, such as beaches, historic sites and other sites of interest. These more passive activities cut across a broad band of people, including residents of inner cities, suburbs and rural areas and low-income to high-income groups. As change continues, the importance of a host of other activities becomes apparent, including activities such as personal water craft use, climbing

and mountain biking, which emerged as growth activities in the 1990s.

An important consideration in the operation of the NSRE is effective communication of findings to outdoor recreation managers in a format that will assist in the increasingly complex task of managing resources for outdoor recreation. We are seeking to improve the effectiveness of data delivery through a number of methods, in addition to the traditional reports and academic articles. These include personal presentations, up-to-date website postings, topic-specific short reports, articles in professional journals, the book described earlier in this chapter, and 'just-in-time' learning media using interactive, computer-based methods.

A general summary report on the 2000/01 NSRE has been produced for publication in book form in 2004 (Cordell *et al.*, 2004). Other reports have been published in different formats and on specific aspects of the survey results, including: shorter general reports (Overdevest and Cordell, 2001; Cordell *et al.*, 2002a); sustaining outdoor recreation (Cordell and Green, 2001); the continued popularity of bird watching (Cordell and Herbert, 2002); sociodemographics, values and attitudes (Tarrant *et al.*, 2002); forest-based outdoor recreation (Cordell and Tarrant, 2002); demographic trends (Cordell and Macie, 2002); and recreation and environment as cultural dimensions (Cordell *et al.*, 2002b). The website for the NSRE is at: http://www.srs.fs.fed.us/trends

Ideally, the National Survey on Recreation and the Environment will continue as this country's on-going survey on outdoor recreation participation. Outdoor recreation growth continues unabated, but how it grows is not always so obvious. NSRE and similar surveys in other countries are essential if we are to keep pace with this growth, the new directions it will take and the issues it will leave in its wake.

References

Audits and Surveys (1972) *The 1972 Survey of Outdoor Recreation Activities.* Audits and Surveys, Washington, DC.

Bergstrom, J.C. (1990) Concepts and measures of economic value of environmental quality: a review. *Journal of Environmental Management* 31(1), 215–228.

Bureau of the Census (1965) *The 1965 Survey of Outdoor Recreation Activities.* Bureau of Outdoor Recreation, Washington, DC.

Bureau of the Census (1970) *The 1970 Survey of Outdoor Recreation Activities.* Bureau of Outdoor Recreation, Washington, DC.

Clawson, M. and Knetsch, J.L. (1966) *The Economics of Outdoor Recreation.* Johns Hopkins Press, Baltimore, Maryland.

Cordell, H.K. and Green, G.T. (2001) Sustaining outdoor recreation in the United States. In: Palo, M., Uusivuori, J. and Mery, G. (eds) *World Forests, Markets, and Policies. World Forests*, Vol. III. Kluwer Academic Publishers, Dordrecht, pp. 395–406.

Cordell, K. and Herbert, N. (2002) The popularity of birding is still growing. *Birding Magazine* 34, 54–61.

Cordell, H.K. and Macie, E.A. (2002) Population and demographic trends. In: Macie, E.A. and Hermansen, L.A. (eds) *Human Influences on Forest Ecosystems: the Southern Wildland-Urban Interface Assessment.* Gen. Tech. Rep. SRS-55. US Department of Agriculture, Forest Service, Southern Research Station, Asheville, North Carolina, pp. 11–35.

Cordell, H.K. and Tarrant, M.A. (2002) Forest-based outdoor recreation. In: Wear, D.N. and Greis, J.G. (eds) *Southern Forest Resource Assessment.* GTR-SRS-53. USDA Forest Service, Southern Research Station, Asheville, North Carolina, pp. 269–282.

Cordell, H.K., McDonald, B.L., Lewis, B., Miles, M., Martin, J. and Bason, J. (1996) United States of America. In: Cushman, G., Veal, A.J. and Zuzanek, J. (eds) *World Leisure Participation: Free Time in the Global Village.* CAB International, Wallingford, UK.

Cordell, H.K., McDonald, B.L., Teasley, R.J., Bergstrom, J.C., Martin, J., Bason, J. and Leeworthy, V.R. (1999) Outdoor recreation participation trends. In: Cordell, H.K. (ed.) *Outdoor Recreation in American Life: a National Assessment of Demand and Supply Trends.* Sagamore Publishing, Champaign, Illinois.

Cordell, K., Betz, C., Green, G., Mou, S., Arndt, P., Redmond, C., Stephens, B.T. and Fly, J.M. (2002a) *Public Survey Report Series*, Web Series SRS-4901-2002-1-5. USDA Forest Service, Southern Research Station, Recreation, Wilderness, Urban Forest, and Demographic Trends Research, Athens, Georgia.

Cordell, H.K., Betz, C.J. and Green, G.T. (2002b) Recreation and the environment as cultural dimensions in contemporary American society. *Leisure Sciences* 24(1), 13–41.

Cordell, H.K., Betz, C.J., Green, G.T., Mou, S., Leeworthy, V.R., Wiley, P.C., Barry, J.J. and Hellerstein, D. (2004) *Outdoor Recreation for 21st Century America.* Venture Publishing, Inc, State College, Pennsylvania.

Outdoor Recreation Resources Review Commission (ORRRC) (1962) *National Recreation Survey. ORRRC Study Report 19.* US Government Printing Office, Washington, DC.

Overdevest, C. and Cordell, H.K. (2001) *Recreation Realignment Report Series.* Web Series SRS-4901-2001-1-14. USDA Forest Service, Southern Research Station, Recreation, Wilderness, Urban Forest, and Demographic Trends Research, Athens, Georgia.

Steeh, C., Kirgis, N., Cannon, B. and DeWitt, J. (2001). Are they really as bad as they seem? Non-response rates at the end of the twentieth century. *Journal of Official Statistics* 17(2), 227–247.

Tarrant, M.A., Porter, R. and Cordell, H.K. (2002) Sociodemographics, values, and attitudes. In: Wear, D.N. and Greis, J.G. (eds) *Southern Forest Resource Assessment.* GTR-SRS-53. USDA Forest Service, Southern Research Station, Asheville, North Carolina, pp. 175–187.

United States Department of the Interior/Heritage, Conservation and Recreation Service (HCRS) (1979) *Third Outdoor Recreation Plan: The Assessment: Appendix 1: Nationwide Outdoor Recreation Survey Summary.* US Government Printing Office, Washington, DC.

United States Department of the Interior, National Park Service (1986) *1982–83 Nationwide*

Recreation Survey. US Government Printing Office, Washington, DC.

Vaske, J.J., Beaman, J., Manfredo, M.J., Covey, D.D. and Knox, R. (1996) Response strategy, recall frame and digit preference in self-reports of angling participation. *Human Dimensions of Wildlife* 1(4), 54–68.

Walsh, R.G. (1986) *Recreation Economic Decisions: Comparing Benefits and Costs.* Venture Publishing, State College, Pennsylvania.

17   United States of America: Time-use and Cultural Activities

John P. Robinson and Geoffrey C. Godbey

Introduction

This chapter reviews national survey data concerning the free-time activities of Americans in the latter third of the 20th century. It focuses both on the amounts of free time Americans have (and its relations to time spent on non-free-time activities) and on the specific activities done in that free time. It brings together data from different sources that sometimes show conflicting trends and conclusions.

Some of the changes in time-use since 1965 are attributable to an increased presence of newer technologies which consumers now had in their homes. Not only did more households contain dishwashers and microwave ovens, but these appliances now featured more options and conveniences. There was a parallel growth in home entertainment systems – CD players, VCRs, larger screen television sets and the like. Cellular phones allowed people to be 'on call' and reachable, any time, any place. Another significant change was the increased diffusion and use of home computers – at first used to streamline household accounting and to play more sophisticated computer games, but more recently allowing people to communicate inexpensively via e-mail and to surf the World Wide Web (Robinson and Kestnbaum, 1999).

As in earlier diary surveys using different modes of data collection, there have been impressive convergences in the various sets of diary data, which are usually well within sampling error of each other. In other words, the data generally point in the same direction, usually indicating an America with somewhat less work and more free time than in the 1960s.

Time-diary Methodology

The main source of the data on free time in this chapter is a comprehensive set of data reported in national probability surveys of respondents aged 18–64 in the form of 24-hour recall time-diaries. In these diary accounts, collected in 1965, 1975, 1985 and 1995, respondents provided complete accounts of what they did for the full 24 hours of a particular day, including the exact time they went to bed, when they got up and started a new day, and all the things they did until midnight of that day. Because they represent complete accounts of daily activity, diary data collected from cross-section samples allow one to estimate how much societal time is spent on the complete range of human behaviour – from work to free time, from travel to time spent at home. Details of these and other surveys referred to in the chapter are provided in Table 17.1.

A time-diary report is fundamentally different from the task of making long-term time estimates, the source of data on more specific detailed free-time activities, as reported later in this chapter. The diary keeper's task is to recall

Table 17.1. National time-use and leisure participation surveys, USA, 1965–2002.

Year	Title of survey	Agency	Sample size	Sample age	Time reference
1965	Americans' Use of Time	Survey Research Center,	1243	18–64	24 h
1975	Project	University of Michigan	2096	18–64	24 h
1985		Survey Research Center,	3729	18–64	24 h
1995		University of Maryland	7249	18–64	24 h
1985	Healthy People 2010/	National Center for Health	132,000	17+	2 weeks
1990	National Health	Statistics (NCHS)	132,000	17+	2 weeks
1998	Interview Survey (NHIS)		132,000	17+	2 weeks
1972–2000	General Social Survey (GSS)	University of Chicago	1500	18+	Year
1982	Survey of Public	US Census Bureau/	5683	18+	Year
1985	Participation	National Endowment	2215	18+	Year
1992	in the Arts (SPPA)	for the Arts	12,726	18+	Year
2002			17,135	18+	Year

only a single day's activities in sequence, with a reporting approach that probably reflects the way the day was structured chronologically for the respondent and to the way most people store their activities in memory. Rather than having to consider a long time period, as with weekly, monthly or annual estimates, the respondent needs only to focus attention on a single day (yesterday). Rather than working from some list of activities whose meanings can vary from respondent to respondent, diary respondents simply describe in their own words the day's activities as recalled (Robinson and Godbey, 1999, Chapter 5).

The diary procedure thus avoids most of the pitfalls of the alternative 'time estimate' approach (Robinson and Godbey, 1999). There are still problems of memory, as when respondents have trouble piecing together a particular period of the day. However, few diary accounts are beset by such structural reporting problems once under way. The final diary figures have been shown to have high reliability, with similar results whether the diary was: conducted by telephone, in person or mailed back; done for the day before (yesterday) or the day after (tomorrow) the contact interview; done in different seasons of the year; or done in different parts of the country. Studies of diary validity include matches of diary times with times estimated from 'beeper studies', 'random hour' accounts, spouse activity reports, video-recorded observations

and 'shadow studies' in which respondents are followed by an observer (Robinson and Godbey, 1999, Chapter 4).

We begin our analysis of free time with a review of the changes in productive and personal care activities, because these are the factors tied so closely to changes in free time.

Recent Changes in Non-free-time Activities

Paid work

There were overall declines in diary work hours, for employed women and for men, between the 1960s and 1990s. These can be contrasted with the more consistent and virtually unchanged figures for *estimated* working weeks, found in the massive estimated work-week data (from 50,000+ respondents per month over the past 30–50 years) collected by the government's Bureau of Labor Statistics (BLS). These changes are shown in Table 17.5.

The lack of much overlap in the work hours of men and women also remained apparent, even if women's overall paid work hours have increased since 1965, due mainly to the *proportions* of American women working, rather than in terms of time they spent on that job when working. This seems true for employed men as well.

Family care

Housework

There were also continual, and predictable, declines in housework by women across the decades since 1965. Alongside that, one can see the countertrend of increased housework time for men. While women's housework hours declined from 26 hours/week in 1965 to just over 15 hours in 1995, men's hours increased from about 5 to about 9 hours/week. Since the decline of more than 11 hours/week of housework for women was almost triple the 4-hour increases for men, it is clear that less housework is being done in America in the 1990s; moreover that gap does not seem to be made up for by paid help or children's help, since neither phenomenon seems more prevalent today.

To some extent, the declines in women's housework were due to societal demographic shifts. First, women in the 1990s were more likely to be employed, and full-time employed women have consistently shown about a 40% decline in housework (Gershuny, 2000). Secondly, women were less likely to be married, and thirdly they were less likely to have children to care for in the household.

None the less, only about half the decline in housework is explained by these demographic shifts. The rest of the decline seems due simply to women reporting less housework in their diaries across time (and apparently not due to technology for doing housework). The same is true for the increase for men. Moreover, these trends appear fairly much across different types of housework activity, from cooking to cleaning to household management. As discussed in more detail in Bianchi and Mattingley (2003), the decline in women's housework time also held true across different categories of women – from the old to the young, from the married to the never married, from those with children to those without, from those with high school to postgraduate education, and among both blacks and whites. The decline was further found among *both* employed women and full-time housewives, although it was not as sharp among employed women as among housewives. It may be that housework has become 'de-valued', as women's educational and job options have broadened. Also, media images of successful women are no longer confined to the happy homemaker but often depict the successful career woman. Since housework has been noted to have lower enjoyment levels and an 'elasticity' about it – it can be done in more or less time, depending upon its perceived importance – time spent on it has declined.

However, the overall trend toward less housework seemed counter to certain factors that might have been thought to have led to increased housework now and in the future. First, American homes were getting larger, averaging over 700 square feet per person, which meant more internal area to keep clean. Secondly, with the ageing of the population and the tendency for older people to do more housework (even as their children leave home), more housework can be predicted from this demographic change as well. Despite these changing conditions, total housework time continued to decline.

Other family care

However, declines were generally *not* in evidence for the other two main categories of family care: shopping and childcare. Thus, it can be seen that the declines in overall family care (housework + shopping + childcare) for women were accounted for almost exclusively by the declines in core housework just described. In other words the hours/week spent on childcare and shopping over the years had hardly changed: 7 hours for shopping and 5 hours for primary activity childcare by mothers. While the childcare figure was an hour lower than in 1965, that was explained entirely by the lower numbers of households with children in the 1990s. In terms of hours for those respondents who were mothers with children in the household, these figures remained virtually unchanged – and they had *increased* when taking into account the greater proportions of working mothers. In the case of men, hours for childcare and shopping were also almost identical to those for 1965, despite the smaller numbers of children. It is still the case, however, that mothers with children in the household reported spending more than three times as much time on childcare as fathers did, in terms of primary activity. (In terms of hours of total *contact* with children, however, 1965 data showed fathers spending closer to 25 hours/week with their children, and mothers 35 hours/week).

Trends in *total family care*, then, for both men and women, simply, and almost entirely, reflected the declines in the housework component of that care. This component seems the only one that changed much over the years. It is well to remember that 30 years ago it looked like nothing would reduce housework time (Robinson and Converse, 1972; Vanek, 1974), since housework hours seemed little different from those reported in the 1920s.

Productive activity

It is possible with time-diary data to sum paid work time and family care to arrive at a figure of total productive time, and this has been calculated in Table 17.2. It shows a significant decline, from 59 hours in 1965 to 50 hours in 1995, or a decline of about 9 hours a week, for both men and women. The decline was especially high for non-employed women, whose productive work hours dropped by 13 hours between 1965 and 1995.

Personal care

We have described personal care as the least interesting, as well as most consistent, set of diary activities across time. This is particularly true for the largest personal care activity, sleep, which did show an increase, but of only by 1 hour/week from 1965 to 1995. Hours

spent eating showed a roughly 1 hour decrease since 1965 among both men and women, although more meals were eaten outside the home. The third personal care category – grooming – showed almost a 2-hour decrease over the decades, a finding consistent with the trend toward 'dressing down' and more casual attire that has been reported in the media. Whether it reflects less frequent bathing or hygiene, or less time getting dressed, the gender gap in grooming time remains – women continue to report spending more than 2 hours/week more grooming time than men – even if their own grooming time has declined.

Travel

Men's travel time in 1995 was about the same as in 1965, but for women it was 2 hours/week higher (mainly due to employment). Whatever the dynamics, women, in general, continued to close the gap in travel time with men, further evidence of the more androgynous lifestyles, in both free time and non-free time, described further below.

Free Time

Given the zero-sum nature of diary time, the decreases in work and housework time shown in Table 17.2 and minimal change in personal care time, means that there was some increase in diary free time from 1965 to 1995. The extent

Table 17.2. Trends in productive activity, USA, 1965–1995.

	Hours/week				
	1965	1975	1985	1995	1965–1995
Women					
Employed	66.6	62.1	59.8	62.9	−4
Non-employed	53.6	44.2	43.2	40.9	−13
Total	59.4	52.3	53.2	50.6	−9
Men					
Employed	62.5	58.6	58.7	59.3	−3
Non-employed	26.8	25.9	32.1	28.7	+1
Total	59.1	53.7	53.1	50.1	−9
Total	59.3	53.0	53.1	50.4	−9

Note: for sample sizes see Appendix Table 1.
Source: Americans' Use of Time Project (see Table 17.1 and Robinson and Godbey (1997)).

Table 17.3. Trends in free time, USA, 1965–1995.

	Hours per week, persons aged 18–64				
	1965	1975	1985	1995	Change, 1965–1995
Women					
Employed	27.2	30.0	34.0	33.8	+6.6
Non-employed	39.2	45.4	46.4	50.8	+11.6
Total	34.0	28.4	38.9	42.3	+8.3
Men					
Employed	33.0	35.3	36.3	40.0	+7.0
Non-employed	61.1	61.6	55.6	63.6	+2.6
Total	35.7	39.2	40.4	46.0	+10.3
Total	34.8	38.7	39.6	44.0	+9.2

Note: for sample sizes see Appendix Table 1.
Source: Americans' Use of Time Project (see Table 17.1) and Robinson and Godbey (1997).

of that increase in free time and how it was used by our four gender-employment categories is shown in Table 17.3.

Non-employed women reported an increase of almost 12 hours free time between 1965 and 1995, from about 39 to 51 hours/week (a figure which is still 12 hours lower than for non-employed men). In contrast, employed women (probably because of their increased work hours) showed a smaller increase of 6–7 hours of free time. Put another way, since 1965, non-employed women have picked up more than 11 hours of free time, compared to 6+ hour increases for employed women (and for employed men). In percentage terms, employed women have increased their free time by 24% compared to 30% for non-employed women. But while employed women have gained less free time than the rest of the population, today's employed woman still enjoyed significantly more free time than her counterpart in the 1960s.

Television and other media

Following the pattern found in earlier studies, we would expect that, as free time goes up, so will television-viewing. However, in the 1990s the gain in free time was not entirely given over to the television set. In contrast to the 3–5 hour gains in free time, TV weekly viewing increased by only about 1.5 hours between 1985 and 1995.

None the less, it is clear that, when examin-ing the last third of the 20th century, the gains in free time have been largely matched by the gains in TV-viewing – for both men and women. These analyses also showed offsetting small declines in reading over the years, and small declines in radio/recording use as well (although radio time as a secondary activity rose to over 10 hours/week in recent times). However, when combined with viewing as a secondary activity, about half of Americans' 40+ hours of free time per week was spent in the company of television.

The home computer

The rapid diffusion of home computers was one of the main factors thought to influence changes in daily life in the 1990s. One does not, however, find much evidence of that in our diaries (at least as of 1995), since the primary activity time reported as computer usage was only about an hour a week. That was not large enough to indi-cate much involvement in other activities, although perhaps larger increases in computer/Internet use may have occurred since 1995.

Social capital and recreation time

For the first time in this diary data series, then, we found gains in non-television free-time activities that kept pace with the gains for television – almost 2 hours/week since 1985. As shown in Table 17.4, the gains came from

Table 17.4. Trends in social capital and other non-media free-time activities, USA, 1965–1995.

	Hours/week, persons aged 18–64				
	1965	1975	1985	1995	Change, 1965–1995
Social capital					
Socializing	8.2	7.1	6.7	7.3	−0.9
Religion	0.9	0.9	0.9	0.9	0.0
Other organizations	1.3	1.5	1.2	0.9	−0.4
Communication	3.6	3.4	4.4	4.6	+1.0
Recreation					
Sports/exercise	1.0	1.6	2.2	3.0	+2.0
Hobbies	2.2	2.8	2.8	2.7	+0.5
Sports/cultural events	1.2	0.6	0.9	1.3	+0.1
Total non-media free time	18.4	19.9	19.3	20.7	+2.3

Source: Americans' Use of Time Project (see Table 17.1) and Robinson and Godbey (1997).

a number of such activities, but particularly fitness activities and socializing. Thus, even in the 'age of television', non-media activities continually managed to consume over 20 hours/week of Americans' free time since 1965. The recent gains in fitness activities meant a dramatic tripling over the past 30 years from 1 to 3 diary hours/week, perhaps a function of health professional and mass media emphases on healthier lifestyles.

Communication in the family and by telephone also gained an hour a week. (Similar continuing gains in attending college and taking other adult education courses of about half an hour a week were also found, although education may now fall more in the category of productive rather than free time.) A further half-hour gain was found for engaging in hobbies (for men), which were now mainly in the form of computer use among men rather than needlework activities (among women). Each of these five categories of recreational activity, then, showed an increase in time.

This stood in marked contrast to the first set of non-media free time activities in Table 17.4 – the three 'social capital' activities to which Putnam (2000) has drawn so much attention. As Putnam has argued, we did find an overall decline in these activities since 1965. The largest decline since 1965, of about an hour per week, was found for socializing – much as would be expected from the findings of the main activities initially affected by television. However, even with that 1995 turnaround, social and visiting time was still at about the

same level as in 1975. In other words, social life seems to have made something of a comeback from the earlier declines in social contact associated with television viewing. Moreover, with the advent of e-mail and cellular telephones, one might have been expected further declines in live social interaction. Perhaps more discretion is beginning to be exercised in regard to television time.

Conversely, the decline of organizational and formal volunteer time in 1995, to less than 1 hour/week, was the first clear indication of decreased social capital in this form of behaviour. The finding that less than an hour a week was spent on these activities (and little of that on actual 'volunteering') contrasted sharply with the recent poll estimate data in which Americans estimate an average of 4–5 hours a week on volunteer activities (Gerson, 1997, p. 27).

Time spent on the third indicator of social capital, religious practice, remained remarkably stable across time – at just under an hour a week, the same amount as for other organizational activity. Here, however, figures on the amount of time hid an important countertrend. As Presser and Stinson (1998) have shown from these same diary data, the *proportion* of Americans attending weekly religious services had significantly declined in recent years – again counter to what respondents in other national surveys report in response to estimate questions. What our constant figures in religious observance conveyed, then, is that for those who attended services, *time per attender* had increased across time. In this case, the greater attendance times per attender provides another example of our 'Newtonian' model ('bodies in motion stay in motion'), in that the religiously rich got richer or more dedicated in their religious observance.

Adding the hours of all three of these social capital activities together provided a total of just over 9 hours/week of social capital, compared to about 10.4 hours/week in the 1960s. That represents a decline of about 15% in such activities. While that may not be seen as dramatic a decline as Putnam (2000) reported, it stands in marked contrast to the increases in TV, exercise, home communication and adult education. In that way, then, any *decline* in social capital takes on added importance – as well as irony, given that these are among the most enjoyable of the activities people report doing in their diary ratings.

Trend summary

In brief, then, the 1965–1995 data comparisons in Table 17.5 tell much the same story as earlier diary trend studies. Hours of paid work were notably lower than in 1965, while women were doing less housework and men more housework. These provided the American public with

Table 17.5. Summary of time-use trends, USA, 1965–1995.

	Change in hours/week	
	Men	Women
Work – employed only	−5.0	−0.5
Work – all	−9.5	+6.0
Family care	+4.5	−12.5
Housework	+4.5	−11.0
Childcare	–	−1.5
Shopping	–	–
Personal care	−2.5	−1.0
Sleep	–	+2.0
Eating	−0.5	−1.0
Grooming	−2.0	−2.0
Free time	+7.5	+7.5
Watch television	+6.0	+6.5
Reading/listen to stereo	−1.0	−0.5
Social capital	−1.5	−1.5
Recreation	+4.0	+3.0

increased free time overall, aided and abetted by the increased free time made possible by decreased marital and parental responsibilities (but separate from them as well).

Unlike earlier gains in free time, the most recent gains are not completely dominated by TV. Indeed, the increased hours Americans reported in fitness, education and home communication activities were a healthy sign, in that not only were they now more active, but they were engaging in activities that they themselves reported as more enjoyable than TV. At the same time, we cannot overlook the finding that TV hours continued to increase and that television remained the focus of virtually half of our free-time activity. The decline in social capital activities was another trend that must be of concern, particularly since there was clearly more free time that could be devoted to such activity.

Table 17.5 shows that both men and women gained nearly 8 hours of free time per week between 1965 and 1995. However, they arrived at this gain from different routes, men's increase having come mainly from about 10 hours/week less paid work, while women's increase came about by almost 12 hours less unpaid work. In men's case, their decreased paid work came from two sources: more men retiring earlier (particularly those aged 55–64) and 5 hours less weekly work for those men who remained in the labour force. Together these totalled nearly 10 hours less paid work for all men aged 18–64, about 10% of whom were not working in 1965 and about 20% of whom were not working in the 1990s. Men had also reduced their eating and grooming time by almost 3 hours since 1965. On the other hand, they had taken on almost 5 more hours of housework during that time, leading to a net gain of about 8 hours in leisure time.

Employed women, on the other hand, had not decreased their work hours since 1965, and had closed the gap between diary and estimated work hours since 1985. Since a higher percentage of women were now working than in 1965, their overall paid working hours increased by 6 hours because of their increased labour-force participation (from 44% of women aged 18–64 in 1965 to 65% in 1996). Their sleep times had also gone up by 2–3 hours a week, but that had been offset by decreased meal and grooming time. It was mainly their 13 hours of decreased family care, then, that provided the opportunity to enjoy an increase of almost 8 hours of free time.

None the less, when it comes to free time and its varied uses, the patterns and trends were much the same for both men and women. The largest increases in the nearly 8 hours of greater free time for both had been in TV-watching – viewing increased by 6–7 hours/week since 1965. More recently, there were some gains in more active recreational pursuits, particularly fitness activities which increased from 1 to 3 hours/week. Offsetting these increases were declines in two types of free-time activities: other media (particularly newspapers) and social capital (especially visiting and socializing, although these showed some resurgence in the 1990s).

While men had 4 hours more free time than women (Table 17.3), women registered 3 hours more weekly hours than men in the personal care activities of grooming and sleeping. Whether this reflected a need for rest and preparation due to more complex and tiring role demands for women in the 1990s, or their preference for sleep and personal appearance over free time, is an issue to examine more closely in the future.

Perhaps the more sobering story in regard to time-use trends is that, despite all the events, technologies and turmoil over the past 30 years, the broad outlines of American daily life were not extensively different from what we found in our 1965 study. It takes a long time for time-use patterns of daily life to change.

Demographic Differences

With few exceptions, the pattern of demographic correlates of activities is much as reported in Robinson and Godbey (1997), so we do not propose to repeat them here. Instead, we draw attention to the changes in two of the main background variables of interest: age and gender.

The changes in age patterns were actually relatively minor, but it is important to note how they have accentuated over time, as more workers have opted for early retirement or shorter working weeks. As they worked fewer hours, older people did put in more time doing housework and sleeping. They also had more free time and used more of that free time for television, reading and other media. It is encouraging, however, to see that, like younger Americans, senior citizens were also more involved in active, non-media activities such as fitness and socializing (Robinson *et al.*, 1997).

In the case of gender, we observed some significant changes over the 1985–1995 decade. Women's diary work hours were now closer to men's – as well as being closer to the work hours those women estimated they put in. Women also continued their reduced time doing housework, and 1990s men showed little evidence of continuing to pick up the resulting slack.

Nevertheless, these 1990s data also provided continuing long-term evidence of the converging androgynous lifestyles of men and women. In Robinson and Godbey (1997), we were impressed by the finding that, on 15 of all 22 activities, men's and women's activities had become more similar between 1965 and 1985. If anything, the 1995 data make this point more clearly, since most of the androgynous trends were stronger in 1995 than in 1985. Using a more quantified and recognized measure of activity similarity, Bianchi and Spain (1996) have calculated that the Euclidian 'distance' between male–female patterns dropped from 24.3 hours in 1965, to 20.7 hours in 1975, to 16.5 hours in 1985 and to 12.5 hours in 1995. On this measure, then, the gap between men's and women's activities had been cut almost in half.

Perceptions of Time Pressure

The clear long-term trends in the increase in free time, as shown in Table 17.3, stand in marked contrast to several measures of subjective perceptions of 'time pressure'. Americans believe that they have less free time than previously. Two measures of this phenomenon are: (i) feelings of 'being rushed', asked in our original 1965 study; and (ii) feelings of 'being stressed', asked first in the 1985 Healthy People 2010 study of the National Health Interview Survey (NHIS). Among the great virtues of the

NHIS survey are the large sample sizes (typically 17,000 respondents annually), the use of very detailed and identically worded questions and the very high response rate obtained (80% or more of those selected into this national probability sample).

In Robinson and Godbey (1997), we noted how the 'always rushed' question response had apparently peaked in the mid-1990s, along with responses to other questions related to feeling more pressured for time. We wondered whether it was perhaps a bellwether for a slow-down in the pace of American life. Since then, the General Social Survey (GSS) also asked the 'rushed' question, and the GSS showed almost identical results to those in our 1995 Maryland survey. The larger sample size and higher response rate in the GSS provides convergent evidence of the turnaround in attitudes about feeling rushed.

Further corroborating evidence came from the release of data from a 1995 NHIS study on responses to its questions about stress. Based on our earlier analyses, we were expecting to see perhaps a levelling of stress feelings. We were therefore quite surprised to find that not only was the 1995 proportion (48%) of American adults saying they had experienced substantial stress in the previous two weeks lower than that reported in 1993 (56%), but also lower than the 50% level reported in the first 1985 survey.

The eight percentage point decline in 1995 feelings of stress was found across the spectrum of social groups (Robinson and Godbey, 1999). Virtually all groups in the survey registered that decline and at about the same level, both the elderly and young adults, for example. Interestingly, women continued to report greater stress than men, but that gender gap had also declined slightly in the 1995 data. Moreover, parallel declines were found in subsequent surveys and on different stress questions in the NHIS, one dealing with stress felt in the previous year, the other with the effects of stress on one's health; thus it was not confined to a single, isolated item.

Could it be that Americans had learned to slow the pace of their lifestyles that most foreign observers consider fast to the point of being almost out of control? Had they become more aware that they in fact did have more free time than previous generations? Had they become familiar with data reported in other mass media accounts? Will they be taking more time to smell the roses in the future?

There were hopeful signs of Americans taking their free time more seriously in our diary data as well. Table 17.4 shows larger gains in non-media free activities (such as socializing and fitness) over the past decade than gains in free time overall. The decline in grooming time may signal lessening concern with fashion and appearance and more concern with dressing comfortably and naturally. The decline in eating time may reflect fewer people in households, now about 2.6, and a higher percentage of households with only one person in them. The increase in sleep may indicate more concern over restoring our energies and our bodies. The decline in housework may be disturbing, but it is unclear if today's households are messier than those in the past.

Observers of American life (including ourselves) have expressed concern about the unbridled materialism of our culture, our slavish responses to the whims of advertising, our sedentary lifestyles and the mindless content of our television shows, popular fiction and feature movies. In the face of mass advertising, however, there were signs in our data that more Americans were appreciating and taking advantage of the greater free time they had. Whether that set of choices will be revealed more clearly in future diary data, when the proportion of the population aged 50 or over may reach 40%, remains to be seen. As this happens, it is likely that free time will continue to increase.

The finding that time spent in behaviours considered to be free time or even leisure has increased from the mid-1960s to the mid-1990s is very much at odds with Americans' 'common knowledge'. So is the slight difference in productive time between females and males, and the miniscule amount of time spent in contemplation or sexual activity. What are we to make of this gap in perception? While all explanations of this contain some element of ideology, the words of a historian seem appropriate.

> The wish to live as intensely as possible has
> subjected humans to the same dilemma as the

waterflea, which lives 108 days at 8 degrees Centigrade, but only twenty-six days at 28 degrees, when its heartbeat is almost four times faster, though in either case its heart beats 15 million times in all. Technology has been a rapid heartbeat, compressing housework, travel, entertainment, squeezing more and more into the allotted span. Nobody expected that it would create the feeling that life moves too fast.

(Zeldin, 1994)

Other Free-time Activity Data Sets

In addition to our diary data, other survey organizations have been collecting data over the past 30 years to track changes in free-time activity. Those with the most commendable methodologies include:

- the General Social Survey (GSS) from the University of Chicago;
- the Survey of Public Participation in the Arts (SPPA) conducted by the US Census Bureau for the National Endowment for the Arts; and
- the Healthy People 2010 surveys conducted by the National Center for Health Statistics.

Further details of the surveys are provided in Table 17.1. All have features of high response rates (70–90%) of those selected into the sample, repeated questions and large sample sizes. Their major advantage over diaries is that the detailed activities studied, such as playing golf or going to a jazz concert, occur very infrequently in daily diary studies. The disadvantage is that all must rely on estimate questions, which are subject to more severe memory recall problems and potentials for social desirability in respondent reporting than the time diary, as noted above. Chase and Godbey (1983), for instance, asked members of specific swimming and tennis clubs to estimate how many times they had used the club during the past 12 months; when their estimates were then checked against the sign-in system each club had, almost one-half of all respondents overestimated their actual occasions of participation by more than 100%!

Unlike the diary data reported above, the estimates here are reported for all respondents 18 and older, including those over 64.

GSS leisure activity questions

The broadest variety of questions and the most frequent (yearly) readings come from the GSS. As shown in Figs 17.1, 17.2 and 17.3, the GSS questions ask about frequency of social interaction, religious participation and mass media use. In Fig. 17.1, for example, it can be seen that, counter to the arguments in Putnam (2000) about declining social capital, the four GSS questions on sociability do not uniformly show declines. Two do: the decline in contact with neighbours and the decline in attending bars, but even the latter's decline stopped about 1985. However, there is no decline in get-togethers with relatives, and an actual increase in seeing friends – almost enough to offset the decline in seeing neighbours. These findings are consistent with the diary findings of relatively little decline in visiting and socializing.

Figure 17.2 does show a slight decline in attending church services across time, not unlike our diary findings – although Presser and Stinson (1998) show notable declines across the years in the *percentage* attending religious services, rather than overall time spent. The GSS data on sex frequency are unique in that no other data source is available. They also show essentially no change over the past 13 years in that activity, further evidence that may be seen to counter Putnam's arguments.

Figure 17.3 shows trends in estimated media use. The estimates for TV hours are relatively constant across time (as they are in the SPPA data below), which is counter to the diary findings of steadily increased viewing across time – especially between 1965 and 1975. The GSS declines in newspaper reading, on the other hand, are quite consistent with the major declines in diary newspaper reading – which is the major free-time activity showing diary time decline. (Diary data on other reading – books, magazines and the like – show much less or no decline.)

Outside of their constant TV-viewing hours, the GSS figures largely corroborate the

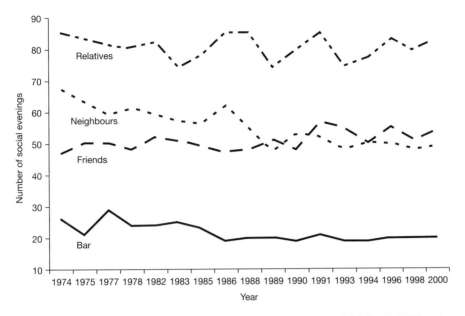

Fig. 17.1. Trends in forms of social contact, USA, 1974–2000. Source: GSS (1972–2000) and Social Sciences Data Collection (nd), see Table 17.1.

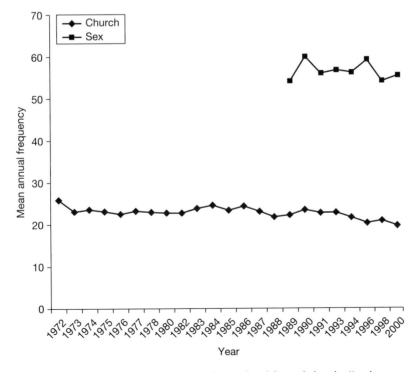

Fig. 17.2. Comparative annual frequency of sexual activity and church attendance, USA, 1972–2000. Social Sciences Data Collection (nd)

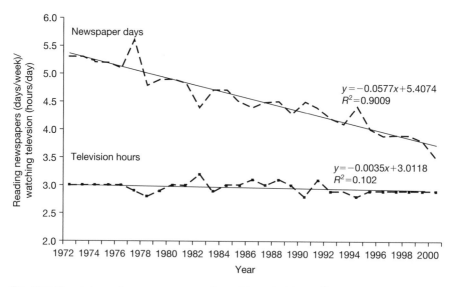

Fig. 17.3. Trends in reading newspapers and watching television, USA, 1972–2000. Missing values were interpolated. Source: GSS (1972–2000), see Table 17.1.

diary free-time trends reported in Tables 17.3 and 17.4.

SPPA – participation in the arts

The SPPA survey covers a variety of free-time activities, but with an arts and culture focus. These are activities highly correlated with level of education, so that it might be expected that these figures would have significantly increased as the population of college graduates in the USA has continued to rise. However, in Table 17.6 it can be seen that, over the period 1982–2002, there was an overall slight drop in the proportion of respondents reporting attendance at cultural events. This is particularly true for visits to historic parks and arts/crafts

Table 17.6. Attendance at arts events, USA, 1982–2002.

Activity	% attending in previous year, persons aged 18+				
	1982	1985	1992	2002	Change 1982–2002
Jazz	9.6	9.5	10.6	10.4	+0.8
Classical music	13.0	12.7	12.5	11.7	−1.3
Opera	3.0	2.6	3.3	3.0	0.0
Musicals	18.6	16.6	17.4	17.1	−1.5
Plays	11.9	11.6	13.5	12.5	−0.6
Ballet	4.2	4.3	4.7	3.7	−0.5
Art museums	22.1	21.9	26.7	26.9	+4.8
Other dance	n/a	n/a	7.1	6.6	(−0.5)
Art/craft fairs	39.0	40.0	40.7	34.6	−4.4
Historic park	39.0	36.0	34.5	31.9	−5.1
Reading literature	56.9	56.1	54.0	57.6	+1.0
Sample size (N)	17,254	13,675	12,736	17,135	
				Average	−0.6

n/a, Not available.
Source: SPPA and NEA (1997) (see Table 17.1).

festivals, and less so for attending live music and theatre performances – but it is clear that more college graduates do not translate into increased participation in the arts. The one optimistic exception appears for increased visits to art museums and galleries.

Table 17.7 shows the same mix of trends for being an active arts/cultural participant or performer. Declines in the arts/crafts activities of pottery and needlework are particularly regular and pronounced.

Table 17.8 shows declines that extend to participation via the mass media, especially for music and theatrical performances on television, which might be surprising given the increased usage and development of new forms of video, such as VCRs and DVD players. It suggests that this may be due to fewer such performances carried on prime-time television. Some encouragement may be found in the increased listening to jazz and classical music on the radio, and the slight increase in watching visual arts on TV.

Table 17.9 shows declines not just in attendance at musical arts events, but in people's attitudes toward different types of music, particularly country-western, easy listening, ethnic and folk music. In this climate, it might be encouraging to see jazz and classical music holding their own. The biggest increase is for rock music, which at 48% liking has surpassed country music as America's favourite.

Finally, the SPPA survey extends to other, non-arts leisure activities, as shown in Table 17.10. Here, one finds even more serious declines in such non-arts activities as home improvements, attending sports events, playing sports and gardening since 1982. There are minor increases in exercising and volunteer work.

NHIS fitness questions

The Healthy People 2010 surveys of the National Center for Health Statistics (NCHS) asks questions about participation in over 20 different physical activities in the previous 2 weeks, mainly related to fitness. As shown in Table 17.11, they show less decline in these fitness activities than suggested in Table 17.10. None the less, there do appear to be small but

Table 17.7. Active participation in the arts, USA, 1982–2002.

	% participating in previous year, persons aged 18+			
Activity	1982	1985	1992	2002
Public music performances				
Play jazz	0.8	0.7	0.7	0.6
Play classical music	0.9	0.9	0.9	1.0
Sing opera	0.1	0.04	0.2	0.1
Sing musicals	0.9	0.8	0.7	0.6
Sing chorale	n/a	n/a	6.3	4.8
Theatre performance				
Act	0.8	0.8	1.6	1.3
Public dance performances				
Modern/other	n/a	n/a	1.2	0.7
Ballet	0.1	0.1	0.03	0.1
Arts/crafts activities				
Pottery	12.0	11.0	8.4	5.9
Needlework	32.0	28.0	24.8	18.1
Photography	11.0	10.0	11.6	11.5
Painting	10.0	9.0	9.6	8.7
Creative writing	7.0	6.0	7.4	7.0
Composing music	n/a	n/a	2.1	2.1

n/a, Not available.
Source: SPPA (see Table 17.1).

Table 17.8. Usage of broadcast and recorded media for arts-related content, USA, 1982–1992.

Art-form/medium	% using in previous year, persons aged 18+				
	1982	1985	1992	2002	Change, 1982–2001
Jazz					
TV	18	17	21	16	−2
Radio	18	18	28	23	+5
Record	20	19	21	17	−3
Classical					
TV	25	24	25	19	−6
Radio	20	21	31	24	+4
Record	22	21	24	20	−2
Opera					
TV	12	12	12	6	−6
Radio	7	7	9	6	−1
Record	8	7	7	6	−2
Musicals					
TV	21	18	15	12	−9
Radio	4	5	4	2	−2
Record	8	7	6	4	−4
Plays					
TV	26	21	17	9	−17
Radio	4	4	3	2	−2
Ballet					
TV	16	15	n/a	n/a	n/a
Dance					
TV	n/a	n/a	19	13	−6
Visual arts					
TV	23	25	32	25	+2
Sample size, N	5683	2215	12,726	17,135	

n/a, Not available.
Source: SPPA (see Table 17.1).

Table 17.9. Music preferences, USA, 1982–2002.

	% of adult population liking each type				
	1982	1985	1992	2002	Change, 1982–2002
Classical/chamber	28	30	33	27	−1
Opera	10	10	12	10	0
Show tunes/operettas	23	24	28	17	−6
Jazz	26	30	34	26	0
Reggae	n/a	n/a	19	15	−4
Rap	n/a	n/a	12	15	+3
Soul			24	29	+3
Blues/R&B	26	33	40		
Latin/salsa	n/a	n/a	20	18	−2
Big band	33	32	35	24	−8
Parade/march	n/a	n/a	18	12	−6
Country-western	58	53	52	43	−15
Bluegrass	25	24	29	21	−4
Rock	35	42	44	48	+13
Ethnic/national	n/a	n/a	22	16	−10

Continued

Table 17.9. *Continued*

	% of adult population liking each type				
	1982	1985	1992	2002	Change, 1982–2002
Folk (contemporary)	25	25	23	15	−10
Mood/easy	48	52	49	30	−18
New age	n/a	n/a	15	12	−3
Choral glee club	n/a	n/a	14	9	−5
Hymns/gospel	36	40	38	27	−9
Heavy metal	–	–	–	22	–
				Average	−4.1

n/a, Not available. Source: SPPA and NEA (1997) (see Table 17.1).

Table 17.10. Participation in leisure activities, USA, 1982–2002.

	% participating in previous year, persons aged 18+				
	1982	1985	1992	2002	Change, 1982–2002
Arts participation	39	39	41	39	0
Exercise	51	57	60	55	+4
Movies	63	59	59	58	−5
Gardening	60	55	55	50	−10
Amusement parks	49	45	50	40	−9
Home improvements	60	58	48	44	−16
Active sports	39	41	39	29	−10
Sports events	48	50	37	33	−15
Outdoor activities	36	37	34	33	−3
Volunteer/charity	28	30	33	30	+2
TV hours/days	3.0	2.8	3.0	2.9	−0.1

Source: SPPA (see Table 17.1).

Table 17.11. Trends in fitness and exercise activities, USA, 1985–1998.

	% participating in previous two weeks, persons aged 17+			
	1985	1990	1998	Change, 1985–1998
Walk for exercise	36	45	43	+7
Jogging	10	8	11	+1
Hiking	4	4	n/a	–
Gardening or yard work	29	26	28	−1
Aerobics or aerobic dancing	8	7	6	−2
Other dancing	10	8	n/a	(−2)
Calisthenics or general exercise	22	18	n/a	(−4)
Golf	4	4	5	+1
Tennis	4	3	2	−2
Bowling	5	4	3	−2
Biking	10	11	12	+2
Swimming or water exercise	9	8	6	−3
Yoga	1	1	n/a	–
Weight lifting or training	9	9	16[a]	+7
Basketball	4	5	6	+2

Continued

Table 17.11. *Continued*

	% participating in previous two weeks, persons aged 17+			
	1985	1990	1998	Change, 1985–1998
Baseball or softball	4	3	3	−1
Football	1	1	1	–
Soccer	1	1	1	–
Volleyball	2	2	2	–
Handball, racquetball or squash	2	2	1	−1
Skating	1	1	n/a	–
Skiing	1	1	1	–

[a] 1998 also includes 'strength training'. n/a, Not available.
Source: Healthy People 2010 Surveys NCHS (nd) (see Table 17.1).

steady declines in aerobics, tennis, bowling, swimming and handball–racquetball–squash. These are offset to some extent by small increases in jogging, golf, biking, basketball, soccer (hidden by rounding of data in Table 17.11) and weight lifting (although the latter increase may be due to an unfortunate change in question wording). There does not appear to be much change in the major NHIS fitness activity of walking for exercise in the 1990s.

While it does not appear that NHIS has repeated these fitness questions since 1998, they do seem to have measured *vigorous* participation with a single question annually since then. The proportions answering 'yes' to this single question on vigorous participation are about the same in 2003 as they were in 1997 (33%), although they are up from the 30% levels found in 1998 and 1999.

In general, these steady NHIS trend figures do not match the steadily increasing amounts of time that respondents report spending in some form of fitness activity in their diaries – one of the most consistent and dramatic increases found in our diary studies.

trends are reported in diary studies in other Western countries). At the same time, US survey respondents increasingly reported being 'rushed' or stressed, since the 1960s, although there are signs of some turnaround in such time-pressured perceptions in the late 1990s.

Regarding other data sources on people's daily behaviour, this time-diary evidence thus conflicts with 'time estimate' or meter data, which show few (or offsetting) changes in paid work time, as well as in specific free-time activities such as TV time, arts participation, fitness activities, religious attendance and social life. In contrast, the diary data show dramatic increases in TV time and fitness activity since 1965, with possible declines in paid work time, as well as in religious, arts and social activity. The estimate and diary data sources do agree that there has been a dramatic decrease in newspaper reading and radio listening, although the latter has made a notable comeback as a secondary activity (for multi-tasking). Future diary data, then, can be expected to show further unique insights into the nature of, or trends in, free-time activity.

Conclusion

Time-diary research in the USA since 1965 has documented several shifts in free time that are surprising or counterintuitive in light of today's perceived 'time famine'. Perhaps most striking is the increase in free time, made possible by decreased paid work (for men) and unpaid 'housework' (for women) (although the same

References

Bianchi, S. and Mattingley, M.T. (2003) Gender differences in quality and quantity of free time. *Social Forces* 81(3), 999–1030.

Bianchi, S. and Spain, D. (1996) *Women, Work and Family in America* Population Bulletin 51(3). Population Reference Bureau, Washington, DC.

Chase, D. and Godbey, G.C. (1983) The accuracy of self-reported participation rates: a research note. *Leisure Studies* 2(2), 231–236.

Gershuny, J. (2000) *Changing Times: Work and Leisure in Postindustrial Society*. Oxford University Press, Oxford, UK.

Gerson, P. (1997) Do do-gooders do too much? *US News and World Report* 122(16), 26–29.

National Center for Health Statistics (NCHS) *Healthy People 2010 Surveys*, NCHS, Washington, DC. www.cdc.gov/nchs/hphome.htm (accessed October 2004).

National Endowment for the Arts (NEA) (1997) *1997 Survey of Public Participation in the Arts: Summary Report*. NEA, Washington, DC. www.nea.gov/pub/Survey/SurveyPDF.html (accessed October 2004).

Presser, S. and Stinson, L. (1998) Estimating the bias in survey reports of religious attendance. Paper to the 53rd Annual Conference of the American Association for Public Opinion Research, Norfolk, Virginia, May.

Putnam, R.D. (2000) *Bowling Alone: the Collapse of American Community*. Simon & Schuster, New York.

Robinson, J. and Converse, P. (1972) Social change as reflected in the use of time. In: Campbell, A. and Converse, P. (eds) *The Human Meaning of Social Change*. Russell Sage Foundation, New York, pp. 17–86.

Robinson, J. and Godbey, G.C. (1997) *Time for Life: the Surprising Ways Americans Use Their Time*. Pennsylvania University Press, University Park, Pennsylvania.

Robinson, J.P. and Kestnbaum, M. (1999) The personal computer, culture, and other uses of free time. *Social Science Computer Review* 17(2), 209–216.

Robinson, J., Werner, P. and Godbey, G. (1997) Freeing up the golden years. *American Demographics* 19(10), 20–24.

Social Sciences Data Collection *General Social Survey*. Social Sciences at Humanities Library, University of California, San Diego, California. http://govt.ucsd.edu/gss/ (accessed October 2004).

Vanek, J. (1974) Time spent in housework. *Scientific American* 11, 116–120.

Zeldin, T. (1994) *An Intimate History of Humanity*. Harper Perennial, New York.

Appendix Table 1. Time-use surveys: sample sizes by gender and employment status, USA, 1965–1995.

	1965	1975	1985	1995
Women				
Employed	306	489	1234	2508
Non-employed	382	618	814	1372
Total	688	1107	2048	3880
Men				
Employed	507	865	1327	2660
Non-employed	54	124	354	709
Total	561	989	1681	3369
Total	1243	2096	3729	7249

18 National Leisure Participation and Time-use Surveys: a Future

Grant Cushman, A.J. Veal and Jiri Zuzanek

Introduction

The contributors to this book were asked to provide information in relation to their respective countries on: (i) national leisure participation and time-use surveys which have been conducted; (ii) overall patterns of leisure participation and leisure time-use arising from the surveys, including, where possible, trends over time; (iii) inequalities in patterns of participation in relation to such factors as gender, age and socio-economic status; and (iv) the effects of globalization on leisure behaviour, including use of the Internet. In this final chapter these four areas are reviewed in turn, in relation to cross-national comparison and the prospect of future surveys.

The Surveys

The contributions to this book reveal a wide range of experience in the conduct of national leisure participation and time-use surveys among the 15 countries represented. Table 18.1 presents information on the latest surveys reported for each of the 15 countries. It shows that 14 out of the 15 have conducted leisure participation surveys and 10 have conducted time-use surveys.

In some cases, notably in the German and Polish contributions, reference is made to

leisure *expenditure*, drawing on data from general household expenditure surveys. Most economically advanced countries conduct household expenditure surveys on a regular basis and a future edition of this book may well draw on such sources more extensively. The following comments may be made on the information presented in the table.

Year of survey

It is too much to expect international agreement on common years for national leisure participation and time-use surveys, but this is arguably not of vital importance, since the social and economic situation which shapes leisure participation is not the same in all countries in any one year. What is more important is that surveys should be carried out periodically on a comparable basis within countries, so that trends may be established and studied.

Time-series

In some countries a series of surveys has been established over a number of years, which enables trends to be established. However, in some of these cases there remain problems of comparability between surveys, and in a number of cases only two surveys are available,

Table 18.1. National survey characteristics.

Country	Leisure participation surveys						Time-use surveys			
	Date of latest survey	Time-series[a]	Activity emphasis	Sample size, '000s	Age range of sample	Reference period	Date of latest survey	Time series[a]	Sample size, '000s	Age range of sample
Australia	2001/02	5	Sport	13	15+	Year	1997	1	9	15+
	2002	3	Cultural	15	18+	Year				
Canada	1992	2	Leisure	12	12+	Year	1998/99	3	11	15+
	2000	5	Sport	12	12+	3 months				
Finland	1991	2	Leisure	4	10+	Year	1999/2000	2	5	10+
France	1997	3	Leisure	3	0–70	Year	1997/98	4	16	15+
	2000	1	Sport	6						
Germany[b]	1991	–	Leisure	3	14+	Often	–		–	–
Great Britain	1996	7	Sport	16	16+	4 weeks	2000/01	4	10	8+
Hong Kong	1993/94	–	Leisure	3	6+	Month	–		–	–
Israel	–		–	–	–	–	1990	1	1	20+
Japan	2003	6	Leisure	3	15+	Year	–		–	–
Netherlands	1999	5	Leisure	?	15+?	Year	2000	5	2	12+
New Zealand	1998/99	1	Sport	4	5+	Year	1998/99	–	9	12+
Poland	1998/99	–	Leisure	4	15+	Year	1996	3	2	–
Russia	c	c	c	c	c	c	1990	c	47	–
Spain	2000	1	Culture	24	–	–	–		–	–
USA	2000	7	Outdoor rec.	50	16+	Year	1995	3	7	18–64
	2002	3	Sport	17	18+	Year				

[a] Number of previous, comparable surveys conducted. [b] Information from first edition of the book. [c] Data in chapter drawn from a variety of sources.

which is not a strong basis for the establishment of trends. The overall picture, in terms of trends, is mixed. Certainly up to the 1980s, leisure time appeared to be increasing, at least for some groups in the community, but there is evidence to suggest that it has declined in the 1990s. There is no clear trend in leisure participation: some activities increase in popularity while others go into decline. As discussed in Chapter 1, most of the surveys are sponsored by government agencies in order to monitor the effects of government policies: in particular, governments would hope to find increasing levels of participation in those types of activity, such as the arts and sport, which they promote. It is clear that, to date, the surveys have not been fully effective in providing data for assessing the effectiveness of such policies. Much more research, with better data, is required to address the question of trends in participation.

Some countries have conducted a number of comparable surveys over time, to establish time-series. In some countries resources exist to conduct surveys annually, but in research terms this is unnecessary, since annual fluctuations are not necessarily a guide to long-term change. Surveys conducted every 4–5 years provide for measurable social changes between surveys and allow a time-series of data to be built up over a reasonable time.

Activity emphasis

The range of activities to be included in the survey presents no problem in the case of time-use surveys, because they cover all activities which people engage in during the course of a day. Challenges arise, however, at the coding stage in clearly identifying and distinguishing leisure from other activities – for example whether to classify travel to a leisure venue as part of the activity or part of the separate activity of 'travel', or whether to count certain meals as leisure or 'personal maintenance'.

In the case of participation surveys, problems of inclusion and exclusion arise from the beginning. Generally such surveys are conducted or sponsored by government departments, or by national statistical agencies with government departments as the main 'clients'. Few governments have single departments with responsibilities across the whole of leisure; typically a myriad of departments – of sport, the arts, the environment, heritage, youth affairs – is involved. Even when a 'whole of government' approach is adopted and the scope of a survey ostensibly encompasses the whole of leisure, the extent of government areas of responsibility may still limit the definition of leisure, often excluding, for example, commercial or home-based activities. In a number of countries, for example, Australia, Great Britain and New Zealand, the scope of the survey is restricted as a result of the dominance of the interests of single departments, such as a Ministry of Sport. In other cases, fragmentation occurs as different departments wish to 'do their own thing' in regard to surveys, resulting in a number of surveys covering different aspects of leisure, which may or may not be comparable and therefore able to be aggregated to produce a comprehensive picture of leisure. Even if such surveys can be aggregated, they may fail to include data on some aspects of leisure that fall outside the purview of *any* government department.

The interest of the *leisure* researcher is in a comprehensive approach to leisure – if this interest is to be served it is necessary to get the message across to government departments and/or statistical agencies that all forms of leisure activity compete for people's time and money: it is only possible to understand one aspect of leisure if the complete picture is available.

When the scope of 'leisure' is agreed, there remains the challenge of listing and coding individual activities. When data are gathered by means of face-to-face interviews or respondent-completion questionnaires substantial lists of activities can be presented to respondents, who can then tick those in which they have participated. The written list has the advantage of acting as a memory prompt, but a long list can be daunting, especially for less literate respondents. In the case of telephone interviews, an open question about 'activities you do in your free time' must be used but, without a visual prompt, this can result in under-reporting of some activities. In both cases a shorter prompting method may be used, referring to activity groupings – such as 'home-based', 'sport' and 'arts and entertainment'.

Table 18.2 lists almost 200 activities which occur in at least one of the participation surveys

Table 18.2. Activities covered in leisure participation surveys in this book.

Arts/cultural activities	Reading newspapers/	Social activities
Art films/cine-clubs	magazines	Special interest courses
Art gallery/art museum	Reading	Sport spectator
Arts crafts	Relax, do nothing	Tea ceremony
Arts (paint, sculpt)	Sewing, knitting, etc.	Travelling overseas
Ballet	Spend time at home/	Visit/be with friends/relatives
Circus	with family	Visitor centre
Classical music concert	Study	Walking
Flower arranging	Talk on telephone	Walking dog
Historic site visit	(15 mins +)	Working for a church group
Jazz concert	Watch TV	Sport/physical recreation
Library visit	Woodwork, carpentry	Aerobics
Movies	Outdoor recreation	Archery/shooting
Museum/historic site visit	Backpacking	Athletics
Museums, galleries	Beach	Australian Rules football
Music recital/opera	Bird watching	Badminton
Opera or ballet	Camping	Ball games
Opera	Kite-flying	Baseball/softball
Other live performances	National park	Basketball
Outdoor concert/play	Parks	Bowls/bowling
Painting, sculpture, pottery	Picnic/barbecue	Boxing/wrestling
Performing arts	Picnic/hike/nature walk	Climbing
Photography	Walk in country/bushwalking/	Cricket
Playing musical instrument	hiking	Cricket: indoor
Playing music	Social/informal recreation	Cricket: outdoor
Pop concerts	Amusement parks, etc.	Curling
Theatre	Auctions	Cycling
Theatre/concert	Bingo	Darts
Making videos	Church/religious activities	Diving
Writing	Club/association member	Exercise, keep fit
Home-based activities	Club visit (licensed/night)	Fencing
Car repairs	Community/voluntary work	Fishing/hunting
Cards, board games	Conversation	Fishing
Chess, checkers	Dancing, discotheque	Football (see also
Collecting (stamps, coins)	Dining out	soccer, etc.)
Computer/video games	Driving for pleasure	Gateball/croquet
Crafts/arts	Electronic/computer games	Golf
Do-it-yourself	Excursions	Gymnastics
Entertaining at home	Exhibitions	Handball
Gardening for pleasure	Fair or festival	Hiking/backpacking
Gourmet cooking	Gambling	Hockey
Household skills	General interest courses	Hockey/lacrosse: indoor
Indoor games	Going out/evening	Hockey/lacrosse: outdoor
Listening to music	Hobbies	Horse riding
Listening to radio	Horse races/trots/dog races	Ice skating
Listening to records/tapes	Karaoke	Informal sport
Model-making	Motor sport	Jet skiing
Outdoor games	Nightclub, disco	Jogging/running
Playing with children	Outings	Judo
Playing with pets	Pachinko	Lawn bowls
Reading books	Pub/café/tea house visit	Martial arts
Reading magazines	Sauna/massage	Netball
Reading newspapers	Shopping for pleasure	Netball: outdoors

Continued

Table 18.2. *Continued*

Netball: indoors	Skating/skiing	Swimming: non-pool
Orienteering	Skiing	Table tennis
Pinball, pool, shuffleboard	Soccer (see also football)	Team sports
Playground games	Soccer: indoor	Tenpin bowling
Pool/snooker/billiards	Soccer: outdoor	Tennis
Rink sports	Softball	Tennis, racquet sports
Roller-skating	Sport (at least one)	Touch football
Rugby	Squash	Volleyball
Rugby League	Strength sports	Water activities: non-power
Rugby Union	(weights, box)	Water-skiing
Sailing	Surfing/lifesaving	Water sport: excluding sailing
Sailing/canoeing/boating	Swim in own/friends' pool	Weight lifting/body building
Self-defence	Swimming	Windsurfing
Shooting/hunting	Swimming: indoor	Yoga
Skateboarding	Swimming: in pool	
Skating	Swimming: outdoor	

represented in this book. No one activity is common to all participation surveys reported, although television-watching and going to the movies come close. In many cases comparability is confounded by the tendency of survey designers to group certain activities together. Examples include opera and concert-going, reading of various types, indoor and outdoor sporting activities and various water-based activities. Groupings of activities may lead to inaccuracies in responses due to the 'inflationary' reporting of participation, where respondents feel that they 'must have' engaged in one or more of a group of activities (e.g. 'performing arts'), even if they cannot recall specific instances. One lesson for the future is for the designers of surveys not to group activities together, but to retain as much detail as possible, to facilitate comparison across surveys.

Future comparative research on leisure participation will depend in part on achieving, as far as possible, an agreed common list of activity codes for analysing participation data. Such an agreement is partially in existence for time-budget surveys; for example, in the Harmonized European Time Use (HETUS) activity coding list (Aliaga and Winqvist, 2003). However, typical time-use coding lists are inadequate for leisure participation surveys because they tend to include only 50–60 separate codes for leisure activities; thus, for example, sports and exercise activities tend to be grouped into just three or four groups.

Sample size

Sample sizes of the surveys referred to in the book vary enormously, from 1000 to 50,000. To a large extent this is a function of the size and political structure of the country, with large samples often called for in countries with federal systems which require results at state or provincial level. But, regardless of the size of the population, small samples are a constraint on analysis of activities which have low participation rates; for example, most individual sports. Thus, with a sample of 1000, a participation rate of 1% is subject to a confidence interval of plus or minus 0.6, that is, the participation rate is estimated to be somewhere between 0.4% and 1.6%. Such a margin makes it very difficult to compare participation rates, both between activities and for the same activity over time. Further, the small overall sample size results in small sub-samples of individual minority-activity participants, making further analysis of the characteristics of participants in such activities difficult. Survey costs are, of course, a limiting factor, exacerbated by the fact that the relationship between sample size and confidence interval is quadratic; that is, to reduce the confidence interval by half requires a fourfold increase in sample size. Arguably, it would be advisable to conduct surveys infrequently with large sample sizes rather than frequently with small sample sizes.

Age range

The 'age threshold' of the samples covered by the surveys varies substantially from country to country, with minimum ages ranging from 6 years to 20 years. In some surveys, therefore, the bulk of teenagers are excluded, and only one includes children under 12 years old. This is highly significant for leisure time as a whole and for certain areas of leisure, such as active sport, popular music and computer and electronic games, where young people are generally very active. Thus even small differences in the age range covered could make comparisons between surveys from different countries invalid. Of course, it would be technically feasible to produce results for all surveys for the highest age cut-off. But this would require special tabulations to be produced by the various survey agencies.

Very few surveys have included an upper age-limit and, with the ageing of Western populations, it would seem increasingly unwise to do so.

In some countries, special surveys have been conducted of children's leisure activities. However, if very young age groups are to be covered, then it is generally necessary to rely on parents' reporting of children's activities; this may introduce inaccuracies for older children, who may have behaviour patterns without parental influence or knowledge.

If international comparability is to be achieved in future, then a common threshold age for surveying and reporting and some common methods for assessing 'under-age' participation will need to be adopted. Given the emerging consensus on the participation reference period discussed below, the varying age ranges of survey samples remains the most significant barrier to cross-national comparison of leisure participation patterns.

Reference period

The major factor preventing comparison between surveys is the activity 'reference period' chosen – that is the time period to which reported participation relates. At one extreme is the 1 or 2 days of the time-diary survey. In participation surveys the period ranges from as little as a week (used, for example, in early Australian surveys) to a year. Clearly the range of activities which an individual engages in during the course of a year is much greater than is possible in a single week or month. The longer the reference period used, therefore, the higher the reported participation rates and the larger the sub-samples of participants in activities. The 1-year reference period is gradually becoming the norm internationally – some three-quarters of the surveys listed in Table 18.1 use this period.

The 1-year reference period has the advantage of covering all seasons of the year in one question, but it can be argued that the scope for error in recalling activities over such a long time period is great. It might be speculated that errors could be made in both directions – under-reporting and over-reporting – and these might cancel each other out, but whether or not this happens is not known. Experiments conducted over 20 years ago by Chase and Godbey (1983) and Chase and Harada (1984) suggested that significant over-reporting was more likely than under-reporting, particularly in activities which are socially approved and which people engage in regularly, but for which they tend to forget the irregular, but possibly frequent, occasions when they missed their 'weekly game'.

A further defect of the 1-year reference period lies in the inclusion of infrequent participants together with frequent participants. For example, the person who has been swimming on just one occasion during the previous year, perhaps for just a few minutes while on holiday, is counted as a participant in swimming, together with the person who swims twice a week throughout the year. For some activities – for example, visiting a zoo – participating just once or twice a year might be a typical attendance pattern. For others, notably sporting activities, regular participation is common, and the desired pattern from the point of view of public policy, so distinguishing between regular and infrequent participants is important. In these cases, the 'headline' figure of total participants is misleading.

To some extent, the problem of the infrequent participant can be overcome by including an additional question on frequency of participation. Typically, rather than being an accurate estimate this will be indicative only;

for example, a person who claims to engage in an activity 'once a week' may not actually do so 52 times a year, due to the normal interruptions to routine, such as sickness and holidays. This makes it possible to deal realistically with individual activities, but since the definition of 'infrequent participant' varies from activity to activity, compilation of an aggregate 'headline' figure for participation in groups of activities, for example sports or the arts, becomes complicated. It is notable that Canadian data on sports participation refer to 'regular' participants only (Table 3.11). Data on frequency of participation are also important for policy or marketing purposes, since increasing frequency of participation can be as important in some situations as increasing the number of participants.

In recent years there has been some attempt to collect data relating to both a shorter and a longer time period in the same survey, and to compare the results. It can be seen in Tables 7.8 and 7.10 in the Great Britain chapter in this book that, for most activities, there is a dramatic difference in the 1-year and the 4-week participation rate. In Canada the 1988 survey was based on a 1-year and subsequent surveys on a 3-month period – it can be seen in Table 3.6 that the impact varies from activity to activity. How much of the differential is due to real differences in the participation rates for the two periods and how much is due to exaggeration of the 1-year participation rate due to inaccuracy of recall is not known. There is, however, a strong incentive to use longer reference periods, particularly the 1-year option, to save on costs. Surveys with shorter reference periods require larger samples to capture minimal samples of participants in minority activities and must be conducted at different times of the year to capture seasonal variation, both features tending to increase the costs of conducting surveys.

Despite its drawbacks, therefore, the 1-year reference period is emerging as the international norm for participation surveys.

Inequality

While absolute levels of participation cannot be compared cross-nationally, some of the patterns of relationships between participation and key socio-economic and demographic variables can be compared in an informal way. In most of the contributed chapters the relationships between participation and a number of traditional social variables, including gender, age and socio-economic status, are examined. These are complex phenomena and their relationships with leisure are the subject of numerous research approaches. The survey data presented in this book represent just one such contribution to the mosaic of data, theory and interpretation available.

In relation to gender, the picture presented is very mixed. Time-budget data indicate that women generally have less leisure time than men, particularly women in the paid work force. As regards participation patterns, women tend to be less active in sport and more active in arts and cultural activities, the differences being more marked in some countries than in others. The finding that women also tend to be more active in home-based activities could be interpreted as a result of choice, but can also be seen as a reflection of lack of freedom of choice, since women's leisure choices are often confined to the home because of childcare and domestic responsibilities, as well as other economic and cultural constraints.

The surveys generally indicate that the range of leisure activities engaged in declines with age. For a few activities, such as television-watching, some arts activities and specific sports, such as golf and bowls, participation rates are higher among the older age groups than among the young, but in general the reverse is the case. Time-budget data present a different picture, with retired people, inevitably, having comparatively large amounts of leisure time available. It is widely accepted that an active leisure life can enhance health and the quality of life generally for older people: the picture of *declining* levels of participation with age may therefore be viewed with concern from the point of view of public policy. It could, of course, be the case that older people choose to engage in fewer activities, but more intensively. But an alternative perspective is that people who drop leisure activities in middle age, due to family and work commitments, often fail to adopt new activities to replace them when leisure time increases with retirement: the result is an increase in time spent on passive 'time fillers', such as watching television, rather than on potentially more rewarding engagement in an activity of choice (Carpenter, 1992; Dodd, 1994).

As regards socio-economic status, based on occupation and education, the general picture emerging from the surveys is that there are marked differences in patterns of leisure participation across the socio-economic spectrum. The economically and educationally advantaged groups in the community generally have higher levels of participation in all activity groups, even though they tend not to have more leisure time. The exception is France, where manual workers have higher participation rates in sport. As with the aged, it is possible that the less advantaged groups adopt a more intensive involvement with fewer activities, but it is also possible that a reduced leisure 'repertoire' results in a lower quality of life. Again the public policy dimension is relevant: it seems clear that the groups who benefit most from government programmes and subsidies in the arts, sport and outdoor recreation are often the economically privileged groups in society. After several decades of implementing modern public leisure policies, the universal rights to leisure, as discussed at the beginning of this book, are some way from being realized in practice.

Use of the Internet

The use of the Internet as a leisure activity has yet to be fully explored in the leisure research literature. Its effects might be anticipated as being no more than an extension, or intensification, of the effects which television has had on society over the past 40 years: a decline in out-of-home commercial leisure activity with associated consequences for social life, an increase in the prevalence of sedentary lifestyles and associated health implications, and an increase in passive absorption of advertising and commercialized popular culture. The last of these is the most controversial and, indeed, there is considerable evidence to suggest that television-watching is, in practice, far from passive (Critcher, 1992). While use of the Internet involves a cathode-ray or similar screen, it is arguably less intellectually passive than watching television or videos, but there is

anecdotal evidence to suggest that its added attraction has increased the amount of time that young people, in particular, spend engaged in physically passive activities.

Data on Internet use are not presented for all countries represented in the book, and not all data are up-to-date, but drawing on post-2000 data only, the following gives a flavour of the findings:

- in Australia the proportion of households with Internet access grew from 16% in 1998 to 46% in 2002, and 57% of males and 51% of females aged 18 and over had used the Internet in the past year;
- in Britain, in early 2003, 54% of the population had used the Internet in the previous 3 months, including 78% of those aged under 25;
- in The Netherlands, a quarter of the population had been using the Internet during their free time in October 2000, spending, on average, 2 hours on the activity in the previous week.

Typically, data on Internet use are derived from special surveys, and it is notable that the reference periods used are even more mixed than for general leisure participation surveys, making comparisons difficult. It is clear that numerous indicators of the extent of Internet use exist, including the proportion of households with home computers with Internet access, the amount of time spent using the Internet, and distinctions between use for work, household or leisure purposes.

Problems and Issues

The major and continuing problems for national leisure participation surveys might be summarized as the 'three Cs': continuity, comparability and comprehensiveness.

Continuity

This refers to the need to conduct surveys on a regular and frequent basis – every 4–5 years at least. As discussed above, in most cases annual surveys, while perhaps useful at the beginning of a survey programme to establish the stability or instability of the data, would seem, in the long term, to be a waste of resources, since most changes in collective behaviour take place over a longer time-period and short-term fluctuations in participation and time-use patterns are just 'noise' in the data.

Comparability

Comparability refers to the need to ensure that surveys *within* countries are comparable, but also to consider ways in which comparability *between* countries might be achieved in future.

Comprehensiveness

This is a reference to the need to cover all aspects of leisure and to include as many activities as possible. However, as Zuzanek suggests (Chapter 3), the long-term accumulation of comparable, standardized data sets is hampered by changes of personnel in key government agencies and the desire of new personnel to make their mark on the process by making changes – which result in loss of comparability.

An issue for promoters of national surveys is to consider the respective roles of time-budget and questionnaire survey methodology. Zuzanek points out that time-budget studies are good at dealing with everyday activities, such as television-watching and other home-based or frequently engaged-in activities, but are less effective in gathering information on activities which, while they may be key indicators of lifestyle, may not take up a great deal of time on a day-to-day basis; for example, theatre going or visiting art galleries. The researcher is, in fact, faced with a spectrum of approaches related to the reference period used, ranging from 1 or 2 days – effectively a time-budget – via a week or a month to 12 months. Beyond 12 months lies the 'personal leisure history' or biographical method, which also has a role to play in leisure research (Hedges, 1986; Smith, 1994). Finding the right balance between these approaches and the advantages and disadvantages they offer, is a challenge for survey researchers around the world.

The Development of Cross-national Comparative Research

The task of the current project was to review the status quo and to bring together information on the availability of data and insights into leisure behaviour and leisure trends from a number of countries. In compiling the first edition of the book, it quickly became clear that the variety of survey vehicles used made comparisons of the results between countries virtually impossible. In the concluding chapter we discussed the merits and possibilities of cross-national research in this area and looked forward to further developments. We, somewhat naively, had a tentative belief that the growing level of activity in conducting national leisure participation and time-use surveys across the world and increasing ease of communication between researchers in different countries, both directly and via conferences, journals and books such as this, would, by now, have improved the level of comparability. Almost a decade later it is clear that this has not happened. While some efforts are being made to increase international liaison in the area of time-use surveys (Pentland *et al.*, 1999; Aliaga and Winqvist, 2003), this has not been the case in leisure participation surveys. Clearly a concerted effort is needed, perhaps under the aegis of an international organization such as UNESCO, if this is to happen.

Looking to the Future

Our discussion in the concluding chapter of the first edition of the book stands as a statement of our thinking on the possible future of cross-national research in this field. For the moment it seems appropriate to make a more succinct statement. The evidence of this book indicates that a wealth of information and insight into patterns of leisure behaviour in contemporary society is being developed at considerable collective cost by a wide range of researchers, in universities and government agencies around the world. But the value of this effort is substantially diminished by the lack of international collaboration in design, analysis and dissemination, resulting in an inability to compare results across more than a handful of countries. More cooperation and collaboration would greatly enhance the value of this work in future. The challenge remains for academic and government researchers to find ways and means to take the necessary steps to achieve this end.

References

Aliaga, C. and Winqvist, K. (2003) *How Women and Men Spend their Time: Results from 13 European Countries.* Statistics in Focus: Population and Social Conditions, Theme 3 B 12/2003 (Cat. No. KS-NK-03-012-EN-N). Eurostat, European Communities, Brussels, accessed via: www.europa.eu.int/comm/eurostat

Carpenter, G. (1992) Adult perceptions of leisure: life experiences and life structure. *Society and Leisure* 15(2), 587–606.

Chase, D.R. and Godbey, G.C. (1983) The accuracy of self-reported participation rates. *Leisure Studies* 2(2), 231–236.

Chase, D. and Harada, M. (1984) Response error in self-reported recreation participation. *Journal of Leisure Research* 16(4), 322–329.

Critcher, C. (1992) Is there anything on the box? Leisure studies and media studies. *Leisure Studies* 11(2), 97–122.

Dodd, J. (1994) The male leisure repertoire, before and after the transition to mid-life. In: Simpson, C. and Gidlow, B. (eds) *Leisure Connections.* Proceedings of the Australian and New Zealand Association for Leisure Studies Second Conference, Canterbury. Lincoln University, New Zealand, pp. 51–56.

Hedges, B. (1986) *Personal Leisure Histories.* Sports Council/ESRC, London.

Pentland, W.E., Harvey, A.S., Powell Lawton, M. and McColl, M.A. (eds) (1999) *Time Use Research in the Social Sciences.* Kluwer/Plenum, New York.

Smith, L.M. (1994) Biographical method. In: Denzin, N.K. and Lincoln, Y.S. (eds) *Handbook of Qualitative Research.* Sage, Thousand Oaks, California, pp. 286–305.

Index

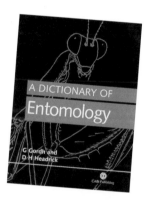
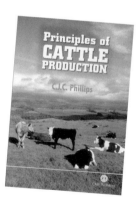